Editors/Advisory Board

P9-ECZ-777

Members of the Advisory Board are instrumental in the final selection of articles for each edition of ANNUAL EDITIONS. Their review of articles for content, level, currentness, and appropriateness provides critical direction to the editor and staff. We think that you will find their careful consideration well reflected in this volume.

Preface

In publishing ANNUAL EDITIONS we recognize the enormous role played by the magazines, newspapers, and journals of the public press in providing current, first-rate educational information in a broad spectrum of interest areas. Many of these articles are appropriate for students, researchers, and professionals seeking accurate, current material to help bridge the gap between principles and theories and the real world. These articles, however, become more useful for study when those of lasting value are carefully collected, organized, indexed, and reproduced in a low-cost format, which provides easy and permanent access when the material is needed. That is the role played by ANNUAL EDITIONS.

Recent events have brought ethics to the forefront as a topic of discussion throughout our nation. And, undoubtedly, the area of society that is getting the closest scrutiny regarding its ethical practices is the business sector. Both the print and broadcast media have offered a constant stream of facts and opinions concerning recent unethical goings-on in the business world. Insider trading scandals on Wall Street, the marketing of unsafe products, money laundering, and questionable contracting practices are just a few examples of events that have recently tarnished the image of business.

As corporate America struggles to find its ethical identity in a business environment that grows increasingly complex, managers are confronted with some poignant questions that have definite ethical ramifications. Does a company have any obligation to help solve social problems such a poverty, pollution, and urban decay? What ethical responsibilities should a multinational corporation assume in foreign countries? What obligation does a manufacturer have to the consumer with respect to product defects and safety?

These are just a few of the issues that make the study of business ethics important and challenging. A significant goal of *Annual Editions: Business Ethics 09/10* is to present some different perspectives on understanding basic concepts and concerns of business ethics and to provide ideas on how to incorporate these concepts into the policies and decision-making processes of businesses. The articles reprinted in this publication have been carefully chosen from a variety of public press sources to furnish current information on business ethics.

This volume contains a number of features designed to make it useful for students, researchers, and professionals.

These include the *table of contents* with summaries of each article and key concepts in italics and a *topic guide* for locating articles on specific subjects related to business ethics.

Also, included in this edition are selected *Internet references* sites that can be used to further explore article topics.

The articles are organized into five units. Selections that focus on similar issues are concentrated into subsections within the broader units. Each unit is preceded by an overview, which provides background for informed reading of the articles, emphasizes critical issues, and presents key points to consider the major themes running through the selections.

Your comments, opinions, and recommendations about *Annual Editions: Business Ethics 09/10* will be greatly appreciated and will help shape future editions. Please take a moment to complete and return the postage-paid *article rating form* on the last page of this book. Any book can be improved, and with your help this one will continue to be.

John E. Richardson
Editor

Contents

UNIT 1
Ethics, Values, and Social Responsibility in Business

The concepts in bold italics are developed in the article. For further expansion, please refer to the Topic Guide.

UNIT 2
Ethical Issues and Dilemmas in the Workplace

The concepts in bold italics are developed in the article. For further expansion, please refer to the Topic Guide.

UNIT 3
Business and Society: Contemporary Ethical Social, and Environmental Issues

The concepts in bold italics are developed in the article. For further expansion, please refer to the Topic Guide.

The concepts in bold italics are developed in the article. For further expansion, please refer to the Topic Guide.

UNIT 4
Ethics and Social Responsibility
in the Marketplace

The concepts in bold italics are developed in the article. For further expansion, please refer to the Topic Guide.

UNIT 5
Developing the Future Ethos and Social Responsibility of Business

The concepts in bold italics are developed in the article. For further expansion, please refer to the Topic Guide.

Correlation Guide

The *Annual Editions* series provides students with convenient, inexpensive access to current, carefully selected articles from the public press. **Annual Editions: Business Ethics 09/10** is an easy-to-use reader that presents articles on important topics such as *workplace misconduct, social and environmental issues, global ethics, ethics in the marketplace,* and many more. For more information on *Annual Editions* and other *McGraw-Hill Contemporary Learning Series* titles, visit www.mhcls.com.

This convenient guide matches the units in **Annual Editions: Business Ethics 09/10** with the corresponding chapters in two of our best-selling McGraw-Hill Business Ethics textbooks by DesJardins and Ghillyer.

Annual Editions: Business Ethics 09/10	An Introduction to Business Ethics, 3/e by DesJardins	Business Ethics: A Real World Approach, 2/e by Ghillyer
Unit 1: Ethics, Values, and Social Responsibility in Business	**Chapter 1:** Why Study Ethics? **Chapter 2:** Ethical Theory and Business **Chapter 3:** Corporate Social Responsibility **Chapter 4:** Corporate Culture, Governance, and Ethical Leadership	**Chapter 1:** Understanding Ethics **Chapter 2:** Defining Business Ethics **Chapter 4:** Corporate Social Responsibility
Unit 2: Ethical Issues and Dilemmas in the Workplace	**Chapter 4:** Corporate Culture, Governance, and Ethical Leadership **Chapter 5:** The Meaning and Value of Work **Chapter 6:** Moral Rights in the Workplace **Chapter 7:** Employee Responsibilities **Chapter 11:** Diversity and Discrimination	**Chapter 2:** Defining Business Ethics **Chapter 3:** Organizational Ethics **Chapter 7:** Blowing the Whistle
Unit 3: Business and Society: Contemporary Ethical, Social, and Environmental Issues	**Chapter 10:** Business' Environmental Responsibilities **Chapter 12:** International Business and Globalization	**Chapter 2:** Defining Business Ethics **Chapter 9:** Ethics and Globalization
Unit 4: Ethics and Social Responsibility in the Marketplace	**Chapter 8:** Marketing Ethics: Product Safety and Pricing **Chapter 9:** Marketing Ethics: Advertising and Target Marketing	**Chapter 3:** Organizational Ethics **Chapter 8:** Ethics and Technology **Chapter 10:** Making It Stick: Doing What's Right in a Competitive Market
Unit 5: Developing the Future Ethos and Social Responsibility of Business	**Chapter 4:** Corporate Culture, Governance, and Ethical Leadership **Chapter 10:** Business' Environmental Responsibilities	**Chapter 10:** Making It Stick: Doing What's Right in a Competitive Market

Topic Guide

This topic guide suggests how the selections in this book relate to the subjects covered in your course. You may want to use the topics listed on these pages to search the Web more easily.

On the following pages a number of Web sites have been gathered specifically for this book. They are arranged to reflect the units of this Annual Editions reader. You can link to these sites by going to *http://www.mhcls.com*.

All the articles that relate to each topic are listed below the bold-faced term.

Brands
26. Trust in the Marketplace
34. Trouble in Toyland
44. Pssssst! Have You Tasted This?

Business and government
4. Building an Ethical Framework
16. The War Over Unconscious Bias
33. Global Diversity: The Next Frontier
34. Trouble in Toyland
39. Marketing, Consumers and Technology: Perspectives for Enhancing Ethical Transactions
41. Dirty Deeds
49. Green Is Good

Business and law
4. Building an Ethical Framework
11. Con Artists' Old Tricks
13. ID Thieves Find a Niche in Online Social Networks
16. The War Over Unconscious Bias
18. Fear of Firing
19. Protecting the Whistleblower
25. The Ethics of Edits: When a Crook Changes the Contract
41. Dirty Deeds

Business environment
4. Building an Ethical Framework
6. Truth or Consequences:The Organizational Importance of Honesty
13. ID Thieves Find a Niche in Online Social Networks
16. The War Over Unconscious Bias
17. Reflecting on Downsizing: What Have Managers Learned?
18. Fear of Firing
20. Learning to Love Whistleblowers
21. On Witnessing a Fraud
33. Global Diversity: The Next Frontier
34. Trouble in Toyland
41. Dirty Deeds
42. Searching for the Top
43. A Word for Older Job-Seekers: Retail
45. Swagland
48. The True Measure of a CEO

Business ethics
3. Business Ethics: Back to Basics
5. Ethical Leadership: Maintain an Ethical Culture
22. His Most Trusted Employee Was a Thief
30. Women and the Labyrinth *of* Leadership
34. Trouble in Toyland

Codes of ethics
3. Business Ethics: Back to Basics
4. Building an Ethical Framework
27. Survey: Unethical Behavior Unreported
36. How Barbie Is Making Business a Little Better

Conflicts of interest
6. Truth or Consequences: The Organizational Importance of Honesty

17. Reflecting on Downsizing: What Have Managers Learned?
19. Protecting the Whistleblower
21. On Witnessing a Fraud
22. His Most Trusted Employee Was a Thief
23. Erasing 'Un' from 'Unemployable'
24. The Parable of the Sadhu
25. The Ethics of Edits: When a Crook Changes the Contract
26. Trust in the Marketplace
27. Survey: Unethical Behavior Unreported
29. Does It Pay to Be Good?
33. Global Diversity: The Next Frontier
42. Searching for the Top
45. Swagland
48. The True Measure of a CEO

Consumer protection
9. Your Privacy for Sale
11. Con Artists' Old Tricks
28. Congress Stops Playing Games with Toy Safety
31. Avoiding Green Marketing Myopia: Ways to Improve Consumer Appeal for Environmentally Preferable Products
34. Trouble in Toyland
37. Is Marketing Ethics an Oxymoron?
39. Marketing, Consumers and Technology: Perspectives for Enhancing Ethical Transactions
41. Dirty Deeds

Crime
4. Building an Ethical Framework
9. Your Privacy for Sale
11. Con Artists' Old Tricks
12. Help! Somebody Save Our Files!: How to Handle and Prevent the Most Common Data Disasters
13. ID Thieves Find a Niche in Online Social Networks
20. Learning to Love Whistleblowers
22. His Most Trusted Employee Was a Thief
26. Trust in the Marketplace
32. The New E-spionage Threat
45. Swagland

Discrimination
7. How to Make Unethical Decisions
10. Are You Too Family Friendly?
15. Hiring Older Workers
16. The War Over Unconscious Bias
18. Fear of Firing
23. Erasing 'Un' from 'Unemployable'
26. Trust in the Marketplace
30. Women and the Labyrinth *of* Leadership
35. Cracks in a Particularly Thick Glass Ceiling
43. A Word for Older Job-Seekers: Retail

Diversity
6. Truth or Consequences: The Organizational Importance of Honesty
16. The War Over Unconscious Bias
18. Fear of Firing
21. On Witnessing a Fraud
43. A Word for Older Job-Seekers: Retail
48. The True Measure of a CEO

Internet References

The following Internet sites have been selected to support the articles found in this reader. These sites were available at the time of publication. However, because Web sites often change their structure and content, the information listed may no longer be available. We invite you to visit *http://www.mhcls.com* for easy access to these sites.

Annual Editions: Business Ethics 09/10

General Sources

Center for the Study of Ethics in the Professions
http://ethics.iit.edu

Sponsored by the Illinois Institute of Technology, this site links to a number of world business ethics centers.

GreenMoney Journal
http://www.greenmoneyjournal.com

The editorial vision of this publication proposes that consumer spending and investment dollars can bring about positive social and environmental change. On this Web site, they'll tell you how.

Markkula Center
http://www.scu.edu/SCU/Centers/Ethics/

Santa Clara University's Markkula Center strives to heighten ethical awareness and to improve ethical decision making on campus and within the community. A list of published resources, links to ethical issues sites, and other data are provided.

U.S. Department of Labor
http://www.dol.gov

Browsing through this site will lead to a vast array of labor-related data and discussions of issues affecting employees and managers, such as the minimum wage.

U.S. Equal Employment Opportunity Commission (EEOC)
http://www.eeoc.gov

The EEOC's mission "is to ensure equality of opportunity by vigorously enforcing federal legislation prohibiting discrimination in employment." Consult this site for facts about employment discrimination, enforcement, and litigation.

Wharton Ethics Program
http://ethics.wharton.upenn.edu/

The Wharton School of the University of Pennsylvania provides an independently managed site that offers links to research, cases, and other business ethics centers.

UNIT 1: Ethics, Values, and Social Responsibility in Business

Association for Moral Education (AME)
http://www.amenetwork.org/

AME is dedicated to fostering communication, cooperation, training, and research that links moral theory with educational practices. From here it is possible to connect to several sites of relevance in the study of business ethics.

Business for Social Responsibility (BSR)
http://www.bsr.org

Core topic areas covered by BSR are listed on this page. They include Corporate Social Responsibility; Business Ethics; Community Investment; the Environment; Governance and Accountability; Human Rights; Marketplace; Mission, Vision, Values; and finally Workplace. New information is added on a regular basis. For each topic or subtopic there is an introduction, examples of large and small company leadership practices, sample company policies, links to helping resources, and other information.

Enron Online
http://www.enron.com/corp/

Explore the Enron Web site to find information about Enron's history, products, and services. Go to the "Press Room" section for Enron's spin on the current investigation.

Ethics Updates/Lawrence Hinman
http://ethics.sandiego.edu/index.html

This site provides both simple concept definitions and complex analysis of ethics, original treatises, and sophisticated search engine capability. Subject matter covers the gamut, from ethical theory to applied ethical venues.

Institute for Business and Professional Ethics
http://commerce.depaul.edu/ethics/

Sponsored by DePaul College of Commerce, this site is interested in research in the field of business and professional ethics. It is still under construction, so check in from time to time.

National Center for Policy Analysis
http://www.ncpa.org

This organization's archive links lead you to interesting materials on a variety of topics that affect managers, from immigration issues, to affirmative action, to regulatory policy.

Open Directory Project
http://dmoz.org/Business/Management/Ethics

As part of the Open Directory Project, this page provides a database of Web sites that address numerous topics on ethics in business.

Working Definitions
http://www.workingdefinitions.co.uk/index.html

This is a British, magazine-style site devoted to discussion and comment on organizations in the wider social context and to supporting and developing people's management skills.

UNIT 2: Ethical Issues and Dilemmas in the Workplace

American Psychological Association
http://www.apa.org/homepage.html

Search this site to find references and discussion of important ethics issues for the workplace of the 1990s, including the impact of restructuring and revitalization of businesses.

International Labour Organization (ILO)
http://www.ilo.org

ILO's home page leads you to links that describe the goals of the organization and summarizes international labor standards and human rights. Its official UN Web site locator can point you to many other useful resources.

Internet References

UNIT 3: Business and Society: Contemporary Ethical, Social, and Environmental Issues

National Immigrant Forum
http://www.immigrationforum.org

The pro-immigrant organization offers this page to examine the effects of immigration on the U.S. economy and society. Click on the links to underground and immigrant economies.

Workopolis.com
http://sympatico.workopolis.com

This Canadian site provides an electronic network with a GripeVine for complaining about work and finding solutions to everyday work problems.

United Nations Environment Programme (UNEP)
http://www.unep.ch

Consult this UNEP site for links to topics such as the impact of trade on the environment. It will direct you to useful databases and global resource information.

United States Trade Representative (USTR)
http://www.ustr.gov

This home page of the U.S. Trade Representative provides links to many U.S. government resources for those interested in ethics in international business.

UNIT 4: Ethics and Social Responsibility in the Marketplace

Business for Social Responsibility (BSR)
http://www.bsr.org/

BSR is a global organization that seeks to help companies "achieve success in ways that respect ethical values, people, communities, and the environment." Links to Services, Resources, and Forum are available.

Total Quality Management Sites
http://www.nku.edu/~lindsay/qualhttp.html

This site points to a variety of interesting Internet sources to aid in the study and application of Total Quality Management principles.

U.S. Navy
http://www.navy.mil

Start at this U.S. Navy page for access to a plethora of interesting stories and analyses related to Total Quality Leadership. It addresses such concerns as how TQL can improve customer service and affect utilization of information technology.

UNIT 5: Developing the Future Ethos and Social Responsibility of Business

International Business Ethics Institute (IBEI)
http://www.business-ethics.org/index.asp

The goal of this educational organization is to promote business ethics and corporate responsibility in response to the growing need for transnationalism in the field of business ethics.

UNU/IAS Project on Global Ethos
http://www.ias.unu.edu/research/globalethos.cfm

The United Nations University Institute of Advanced Studies (UNU/IAS) has issued this project abstract, which concerns governance and multilateralism. The main aim of the project is to initiate a process by which to generate jointly, with the involvement of factors from both state- and nonstate institutions in developed and developing countries, a global ethos that could provide or support a set of guiding principles for the emerging global community.

UNIT 1

Ethics, Values, and Social Responsibility in Business

Unit Selections

Key Points to Consider

- Do you believe that corporations are more socially responsible today than they were 10 years ago? Why or why not?

- In what specific ways do you see companies practicing social responsibility? Do you think most companies are overt or covert in their social responsibility activities? Explain your answer.

- What are the economic and social implications of "management accountability" as part of the decision-making process? Does a company have any obligation to help remedy social problems, such as poverty, urban decay, and pollution? Defend your response.

- Using recent examples of stock, financial, and accounting debacles, discuss the flaws in America's financial system that allow companies to disregard ethics, values, and social responsibility in business.

Student Web Site

www.mhcls.com

Internet References

Association for Moral Education (AME)
   http://www.amenetwork.org/
Business for Social Responsibility (BSR)
   http://www.bsr.org
Enron Online
   http://www.enron.com/corp/
Ethics Updates/Lawrence Hinman
   http://ethics.sandiego.edu/index.html
Institute for Business and Professional Ethics
   http://commerce.depaul.edu/ethics/
National Center for Policy Analysis
   http://www.ncpa.org
Open Directory Project
   http://dmoz.org/Business/Management/Ethics
Working Definitions
   http://www.workingdefinitions.co.uk/index.html

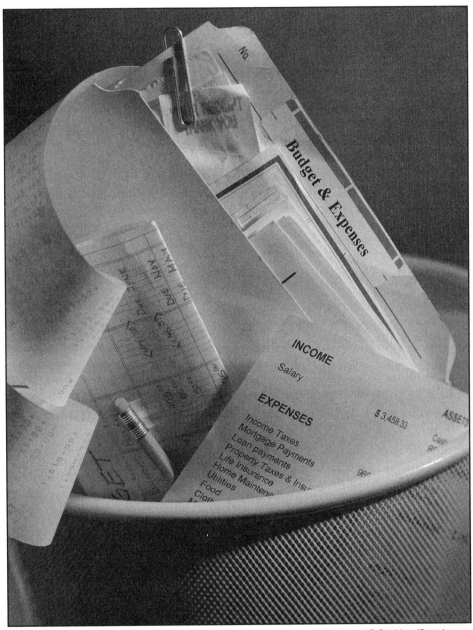

© Stockbyte/Getty Images

Ethical decision making in an organization does not occur in a vacuum. As individuals and as managers, we formulate our ethics (that is, the standards of "right" and "wrong" behavior that we set for ourselves) based upon family, peer, and religious influences, our past experiences, and our own unique value systems. When we make ethical decisions within the organizational context, many times there are situational factors and potential conflicts of interest that further complicate the process.

Decisions do not only have personal ramifications—they also have social consequences. Social responsibility is really ethics at the organizational level, since it refers to the obligation that an organization has to make choices and take actions that will contribute to the good of society as well as the good of the organization. Authentic social responsibility is not initiated because of forced compliance to specific laws and regulations. In contrast to legal responsibility, social responsibility involves a voluntary response from an organization that is above and beyond what is specified by the law.

The nine selections in this unit provide an overview of the interrelationships of ethics, values, and social responsibility in business. These essays offer practical and insightful principles and suggestions to managers, enabling them to approach the subject of business ethics with more confidence. They also point out the complexity and the significance of making ethical decisions.

Thinking Ethically
A Framework for Moral Decision Making

Manuel Velasquez et al.

Moral issues greet us each morning in the newspaper, confront us in the memos on our desks, nag us from our children's soccer fields, and bid us good night on the evening news. We are bombarded daily with questions about the justice of our foreign policy, the morality of medical technologies that can prolong our lives, the rights of the homeless, the fairness of our children's teachers to the diverse students in their classrooms.

Dealing with these moral issues is often perplexing. How, exactly, should we think through an ethical issue? What questions should we ask? What factors should we consider?

The first step in analyzing moral issues is obvious but not always easy: Get the facts.

The first step in analyzing moral issues is obvious but not always easy: Get the facts. Some moral issues create controversies simply because we do not bother to check the facts. This first step, although obvious, is also among the most important and the most frequently overlooked.

But having the facts is not enough. Facts by themselves only tell us what *is*; they do not tell us what *ought* to be. In addition to getting the facts, resolving an ethical issue also requires an appeal to values. Philosophers have developed five different approaches to values to deal with moral issues.

The Utilitarian Approach

Utilitarianism was conceived in the 19th century by Jeremy Bentham and John Stuart Mill to help legislators determine which laws were morally best. Both Bentham and Mill suggested that ethical actions are those that provide the greatest balance of good over evil.

To analyze an issue using the utilitarian approach, we first identify the various courses of action available to us. Second, we ask who will be affected by each action and what benefits or harms will be derived from each. And third, we choose the action that will produce the greatest benefits and the least harm. The ethical action is the one that provides the greatest good for the greatest number.

The Rights Approach

The second important approach to ethics has its roots in the philosophy of the 18th-century thinker Immanuel Kant and others like him, who focused on the individual's right to choose for herself or himself. According to these philosophers, what makes human beings different from mere things is that people have dignity based on their ability to choose freely what they will do with their lives, and they have a fundamental moral right to have these choices respected. People are not objects to be manipulated; it is a violation of human dignity to use people in ways they do not freely choose.

Of course, many different, but related, rights exist besides this basic one. These other rights (an incomplete list below) can be thought of as different aspects of the basic right to be treated as we choose.

- *The right to the truth*: We have a right to be told the truth and to be informed about matters that significantly affect our choices.
- *The right of privacy*: We have the right to do, believe, and say whatever we choose in our personal lives so long as we do not violate the rights of others.
- *The right not to be injured*: We have the right not to be harmed or injured unless we freely and knowingly do something to deserve punishment or we freely and knowingly choose to risk such injuries.
- *The right to what is agreed:* We have a right to what has been promised by those with whom we have freely entered into a contract or agreement.

In deciding whether an action is moral or immoral using this second approach, then, we must ask, Does the action respect the moral rights of everyone? Actions are wrong to the extent

The Case of Maria Elena

Maria Elena has cleaned your house each week for more than a year. You agree with your friend who recommended her that she does an excellent job and is well worth the $30 cash you pay her for three hours' work. You've also come to like her, and you think she likes you, especially as her English has become better and you've been able to have some pleasant conversations.

Over the past three weeks, however, you've noticed Maria Elena becoming more and more distracted. One day, you ask her if something is wrong, and she tells you she really needs to make additional money. She hastens to say she is not asking you for a raise, becomes upset, and begins to cry. When she calms down a little, she tells you her story:

She came to the United States six years ago from Mexico with her child, Miguel, who is now 7 years old. They entered the country on a visitor's visa that has expired, and Maria Elena now uses a Social Security number she made up.

Her common-law husband, Luis, came to the United States first. He entered the country illegally, after paying smugglers $500 to hide him under piles of grass cuttings for a six-hour truck ride across the border. When he had made enough money from low-paying day jobs, he sent for Maria Elena. Using a false green card, Luis now works as a busboy for a restaurant, which withholds part of his salary for taxes. When Maria Elena comes to work at your house, she takes the bus and Luis baby-sits.

In Mexico, Maria Elena and Luis lived in a small village where it was impossible to earn more than $3 a day. Both had sixth-grade educations, common in their village. Life was difficult, but they did not decide to leave until they realized the future would be bleak for their child and for the other children they wanted to have. Luis had a cousin in San Jose who visited and told Luis and Maria Elena how well his life was going. After his visit, Luis and Maria Elena decided to come to the United States.

Luis quickly discovered, as did Maria Elena, that life in San Jose was not the way they had heard. The cousin did not tell them they would be able to afford to live only in a run-down three-room apartment with two other couples and their children. He did not tell them they would always live in fear of INS raids.

After they entered the United States, Maria Elena and Luis had a second child, Jose, who is 5 years old. The birth was difficult because she didn't use the health-care system or welfare for fear of being discovered as undocumented. But, she tells you, she is willing to put up with anything so that her children can have a better life. "All the money we make is for Miguel and Jose," she tells you. "We work hard for their education and their future."

Now, however, her mother in Mexico is dying, and Maria Elena must return home, leaving Luis and the children. She does not want to leave them because she might not be able to get back into the United States, but she is pretty sure she can find a way to return if she has enough money. That is her problem: She doesn't have enough money to make certain she can get back.

After she tells you her story, she becomes too distraught to continue talking. You now know she is an undocumented immigrant, working in your home. What is the ethical thing for you to do?

This case was developed by Tom Shanks, S.J., director of the Markkula Center for Applied Ethics. Maria Elena is a composite drawn from several real people, and her story represents some of the ethical dilemmas behind the immigration issue.

This case can be accessed through the Ethics Center home page on the World Wide Web: http://www.scu.edu/Ethics/. You can also contact us by e-mail, ethics@scu.edu, or regular mail: Markkula Center for Applied Ethics, Santa Clara University, Santa Clara, CA 95053. Our voice mail number is (408) 554-7898. We have also posted on our homepage a new case involving managed health care.

---

that they violate the rights of individuals; the more serious the violation, the more wrongful the action.

The Fairness or Justice Approach

The fairness or justice approach to ethics has its roots in the teachings of the ancient Greek philosopher Aristotle, who said that "equals should be treated equally and unequals unequally." The basic moral question in this approach is: How fair is an action? Does it treat everyone in the same way, or does it show favoritism and discrimination?

Favoritism gives benefits to some people without a justifiable reason for singling them out; discrimination imposes burdens on people who are no different from those on whom burdens

are not imposed. Both favoritism and discrimination are unjust and wrong.

The Common-Good Approach

This approach to ethics presents a vision of society as a community whose members are joined in the shared pursuit of values and goals they hold in common. This community comprises individuals whose own good is inextricably bound to the good of the whole.

The common good is a notion that originated more than 2,000 years ago in the writings of Plato, Aristotle, and Cicero. More recently, contemporary ethicist John Rawls defined the common good as "certain general conditions that are . . . equally to everyone's advantage."

In this approach, we focus on ensuring that the social policies, social systems, institutions, and environments on which we depend are beneficial to all. Examples of goods common to all include affordable health care, effective public safety, peace among nations, a just legal system, and an unpolluted environment.

Appeals to the common good urge us to view ourselves as members of the same community, reflecting on broad questions concerning the kind of society we want to become and how we are to achieve that society. While respecting and valuing the freedom of individuals to pursue their own goals, the common-good approach challenges us also to recognize and further those goals we share in common.

The Virtue Approach

The virtue approach to ethics assumes that there are certain ideals toward which we should strive, which provide for the full development of our humanity. These ideals are discovered through thoughtful reflection on what kind of people we have the potential to become.

Virtues are attitudes or character traits that enable us to be and to act in ways that develop our highest potential. They enable us to pursue the ideals we have adopted.

Honesty, courage, compassion, generosity, fidelity, integrity, fairness, self-control, and prudence are all examples of virtues.

Virtues are like habits; that is, once acquired, they become characteristic of a person. Moreover, a person who has developed virtues will be naturally disposed to act in ways consistent with moral principles. The virtuous person is the ethical person.

In dealing with an ethical problem using the virtue approach, we might ask, What kind of person should I be? What will promote the development of character within myself and my community?

Ethical Problem Solving

These five approaches suggest that once we have ascertained the facts, we should ask ourselves five questions when trying to resolve a moral issue:

- What benefits and what harms will each course of action produce, and which alternative will lead to the best overall consequences?
- What moral rights do the affected parties have, and which course of action best respects those rights?
- Which course of action treats everyone the same, except where there is a morally justifiable reason not to, and does not show favoritism or discrimination?
- Which course of action advances the common good?
- Which course of action develops moral virtues?

This method, of course, does not provide an automatic solution to moral problems. It is not meant to. The method is merely meant to help identify most of the important ethical considerations. In the end, we must deliberate on moral issues for ourselves, keeping a careful eye on both the facts and on the ethical considerations involved.

This article updates several previous pieces from *Issues in Ethics* by **MANUEL VELASQUEZ**—Dirksen Professor of Business Ethics at SCU and former Center director—and **CLAIRE ANDRE,** associate Center director. "Thinking Ethically" is based on a framework developed by the authors in collaboration with Center Director **THOMAS SHANKS, S. J.,** Presidential Professor of Ethics and the Common Good **MICHAEL J. MEYER,** and others. The framework is used as the basis for many Center programs and presentations.

Create a Culture of Trust

Take 10 actions to cultivate a spirit of reciprocity.

Noreen Kelly

Creating a culture of trust starts at the top. Leaders are responsible for creating a culture of shared values and meaning, promoting ethical behavior, and looking after their brand and reputation.

Edgar Schein, an expert on culture, states: "Culture defines leadership. Leaders should be conscious of culture; otherwise, it will manage them."

As guardians of culture, leaders need to live the values. Enron's espoused "values" of respect, integrity, communication and excellence, meant nothing. In a values-based organization, a leader's actions and behaviors align with stated values and beliefs. The leaders at Google, #1 on the list of the *100 Best Companies to Work For,* figured out the formula that works for them: treat people with respect, support their creative endeavors, and adhere to the motto of "Don't be evil."

Another basis for trust is the belief that you, as a leader, are acting in an ethical manner and promoting ethical ideas and practices. Culture plays a greater role than formal ethics and compliance programs when it comes to preventing unethical behaviors. Even after Enron and other scandals and enactment of Sarbanes-Oxley, few leaders have changed their culture to be one where ethical violations are simply not tolerated. This change can only come from the top, and leaders must involve employees at all levels.

Leaders must adopt an enterprise-wide cultural approach to ethics that extends beyond a compliance mentality. By creating a strong ethical culture, shaped by ethical leadership and values, you dramatically reduce misconduct. A well-implemented ethics and compliance program and a strong ethical culture greatly reduce ethics risk.

Reputation is a company's most important asset and a critical factor in earning and creating trust. Based on actions rather than words, reputation is about staying true to who you are. Companies that set high aspirations through their branding and marketing need to live up to that promise. When a gap exists between who a company is and who they say they are, an environment of distrust is created.

In promoting social responsibility, leaders must do right by employees. While protecting the environment, supporting the community, and adopting socially responsible practices are all important, leaders should be first committed to their own employees.

10 Actions Cultivate Trust

To cultivate a culture of trust, follow 10 actions:

1. *Live the values.* Match actions with words. Walk the talk. Live up to the values you espouse. Inspire people through leading by example. Practice and promote alignment with the values daily and send clear signals about what the values are. Make ethics a priority. Model ethical behavior and support those who uphold standards.

2. *Tell the truth.* Be honest. Get rid of hidden agendas. Be simple, straightforward, and consistent. Admit what you don't know when asked a question, and promise to find out. Share what you know, when you know it. If you don't know, say so. If you can't tell, say so.

3. *Communicate, communicate, communicate.* Encourage open communication. Keep employees informed and address issues when you observe them. Create a dialogue. Listen. Engage and involve people at the grassroots of a project or decision when possible. Value people's input and opinions. Communicate the importance of ethics and integrity, along with shared vision and values. Provide clear and consistent communication to key stakeholders.

4. *Be in integrity.* Make good on your promises and commitments. Be realistic. Don't overpromise. Do what you say you're going to do. Take responsibility for your actions and act ethically.

5. *Be authentic.* Engage in honest conversations. Be credible. Be who you say you are. Demonstrate company values through thoughts, words, intentions and actions. Bring words and actions into alignment.

6. *Be accountable.* Admit mistakes. Hold yourself accountable for your actions, words, and decisions to your employees and customers.

7. *Be transparent.* Be visible. Disclose information as needed. Clearly communicate facts to build trust and credibility with stakeholders.

8. *Respect the individual.* Promote mutual trust and respect. Be inclusive. Show empathy. Acknowledge and honor people's feelings and concerns.

9. ***Share information.*** Keep employees informed and address issues when they are observed. Note that decisions may change, and provide timely feedback. Involve people at the grassroots level of a project or decision whenever possible. Involve those who are or could be affected. Sharing of information within and between teams creates dialogue, promotes cooperation, and helps build community over time.

10. ***Do the right thing.*** Much evidence supports the impact of values, ethics and reputation on the bottom line: Values driven companies are the most successful. Companies that fail to look after the reputation aspects of performance ultimately suffer financially. Companies that are great places to work are more financially successful. Organizations with high trust benefit from increased profitability, market value, and lower costs.

Beyond bottom-line implications, leaders should create a culture of trust simply because it's the right thing to do. Adam Smith, author of *The Theory of Moral Sentiments* (1759), believed that virtues like trust, fairness and reciprocity are vital for the functioning of a market economy. Consider the high costs of breaking trust, risking reputation, and sacrificing ethical standards.

Creating a trust culture takes commitment and action. Trust begets trust. Trust sustains trust and repairs lost trust.

Leaders who choose to trust, value, respect, and empower their people are rewarded with motivated and productive people and greater profitability. Leaders who communicate openly and honestly create mutual trust, bolster credibility and engage their people.

Move away from fear-based values toward positive values, and create connections and conversations that maintain trust. In a spirit of reciprocity, participation, dialogue and hope, a culture of trust can be achieved.

NOREEN KELLY is president of Trust Matters. Call 312.988.7562, email noreen@noreenkelly.com. Visit www.noreenkelly.com.

Business Ethics
Back to Basics

With business news dominated in recent years by some spectacular examples of ethical malfeasance, confidence in the business world has been shaken. Never mind that the Enrons of the world are actually few and far between. No business or organization can afford even a suspicion of unethical behavior and must take proactive steps to ensure that no suspicions arise. Ethical behavior begins at the top with actions and statements that are beyond reproach and ambiguity. Managements may want to follow an eight-point action list presented here for establishing a strong ethical culture and also a decision checklist when ethical dilemmas loom. Sterling reputations are valuable business assets: they are earned over time but can be lost almost overnight.

WILLIAM I. SAUSER, JR.

Introduction

Enron, Arthur Andersen, Tyco, ImClone, Martha Stewart, WorldCom, Global Crossing, Merrill Lynch, Rite-Aid, Qwest, Adelphia, Kmart, HealthSouth—the list of formerly respected businesses (and business leaders) being charged with breaches of ethical conduct seems to be growing by the day. This is having adverse effects on our economic well-being, on investor confidence, and on the perceived desirability of pursuing business as a respectable calling.

Commenting on the ethical crisis in business leadership, Eileen Kelly (2002) observed, "Recently a new business scandal seems to surface each day. The current volatility of the market reflects the apprehension, the sense of betrayal, and the lack of confidence that investors have in many large corporations and their managements" (p. 4). Marcy Gordon (2002), reporting on a speech by United States Securities and Exchange Commissioner Paul Atkins, noted, "The string of accounting failures at big companies in the last year has cost U.S. households nearly $60,000 on average as some $5 trillion in market value was lost."

Accounting failures are not the only ethical concerns facing modern business organizations. The Southern Institute for Business and Professional Ethics (2002) lists on its Web site an array of issues that put pressures on business enterprises. These include the globalization of business, work force diversification, employment practices and policies, civil litigation and government regulation, and concerns about environmental stewardship. The institute (on the same Web site) concluded, "Despite such powerful trends, few managers have been adequately equipped by traditional education to recognize, evaluate, and act upon the ethical dimension of their work."

Columnist Malcolm Cutchins (2002), an emeritus professor of engineering at Auburn University, summed up the problem concisely: "We have seen the effect of not teaching good ethics in business schools. If we continue to neglect the teaching of good principles on a broad scale, we all reap the bad consequences."

Business Ethics

Ethics has to do with behavior—specifically, an individual's moral behavior with respect to society. The extent to which behavior measures up to societal standards is typically used as a gauge of ethicality. Since there are a variety of standards for societal behavior, ethical behavior is often characterized with respect to certain contexts. The Ethics Resource Center says, "*Business Ethics* refers to clear standards and norms that help employees to distinguish right from wrong behavior at work" (Joseph, 2003, p. 2). In the business context, ethics has to do with the extent to which a person's behavior measures up to such standards as the law, organizational policies, professional and trade association codes, popular expectations regarding fairness and rightness, plus an individual's internalized moral standards.

Business ethics, then, is not distinct from ethics in general, but rather a subfield (Desjardins, 2003, p. 8). The subfield refers to the examination and application of moral standards within the context of finance; commerce; production, distribution, and sale of goods and services; and other business activities.

It can be argued that an ethical person behaves appropriately in all societal contexts. This may be so, in which case one might prefer the term "ethics in business" to "business ethics." The distinction is subtle, but serves as a reminder that morality may be generalized from context to context. Adam Smith, for example, saw no need for ethical relativism when it comes to business. "It is impossible to determine just how business became separated from ethics in history. If we go back to Adam Smith, we find no such separation. In addition to his famous book on business and capitalism, *The Wealth of Nations*, Adam Smith also wrote *The Theory of Moral Sentiments*, a book about our ethical obligations to one another. It is clear that Smith believed that business and commerce worked well only if people took seriously their obligations and, in particular, their sense of justice" (Bruner, Eaker, Freeman, Spekman, and Teisberg, 1998, p. 46).

May (1995) echoed this important point: "The marketplace breaks down unless it can presuppose the virtue of industry, without which goods will not be produced; and the virtues of "honesty and integrity, without which their free and fair exchange cannot take place."

Standards of Behavior

The law (including statutory, administrative, and case law) is an important and legitimate source of ethical guidance. Federal, state, and local laws establish the parameters (Fieser, 1996), and violation of the law is almost always considered unethical (with the possible exception of civil disobedience as a mechanism for putting the law itself on trial). Pursuing business outside the law is regarded as an obstructionist approach to business ethics (Schermerhorn, 2005, p. 75). Such an individual would almost certainly be labeled unethical.

A second important source of authority is organizational policies, which are standards for behavior established by the employing organization. Typically they are aligned with the law (which takes precedence over them) and spell out in detail how things are done. All employees are expected to adhere to organizational policies. It is very important that managers at the highest level set the example for others by always working within the law and the policies of the organization.

Another important source of ethical guidance is the code of behavior adopted by professional and trade associations. These codes are often aspirational in nature and frequently establish higher standards for behavior than the law requires. Members of a profession or trade association typically aspire to meet these higher standards in order to establish and uphold the reputation of a profession or trade.

A fourth type of standard—often unwritten and commonly the community's concept of morality. These social mores, based on commonly held beliefs about what is right and wrong and fair and unfair, can be powerful determinants of a person's reputation. Behavior that—in the strictest sense—meets legal requirements, organizational policies, and even professional standards may still be viewed by the general public as unfair and wrong (Krech, Crutchfield, and Ballachey, 1962).

A fifth set of standards reflects the individual conscience. Coleman, Butcher and Carson (1980, p. Glossary IV) define "the conscience" as "the functioning of an individual's moral values in the approval or disapproval of his or her own thoughts and actions," and equate it roughly with the Freudian concept of the superego. Highly ethical business leaders typically have moral standards that exceed all four of the lesser standards just listed. These values, learned early in life and reinforced by life's experiences, are internalized standards often based on personal, religious or philosophical understandings of morality (Baelz, 1977, pp. 41–55).

Ethical Dilemmas

An ethical dilemma is a situation where a potential course of action offers potential benefit or gain but is unethical, in that it violates one or more of the standards just described. Behaviors violating laws are, by definition, illegal as well as unethical. The key question for the business leader when presented with an ethical dilemma is: "What to do?" Behavior determines a person's ethical reputation, after all. Ethical leadership is exhibited when ethical dilemmas are resolved in an appropriate manner.

Here is a sampling of some ethical dilemmas that frequently rise in the business setting. Many of these behaviors are illegal as well as unethical.

- Providing a product or service you know is harmful or unsafe
- Misleading someone through false statements or omissions
- Using insider information for personal gain
- Playing favorites
- Manipulating and using people
- Benefiting personally from a position of trust
- Violating confidentiality
- Misusing company property or equipment
- Falsifying documents
- Padding expenses
- Taking bribes or kickbacks
- Participating in a cover-up
- Theft or sabotage
- Committing an act of violence
- Substance abuse
- Negligence or inappropriate behavior in the workplace.

Poor Ethical Choices

Why do people sometimes make poor choices when faced with ethical dilemmas? One set of reasons has to do with flaws of *character*. Such character defects include malice (intentional evil); sociopathy (lack of conscience); personal greed; envy, jealousy, resentment; the will to win or achieve at any cost; and fear of failure. There are also flaws in *corporate culture* that lead even good people to make poor ethical judgments. Weaknesses in corporate culture include indifference, a lack of knowledge or understanding of standards on the part of employees; poor or inappropriate incentive systems; and poor leadership, including the use of mixed signals such as:

- I don't care how you do it, just get it done.
- Don't ever bring me bad news.
- Don' t bother me with the details, you know what to do.

8

- Remember, we always meet our financial goals somehow.
- No one gets injured on this worksite . . . period. Understand?
- Ask me no questions, I'll tell you no lies.

Such statements by managers to their subordinates too often imply that unethical behaviors that obtain the intended results are acceptable to the organization. While it may be difficult—other than through termination or other sanctions—to rid the organization of employees with character flaws, correcting a poor organizational culture is clearly a matter of leadership.

Establishing a Strong Ethical Culture

Business leaders who wish to take proactive measures to establish and maintain a corporate culture that emphasizes strong moral leadership are advised to take the following steps:

1. **Adopt a code of ethics.** The code need not be long and elaborate with flowery words and phrases. In fact, the best ethical codes use language anyone can understand. A good way to produce such a code is to ask all employees of the firm (or a representative group) to participate in its creation (Kuchar, 2003). Identify the commonly-held moral beliefs and values of the members of the firm and codify them into a written document all can understand and support. Post the code of ethics in prominent places around the worksite. Make certain that all employees subscribe to it by asking them to sign it.

2. **Provide ethics training.** From time to time a leader should conduct ethics training sessions. These may be led by experts in business ethics, or they may be informal in nature and led by the manager or employees themselves. A highly effective way to conduct an ethics training session is to provide "what if" cases for discussion and resolution. The leader would present a "real world" scenario in which an ethical dilemma is encountered. Using the organization's code of ethics as a guide, participants would explore options and seek a consensus ethical solution. This kind of training sharpens the written ethical code and brings it to life.

3. **Hire and promote ethical people.** This, in concert with step four, is probably the best defense against putting the business at risk through ethical lapses by employees. When making human resources decisions it is critical to reward ethical behavior and punish unethical behavior. Investigate the character of the people you hire, and do your best to hire people who have exhibited high moral standards in the past. Remember that past behavior is the best predictor of future behavior, so check references carefully. Formal background investigations may be warranted for positions of fiduciary responsibility or significant risk exposure. Base promotional decisions on matters of character in addition to technical competence. Demonstrate to your employees that high ethical standards are a requirement for advancement.

4. **Correct unethical behavior.** This complements step three. When the organization's ethical code is breached, those responsible must be punished. Many businesses use progressive discipline, with an oral warning (intended to advise the employee of what is and is not acceptable behavior) as the first step, followed by a written reprimand, suspension without pay, and termination if unethical behavior persists. Of course, some ethical lapses are so egregious that they require suspension—or even termination—following the first offense. Through consistent and firm application of sanctions to correct unethical behavior, the manager will signal to all employees that substandard moral behavior will not be tolerated.

5. **Be proactive.** Businesses wishing to establish a reputation for ethicality and good corporate citizenship in the community will often organize and support programs intended to give something back to the community. Programs that promote continuing education, wholesome recreation, good health and hygiene, environmental quality, adequate housing, and other community benefits may demonstrate the extent to which the business promotes concern for human welfare. Seeking and adopting best practices from other businesses in the community is also a proactive strategy.

6. **Conduct a social audit.** Most businesses are familiar with financial audits. This concept can be employed in the context of ethics and corporate responsibility as well. From time to time the leader of the business might invite responsible parties to examine the organization's product design, purchasing, production, marketing, distribution, customer relations, and human resources functions with an eye toward identifying and correcting any areas of policy or practice that raise ethical concerns. Similarly, programs of corporate responsibility (such as those mentioned in step five) should be reviewed for effectiveness and improved as needed.

7. **Protect whistle blowers.** A whistle blower is a person within the firm who points out ethically questionable actions taken by other employees—or even by managers—within the organization. Too often corporate whistle blowers are ignored—or even punished—by those who receive the unfortunate news of wrongdoing within the business. All this does is discourage revelation of ethical problems. Instead the whistle blower should be protected and even honored. When unethical actions are uncovered within a firm by one of the employees, managers should step forward and take corrective action (as described in step four). Employees learn from one another. If the owners and managers of a business turn a blind eye toward wrongdoing, a signal is sent to everyone within the firm that ethicality is not characteristic of that organization's culture. A downward spiral of moral behavior is likely to follow.

8. **Empower the guardians of integrity.** The business leader's chief task is to lead by example and to empower every member of the organization to demonstrate the firm's commitment to ethics in its relationships with suppliers, customers, employees, and shareholders. Turn each employee of the firm, no matter what that individual's position, into a guardian of the firm's integrity. When maliciousness and indifference are replaced with a culture of integrity, honesty, and ethicality, the business will reap long-term benefits from all quarters.

A Checklist for Making Good Ethical Decisions

A business leader who takes seriously the challenge of creating a strong ethical culture for the firm must, of course, make good decisions when faced personally with ethical dilemmas. Here is a checklist a manager might wish to follow:

1. Recognize the ethical dilemma.
2. Get the facts.
3. Identify your options.
4. Test each option: Is it legal, right, beneficial? Note: Get some counsel.
5. Decide which option to follow.
6. Double-check your decision.
7. Take action.
8. Follow up and monitor decision implementation.

Number six is key: Double-check your decision. When in doubt consider how each of the following might guide you. Take the action that would allow you to maintain your reputation with those on this list you believe adhere to the highest ethical standards: Your attorney, accountant, boss, co-workers, stakeholders, family, newspaper, television news, religious leader, and Deity.

How would you feel if you had to explain your decision—and your actions—to each of these? If you would not feel good about this, then it is quite likely that you are about to make a poor decision. Double check your decision in this manner before you take any action you may later regret.

Conclusion

A firm's reputation may take years—even decades—to establish, but can be destroyed in an instant through unethical behavior. That is why it is so important for business leaders to be very careful about the things they say and do. Taking the time and effort to establish and maintain a corporate culture of morality, integrity, honesty, and ethicality will pay important dividends throughout the life of the firm. While taking ethical shortcuts may appear to lead to gains in the short term, this type of corporate strategy almost always proves tragic in the longer term.

Every business leader will be faced at one time or another with an ethical dilemma. Many face even daily temptations. How the leader manifests moral integrity when faced with ethical dilemmas sets the tone for everyone else in the organization.

This is why it is so important to "walk the talk" by making good ethical decisions every day. Understanding and applying the concepts presented in this article will enable you, as a business leader, to create and maintain an ethical corporate culture in your business. As Carl Skoogland, the former vice president and ethics director for Texas Instruments, recently advised, if you want to create an ethical business, you must *know what's right, value what's right, and do what's right* (Skoogland, 2003).

References

Baelz, P. (1977). *Ethics and belief.* New York: The Seabury Press.

Bruner, R. F., Eaker, M. R., Freeman, E., Spekman, R.E., and Teisberg, E. O. (1998). *The portable MBA, 3rd ed.* New York: Wiley.

Coleman, J. C., Butcher, J. N., and Carson, R. (1980). *Abnormal psychology and modern life, 6th ed,* Glenview, IL: Scott Foresman.

Cutchins, M. (2002, November 20). Business ethics must be taught or we all pay. *Opelika-Auburn News,* p. A4.

Desjardins, J. (2003). *An introduction to business ethics.* Boston: McGraw-Hill.

Fieser, J. (1996). Do businesses have moral obligations beyond what the law requires? *Journal of Business Ethics, 15,* 457–468.

Gordon, M. (2002, November 18). Accounting failures cost $60,000 on average, SEC commissioner says. *Opelika-Auburn News,* p. C4.

Joseph, J. (2003). *National business ethics survey 2003: How employees view ethics in their organizations.* Washington, DC: Ethics Resource Center.

Kelly, E. P. (2002). Business ethics—An oxymoron? *Phi Kappa Phi Forum, 82*(4), 4–5.

Krech, D., Crutchfield, R. S., and Ballachey, E. L. (1962). Culture. Chapter 10 in *Individual in society* (pp. 339–380). New York: McGraw-Hill.

Kuchar, C. (2003). Tips on developing ethics codes for private companies. *GoodBusiness,* 2(3), pages unnumbered.

May, W. F. (1995). The virtues of the business leader. In M. L. Stackhouse, D. P. McCann, S. J, Roels, and P. N. Williams (Eds.), *On moral business* (pp. 692–700). Grand Rapids, MI: Eerdmans.

Schermerhorn, J. R., Jr. (2005). *Management, 8th ed.* New York: Wiley.

Skoogland, C. (2003, October 16). *Establishing an ethical organization.* Plenary address at the Conference on Ethics and Social Responsibility in Engineering and Technology, New Orleans, LA.

The Southern Institute for Business and Professional Ethics. (2002). *The certificate in managerial ethics.* Retrieved August, 14, 2002, from http://www.southerninstitute.org.

DR. SAUSER is Associate Dean for Business and Engineering Outreach and Professor of Management at Auburn University. His interests include organization development, strategic planning, human relations in the workplace, business ethics, and continuing professional education. He is a Fellow of the American Council on Education and the Society for Advancement of Management (SAM). In 2003, he was awarded the Frederick W. Taylor Key by SAM for his career achievements.

From *SAM Advanced Management Journal,* 2005, No. 2, pp. 1–4. Copyright © 2005 Society for Advancement of Management. Reprinted with permission.

Building an Ethical Framework

10 questions to consider in encouraging an ethical corporate culture.

THOMAS R. KRAUSE AND PAUL J. VOSS

Although we are now several years into the new and landmark regulatory environment that mandates an organizational culture of ethical conduct, there remains little guidance on how to get there. Many companies are engaged in a scramble to create a paper and electronic trail to ward off prosecution, rather than in a well-designed effort to promote or govern the culture of their organizations. While procedure is essential, the lesson we have learned from organizational change efforts is that leadership, rather than rules, finally determines behaviors and their outcomes.

This article suggests 10 primary questions every executive should ask—and expect to have answered thoroughly and well—in order to initiate a culture that encourages and sustains ethical conduct. These questions are meant to be asked and answered among leaders themselves, as well as with employees throughout the organization.

1. What is the relationship between ethics and other performance metrics in the company?

The relative cost of preventing a protracted ethical dilemma or full-fledged scandal is exponentially lower than the costs associated with fixing ethical problems. For example, see "The Cost to Firms of Cooking the Books," by J. Karpoff, D. Lee and G. Martin, forthcoming in *The Journal of Financial and Quantitative Analysis,* for a study of the substantial costs in fines and lost market value to almost 600 firms subject to SEC enforcement before the enactment of the Sarbanes-Oxley Act. Current research demonstrates that ethical companies are more competitive, profitable and sustaining than unethical companies. The challenge for the ethical leader is to find that connection and reveal it to the organization.

2. Have we, as required by the 2004 federal sentencing guidelines, offered ethics training for all of our employees? Does the training provide more than rote introduction of the company's code of conduct?

Ethics training comes in all shapes and sizes, with the most successful moving from theory to practice and from the conceptual to the real. Companies must first settle on an ethical vocabulary, define terms and establish core values. Live case studies can then help leadership and management "solve" relevant ethical dilemmas, both real and hypothetical.

3. What is the relationship between exercising sound ethics and retaining great talent?

Fortune magazine's annual list of the top 100 companies to work for contains a wide variety of companies with no obvious common denominator. Salary, benefits, career opportunities, location and profession all vary. What they do have in common is trust between employee and employer. Ethical behavior with and among employees, then, can lay the groundwork for attracting and retaining the best talent.

4. Have we conducted a "risk assessment" to determine our exposure to major ethical damage? What is our potential Enron?

While each company may have its unique "ethical nightmare," most companies face similar ethical exposures (e.g., to theft and accounting irregularities). Companies must examine the potential hazards of perverse incentives (e.g., compensation based 100 percent on financial goals) and the various "unintended consequences" of policy, procedures and protocols. Companies can reduce or eliminate adverse incentives by never rewarding, intentionally or unintentionally, improper behavior.

Research literature identifies several characteristics predictive of ethical outcomes: management credibility, upward communication, perceived organizational support, procedural justice and teamwork.

5. How can we be proactive in the area of ethics, culture and corporate citizenship?

Leaders need to own and shape the culture as much as they manage, for example, quality initiatives. Research literature identifies several characteristics predictive of ethical outcomes: management credibility, upward communication, perceived organizational support, procedural justice and teamwork. Well-tested diagnostic tools allow leaders to measure these characteristics and specific behaviors that foster the culture desired.

6. What tone should executive leadership set regarding ethics, integrity and transparency?

Setting an example is just one part of the executive leadership's responsibility. What leaders say, think and feel affects the tone as much as their actions. Mistrust, cynicism or indifference from topmost leaders can erode others' loyalty to the organization, to its mission, to employees and to shareholders. Left unchecked, this tone from the top can also potentially push ethical leaders out the door.

7. What does management need from the board of directors and senior leadership to enhance and buttress corporate ethics?

Employees who see the governing board and executive leadership as unconcerned will discount any directives about ethics that come from them. Consistency and authenticity from the board and executive leadership play a signal role in establishing an ethics initiative. At a minimum this means providing a reasonable budget of time, talent and money.

8. Who is driving ethics and compliance in the company?

The recent American Management Association report *The Ethical Enterprise* (2006) shows that ethical companies do not happen by accident. Companies need to designate internal drivers who move along the discussions, training and initiatives, producing ethical outcomes.

9. Do we have consistency of message between and among the board, the CEO, the senior executive team and the associates in terms of ethics and culture?

We all need to be on the same page, but finding the proper tone and guidance can be tricky. Establishing a common vocabulary can help with this process. For example, what does it mean to act unethically? What is an ethical dilemma? Who were Aristotle, Plato and Machiavelli, and how can they help provide a vocabulary for our company? What ethical model do we want to follow? What can we do to make it stick?

10. What roadblocks now discourage ethical conversations and the implementation of ethical practices, procedures and protocols?

Most people want to act with ethics and integrity, "to do the right thing." Yet our current approach to ethical conversation often does not advance our thinking or practice past our own perspectives. The object of dialogue, as advocated by physicist David Bohm, is "not to analyze things, or to win an argument, or to exchange opinions. Rather, it is to suspend your opinions and . . . to listen to everybody's opinions, to suspend them, and to see what all that means. . . . And if we can see them all, we may then move more creatively in a different direction." (For more information, see "On Dialogue," Ojai, Calif.: David Bohm Seminars, 1990.)

> **Most people want . . . "to do the right thing." Yet our current approach to ethical conversation often does not advance our thinking past our own perspectives.**

Starting the Conversation

Asking these 10 questions at board meetings, in leadership team meetings, and in the course of day-to-day interactions with employees engenders a climate that leads, over time, to zero tolerance for ethical lapses and impropriety. They also help executives assure their own diligence and oversight of ethical risks and threats, and deliver on their promise to employees, shareholders, customers and the community at large.

THOMAS R. KRAUSE, PhD is author of several books and Chairman and Co-founder of Behavioral Science Technology, Inc. (BST), an international performance solutions consulting company. He focuses on executive leadership development and coaching for clients including NASA, BHP Billiton and the FAA. PAUL J. VOSS, PhD is Ethics Practice Leader with BST. An author, scholar and lecturer, Dr. Voss' clients include Home Depot, the FBI lab, General Electric and Russell Athletics.

Ethical Leadership
Maintain an Ethical Culture

RONALD E. BERENBEIM

I n the United States, the consensus regarding the need for ethical business practice has been codified in *The Revised Sentencing Guidelines,* which is widely accepted as an authoritative business conduct guidance document in the United States and elsewhere—a template for sound business practice.

Compliance with the *Guidelines* requires that a high-level person be responsible for the company's ethics program and foster an ethical culture within the company. Such an environment affords assurance that people are free to ask questions and raise concerns. Meeting the demands of the *Guidelines* demands ethical leadership. For example, in Australia, a company can be criminally liable if it fails to maintain a culture that requires compliance with the law—if the culture directs, tolerates, or leads to noncompliance with the criminal provisions proscribing the bribery of foreign public officials. This standard helps companies avoid these problems with descriptions of the necessary structural, operational, and maintenance elements for effective compliance.

Three Lessons from Nehru

As an example of ethical leadership of the highest order, consider the case of Jawaharlal Nehru. In 1937, Nehru had just been elected to a second, consecutive term as President of the Indian National Parliament. Rabindrath Tagore, the Indian poet, philosopher, writer, and Nobel laureate hailed him as "representing the season of youth and triumphant joy." Even a British official wrote of him at the time, "there is no doubt that his manliness, frankness, and reputation for sacrifice attracts a large public."

Though widely held, this favorable view was not unanimous. One anonymous writer vigorously dissented. In a severe attack published in the *Modern Review,* the critic said: "He has all the makings of a dictator in him—vast popularity, a strong will directed to a well-defined purpose, energy, pride, organizational capacity, ability, hardness, and with his love of the crowd, an intolerance of others and a certain contempt for the weak and inefficient. His conceit is formidable. He must be checked. We want no Caesars."

The author of this vitriolic article was none other than Nehru himself. Recalling this episode is not to make a judgment about Nehru but to demonstrate how his behavior in this situation shows an intuitive grasp of the essence of ethical leadership. Nehru understood that a leader is most ethical and effective when his or her power is limited—by institutional arrangements and the criticism that results from harsh public scrutiny. If the Congress Party and the Indian press lacked these resources, he believed that it was necessary for him to supply the discipline that these countervailing forces ordinarily would have imposed.

From this great example of ethical leadership, I draw three lessons:

1. *Ethical leaders don't hide from debate.* An ethical leader understands that open and contentious debate is essential to making the best possible decisions. And openly debated decisions result in better outcomes. Some years ago, a research study focused on the behavior of members of investment clubs, small and somewhat informal gatherings of private individual investors, in the United States. Those groups in which the members enjoyed one another's company, reached consensus quickly, and were polite and civil, had a much poorer performance record than the clubs whose investment choices were the result of contentious debate.

An ethical leader understands that open and contentious debate is essential to making the best possible decisions. Although encouraging debate is essential, ethical leadership must balance the need for robust discussion with the requirement of commitment to a common purpose. Where such a consensus is lacking there is a danger of polarization, which will cause people to avoid the risk of winding up on the wrong side and in so doing limit their comments to information that everyone already has.

These findings tell us something that most of us already know—and often forget—or at least choose to believe is good advice for other organizations (perhaps even our competitors), but not our own. Leaders who ignore this wisdom put their enterprises at great risk. For confirmation of this view, one need look no further than the U.S. Presidential Commission report released March 30, 2005, on the intelligence failures in Iraq. The report recommended moving "away from the intelligence community's tradition of searching for consensus, in favor of opening up internal debate and including a more diverse spectrum of views."

2. *Ethical leaders are active participants.* Leaders need to be active participants in the debate over alternatives. In some circles, it has become a fashionable corporate model for the CEO to say to the senior executives, "You people thrash it out, reach a consensus, and send me your recommendation." Such a decision-making process has serious flaws. The most robust internal processes are of no avail if the leader is exempt from them. Good leaders don't just subject themselves to the need to test their ideas—they welcome the opportunity and have a zest for intellectual combat. They realize that there is more to leadership than giving orders. Ethical leaders understand that their views and decisions are in large measure determined by their contact with the people they lead.

Among other advantages, these discussions provide a necessary dose of reality. Nehru's self-criticism attacked his own "conceit" and what he believed to be his "intolerance of others and [a certain] contempt for the weak and the inefficient." He seemed to understand that however decisive and effective a leader's decision-making powers may be, the implementation of a decision requires great patience and tolerance. Or to put it another way, as the 19th-century Prussian general Helmuth von Moltke once said, "No plan survives contact with the enemy." And one can only add that untested ideas are likely to be a plan's first casualty.

Another consequence of the arrogance resulting from a leader's isolation and immunity from full disclosure and accountability is a loss of the public esteem that is essential for maintaining power. In the end, Enron was destroyed by the incompetence of its leadership. Had that not been the case, it is still entirely possible that the company would have met a similar fate anyway if and when the public learned of senior management's greed and wanton extravagance.

3. *Institutional sustainability comes first.* This principle entails an understanding of limits—not those that are imposed by institutional arrangements, the need for public approval, or even self discipline—but rather the limits of human mortality. The final task of ethical leadership is to put in place the requirements for institutional sustainability that survives the loss of any one person. Perhaps the best test of leadership is the state of the enterprise 20 years after the leader has left. Are decisions made in an orderly way? Is the leadership accountable? Is the transfer of power completed without serious disruption? Has the founding vision survived but also accommodated itself to changing economic, social, and political realities? The final task of ethical leadership is to put in place the requirements for institutional sustainability that survives the loss of any one person.

Judged by those standards, Nehru gets high marks. He understood that leaders function best when they are subject to limits, understand those constraints, and strive in a human way to function within these boundaries. And as Nehru concluded somberly, the ultimate limit is mortality. At the head of the epilogue to his autobiography, he placed this epigraph from the Talmud: "We are enjoined to labor; but it is not granted to us to complete our labors."

RONALD E. BERENBEIM is a principal researcher and director of The Conference Board's Working Group on Global Business Ethics Principles. This article is based on his presentation at The Conference Board 2005 Global Leadership Development Conference in Mumbai, India, and used with permission.

Truth or Consequences
The Organizational Importance of Honesty

ERLINE BELTON

"We do not err because truth is difficult to see. It is visible at a glance. We err because this is more comfortable."
—Alexander Solzhenitsyn, Nobel Prize Winner, Soviet Writer and U.S. Citizen

We have all experienced the public lie that goes unchallenged. It may be baldly untrue but somehow accepted as the basis for action with life and death consequences. Some of our experience of public lies may be based on differences in values or perceptions, but sometimes what is said just simply violates the facts—this is disheartening and drives people out of public participation.

The same may be said of organizations. A nonprofit may, on the surface, be making every effort to promote teamwork and "the higher good," but if its people continue to perceive a culture that supports a different and less reliable set of operating norms and assumptions than what is written or espoused, they will not bring themselves wholly to our efforts.

Here are some typical reasons for telling lies:

- to avoid pain or unpleasant consequences;
- to promote self-interest and a particular point of view;
- to protect the leaders or the organization;
- to perpetuate myths that hold the organization or a point of view together.

Regardless of why they are told, untruths and lies can cause people to disengage—and they can also diminish the spirit people bring into the workplace. This leads to a sometimes massive loss of applied human intellectual and physical capital assets. A disinvestment of human spirit results in what I refer to as a Gross National People Divestiture (GNPD). The GNPD index in any organization or society can be directly related to the prevalence and magnitude of untruths told and allowed to stand. GNPD occurs when your organization's tolerance of untruth creates a climate of cynical disbelief engendering a lack of trust in information and relationships. This automatically creates management problems that are sometimes difficult to put your finger on but are often very powerfully present nonetheless.

Our challenge is to buck the culture and engage people in building a climate of truth telling that will lead to a newly revived work ethic and heightened individual and collective energy. In order to do this effectively, we must understand the conditions that support the emergence of truth, and understand and eliminate those that routinely undermine its presence in our organizations.

Staying Safe: Are You Avoiding Pain, but Inviting Extinction?

According to psychologist Abraham Maslow, our strongest mutual instinct is to be safe from harm and to protect our sense of well-being. It is this instinct that guides us to avoid risk (or what we perceive to be risk), and to respond cautiously to changes in our environment, relying heavily on familiar patterns of behavior in an effort to promote and sustain a sense of equilibrium. As coworkers or managers, this instinct often propels us to play it safe and go along with the program. Ironically, in a quickly changing environment this is obviously counterproductive.

Thus, too often, we opt for the illusion of stability in order to promote a sense of psychological well-being. This sense is acquired in exchange for at least a fragment of the whole truth; and since we all know "the truth" is relative anyway, we hardly notice the cost. It is true that we all seek solid ground when in doubt. But does that solid ground need to be sameness? Solid ground might be, for instance, a place to stand for something we can believe in and whose integrity we can rely on when all else appears undependable and unpredictable.

Over time illusions dissolve and evaporate. When they do, those who have used them for grounding are left less safe, less secure than ever. And those who have allowed even the smallest of illusions to inform our management decisions, have placed entire organizations, teams and ourselves at risk.

Because of the diversity of perspectives and information available in any group, a collective organizational "truth" has the potential to be stronger and more accurate than any one individual's truth. But it is only when we have the combination of individual as well as collective seeking of truth, that organizational potential is realized. This requires an open atmosphere where people can depend upon one another to engage honestly, respectfully, and with spirit intact. It requires the testing of personal assumptions among people and that requires a level of trust.

More often than not, organizational potential is not realized. Why? Team meetings, team coordination, and team feedback all involve a diversity of people and personalities that have at least one thing in common: they don't want to get hurt; they don't want unpleasant things to happen; they want to feel safe; and they want to contribute. We, as fallible individuals create the environment, and environmental conditions can support either truth or lies.

Conditions That Support Untruths

Groupthink. The tendency to just go along with the crowd, avoid drawing criticism to ourselves, and assume that everyone agrees, is so subtle and unconscious that we are generally unaware of it. As a result, we often all wind up somewhere nobody really wanted to be. For instance, imagine the scenario of an organization trying to decide on whether to apply for a major contract. Most staff members are in favor of going forward while a few are privately concerned that the organization does not have the capacity to handle the work or the money. The push toward acquiring the contract is so strong that the isolated few remain silent for fear of being characterized as pessimists or naysayers. The organization lands the contract and finds itself in terrible straits trying to handle the management challenge. One variation on this is situations in which everyone knows something but there is an undercurrent of pressure not to state it aloud. Colluding in lies can be crippling. In one organization I know, the staff was asked about the biggest lie inhabiting the organization. After much hemming and hawing, one man finally blurted out, "The lie is that we provide good services that the community wants. We don't and we treat any client who complains like a troublemaker." He went on to provide examples. Everyone else around the table nodded agreement immediately. Consider the enormous cost of having kept this silent for years! This was a key organization, serving an isolated immigrant community. Unfortunately the dialogue group did not include the executive director or board members who later did not allow the conversation to progress further. This was seven years ago, and to this day, funders see the organization as "chronically in trouble."

Imaginary conflicts. People often choose their words and edit their facts to protect themselves from anticipated reactions. One person's imaginary conflicts can warp the way information is exchanged. In a team, the distortion is amplified by the processes of repetition and groupthink. Eventually, the distorted facts may culminate in a "self-fulfilling prophecy" where our worst fears materialize precisely because we acted in fear. Think about the executive director that everyone soft pedals around for fear of hitting one of her sacred organizational cows. Rather than gently prodding for potential change or aiming for a more open debate about organizational myths, staff members assume that some topics are "off limits" and live in silence with the uncomfortable consequences. Of course, this only fulfills the idea of the executive director as a leader entrenched in her ways, and prevents her from getting accurate feedback—and so it goes.

Hidden agendas. When individuals have their own interests at heart, or believe that something is true but fail to disclose this fact, seemingly straightforward discussions have a way of going wrong. Unexpected disunity and conflict can undermine team spirit and group confidence, preventing the group from working efficiently and effectively. Self-interest isn't so bad in itself, but when kept underground it acts like a dark matter pulling everything in its direction—down. The most distressing of these situations occur when individuals see themselves as self-righteous warriors using any means necessary in their "struggle for justice."

The Spectrum of Everyday Lies

Exaggerating or underplaying the truth. This is often done for one's own benefit, for that of the team, or for a teammate. These lies usually reflect (or exceed) desired expected outcomes.

Shading the truth. This is usually done to make a point or to protect yourself, your team, or your teammate. Again, such a lie is used to make the impression that things are more like you want or expect them to be than they actually are. These lies are often used in a noble effort to protect others from the truth.

Beating around the bush or throwing up a smoke screen. This is a delay tactic used to enlarge the insulation or cushion of safety between you and somebody who makes you uncomfortable. This category includes situations in which you withhold an opinion or fail to tell a person where he or she really stands with you for fear of creating complications or undesired reactions. It also includes instances when you fail to say no directly, when no is what you mean.

Pretending certainty or expertise. There is a lot of pressure in the work-place to provide answers now, to know the facts, the status, the scoop. These lies are often passed off as bravado, but they create unfounded expectations and dependencies in others, thus setting them up for unpleasant surprises.

Not letting others know your true position. Especially in times of ambiguity or controversy, there is a temptation to cover yourself by either making your stand unclear, or stating it in such a way that it sounds as if you are in agreement with others when, in fact, you are not. This is a common feature of groupthink and often leads to outcomes nobody really wanted, but everybody assumed they did!

Consciously withholding relevant information. This is often used as a kind of power play to leverage the value and impact of information that you have. By not fully disclosing your knowledge, you are in fact manipulating people for your own purposes (whatever they may be).

Perceptions of powerlessness. Especially in teams with strong leaders, people may feel they have no legitimate voice and are vulnerable (by proximity) to the "powers that be." Opting to assume that others know best, some people often let others make choices and decisions for them, and withhold information that might influence the discussion. Once this happens, these people have made themselves powerless to do anything but accept the consequences.

Perceptions of invulnerability. Belonging to a successful team can be exhilarating—so exhilarating that maxims such as "success sows the seeds of its own failure" seem irrelevant and only applicable to somebody else. There is a strong sense of being "in the know" and having a unique advantage over others who are outside the circle of your team. This can lead to carelessness, letting perceptions, communications, and facts slide by without diligent examination and discussion.

Misplaced loyalty or dysfunctional rescuing. Relationships that have longevity often interfere with the ability to be objective about performance, and ultimately one's competence to do the job. Loyalty to these relationships can cause individuals to look the other way and avoid listening to obvious data that suggests that either the person is in the wrong position, or that it is time to move on. Silence on the issues of lack of performance is a major untruth. If unacknowledged it creates disharmony and reduces leadership's credibility. Once acknowledged, and once actions have been taken, an environmental unfreezing occurs that revitalizes human spirit and performance.

Failing to give due credit. A common way of self-promotion in a group setting, this denies or diminishes the value of others' input and contributions. It disempowers people and leads to the inappropriate use of human resources.

Deluding yourself—self-deception. This is perhaps the most common source of everyday lies. You have both conscious and unconscious internal mechanisms that operate to protect you from cold hard facts in the misguided belief that what you don't know won't hurt you. These self-deceptions set you up for hard falls, and introduce faulty information into whatever team dynamic you are part of.

Conditions That Support Truth Telling

Individual examination/accountability. Individual organizations and teams can "build better truths." Since untruths can be intentional, the truth must be intentional. Collective truth for a team is the result of individual encouragement through consent that is informed, uncompelled, and mutual. The leader has a critical and essential role as role model and must understand that his or her behavior is under more scrutiny and will be given more weight than that of the others. If the leader fails at this, the organizational setting will also fail.

Visible commitment to truth telling. Relentlessly stating that truth telling has value is only the first step. Explaining thoughts, acknowledging the power of our words, and being accountable to one another for our actions will demonstrate that concept. In spite of our fear about telling the truth, relationships can be consistently strengthened with truth as the foundation.

Collective truths and collective responsibility. All team members need to collaborate in a dialogue that sets the foundation for an agreed-upon definition and description of "reality." This vision of reality is not complete until each member gives explicit consent and can accept the idea that the view of reality presented, even with qualifications, is one that they can sign on to. Once there is ownership and a feeling of collective responsibility, a future can be created. This kind of dialogue requires personal risk, courage, and time.

The whole truth. Access to reliable, solid, and truthful information is the one commodity every person, regardless of role or position, needs in order to succeed. As people who live or work together, we require information that is communicated openly and freely. Information based on the "whole truth" informs decisions, actions, behavior, and dialogue to support an outcome. Organizations that support truth telling understand that there are four critical components to the whole truth, and to laying the foundation for achieving outcomes that have meaningful results and credibility: information must be complete, timely, accurate, and true.

Information flow. Information creates its leaders' legacies and the values they stand for. Consider an organization's values and beliefs in the context of its history and current reality. All available facts and information (including personal stories, feelings, and visible and invisible reactions) are on the table in an accurate and accessible way; all information is understood and shared.

Free choice, sustained environmental spirit, safety. In organizations that value truth telling, each individual is free to evaluate and decide based solely on the merit of available truthful facts; there isn't even a hint of social, political, or economic coercion. The environment must show evidence that it is "safe" to tell the truth. There must be visible examples of situations where the truth was told, acknowledged, and acted on—and the consequences were *not* punitive. This does not mean that the truth may not bring a fallout; that could very well happen. People will leave organizations in which they don't fit, and that is a positive thing for the organization and the individuals involved.

Laying a Solid Foundation

Running an organization based on truth requires—and demands—the taking of personal risks and time. The perception that time is limited, or the fear that the truth will hurt us, or hurt someone or something we care about, are perhaps the greatest obstacles to organizational truth telling.

Busy men and women are always looking for shortcuts and abbreviations to help speed things along. But truth lies at the very foundation of a successful organization, and you can't lay a solid foundation when you cut corners; doing so places the whole structure in danger of eventual collapse. But if your culture now includes a tolerance for and comfort with lying (as it is described in the above "spectrum"), you have to be explicit about changing your culture and about what the "whole truth" must include. And then you must patiently and persistently inch your way toward it, in practice. Organizational healing and reconciliation are the natural first steps toward restoring a culture where truth telling is a value. It is through the process of making the change as an organization-wide effort that we reclaim the vital human spirit necessary for renewing our organizations, communities and country. Truth telling leads to freedom. Freedom requires that we challenge the way things are in organizations if we truly want them to accomplish what is in our collective hearts.

ERLINE BELTON is the CEO of the Lyceum Group in Boston. She has been identified by clients as an organization healer, and feels honored to be of service as she practices organization development from her heart and head.

Editors' Note—Recent *NPQ* articles on organizational conflict ("Brave Leadership in Organizational Conflict," by Kenneth Bailey, Winter 2004) and defensive behavior ("Defending Defensiveness," by Sandra Janoff, Spring 2004) have brought a terrific response from readers throughout the country. It is clear that interpersonal skills and behavior, and the organizational systems that either support or undermine a healthy exchange, continue to be of central concern to people in nonprofits. The following piece by Erline Belton serves as a companion to these other articles, presenting a complementary vision of the group and personal skills that are needed to propel our organizations forward.

How to Make Unethical Decisions

ANDREW SIKULA, SR. AND JOHN SIKULA

People make decisions and solve problems in a variety of ways. Oftentimes, little if any thought goes into choice selection. Sometimes, even very important decisions are made without serious contemplation of potential alternatives and their consequences. Many different tools/techniques and rationales are utilized in problem solving and decision making with little or no regard to ethical judgment and/or aftermaths. Some ways of making choices are worse than others when using pity parameters. This article discusses commonly used but ethically unsound methods of making selections. Later in the writing, appropriate standards and benchmarks for determining ethical action will be presented.

Unlawful Discrimination

For starters, we can begin by recognizing that all forms of illegal discrimination involve unethical decisions. In general, all unlawful acts are also unethical activities. There are some exceptions to this statement, such as the homeless sleeping in public parks, but such examples and exceptions go beyond the main emphasis of this writing. Later in this article the authors will discuss the fact that legality and morality are not identical. For openers, however, please recognize that personal and personnel employment discrimination in decision making based upon human characteristics of race, color, creed, religion, gender, age, sexual orientation, and/or disability is both unlawful and unethical. More debatable for example, is whether nepotism, that is, giving hiring, promotion and pay preferences to relatives, is legal and/or moral. In most settings, nepotism is legal, although it may violate company policy especially if direct supervision is involved. However, most ethic experts consider nepotism to be immoral because it violates the ethical principles of human fairness, justice, and equal employment opportunity.

Unsophisticated Decision Making Tools & Techniques

Sometimes silly and senseless methods are used to pick among available alternatives. If you want to make unethical decisions, frequently use such popular games as: enee, meenie, minee, mo; pick a number; rock, paper, scissors; and drawing straws. Just as bad ethically but much more frequently used are the ten determination discriminators listed below:

1. Flipping a coin
2. Crystal ball
3. Spinning a wheel
4. Cutting a deck of cards
5. Reading tea leaves, Tarot cards, palms, head bumps, etc.
6. Ouija board
7. Farmer's Almanac
8. Astrology/horoscopes
9. Sorcery/witchcraft
10. Doing nothing and/or relying on past practices

These ten techniques do not need much additional explanation because we all know what they mean and what they involve. As formally trained educators, the authors are amazed as to the frequency with which people admit to relying on such methods, even in very important matters. It should go without saying, but we will nonetheless here state, that ethical excellence and moral management cannot be achieved by utilizing these methods.

Many people are immobilized by difficult decisions. They procrastinate indefinitely, do nothing, and let the chips fall where they may. They may allow others to make decisions for them, or rely on game-like decision making techniques to avoid stress. Such individuals relinquish their free will, which is mankind's most valued asset. Unfortunately, this can then lead to a victim or entitlement mentality where one sees an organization as a villain or enemy causing personal harm or loss to oneself which, they think, preferably can be remedied only by litigation.

Regarding past practices, many people think that it is safe to simply rely on the past and to repeat the same decision(s) made previously. It worked once and might work again. This is a dangerous tactic/strategy because nothing in life is as certain as change. People change, circumstances vary, and timing needs to be adjusted. Making identical decisions and doing things the same way year after year can lead to failure much of the time. It is also boring.

Commonly Used Choice Rationales

Much more complicated and controversial than the previous ten decision techniques are another set of rationalizations used by human beings to justify their choices. These solutions involve cognitions and are much more difficult to recognize as improper preference parameters. It takes serious study and often data-based research findings to convince someone that the following ten rationales are unreliable and anti-intellectual guides for determining or interpreting past, present and/or future ethical behaviors. This is because one's ego and personality are involved, and stating that such directors are not sound ethical indicators is often viewed as a personal attack on one's character and/or integrity. But, after each of the authors having spent over 45 years in higher education, we are convinced, and data-based research supports, that the following rationales are not reliable or sound ethical pointers.

1. First impressions
2. Common sense
3. Feelings
4. Instincts
5. Gut reaction
6. Human nature
7. Groupthink
8. Everyone's doing it
9. Self-interest
10. Conscience

Several items on this list may surprise and/or offend the reader. Additional explanation is needed to clarify these listing inclusions. Abundant research is available proving that first impressions are just as likely to be wrong as right. Common sense is neither common nor sensical. If common sense existed, individuals and institutions would not be having so much difficulty making proper choices. Human feelings, personal instincts, and individual gut reactions are all individually and collectively poor decision determinants. None can withstand the scrutiny of the scientific method when tested empirically. Sometimes, the first five items of this ten-item listing are recognized as being poor ways for others to make decisions. However, to recognize that these five mistakes pertain also to ourselves, is a much more difficult acknowledgement. Seeing faults in others is easy. Recognizing these same deficiencies in ourselves is at least tenfold as challenging.

The next three listed items are collective rather than individual in character. Some people trick themselves into believing that it is human nature to be ethical and to do right and proper things. The opposite is true. Believers accept the concept of original sin where mankind is viewed as sinners in need of repentance. For generations now, schools and colleges, buying into Adam Smith historically and Milton Fiedman et al. presently, have taught that each and every person pursuing their own self-interest will lead to the greater good of corporations, society and the world as a whole. But contrary to popular opinion, greed is not good. And what is best for an individual is not always best for a community. In a free market economy this might be true in

theory, but it is a falsehood in actual global practice. Perfect markets assume the free flow of information, goods, services, money and personnel—none of which happens in the real world. Because absolute power corrupts people absolutely, governments have a legitimate role to play in society, and these governments operate ethically best when they are limited and democratic rather than expansive and autocratic in oversight and rule. Self-interest is a justification that needs to be risen above. Higher order decision making requires one to put aside self-interest for the good of a larger group or calling. Needless to say, this is difficult, and it is a very hard lesson to teach and to learn.

Just because a group thinks some way, or everyone seems to be acting in a certain manner, does not constitute ethical behavior. John Gardner has warned us that "the moral majority is neither." The majority of people may not act morally. Laws represent majority opinion, but not always morality reasoning. Laws change over time and geography. Prostitution and gambling are legal in some states but not others. Slavery and polygamy laws have changed over time in different countries and settings. Legality is not morality. Morality is a higher calling and often runs counter to groupthink and community sentiment.

The most difficult truism to buy into from this listing is the fact that your conscience may not always be a proper guide to ethical behavior. A conscience is acquired over time. It is not inherited or part of one's chromosomes or DNA. The conscience is developed over time through education and experience. Some people have learned unethical behavior and they suffer from negative past happenings. A person may have no conscience, or possess one deranged by evil. The conscience is the best ethical guide from the previously listed ten commonly used choice rationales, but it is not a perfect guidance system.

So far we have discussed "How To Make Unethical Decisions" using "Unsophisticated Decision Making Tools and Techniques," and by utilizing "Commonly Used Choice Rationales." If these methodologies do not produce ethical decisions and behaviors, what means can we use to improve and enhance ethical actions?

Appropriate Guides for Determining Ethical Actions

No guidance system is perfect because human misinterpretations of advice can always happen. Given that there may be some human communication problems and limitations, nonetheless, the authors offer the following ten ethical guidance suggestions:

1. Scripture
2. Prayer
3. Learned knowledge
4. Formal education
5. Innate intelligence/wisdom
6. Past experience
7. Correct consultation
8. Meritorious mentoring
9. Positive role modeling
10. Pooled judgment

One of the problems with decision games, tools, and rationales is that they tend to be implemented very quickly or over a very short period of time. Appropriate ethical guidance systems, on the other hand, involve thought, reflection and/or observation often covering months or years of time. Ethical decisions are not made instantaneously. Moral management is a process involving deliberative thought and action. Ethical excellence is achieved by using virtuous values as benchmark standards. These benchmarks provide direction to appropriate behavior.

Although not discussed much in the management and supervision literature, it is an undisputable fact that people use prayer, meditation and/or reflection before making major personal and professional decisions. Scripture, the Bible, and/or the Words of God and Jesus are studied and implemented by Christian decision makers. Other faiths use other sources which they believe provide divine inspiration and guidance.

Human beings also have innate intelligence, learned knowledge, and formal education upon which they rely to help them choose proper alternative actions. Wisdom is developed over time and often comes from the school of hard knocks, past experiences, former failures, and/or selective success stories.

Ethical choices may often result from following the trusted advice of persons with highly developed individual integrity and personal character. The open scrutiny of others, (be it your parents, children, news reporters, et al.), often helps to purify chosen options. This scrutiny, openness, and/or transparency can come from a variety of ethical expert sources including consultants, mentors, and role models. These outsiders must be "correct," "meritorious," and "positive." The authors realize that these are value laden terms, but consensus can be reached on each. Advisors must be righteous, virtuous and exemplar if they are to effectively serve as ethics advocates. Never use advisors with questionable reputations. When utilized properly, ethics experts help to ensure that a person assumes both responsibility for one's behavior, and accountability to others for consequences of individual actions.

Sometimes it is wise to get the counsel of more than one trusted colleague or moral mentor. The best and most ethical decisions can come as a result of the pooled judgment of several monitors. However, it is cautioned here that pooled judgment works best when the consultants number 3-5 in total. Larger groups tend to compromise solutions and average down ethics and decision quality due to groupthink and negotiations. One should not attempt to negotiate between right and wrong. Compromise may be a resolution to a confrontation, but it never results in better ethics and/or a heightened level of integrity.

Conclusion

There are many ways to make unethical decisions. Breaking the law of the land is unethical. Using gamesmanship and quickie tools and techniques also are examples of poor ways to make decisions and to select options. More commonly used are a variety of human rationales which when tested scientifically can prove to be faulty. It is difficult for most people to persistently practice procedural propriety and to exclusively execute ethical excellence. Moral management takes time, tenacity and transparency to implement, but with practice over time, individuals and institutions can learn to replace defective decisions with successful selections.

ANDREW SIKULA, Sr. is the Director of the Graduate School of Management at Marshall University's South Charleston Campus. **JOHN SIKULA** is the Vice President for Regional Centers and Outreach at Ashland University in Ashland, Ohio. Andrew and John Sikula are identical twin brothers and co-authors of the above article.

Best Resources for Corporate Social Responsibility

Karen McNichol

What most of us lack these days isn't data but time. The World Wide Web is a marvelous research tool, but the sheer amount of information available can be overwhelming. How do you weed through it to find the very best sites, where someone has already synthesized masses of material for you? Well, consider the offerings below a garden without the weeds: a selection of the best of the best sites in corporate social responsibility (CSR).

1. Best Practices and Company Profiles

www.bsr.org—This may well be the best CSR site of all. Run by the business membership organization Business for Social Responsibility, its focus is on giving business hands-on guidance in setting up social programs, but data is useful to researchers as well, particularly because of "best practice" examples. Topics include social auditing, community involvement, business ethics, governance, the environment, employee relations, and corporate citizenship. New topics are being researched all the time. One recent report, for example, looked at companies linking executive pay to social performance, while others have looked at how to implement flexible scheduling, or become an "employer of choice." Visitors can create their own printer-friendly custom report on each topic, selecting from sections like Business Importance, Recent Developments, Implementation Steps, Best Practices, and Links to Helping Resources. To receive notices about updates, plus other CSR news, subscribe

Figure 1 www.worldcsr.com offers one-stop access to the leading business-led organizations on corporate social responsibility in Europe and the U.S.

to BSR Resource Center Newsletter by sending a message to centerupdates@bsr.org with "subscribe" in the subject line.

www.ebnsc.org—You might call this the BSR site from Europe. It is sponsored by Corporate Social Responsibility Europe, whose mission is to help put CSR into the mainstream of business. This site includes a databank of best practices from all over Europe on topics like human rights, cause-related marketing, ethical principles, and community involvement. To give just one example of the site's capability, a search on the topic "reporting on CSR" came up with a dozen news articles available in full, plus a case study, and a list of 20 books and reports on the topic. One unique feature is the "CSR Matrix," which allows visitors to call up a complete social report on companies like IBM, Levi Strauss, or Procter & Gamble. The "matrix" is a grid, where the visitor clicks on one box to view the company's code of conduct, another box to see how the company interacts with public stakeholders, a third box to access the company's sustainability report, and so forth.

www.worldcsr.com is a World CSR portal offering one-stop access to the leading business-led organizations on corporate social responsibility in Europe and the U.S., including the two sites mentioned above. Another site on the portal—www. businessimpact.org—offers a useful databank of links to related organizations, such as the Global Reporting Initiative, Institute for Global Ethics, and World Business Council for Sustainable Development. Readers can also subscribe to the Business Impact News e-mail newsletter.

www.responsibleshopper.org—For individuals wishing to shop with or research responsible companies, Responsible Shopper from Co-op America offers in-depth social profiles on countless companies. A report on IBM, for example, looks at everything from Superfund sites, toxic emissions, and worker benefits to laudatory activities. Different brand names for each company are listed, and social performance is summarized in letter ratings—as with IBM, which got an "A" in Disclosure, and a "B" in the Environment.

2. Social Investing

www.socialfunds.com—Run by SRI World Group, Social Funds is the best social investing site on the web. A staff of reporters researches breaking news and posts it without charge. For socially responsible mutual funds, the site offers performance statistics plus fund descriptions. There's an investing center where you can build your own basket of social companies, plus a community banking center with information on savings accounts and money market funds with responsible banking organizations. A shareholder activism section offers a status report on social resolutions and is searchable by topic (equality, tobacco, militarism, etc.). Also available is a free weekly e-mail newsletter, SRI News Alert—which goes beyond social investing. One recent issue, for example, looked at new labeling programs for clean-air office construction, an Arctic Wildlife Refuge resolution against BP Amoco, and why greener multinationals have higher market value. A new service from SRI World Group, offered jointly with Innovest Strategic Advisors, offers subscribers ($100 annually) ratings of companies

in various industries, based on environmental and financial performance.

www.socialinvest.org—This is the site of the nonprofit professional membership association, the Social Investment Forum, and is a useful pair to the above site. One unique feature is the collection of Moskowitz Prize-winning papers on research in social investing. The 2000 winner, for example, was "Pure Profit: The Financial Implications of Environmental Performance." Also available is a directory to help visitors find a financial adviser anywhere in the country; a mutual funds chart; a guide to community investing (showing resources by state and by type); and materials on SIF's campaign to end predatory lending. You can also access the Shareholder Action Network-which shows how to submit shareholder resolutions, and offers information on both current campaigns and past successes.

www.goodmoney.com.—Offering some unique investing features of its own is the Good Money site, which showcases the Good Money Industrial Average: a screened index which outperformed the Dow in 2000. Also available are social profiles and performance data for a variety of public companies—including the 400 companies in the Domini Social Index, companies with the best diversity record, the Council on Economic Priorities "honor roll" list, and signers of the CERES Principles (a voluntary environmental code of conduct). Another section on Eco Travel has dozens of links and articles.

3. Corporate Watchdogs

www.corpwatch.org—For activists, this may be the best site of all. Calling itself "The Watchdog on the Web," CorpWatch offers news you may not find elsewhere on human rights abuses abroad, public policy; and environmental news—plus on-site reporting of protests. Its director Josh Karliner was nominated by AlterNet.org (an alternative news service) as a Media Hero 2000, for using the web to fight the excesses of corporate globalization. CorpWatch puts out the bimonthly Greenwash Awards, and runs a Climate Justice Initiative, as well as the Alliance for a Corporate-Free UN. An Issue Library covers topics like the WTO and sweatshops, while the Hands-on Guide to On-line Corporate Research is useful for research ideas. A free twice-monthly e-mail newsletter updates readers on recent CorpWatch headlines. One recent issue of "What's New on CorpWatch" looked at topics like the World Bank's record, the protests at the World Economic Forum, California's deregulation troubles, plus the regular "Take Action" feature urging readers to send e-mails or faxes on a specific issue. To subscribe to the e-letter, send blank message to corp-watchers-subscribe@igc.topica.com.

www.corporatepredators.org—Featuring Russell Mokhiber, editor of the weekly newsletter Corporate Crime Reporter, this site offers a compilation of weekly e-mail columns called "Focus on the Corporation," written by Mokhiber and Robert Weissman. They offer a valuable, quirky voice in corporate responsibility. Taking on topics not covered elsewhere, the columns have looked at how the chemical industry responded to Bill Moyers TV program on industry coverup, how little academic research focuses on corporate crime, and why it's inappropriate to legally view corporations as "persons." At this site (which also features

Figure 2 For activists, www.corpwatch.org may be the best site of all.

the book *Corporate Predators* by Mokhiber and Weissman), readers can access weekly columns back through 1998. Subscribe free to the column by sending an e-mail message to corp-focus-request@lists.essential.org with the text "subscribe."

4. Labor and Human Rights

http://oracle02.ilo.org/vpi/welcome—Sponsored by the International Labor Organization, this web site offers a new Business and Social Initiatives Database, compiling Internet sources on employment and labor issues. It covers topics like child labor, living wage, dismissal, investment screens, monitoring, international labor standards, glass ceilings, safe work, and so forth. It features information on corporate policies and reports, codes of conduct, certification criteria, labeling and other programs. A search feature allows visitors to retrieve information on specific companies, regions, and business sectors. This is one of the most comprehensive labor sites out there.

www.summersault.com/~agj/clr/—Sponsored by the Campaign for Labor Rights, this site keeps activists up to date on anti-sweatshop struggles and other pro-labor activities around the world. Particularly useful is the free e-mail newsletter Labor Alerts, which updates readers on recent news about

trade treaties, plant shutdowns, labor organizing, job postings, upcoming protests, recent books, and so forth. One recent issue contained a "webliography" of sites about the pending creation of the Free Trade Area of the Americas (FTAA). To subscribe contact clrmain@afgj.org.

5. Progressive Economics

www.epn.org—For the best thinking in progressive economic policy, this site managed by *The American Prospect* magazine is a one-stop source. It's the Electronic Policy Network, an on-line consortium of over 100 progressive policy centers nationwide, like the Center for Public Integrity, the Brookings Institution, the Financial Markets Center, and many more. (The focus of member groups is heavily though not exclusively economic.) A feature called Idea Central offers on-line bibliographies on topics like globalization, poverty, and livable cities. Certain topics get "Issues in Depth" treatment: One, for example, looks at campaign finance reform—including history, alternatives, and legal background, with numerous links to sites like a database of soft-money contribution, research from the Center for Responsive Politics, ACLU factsheets, and more. Another feature, "What's New," looks at recent reports and research papers by member

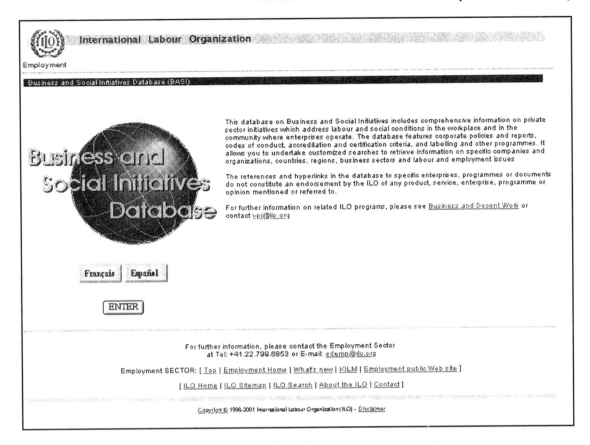

Figure 3 The Business and Social Initiatives Database (http://oracle02.ilo.org/vpi/welcome) is one of the most comprehensive labor compilations out there.

policy centers—like a recent report from the Economic Policy Institute on privatization, or a report on state initiatives for children from the National Center for Children in Poverty. Readers can receive summaries of new research reports by subscribing to the e-mail EPN News; send an e-mail to majordomo@epn.org with "subscribe epnnews" in the message body.

www.neweconomics.org—This valuable site is run by The New Economics Foundation (NEF), a UK nonprofit think tank created in 1986 to focus on "constructing a new economy centered on people and the environment." Different areas on the site focus on powerful tools for economic change, like alternative currencies, social investment, indicators for sustainability, and social accounting. A monthly web-based newsletter reports on topics like Jubilee 2000 (the movement to cancel the debt of developing nations), May Day plans, an "indicator of the month," and more. A new bimonthly e-briefing is called "mergerwatch," which looks at the hidden costs behind mergers, and who pays the price. Its first issue in April 2001 reported, for example, that a 1999 KPMG study showed 53 percent of mergers destroy shareholder value, and a further 30 percent bring no measurable benefit.

6. Employee Ownership

http://cog.kent.edu—For researchers in employee ownership, the Capital Ownership Group site is indispensable. COG is a virtual think tank of individuals—including academics, employee ownership specialists, and business leaders worldwide—who aim to promote broadened ownership of productive capital. The site's library allows visitors to browse ongoing discussions, on topics like promoting employee ownership globally, getting economists more involved in issues of capital ownership, the role of labor in employee ownership, and more. The library offers hundreds of papers and research reports, on topics like labor-sponsored venture capital, employee governance, case studies, and much more.

www.nceo.org—This is the site of the National Center for Employee Ownership, a nonprofit research and membership organization that is one of the best sources for employee ownership information. Its web library features a valuable introduction to the history of Employee Stock Ownership Plans (ESOPs), plus information on open book management, stock options, and alternatives to ESOPs. An "Interactive Introduction to ESOPs" lets visitors "chat" with an expert in the same way as if they spent fifteen minutes on the phone with a lawyer. Also available are a wealth of links to related sites, plus news and statistics on employee ownership.

www.fed.org—The sponsor of this site is the Foundation for Enterprise Development—a nonprofit started by Robert Beyster, founder of employee-owned SAIC—which is an organization that aims to promote employee ownership. Its focus is not ESOPs but stock options and other forms of equity ownership. A monthly online magazine features profiles of employee ownership at specific companies, articles on developing an ownership culture, plus news. An e-mail service updates readers on headlines.

www.the-esop-emplowner.org—From the ESOP Association—a membership and lobbying organization—this site offers a resource library, news of events, reports on legislative victories, and information on legislative initiatives. The site also offers information on the ESOP Association's political action committee, which since 1988 has helped candidates for federal office who support ESOPs and ESOP law.

7. Sustainability

www.GreenBiz.com—Run by Joel Makower, editor of *The Green Business Letter*, Green Biz is the best site on progressive environmental business activities. It enables visitors to discover what companies are doing, and to access citations of countless web resources and reports, on topics like sustainable management, green auditing, EPA programs, pending legislation, clean technologies, recycling, and all things green. A new service features free job listing for environmental professionals. Get regular updates from a free e-mail newsletter, GreenBiz, published every other week.

www.rprogress.org—Run by the nonprofit Redefining Progress—which produces the Genuine Progress Indicator (as a counterpoint to GDP)—this site offers news on topics like climate change, forest-land protection, tax reform, and congressional influence peddling. Recent stories featured a proposal to promote market-based policies for reducing sprawl, a better way to return the government surplus, plus a look at Living Planet 2000—calculating the ecological footprints of the world's largest 150 countries. Numerous studies on environmental justice, tax fairness, and community indicators are available, plus links to other climate change sites.

www.sustainablebusiness.com—The monthly on-line magazine Sustainable Business offers news on the "green economy," covering recycling, product take-back, legislative developments, and so forth. Other features are a database of "Green Dream Job" openings; plus a section to help green businesses find venture capital. A library features web sites, reports, and books.

www.cleanedge.com—The new organization Clean Edge focuses on helping investors, industry, and society understand and profit from clean technology, like wind, solar, energy

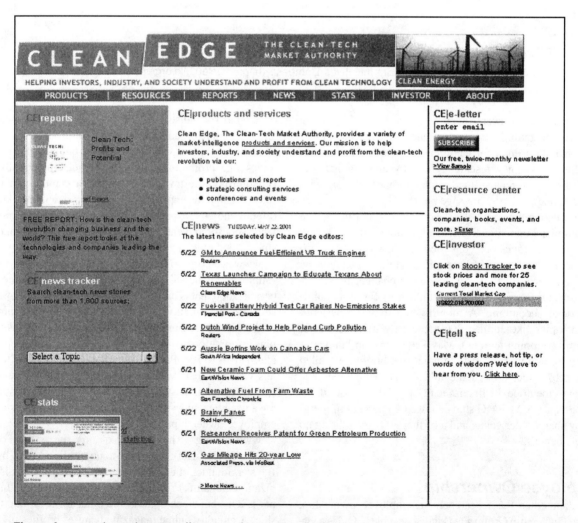

Figure 4 www.cleanedge.com offers news from 1,800 sources, stock trading information on 25 companies, plus lists of conferences, trade associations and research centers.

efficiency, and alternative fuels. The site offers news from 1,800 sources, stock trading information on 25 companies, plus lists of conferences, trade associations and research centers. The group's premier publication, "Clean Tech: Profits and Potential," reports that clean energy technologies will grow from less than $7 billion today to $82 billion by 2010.

8. Ethics

www.depaul.edu/ethics—Sponsored by the Institute for Business and Professional Ethics at DePaul University, this site offers a large compilation of ethics resources on the web, categorized by topic; educational resources for teachers and trainers, including syllabi; faculty position announcements; calls for papers; a calendar of events; a list of other ethics institutes, and much more.

www.ethics.ubc.ca—From the Center for Applied Ethics at the University of British Columbia in Canada, this site offers a particularly valuable compilation about ethics codes—featuring sample codes, guidance on writing a code, plus books and articles on the topic. Other features are links to ethics institutes, consultants, course materials, publications, and collections of articles.

www.ethics.org/businessethics.html—Sponsored by the Ethics Resource Center, this site features valuable data from several business ethics surveys 1994–2000, information on character education for youth, a compendium of codes (coming soon), plus links to many ethics centers and organizations. A research bibliography covers topics like measuring success in an ethics program, or ethics in a global economy. And a provocative "Ethics Quick Test" can be taken on-line, with results available by e-mail.

UNIT 2

Ethical Issues and Dilemmas in the Workplace

Unit Selections

Key Points to Consider

- What ethical dilemmas do *managers* face most frequently? What ethical dilemmas do *employees* face most often?

- What forms of gender and minority discrimination are most prevalent in today's workplace? In what particular job situations or occupations is discrimination more widespread and conspicuous? Why?

- Whistle-blowing occurs when an employee discloses illegal, immoral, or illegitimate organizational practices or activities. Under what circumstances do you believe whistle-blowing is appropriate? Why?

- Given the complexities of an organization, where an ethical dilemma often cannot be optimally resolved by one person alone, how can an individual secure the support of the group and help it to reach a consensus as to the appropriate resolution of the dilemma?

Student Web Site

www.mhcls.com

Internet References

American Psychological Association
http://www.apa.org/homepage.html
International Labour Organization (ILO)
http://www.ilo.org

LaRue Tone Hosmer, in *The Ethics of Management,* lucidly states that ethical problems in business are truly managerial dilemmas because they represent a conflict, or at least the possibility of a conflict, between the *economic performance* of an organization and its *social performance.* Whereas the economic performance is measured by revenues, costs, and profits, the social performance is judged by the fulfillment of obligations to persons both within and outside the organization.

Units 2 to 4 discuss some of the critical ethical dilemmas that management faces in making decisions in the workplace, in the marketplace, and within the global society. This unit focuses on the relationships and obligations of employers and employees to each other as well as to those they serve.

Organizational decisionmakers are ethical when they act with equity, fairness, and impartiality, treating with respect the rights of their employees. Organizations' hiring and firing practices, treatment of women and minorities, tolerance of employees' privacy, and wages and working conditions are areas in which it has ethical responsibilities.

The employee also has ethical obligations in his or her relationship to the employer. A conflict of interest can occur when an employee allows a gratuity or favor to sway him or her in selecting a contract or purchasing a piece of equipment, making a choice that may not be in the best interests of the organization. Other possible ethical dilemmas for employees include espionage and the betrayal of secrets (especially to competitors), the theft of equipment, and the abuse of expense accounts.

The articles in this unit are broken down into seven sections representing various types of ethical dilemmas in the workplace. The first article in the initial section describes the way our personal information is being bought, sold, and sometimes stolen. The next article examines how companies have become more vigilant in the surveillance of employees with new high-tech tools.

In the subsection entitled *Organizational Misconduct and Crime,* articles explore how seniors are victimized by fraud and suggests how to help deter hackers and scam artists and prevent common data disasters.

The selection under *Sexual Treatment of Employees* takes a close look at how women are treated in the workplace and the expansion of sex-discrimination lawsuits.

The readings in the *Discriminatory and Prejudicial Practices* section scrutinize how hiring older workers can contribute to a reliable and dedicated workforce and how Wal-Mart and others are facing class-action lawsuits for job discrimination.

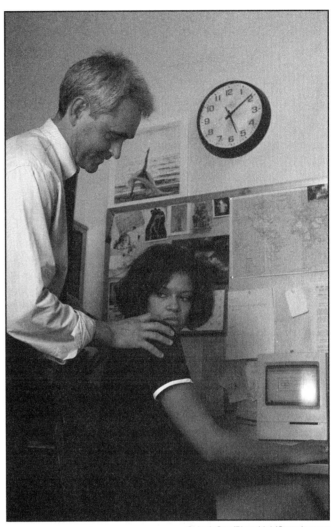

© Jack Star/PhotoLink/Getty Images

In the next subsection entitled *Downsizing of the Work Force,* articles consider why some companies are fearful of firing certain types of employees.

The selections included under the heading *Whistle-blowing in the Organization* disclose why some businesses that once feared whistleblowers are now finding new ways for employees to report wrongdoing and analyzes the ethical dilemmas and possible ramifications of whistle-blowing activities.

In the last subsection, Handling Ethical Dilemmas at Work, some cases are presented for the reader to wrestle with actual ethical dilemmas, and also covered is how the Walgreen Corporation trains the disabled to take on regular wage-paying jobs.

Your Privacy for Sale

Until Valentine's Day weekend 2005, Elizabeth Rosen had never heard of ChoicePoint. But ChoicePoint, it turns out, knew plenty about her.

That's when Rosen, a nurse, received a letter and found out that the Alpharetta, Ga., company had collected information about her. Among the sensitive items it had: her Social Security number, records of her insurance claims, her current and past addresses, and her employment history. Now Choice-Point was informing her that it had inadvertently disclosed her information—and that of 165,000 other Americans—to a group of criminals. What galls Rosen more, she says, is that all along, ChoicePoint itself "was profiting by collecting and selling confidential information about me without my knowledge or consent."

ChoicePoint, which has $1 billion in annual revenues, is only one entity in a vast and secretive data industry that feeds on private information about you and millions of other Americans. Its inhabitants include corporate mastodons with access to millions of public records; swarms of private investigators, some of whom lie to obtain confidential information; and hundreds of companies selling background checks, profiles, and address lists, all to meet the surging demand from business, law enforcement, and, increasingly since 9/11, the federal government.

The data collectors say that they're not prying but speeding the retrieval of public records for both consumers and law enforcement, allowing businesses to cut their risks for fraud and helping marketers to zero in on customers who really want their products. "More than two-thirds of what we do is regulated by state and/or federal law," says Chuck Jones, a spokesman for ChoicePoint.

Federal privacy and data-security laws such as the Fair Credit Reporting Act and the Gramm-Leach-Bliley Act do guard some categories of data, including information used to determine eligibility for credit or insurance. But a 2006 investigation by the U.S. Government Accountability Office (GAO) concluded that such protections are limited and that Congress should require information resellers to safeguard all sensitive personal information.

Indeed, CR's three-month investigation found that the practices of the data collectors can rob you of your privacy, threaten you with ID theft, and profile you as, say, a deadbeat or a security risk. Worse, there's no way to find out what they are telling others about you. When our reporters requested their own records, they were told that they could not see everything that was routinely sold to businesses. The meager information they did receive was punctuated with errors.

CR Quick Take

Large data brokers have your numbers—Social Security, phone, and credit cards. They might also know about the drugs you take, what you buy, your political party, and your sexual orientation. When we investigated this secretive industry, we discovered:

- Data brokers are willing to sell even your most sensitive information to paying customers, some of them crooks.
- When CR staffers asked to see their own files, they received scant information. One report contained 31 errors.
- The federal government is a steady customer of the data collectors, but there's no way to know what it collects or exactly how much it pays.
- Pretexters, who lie to get information about you and sell it to anybody, operate largely free of regulation.

The Data Food Chain

Data and list brokers of all stripes and sizes have collected information about individuals for decades. In recent years, however, faster computers and cheaper electronic data storage have fueled the growth of giant information aggregators, such as ChoicePoint. They have put the industry on steroids by feeding on public record databases, acquiring companies with analytic software, and consolidating it all in a centralized online resource where it can be categorized, searched, and sliced into customized slabs for resale.

Among the horde of data brokers, Acxiom, LexisNexis, and ChoicePoint are some of the most prominent. Acxiom, a giant with $1.2 billion in annual revenues, processes a billion records a day. Major clients include American Express, Bank of America, Federated Department Stores—and Consumers Union, the nonprofit publisher of CONSUMER REPORTS. Acxiom officials turned down CR's request for an interview.

LexisNexis, with $2 billion a year in revenues, got its start in Dayton, Ohio, supplying data to the U.S. Air Force. It has long aggregated news, business, and legal documents, but with its acquisition last year of Seisint, which resells public records to law enforcement and private investigators, it is focusing on security. "LexisNexis products and services help to power the consumer economy, fight terrorism, and keep our streets and homes safe," says David Kurt, a company spokesman.

Her Information Sold to Crooks

WHO: Elizabeth Rosen, nurse, California
WHAT HAPPENED: Rosen learned in February 2005 that she was a victim of a large ChoicePoint data breach. Her credit report revealed no problems initially, but she recently has been hounded by calls from bill collectors who ask for other people. ID theft experts say that those calls may indicate a thief has been using her Social Security number under a different name and address—a growing trend in ID fraud.

A Murder from $150 of Data

WHO: Viola Berkeyheiser, Washington Crossing, Pa.
WHAT HAPPENED: Berkeyheiser's husband, William, was murdered in 2005 by Stanford Douglas, a mentally ill former co-worker who held a grudge against him for a joke Douglas claimed Berkeyheiser told years earlier. A civil suit filed by Viola Berkeyheiser charges that Douglas located Berkeyheiser through A-Plus Investigations, which bought his address from IRBsearch, another data broker, for a few dollars. Douglas paid A-Plus $150. IRBsearch says, "We have no proof of any of the facts." A-Plus chief executive officer John Ciaccio says that Douglas said he wanted the data for "a legal purpose."

ChoicePoint, which was spun off by Equifax, the credit bureau, in 1997, allows law enforcement to tap its data over the Internet. As the U.S. Marshals Service said in an internal document, "With as little as a first name or a partial address, you can obtain a comprehensive personal profile in minutes." ChoicePoint also keeps claims histories on your auto and homeowners policies and provides access to birth certificates and other vital records, a service it manages for many states.

What They Feed On

The big aggregators (and fleets of smaller ones, including LocatePlus and Intelius) wouldn't exist if there weren't data for them to ingest. Fortunately, for them, the richest resources—public records—are increasingly accessible. Some hire researchers to visit courthouses and county clerks' offices to retrieve information from paper records, but increasingly, state and local governments post records online, making data gathering simpler and less costly for everyone. Open access also increases the potential for misuse of sensitive information. Property deeds, tax liens, and marriage and divorce documents often contain Social Security numbers, dates of birth, and other sensitive information that are golden keys for identity thieves.

A 2004 GAO study found that up to 28 percent of counties in the U.S. posted records with Social Security numbers online. When we checked documents online for Maricopa County, Ariz., an area with the highest per-capita rate of ID theft in 2005, we found individuals' Social Security numbers on deeds, death certificates, federal tax liens, and divorce filings, one of which also included the couple's credit-card account numbers.

Consumers supply tons of data themselves, often unwittingly, because information about purchases, donations, and memberships is now widely shared. "People are surprised that their name even exists on lists," says Greg Branstetter, founder of Hippo Direct, a mailing-list broker in Cleveland. "But most of list creation comes from consumer behavior, whether it is buying from catalogs, ordering magazines, joining associations, or filling out warranty cards." Branstetter recently completed a project that required him to "track down gay-oriented business publications and Web sites" to provide mailing lists for a client who wanted to market to gay men.

Selling Your Info

Data brokers provide individual background searches for employers and others. They also take in hefty revenues from slicing and dicing your information with data-mining software to create targeted lists to appeal to marketers.

Remember all those colorful bits of detail about your ailments and hobbies that you supplied on warranty cards? In the data industry, they are combined with information drawn from other sources such as public records and credit transactions to provide what Focus USA, a data broker, describes as a "three-dimensional view." Focus's own database covers 105 million U.S. households, with labels such as "Christian Donors," who give twice the portion of their incomes that non-religious households give to politicians and causes, and a group it calls "Hooked on Plastic," consisting of 4.2 million American families for whom "using credit cards doesn't feel like they're spending money."

Data brokers are not above selling your most sensitive information. InfoUSA, a database marketer with $400 million in sales, promises on its Web site to "find people who suffer from health conditions such as diabetes" or "search for people taking a certain medication." Clients can order a mailing list of, say, Prozac users or refine the list to include only those with incomes over $100,000 a year. Rakesh Gupta, InfoUSA's database president, says that only "legitimate companies," primarily large pharmaceutical manufacturers, are permitted to buy the lists.

Keeping Your Secrets

Federal law gives you the right to view data that will be used for certain purposes, such as background screening to determine your eligibility for insurance, a job, or an apartment rental. But there's a lot that the law doesn't cover.

Two CONSUMER REPORTS staffers requested copies of their own reports. Acxiom's report for consumers (cost: $5) provided five pages of bare-bones facts such as name, address, phone number, and age. The company included a separate sheet summarizing the range of information that consumers could not view but that the company's business clients could. Among those tidbits: e-mail address, occupation, political party, categories of retail purchases, estimated net worth, and details on their cars. ChoicePoint's free basic report was also skimpy. Only LexisNexis' "Person Report" (cost: $8) provided a little more, listing addresses and birth dates for relatives and neighbors.

The reports also contained several errors, including incorrect addresses, misspellings of names, and an incorrect Social Security number. Data brokers say, however, that they are not in the business of correcting inaccuracies. A letter accompanying the report from LexisNexis, for example, says, "We do not examine or verify our data, nor is it possible for our computers to correct or change data that is incorrect."

"It's easy to see how an ordinary consumer could fail to get a job or an apartment," says Richard Smith, a Boston Internet security consultant, "or even end up on a no-fly list, now that the government is becoming such a big client, too."

Given the sensitivity of the information that brokers distribute, ensuring its security should be a top priority. The three major data brokers have all suffered major breaches in recent years, although only ChoicePoint's thus far has led to censure by the Federal Trade Commission. It slapped the company with a $10 million fine, the largest civil penalty in agency history. It also harshly criticized the company's security and record-handling procedures. Instead of limiting access to legitimate businesses or government agencies, the company released data to crooks whose requests used commercial mail drops as business addresses, "an obvious red flag," the FTC said. As it turned out, a Nigerian fraud ring was behind the breach.

In February 2005 consumers began to learn about the data breach. To date, says Brian Hoffstadt, an assistant U.S. attorney who co-prosecuted the case against the data thieves, $600,000 worth of fraudulent credit-card charges have been documented involving an estimated 100 individual victims. "For the consumers involved, there could be a ripple effect, and we may not know the true impact for quite a while," Hoffstadt says.

Elizabeth Rosen, the nurse whose information was stolen in the ChoicePoint breach, encountered no problems initially. But more than a year later, she began to be hounded by calls from various bill collectors asking for other people. ID theft experts say that's a bad sign, indicating that a thief might have set up accounts using her Social Security number under other names and addresses—a new and growing trend in ID fraud.

In response to the FTC, ChoicePoint has tightened its security procedures, following mandates to verify the identities of businesses seeking to obtain consumer reports, even visiting some and auditing their use of those reports.

A Steady Customer

Since 2002, a rule change at the U.S. Department of Justice has allowed unrelated bits of personal data to be pieced together to target American citizens as potential threats who merit surveillance or investigation, even if no reasonable suspicion of criminal activity exists. The federal government has become a steady buyer of this kind of information. In fiscal 2005, the departments of Justice, Homeland Security, and State, and the Social Security Administration spent $30 million on data-broker contracts, according to a 2006 GAO report, which also suggested that the data-broker business was at odds with widely accepted principles for protecting personal data.

Another example: To help sell military careers to young people, the Pentagon has bought data from brokers. According to the Electronic Privacy Information Center (EPIC), they include American Student List, a company that signed a consent agreement in 2002 with the FTC promising not to distribute student data to brokers for noneducational marketing without disclosing it to students.

The Pentagon's database has accumulated information on the ethnicities, grade-point averages, intended fields of college study, phone numbers, and e-mail addresses of about 30 million Americans between ages 16 and 25. Those in the database can request by letter that the Pentagon not send direct-mail or telemarketing pitches, but they are not permitted to opt out of the database.

Activist groups, such as Leave My Child Alone, based in San Francisco, complain that recruiters repeatedly call students at home or on cell phones. Felicity Crush, the group's spokeswoman, says, "They have the money to farm this out to a private company, but when we asked the Pentagon to establish a toll-free number for opting out, they claim they didn't have money in the budget."

Finding out what the government is buying has proven impossible. When EPIC filed a request under the Freedom of Information Act in 2001 to obtain copies of records relating to federal agencies' use of data brokers, among the documents it received was a Jan. 13, 2000, PowerPoint slide presentation with the ChoicePoint and Federal Bureau of Investigation logos displayed together above the report's title: "A Partnership for the New Millennium." All other text on the slides had been blacked out, and to date, the FBI has failed to deliver 5,000 additional pages of ChoicePoint contracting documents.

"Over the past several years, we've learned about huge databases of information on law-abiding Americans being assembled by the government directly or purchased by the government from private vendors," Sen. Ron Wyden, D-Ore., recently told CR. "These reports raise serious concerns about privacy and consumer rights." In 2003, he introduced legislation to require the FBI and other federal agencies to provide detailed reports to Congress explaining their use of public and private databases. The bill failed to pass, though Wyden hopes to take up the issue again.

On a Pretext

The data industry has a shady element that includes private investigators and others who practice so-called pretexting: impersonating relatives, company officials, or even law-enforcement personnel to obtain confidential consumer information.

The results can be deadly. Case in point: Amy Boyer of Nashua, N.H., was fatally gunned down by Liam Youens, a stalker, as she left work. Youens had obtained, for less than $200, all of the information he needed to track her from Docusearch.com, an online data broker that, court papers say, hired a pretexter to find out where she worked. A civil suit filed against the company charged that Youens maintained a Web site describing his plans to kill Boyer. The case was settled out of court. Dan Cohn, president of Docusearch, says, "Our policies and the way we do business has changed as a result."

The murder occurred in 1999, but Docusearch and similar "backgrounding" services have only grown. Rob Douglas, founder of PrivacyToday.com, information security consultants, says, "With the advent of the Internet, data brokers learned how much money could be made selling phone and bank records to customers online, and the feeding frenzy was on."

While some Web sites require that customers complete a "permissible purpose form" stating that they have a legitimate legal reason for requesting someone's confidential information, Douglas says such requirements are usually nothing more than "legal mumbo jumbo" the brokers use to cover themselves in case something goes awry later. He says faxing a fake letterhead identifying you as a member of a law firm or a potential employer usually can get you what you want.

Customers buying covertly obtained information range from large corporations tracking deadbeat customers to snoops checking up on potential mates. According to statements that some data brokers have provided to congressional investigators, their customers also include local and federal law-enforcement personnel who in this way obtain cell-phone records without subpoenas or warrants. "This illicit marriage between law enforcement and black-market information thieves deserves to be fully investigated," Douglas says.

David Gandal, a Loveland, Colo., investigator who has used pretexting to track debtors skipping out on car loans, says, "Just about every major financial institution has paid for this kind of work." He told CR that armed with a few bits of identifying information readily available to most investigators through large commercial databases, a pretexter calls customer service representatives at a phone company or utility. The person then tricks them into revealing account numbers, passwords, and other sensitive information by pretending to be the customer or another company employee, say, someone in tech support. "I'm a man of many voices," Gandal says. "Sometimes I would pretend to be a stroke victim having trouble getting my words out and they'd help by volunteering whatever information I needed."

While pretexting to obtain access to bank records was outlawed in 1999 with the passage of the Gramm-Leach-Bliley Act, no federal law specifically prohibits using such deception to obtain phone, utility, or other customer records.

Fighting Back

A few fledgling efforts to combat the release of personal information have made headway. B. J. Ostergren, a former insurance claims supervisor, launched an effective one-woman campaign to keep her home county in Virginia from posting its

What You Can Do

While you have no control over much of the data collection and sharing that occurs, you can limit the amount of information circulating about you. Also, checking the accuracy of those records that you're entitled to see allows you to spot signs of ID theft and fraud.

Opt out of:

Telemarketing. Put your name on the Federal Trade Commission's Do Not Call registry by going to www.donotcall.gov or calling 888-382-1222.

Unwanted solicitations. Ask financial institutions, retailers, and Web sites not to share your information with other nonaffiliated companies. Contact the Direct Marketing Association at www.dmaconsumers.org/consumer assistance.html; for unsolicited e-mail, www.dmaconsumers.org/consumers/optoutform_emps.shtml.

Sales of your information to others. The Privacy Rights Clearinghouse lists data brokers that offer limited opt-out policies at www.privacyrights.org/ar/infobrokers.htm.

Keep your information private:

Don't fill out surveys on warranty cards. Just provide your name, address, and necessary product information, and your warranty will be honored. Be careful with direct-mail surveys that don't come from companies with which you already do business.

Don't provide sensitive information on the phone, through the mail, or over the Internet unless you've initiated the contact or you're sure that it's from an organization you trust. If in doubt, contact the organization.

Check what's on file about you:

Order your free annual report from each of the major nationwide credit-reporting companies once every 12 months at www.annualcreditreport.com.

Request your files from the major data brokers: ChoicePoint at www.choicetrust.com and LexisNexis at www.lexisnexis.com/terms/privacy/data/obtain.asp. You can call Acxiom at 877-774-2094 or send e-mail to reference report@acxiom.com.

Get medical information. If you've applied for individual health- or life-insurance policies within the past seven years, the MIB Group keeps data that insurers use to help determine your rates. Get a report by calling MIB toll-free at 866-692-6901.

public records on the Internet. To get legislators' attention, she demonstrated the potential for harm in January 2005 by posting on her own Web site *(www.thevirginiawatchdog.com)* a few Social Security numbers for people whose records she spotted online. Among them: former CIA Director Porter Goss, former Secretary of State Colin Powell, and Florida Gov. Jeb Bush, whose number was blacked out on Dade County online records after she drew attention to it. "I understand why he'd want to black out his number," Ostergren says. "But shouldn't everyone have that right?"

Are You Too Family Friendly?

As the proportion of single and childless workers increases, so do complaints of unfairness in employers' benefits and policies.

SUSAN J. WELLS

S ingle employees' inner resentment about married peers' family needs can surface innocently enough.

Thomas Harpointner, chief executive officer of AIS Media Inc., recalls the time an employee of his Atlanta-based technology company left work early on Halloween to go trick-or-treating with his children.

"It did raise a few eyebrows," he says, "and some people poked fun about it." Half of AIS Media's employees are unmarried.

Harpointner got the message.

"We realized that this was no joke—it was a real issue," he says. "If someone needs an afternoon off, it shouldn't matter what the reason is. And if one employee gets the privilege, then everyone should—and we should make it a policy," he concluded.

Harpointner did just that, along with attractive enhancements to a set of employee-friendly—not solely family-friendly—benefits that apply to everyone equally and strive to reward everyone fairly by matching employees' individual priorities, "regardless of their lives or career stages, personal situations, whatever," he says.

More employers, and their HR leaders, would be wise to do the same. According to the latest available U.S. Census Bureau data, the nation grows more unmarried with each passing year.

The Shifting Majority

Unmarried and single U.S. residents numbered 92 million in 2006, making up 42 percent of all people 18 and older. That's up from 89 million, or 41 percent, in 2005. Sixty percent of the unmarried and single adult men and women in 2006 had never been married, up from 50 percent in 1970. Another 25 percent were divorced, and 15 percent were widowed.

Slightly more than one in four households, 26 percent, consisted of a person living alone in 2006, up from 17 percent in 1970. And of the nation's 114 million households in 2006, 47.3 percent were headed by unmarried individuals. That figure fluctuates around 50 percent; it hit 50.3 percent in 2005, for instance.

Essentially, more people live together, marry at older ages or not at all, and rear children in cohabiting or solo-parent households, says David Popenoe, professor of sociology emeritus at the

New Brunswick, N.J., campus of Rutgers University. Popenoe is founder and co-director of the National Marriage Project, a nonpartisan research organization at the school.

His July 2007 report, *The Future of Marriage in America,* tracks a decline of nearly 50 percent in the annual number of marriages per 1,000 unmarried adult women from 1970 to 2005. It also notes the rise in households without minor children. In 1960, for example, nearly half of all households had children under 18. By 2000, the portion had fallen to less than a third. In a few more years, it's projected to drop to a quarter, according to the report.

These trends contribute to a burgeoning movement to promote singles' rights, with a growing number of advocacy organizations becoming more vocal about what they perceive as unfair treatment by employers, government and society.

The Backlash

Nicky Grist, executive director of the 9,200-member Alternatives to Marriage Project Inc. (AtMP), a nonprofit advocacy organization in Brooklyn, N.Y., insists that the census data should make policy-makers and corporate decision-makers question and address some longtime, commonly held beliefs.

Marital status simply isn't a meaningful or reliable indicator of what's really going on in employees' lives.

"More of the workforce is going to be single, unmarried or childless—or some combination," she says. "Employers—especially now—need to recognize that marital status isn't a defining characteristic of the workplace any longer. It simply isn't a meaningful or reliable indicator of what's really going on in employees' lives."

The trends reignite some of the work/life backlash that first greeted employers' widespread adoption of "family-friendly" benefits decades ago.

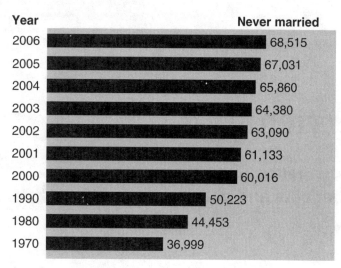

Year	Never married
2006	68,515
2005	67,031
2004	65,860
2003	64,380
2002	63,090
2001	61,133
2000	60,016
1990	50,223
1980	44,453
1970	36,999

Americans Who Have Never Married, 1970–2006. Total men and women in the U.S. population in thousands.

Source: U.S. Census Bureau, Current Population Survey, 2006 Annual Social and Economic Supplements (released March 2007), and earlier reports.

While 88 percent of 1,909 employees surveyed this spring by staffing and recruitment firm Adecco USA of Melville, N.Y., said they admire working parents' ability to "do it all" when it comes to work and family, 36 percent of men and women said parents' flexibility at work negatively affected team dynamics, and 31 percent said employee morale suffered. Working men ages 35 to 44 reported an even greater negative perception: 59 percent of them said flexibility for working mothers caused resentment among co-workers.

Fueling the Tension

What causes this workplace unease to boil over? Childless singles feel put upon, taken for granted and exploited—whether because of fewer benefits, less compensation, longer hours, mandatory overtime, or less flexible schedules or leaves—by married and child-rearing co-workers.

"The overall assumption tends to be that if you're single, you have nothing better to do—or nothing that qualifies as more important than what your married co-workers have to do—and so you're going to have to pick up what the rest of the workforce can't or won't," explains Bella DePaulo, Ph.D., a visiting professor of psychology at the University of California-Santa Barbara, and author of *Singled Out: How Singles are Stereotyped, Stigmatized, and Ignored, and Still Live Happily Ever After* (St. Martin's Press, 2006).

On her web site, DePaulo collects experiences and complaints from single employees regarding all kinds of perceived work and benefits inequities—and she finds they're frustrated.

"If a single worker complains to a boss or co-worker about such things, they say they often get a hostile response," she says. "No one wants to be unfair—but when the issue's brought out into the open, it's obviously hitting a nerve with both parties."

Even policies dealing with office perks meant to foster employee relations can backfire. For example, DePaulo recalls an annual department picnic at a previous teaching job. Every employee was asked to pay a flat fee—no matter whether they were single or were bringing a spouse and five kids. Although the policy was unfair to singles, effectively causing them to subsidize colleagues' families, confronting the problem without sounding insensitive was a challenge, she says.

Fostering a Singles-Friendly Environment

Wendy Casper, Ph.D., assistant professor of management in the College of Business Administration, University of Texas at Arlington, has researched single employees' perceptions of how their organizations support their work/life balance in comparison to employees with families.

In a study of 543 singles without children published in the June 2007 issue of the *Journal of Vocational Behavior,* Casper and her colleagues documented that singles viewed more inequity in benefits policies and work/life support from their employers than did employees with families.

"Singles are more in tune with these perceptions than marrieds are," she says. "And company decision-makers, who may have greater access to work/life policies themselves, may not be as intuitive or sensitive to their single employees' views."

As part of the research, Casper identified five measures of a "singles-friendly culture." Social inclusion, equal work opportunities, equal access to benefits, equal respect for nonwork life and equal work expectations are the key, defining characteristics that employers should address, assess and evaluate, the researchers suggest.

They also point to evidence that nonmonetary and more informal elements of employee relations may be as important to equalizing the varied needs of the singles workforce.

"The social inclusion factor had much greater consequences than the other issues did in terms of driving a backlash," says Casper. "Social inclusion plays a big role: When single employees have a sense of attachment and feel more supported at work, it tends to lead to greater retention, productivity and job performance."

Casper speculates that single and childless workers have stronger needs for workplace social inclusion because their relationships and overall sense of community are more likely to be connected to their jobs.

Technology company Texas Instruments Inc. numbers among the employers who have made an effort to increase such inclusive strategies.

To help new employees connect, for example, it started a support group in its IT Services division five years ago. The group sponsors professional development, with "lunch and learn" programs, seminars and mentoring; networking, with happy hours and other events; social events such as WhirlyBall, movies and bowling; and community services such as volunteering and charitable outreach.

Since then, there has been interest among Texas Instruments' other business groups in forming "New Employee Initiative" groups. "It can mean a lot to have a peer group within the company," says Betty Purkey, manager of work/life strategies at the Dallas-based company.

Creating a Wider View

To encourage a sense of equality among all demographic groups, more company officials take a wider view of the benefits and work/life programs they provide—with an eye toward diversity, flexibility, neutrality and choice.

"The buzzword shouldn't be 'family-friendly,' " says social psychologist DePaulo. "It should be 'employee-friendly' or 'life-friendly.' "

Indeed, many employers already have renamed their benefits "work/life" or "personal benefits" or have simply gotten rid of the distinction, she notes.

Some employers move to types of benefits that level the playing field by offering something for everyone.

For instance, 70 percent of 326 HR executives surveyed in 2006 by CCH and Harris Interactive said their organizations offer paid-time-off programs bundling vacation, sick and personal leave into one bank of time off that employees can manage more flexibly. In addition, 37 percent of 590 HR professionals polled for the Society for Human Resource Management's 2007 Benefits Survey said their companies offer flexible or cafeteria-benefits plans allowing employees to choose from a variety of benefits and designate a set amount of money to pay for the benefits. These types of plans can allow for different lifestyles without rewarding employees having larger families with more benefits for the same job, for example.

Yet unequal access to employer-sponsored health insurance remains one of the top complaints of many unmarried workers with partners, including AtMP members, says Grist.

According to research by the Human Rights Coalition (HRC), a Washington, D.C., civil rights organization, a majority of *Fortune* 500 companies provided benefits to same-sex domestic partners in 2006. Since then, 17 more companies have added the benefits, bringing the total to 267—or 53 percent of *Fortune* 500 companies, the HRC says.

But while same-sex benefits have been more widely adopted among large organizations, opposite-sex domestic-partner coverage generally has seen slower adoption. In fact, all unmarried couples are still significantly less likely to have health insurance than married people, according to a 2006 study by The Williams Institute on Sexual Orientation Law and Public Policy at the University of California-Los Angeles Law School.

"We found that 20 percent of people in same-sex couples are uninsured, compared with only 10 percent of married people or 15 percent of the overall population," says M.V. Lee Badgett, the institute's research director and co-author of the study. "Unmarried heterosexuals with partners are even worse off, with almost one-third uninsured."

This results in a continuing health-benefits gap for unmarried employees who may be in committed relationships or have other family members they'd like to cover but can't, says Grist. "Access to domestic-partner coverage depends on the definition of your relationship—and whether it's legally recognized," she says. "There's not a clear, legal status that currently describes a lot of these interdependent relationships." Only a few states currently recognize unmarried relationships.

Wayne Wright, Ph.D., and his partner of eight years, Madeline Holler, fell into that gap two years ago after relocating to Southern California from St. Louis. He had accepted a job as an assistant professor of philosophy at a state university. It was his understanding, he says, that his new job's benefits package included coverage for domestic partners—a perk that he and Holler had enjoyed at his previous employer.

Shortly after their move, however, "our 'unmarriage' began to unravel," Holler says.

It wasn't until orientation for new faculty members, Wright says, that he learned that his employer's domestic-partner coverage applied only to same-sex couples—a distinction that wasn't initially described.

And with the first $400 health insurance premium coming due to continue coverage under COBRA for Holler, Wright felt they had no choice, he says. He booked a hotel room in Las Vegas for the following weekend, and he and Holler were married at the celebrated drive-through on the Strip called The Little White Wedding Chapel.

While they hold no grudges and are secure in their relationship, Wright and Holler also say they felt powerless over what should be a personal life decision. "We absolutely felt forced to do it," Wright says.

Ending Special Deals and Stigma

While companies continue to diversify their benefits, some employers strive to custom tailor the entire employment relationship—including responsibilities, scheduling, workload and benefits—in an effort to end perceived tensions between employee groups and to improve recruitment and retention.

"In the past, an employee who wanted to work in a different way might have made a personal deal with his or her boss," says Ellen Galinsky, president and co-founder of the Families and Work Institute in New York. "Today, employees and employers are working together to find new ways to restructure the workplace in unique ways to give people the flexibility they need and to improve bottom-line business measures like productivity and retention."

Take ARUP Laboratories in Salt Lake City, where employees suggested the unusual idea of a seven-days-on, seven-days-off scheme. Workdays are 10 hours each, so employees log 70 hours in all during any given two-week period. They're paid, however, for two 40-hour weeks.

This flexible scheduling, and other forms of flexibility, help the medical-testing company recruit employees in the face of a national health care talent shortage.

Each worker is paired with a counterpart handling the opposite schedule; the two cover for each other if they have conflicts.

"We've created a self-functioning, stable team in which employees essentially get 26 free weeks a year to do with what they choose or need—take time with children, take a class, do volunteer work or go skiing," says Von Madsen, assistant vice president, human resources manager. Along with its menu of equal and neutral employee benefits, the flexible-schedule policy has helped the 2,100-employee company reduce turnover from an industry average of 22 percent to about 14 percent, Madsen says.

The flexibility also has had a positive effect on perceived scheduling and time-off inequities among singles and families.

"It helped eliminate the rift between employees with children and those without, who sometimes felt they had to cover the workload for parents who took additional time off for their children's needs," Madsen says. "It's created a more even footing."

At accounting giant Deloitte & Touche USA LLP, a new approach to career planning will become a corporate mandate in the next year.

Called "mass career customization," the initiative encourages every employee to engage in upfront, open discussion and custom planning about the course of his or her career and life-balance needs, according to Cathleen Benko, vice chairman and managing principal of talent, and co-author of a book about the program, *Mass Career Customization: Aligning the Workforce with Today's Nontraditional Workforce* (Harvard Business School Press, September 2007).

Changing demographics played a part in the design.

"The family structure has fundamentally changed in this country—83 percent of U.S. households are now considered 'nontraditional,' and singles are certainly a part," Benko says. "There's little wonder why many executives are either sensing or already confronting mounting tensions."

Benko suspects these tensions are rooted in the misalignment between the traditional workplace and the largely nontraditional workforce, explaining, "The one-size-fits-all approach no longer works."

Her model divides work into four dimensions—pace, workload, location and schedule, and role—and then builds career objectives in each dimension that match employees' life circumstances along the way, allowing employees to "dial up and down," she says, and then revisiting these choices periodically as circumstances change.

Since 2005, the concept has been pilot tested and is now in the midst of a phased, 12-month rollout companywide, Benko says. Eventually, all 42,000 employees will be enrolled.

U.S. households in thousands

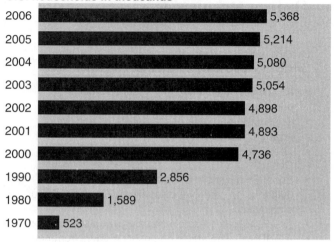

Year	Households
2006	5,368
2005	5,214
2004	5,080
2003	5,054
2002	4,898
2001	4,893
2000	4,736
1990	2,856
1980	1,589
1970	523

The Number of Unmarried-Couple Households Increases . . . , 1970–2006.

Sources: U.S. Census Bureau, Current Population Survey, 2006 Annual Social and Economic Supplement (released March 2007), and earlier reports.

Children under 18

Year	Percent
2005	32.3%
2000	32.8%
1990	34.6%
1980	38.4%
1970	42.2%

. . . While the Percentage of Households with One or More Children Decreases, 1970–2006.

Source: U.S. Census Bureau, Statistical Abstract of the U.S., various years.

Interestingly, she notes, the pilots so far have found that "rather than dialing down on their careers, many employees were choosing to dial up," reflecting, in part, the fact that 65 percent of Deloitte's employees are under the age of 35. "Dialing up" refers to increasing one's professional commitment, perhaps by returning to full-time hours or adding hours, seeking the promotion fast-track, or going after opportunities for higher rewards and compensation.

During the pilots, Benko says, employee job satisfaction and retention also rose.

"This approach works because it takes a lattice, rather than ladder, approach to job moves," she says. "Work doesn't have to be an 'up or out' route, and we have a system here that's fluid and adaptable through all life and career stages."

Including All Perspectives

As Deloitte & Touche and other employers test employment customization, one thing is certain: Employment and work/life policies will continue to evolve, as different demographic groups force change and inclusion. And unlike the personal demographic characteristics that workers bring to their jobs, experts say that employers hold the power to create supportive workplace policies.

Demographics change in a clear direction, says DePaulo. Raising awareness and thinking in a broader perspective about the makeup of the workplace become more important. "A singles perspective should be acknowledged right along with the other perspectives. It's not the *only* perspective, but it should be one of them."

Susan J. Wells, a business journalist in the Washington, D.C., area and a contributing editor of *HR Magazine,* has more than 20 years of experience covering business news and workforce issues.

Con Artists' Old Tricks

A no-risk investment? A 'nephew' in distress? Don't believe them. Senior citizens need to be vigilant.

KATHY M. KRISTOF

Walter Kincherlow Sr., 69, never expected to retire a millionaire. But during his 29 years as a maintenance worker, he managed to sock away more than $80,000. He invested pretty well too, until an "estate planner" took a look at his portfolio while updating his living trust and clucked that Kincherlow's investment returns were paltry.

Claiming that Kincherlow could earn 20% per year safely, he persuaded the widower to pour his life savings into real estate investments with an El Segundo investment firm called Jon W. James & Associates. Kincherlow said he was assured that his principal was safe. But signs of trouble emerged when he wanted to start spending some of his savings. Then, company managers either couldn't be reached or talked him out of withdrawal, he said. Meanwhile, they tried to persuade him to secure a huge home equity loan to invest even more.

Securities regulators filed an emergency action last summer to shut down the firm, which they claimed was operating a $22-million fraud. James maintained in legal filings that the company's investments simply had insufficient time to pan out. In any event, a court-appointed receiver says investors are owed about $13 million, but the company has less than $4 million in assets to repay investors.

"They're telling me that I might end up with $6,000 or $7,000 out of all of the money I invested," said Kincherlow, who now lives in Victorville. "I wish I never had done this."

He has plenty of company. More than 200 investors are in similar straits with Jon W. James & Associates, and that's just the tip of the iceberg.

About 5 million seniors are victimized by some sort of financial fraud each year, according to the Securities and Exchange Commission. California law enforcement authorities believe that about a million of those victims live in the Golden State. Fraud against seniors is rising, experts add, but precise numbers are impossible to come by, partly because authorities believe that only 1 in 5 such frauds are ever reported.

The tragic part: Once a senior gets taken, there's little chance he or she will ever get the money back. And experts maintain that most of the fraud is easily avoided.

Karen Liebig of Torrance runs a nonprofit group called the Keep Safe Coalition. Its mission is to arm seniors with the information necessary to protect them from scams. They go everywhere: convalescent homes, senior centers, libraries, bridge clubs. Anywhere seniors gather and might want information about the hallmarks of elder abuse—financial or physical—will draw Liebig and her reams of tip sheets and little giveaways, such as pens and whistles with a message: "Blow the whistle on fraud!"

With PowerPoint presentations and gentle talks, she explains to people like Kincherlow that there is no such thing as a "safe" or "guaranteed" investment that pays 20% annually. She cajoles them to beware of "trust officers" bearing investment advice. She pulls in district attorneys and detectives to talk about salesmen who are willing to take seniors to the store and run errands for them as a way of gaining their trust before they sell them investments that could bankrupt them.

"We have a case now where the girlfriend of the grandson served as a caregiver and she's taken money out of this woman's account; she's taken home equity loans in her name," Liebig said. "The lady, who is in her late 80s or 90s, is never going to get her money back."

More than anything, Liebig urges seniors to seek help when they're being pressured to buy something and report it when someone takes advantage. And she counsels friends and family members of older folks living alone—the most vulnerable targets—to keep in close touch and look for telltale signs of trouble.

Just as you watch the people your teenagers hang out with, friends and relatives of senior citizens should be watchful when the senior takes up with new caregivers and friends. They should also worry if the family's "lost soul" takes such good care of grandma that everybody else loses contact.

"We have had immediate family members, who are in line to inherit the money anyway," said Det. Sgt. Peter Grimm of the Redondo Beach Police Department. "But the greed factor kicks in, and they say, 'I want it now.'"

That's one reason seniors are such attractive targets, officials say. Because they're embarrassed or infirm or have such a close emotional connection to the con artist, they're far less likely to report and pursue prosecution of the criminal. They're also, demographically, a wealthy group, holding billions in assets and home equity.

"It's just like Willie Sutton," said Donn Hoffman, a Los Angeles County deputy district attorney who prosecutes cases of elder abuse. Crooks "go where the money is."

Many of the crimes that affect the elderly are scams that can hit people of any age: identity theft, bogus lotteries, "free" gifts that require you to send money for shipping and Ponzi schemes that use new investor money to pay off old investors until they run out of victims and the schemes collapse.

The company that Kincherlow fell prey to didn't exclusively target seniors, just retirement assets. But he was nabbed through a "trust update," a common gambit aimed at seniors. Although living trusts can help avoid probate, state securities authorities maintain that con artists establish "trust mills" to simply get a good look at a senior's assets. They then convince the victim that their investments are either too risky or too low-yielding, and talk them into buying bogus or unsuitable investments that pay off for the broker while they impoverish the client.

The same technique is frequently used to sell seniors into variable annuities, which pay high commissions to the brokers, but can lock the investor's money up for decades.

Although these investments arguably are viable for younger individuals, they're almost always unsuitable for the over-70 set, to whom they're often sold, Hoffman said.

Riffling through pending investigations on his desk, Hoffman pulled out three involving the sale of annuities to elderly individuals and couples.

In one, a 74-year-old woman who told her agent she needed regular income from her investments was sold an annuity that provided no regular income. If she pulls money out during the next 10 years, she'll lose 20% of her principal to "surrender" penalties.

A similar case involved a couple in their late 60s who were both in ill health with diabetes and heart disease. Instead of an investment that would generate the income they needed to buy medications, they got an annuity that doesn't provide access to their savings until the husband turns 98.

In the third, a 71-year old woman with Alzheimer's was befriended by an agent who talked her into transferring her

Signs of Trouble

About 5 million seniors are victims of financial fraud each year, according to the Securities and Exchange Commission. California authorities estimate that 1 million of those victims live in the Golden State. Red flags include:

"Guaranteed" Investments That Pay Double-digit Returns

Any investment that promises to pay more than a certificate of deposit or Treasury bill bears substantial risk. Most "guarantees" offered on high-return investments aren't worth the paper they're written on.

Living-trust Officers Bearing Investment Advice

Regulators maintain that many companies that update living trusts are really just seeking a close look at a senior's portfolio to sell them high-cost and, often, inappropriate investments. Buy legal advice and investment advice separately. Not sure if you need a trust? Contact Healthcare and Elder Law Programs Corp., a nonprofit education and counseling group, at (310) 533-1996 or http://www.help4srs.org.

Free Lunch Seminars

Securities regulators say seminars offering seniors a free meal are too often come-ons for high-pressure salespeople to pitch annuities that can lock up your assets for decades, while paying huge fees to the salesperson. You can go to lunch, but don't invest until you've had a savvy friend or impartial investment advisor review the prospectus or offering circular. If the salesperson says the "opportunity" can't wait for you to examine the details, pass it up.

"Free Gifts" and Foreign Lottery Winnings

If you need to send a payment for "postage" or "taxes," you haven't won a "free gift" or a foreign lottery, you're being reeled in on a scam. Your winnings won't arrive; and you'll lose the amount you sent—or more. Some crooks use these scams to steal your banking information.

E-mailed Bank "Updates," IRS Refund Notices and "Account Warnings"

Your banker, the federal government and even PayPal are not going to ask you to update your account information by clicking on a link in an e-mail, but a con artist wanting your credit card numbers or Social Security number to commit identity theft will. Don't click through. If you think your banker needs to update your account information, call your bank directly. If you're wondering about a federal tax refund, contact the Internal Revenue Service at (800) 829-1040 or http://www.irs.gov.

Relatives and Caregivers Who Take Your Mail or Isolate You

Relatives and caregivers are often a tremendous help, but some bad apples take advantage of their trusted positions to commit identity theft and steal from seniors' bank accounts. Beware of anyone who discourages you from seeing others or who won't let you see your mail.

Call for Help

Seniors who are concerned about a caregiver, or friends or neighbors who worry that a senior may be in trouble, should call their county's adult protective services agency.

investments into annuities. She lost $30,000 to surrender fees on the first transfer and lost access to her money.

"I didn't dig through the complaints looking for the good ones," Hoffman said. "These are just typical."

Some frauds are tailor-made to ensnare senior citizens.

Consider, for example, the "nephew scam" that hit dozens of South Bay seniors. Someone would call with a friendly greeting such as, "Hi, Auntie! It's your favorite nephew. You remember me, don't you?"

The older person, often hard of hearing and not wanting to admit he or she might have forgotten a relative, would volunteer something along the lines of, "Is that you, Johnny?," giving the con artist a name to work with, Liebig said.

The bogus nephew then says he's at a local airport on his way to a business meeting but just got robbed and doesn't even have cab fare. The "favorite aunt" is asked to lend him a substantial sum, which will be picked up by one of the nephew's associates and repaid promptly. Naturally, neither the money nor the "nephew" is ever seen again.

Although this "nephew" is a bogus one, Liebig said, too often seniors are taken by their own relatives. Adult children, grandchildren, nieces and nephews can perpetrate identity fraud or mortgage fraud or simply raid the senior's bank account.

Although experts can tell seniors to be cautious of telemarketers and strangers offering investment advice, it's difficult to warn them about their own families.

"We tell people that we're not trying to scare them, but if someone is attempting to isolate them from other friends and family members—if they take your mail—you've got to be cautious no matter who they are," Liebig said.

On the bright side, regulators of all stripes are paying more attention to fraud against seniors.

Many states, including California, have passed laws to stiffen penalties for defrauding seniors, whether through Ponzi schemes or simply recommending unsuitable investments. Police departments and district attorney's offices in many major cities all over the country have launched units focused solely on senior abuse.

California insurance regulators are contemplating new rules that would impose stricter standards on the sale of variable annuities to anyone over age 65. The Securities and Exchange Commission has been investigating companies offering "free lunch" seminars, which are often used to lure elderly investors. And the SEC has teamed up with the National Assn. of Securities Dealers and AARP to host a "senior summit" next month aimed at getting regulators, law enforcement and community groups in the same room to find ways to combat senior fraud.

In the meantime, Liebig said, seniors need nosy neighbors to protect them.

"If there was somebody that used to sit on the porch and wave at you every day and you don't see them for a while, you need to knock on the door and check on them," she said.

If you suspect there's something wrong, call local law enforcement or adult protective services, she added.

kathy.kristof@latimes.com

Help! Somebody Save Our Files!

How to Handle and Prevent the Most Common Data Disasters

Michael Fitzgerald

D ustin Britt was working at his desk last Halloween when a huge explosion outside his window shook the building. The lights went out, and one of his co-workers screamed, "Oh, my God, I think we're going to die!"

But no one in the office was injured. The explosion had been caused by a car crashing into a telephone pole. Matchstic, the Atlanta design firm where Britt is a project manager, did lose power for more than a day. But it was prepared. Matchstic's computers either were laptops or had backup power supplies, which allowed them to be powered down without the loss of any work. And the company's servers are backed up once a day. Employees worked from home until power was restored, and a presentation had to be held in a nearby coffee shop, but otherwise the company was unaffected.

Other companies haven't been so lucky. No one comes to work expecting an IT crisis, but heart-stopping technical meltdowns happen every day—important files get wiped out, or thieves get hold of sensitive data. And data disasters of all sorts hit especially hard at small and midsize companies, where file backups, data security, and sometimes even basic protections like antivirus software frequently get overlooked in the scramble to make payroll and meet project deadlines. We've put together a guide to help you handle and possibly prevent four of the most common IT catastrophes.

1. Laptop Theft

Half of all organizations had a laptop or other mobile device stolen last year, according to a recent survey by the Computer Security Institute. And if the next stolen notebook belongs to your company, the replacement cost is the least of your worries. Most states have laws requiring businesses to tell customers when a laptop containing unencrypted sensitive data, such as Social Security numbers and credit card numbers, goes missing. Technology research firm Gartner estimates that each customer record lost costs a company from $150 to $250 in legal fees, notification costs, and other expenses. Plus, laptops often contain company intellectual property and other files that you wouldn't like bad guys leafing through.

Each stolen customer record costs from $150 to $250 in legal fees, notification costs, and other expenses.

How to respond. Your response depends on what you have done up front. For about $40 and up per laptop per year, services such as MyLaptopGPS and Absolute Software's Computrace LoJack for Laptops may be able to get the computer back. If you have installed one of these programs, the stolen machine will report its location to the authorities as soon as the thief connects to the Internet. Some services let you remotely wipe all data from the hard drive or will even covertly download files from the stolen laptop for you. If you don't have a tracing program, the best you can do is report the serial number to the police and the manufacturer and hope it winds up at a repair shop.

Preventive measures. In addition to installing tracing software, make sure to encrypt the hard drive. "If the data's encrypted, thieves can't use it, and you'll save yourself notice costs and bad public relations," says Randy Gainer, who deals with many privacy and security cases as a partner in Davis Wright Tremaine, a Seattle law firm. The enterprise edition of the Windows Vista operating system has an encryption feature, BitLocker, built in. Other encryption programs, such as PGP Whole Disk Encryption or Veridis' FileCrypt, can run about $50 to $120 per computer. Other tips: Record your laptops' serial numbers in a handy place. And advise employees to treat a laptop like a wallet. You wouldn't leave your wallet in the car, and you shouldn't leave your laptop there, either.

2. Hard Drive Failures

Shortness of breath, nausea, and intense feelings of dread. If you're experiencing these symptoms, you may be having a heart attack—or you may be reacting to the death of your computer's hard drive. Sean Marx recently suffered through the latter. He's CEO and co-founder of Give Something Back, an Oakland, California, supplier of environmentally friendly office supplies. When he suddenly couldn't get his computer to turn on, he knew he was in trouble. Marx's computer holds very large spreadsheets that track the company's sales and accounting, and he is often the only person with up-to-date versions of those files. He hadn't backed up in six months, even though he knew better. "I very quickly had that sinking feeling," says Marx.

How to respond. If your IT team can't bring your computer back to life, the only option is to send the drive to a data recovery service, which can charge anywhere from several hundred to several thousand dollars to rescue your files. The services aren't always successful. In Marx's case, he spent $1,500 at a local data recovery shop, but almost all the files were corrupted. He was able to recover many files attached to e-mails that were archived on the company's server.

Preventive measures. Back up your hard drive often, and use online services such as Mozy, iBackup, or EVault, which charge monthly fees of about $10 and up per employee. That way, even if a fire or flood ravages your server room, the data will be fine. You could also swap your current hard drive for a system that uses two drives to store two sets of your data, otherwise known as a RAID. So if one of the hard drives were to fail, you would still have the other.

3. Virus Outbreaks

"Your files are encrypted with RSA-1024 algorithm. To recovery your files you need to buy our decryptor." This is the error message, misspelling and all, created by a recent version of Gpcode.ak, a so-called blackmail Trojan horse. Gpcode.ak sneaks onto your computer, encrypts your files so you can't open them, and then demands a ransom for them. About eight years ago, in the heyday of virus outbreaks, malware writers seemed to compete for the most attention. Now, many virus writers have moved on to lower-profile—and more profitable—activities, like phishing, which tricks people into giving up their passwords, account numbers, and other personal data. Viruses remain one of the most common data problems, according to the Computer Security Institute.

How to respond. Many viruses can be contained or removed with antivirus software. The Gpcode.ak virus is an exception. However, Kaspersky Lab, which sells antivirus programs, recently released a free program, StopGpcode, that may help you unlock your files without capitulating to the blackmailers.

Preventive measures. Install antivirus software on all company computers and keep the virus definitions up to date. And make sure to back up your data frequently, just in case you need to revert to the last system-restore point before the virus hit. You can also use services like Postini, which, for about $12 per user per year, will remove viruses from e-mails

before they reach your inbox. Companies of a certain size can try something called application whitelisting. Programs like Bit9's Parity, which is available for about $30 per computer for a minimum of 100 machines, allow only software approved by the IT department to run on employee computers.

4. System Hacks

It's tough to keep up with hackers, because they are constantly finding new ways to infiltrate databases. In January, Davidson Companies, a financial services firm based in Great Falls, Montana, announced that a hacker may have been able to access personal data on its current and former customers. A handful of the estimated 226,000 affected customers have since filed a lawsuit. Davidson Companies would not comment.

Hackers often target financial companies. They also have an eye for e-commerce sites. In January, the Federal Trade Commission announced a settlement with Life Is Good, a Boston-based apparel maker. The agency criticized the company's e-commerce security after a 2006 incident, in which a hacker used an "SQL injection attack"—an attempt to gain control of the database by typing code into areas like search boxes—to grab customers' credit card numbers and expiration dates. The terms of the settlement require Life Is Good to beef up security and hire an independent security auditor to evaluate its systems for the next 20 years. The company declined to comment on the settlement, but an FTC representative says the agency learns about the cases it investigates through a variety of sources, including suppliers and customers.

Seventy percent of firms didn't know they had been hacked until someone else reported suspicious activity.

Often companies don't even realize they have been hacked until well after the fact. According to a recent security report by Verizon Business, 70 percent of firms didn't know they had been hacked until someone else—a customer or a bank—reported suspicious activity.

How to respond. If you think there has been a breach, take action right away. Davidson Companies immediately took its website offline, hired a security firm to investigate, and contacted the authorities, the credit bureaus, and its customers. You'll need to do the same, and also contact your attorney, if hackers may have gained access to credit card numbers or other sensitive information. It has become the norm to offer customers a year of credit monitoring services, which can cost about $10 a month per customer. Brace for customer defections, lawsuits, and possible fines from the FTC.

Preventive measures. There is no foolproof way to stop all hacks. So make sure your website encrypts your customers' credit card numbers and passwords (as opposed to storing them in a readable text format, which is what Life Is Good did before the attack). That way, even if hackers get in, they won't be able to see the information. And make sure that you apply the latest security patches to your software to protect against known vulnerabilities. One in five hacks exploits a security hole that's been public knowledge for six months or longer. McAfee offers a service called McAfee Secure, which scans your website daily for known security vulnerabilities. The service starts at about $1,700 to $2,800 a year for sites with fewer than 30,000 daily page views. Sophisticated techies may also be able to create what's known as a honeypot, phony files and decoy servers that are used to trap hackers. It's sort of like leaving a fake pile of gold out in the open—if anyone tries to take it, you will know the system is under attack.

ID Thieves Find a Niche in Online Social Networks

Scam artists are taking advantage of a trusting arena to get members to divulge passwords and other information.

Joseph Menn

Michael Maris became an unwitting spammer.
The 22-year-old college student from Chicago received messages last year from annoyed friends on MySpace, wondering why he had used the social networking site to send them pitches for male enhancement products.

He checked his outgoing mail folder and discovered that someone had hacked into his account, then blasted the unsolicited messages to each of his 70 MySpace pals. Among the recipients were his nieces, ages 14 and 16.

"I couldn't believe that it happened," he said.

Social networking sites, which let users create detailed profile pages and connect with friends, are becoming the hot new thing for identity thieves, both amateur and professional. As improved spam filters and skeptical consumers make bogus e-mail less successful, scam artists are taking advantage of the atmosphere of trust that exists within these online circles of friends.

Symantec Corp., a tech security firm, recently reported that 91% of the bogus U.S.-based websites used in so-called phishing attacks during the second half of 2007 imitated the log-in pages of two unnamed social networking sites—believed by industry executives to be the two biggest, MySpace and Facebook. Phishing tries to trick recipients into visiting phony websites and disclosing account numbers, passwords and other personal data.

"The bad guys are very adaptable. If something doesn't work, they come up with something new," said Kevin Haley, a product executive at Symantec. "Users feel more comfortable surrounded by their friends online—what could be safer?"

Sometimes financial gain isn't the objective. Cyber-bullies have taken over the social networking accounts of acquaintances to post vicious rants or engage in mischief.

Frank Nein, a new-media executive in Los Angeles, is still perturbed that a man showed up at the home of his 12-year-old daughter after another girl impersonated her during MySpace chats.

Nicole Whiting, a 19-year-old nanny from Charlotte, N.C., fielded questions from friends about her new boyfriend, Patrick.

Protecting Your ID

Here are ways to reduce the risk of identity theft on social networks:

- Post few identifying facts, such as the city and date of your birth. The more you say about yourself, the easier it is for a scammer to pretend to be you or to have a relationship with you.
- Use a different password for each website. Passwords can be easy to remember if you use the same combination of letters but, for example, add MS for MySpace or FB for Facebook.
- If you have already logged on to a site and then click a link within it, you should not be prompted to log in again. When in doubt, type the address, such as www.facebook.com, and start all over there.
- Before putting applications or the mini-programs known as widgets on your profile page, find out what others have said about those features. If the providers require a user name and password, use a new one.
- Be wary when strangers ask you to link up with them as a "friend."
- Make sure you have a computer operating system, firewall and anti-virus program that update automatically.

Source: Times research.

They learned of the relationship on what they thought was her Facebook page.

One problem, she said: "I don't even know a Patrick."

It turned out that "some lonely guy" had copied her pictures from her MySpace page, borrowed her first name and created a Facebook profile for an imaginary girlfriend. Her problem ended after she tracked down Patrick and complained.

But experts warn that victims of more sophisticated scams won't get off so easy. The same kind of hucksters who dreamed up e-mail scams featuring Nigerian dictators are now focused on cracking social networks to peddle products and engage in identity theft.

Crooks surreptitiously install software that records keystrokes to steal financial data, or they use personal details gleaned from the profiles to make fraud attempts more credible.

In more organized campaigns, scammers distribute free widgets that purport to help users decorate their profile pages but secretly use the log-on information to spam their friends, as happened to Maris. Other crooks surreptitiously install software that records keystrokes to steal financial data; or they use personal details gleaned from the profiles to make e-mail fraud attempts more credible.

One common technique on social networking sites involves sending messages that appear to come from an online buddy, inviting the recipient to check out a new profile page. The page then asks the recipient to log in.

It's a scam. Although the page looks as if it's on MySpace or Facebook, thieves have set it up to capture log-in names and passwords. The con artists can then try those names and Passwords to gain access to e-mail accounts, financial accounts and other websites, given that many people use the same password widely.

For scammers, knowing the names of a target's friends can be a powerful tool. Last year researchers at Indiana University used simple tools to crawl through major networking sites and record the connections among Indiana students they found. They then sent e-mails that appeared to come from a friend also enrolled at the school.

About 72% of the recipients clicked on the e-mailed link and then entered their university user names and passwords at a fake site. In a control group where the e-mails came from strangers at the university, only 16% fell for it.

MySpace and other sites that rely on outside advertising networks also have been compromised by malicious banner ads that take advantage of security holes in users' Web browsers to install spyware. In addition, both MySpace and Facebook recently had security vulnerabilities in their systems for uploading photos. "Tool-kits" for exploiting those vulnerabilities to forcibly install "malware" circulated rapidly in hacker communities.

Most attacks work only against people who lack updated firewalls, anti-virus systems and anti-spyware programs, but some can victimize anyone clicking the wrong link.

Parry Aftab, executive director of the nonprofit group WiredSafety, said the most pernicious attempts to get log-on information or install spyware remained phishing e-mails that appear to come from financial institutions. The account takeover at social sites, by contrast, usually aim to send spam within a network, drawing people to porn sites or those selling questionable wares.

Major social networking sites are stepping up their defenses. Beverly Hills-based MySpace, which is owned by Rupert Murdoch's News Corp., now tries to have the Web links from its pages go through a sort of quarantine. When it recognizes that users are about to follow a link away from the site, MySpace flashes an explanation of the potential for fraud.

"MySpace employs a variety of technological, legal and policy solutions to protect our users from phishing attempts," Chief Security Officer Hemanshu Nigam said in a statement.

MySpace and Palo Alto-based Facebook Inc. declined to make executives available for comment.

"Facebook is committed to user safety and security and is constantly improving the site to provide new technology to catch phishers quickly and limit the damage they can do," it said in a statement. "We always encourage users to take precautions when clicking on any suspicious links and to only log in to Facebook from pages they know are legitimate."

Security experts said they expected identity theft and other scams on social networking sites to escalate.

Spam has evolved from advertising pitches to take e-mails from banks and, most recently, highly targeted phishing attacks that focus on a given company's executives or customers. Some instances of that tactic, known as spear-phishing, rely on information about the targets gleaned from postings on Facebook, LinkedIn and other sites favored by Professionals, experts said.

As the social networks do better at blocking fake or captured user accounts, the scams will become more harmful by automatically installing key-loggers and other data-stealing software, said Adam O'Donnell, director of emerging technologies at anti-spam firm Cloudmark Inc.

"As anti-spam improves, all the techniques they use for e-mail will work on social networks," he said. "This time, those techniques are going to have a much higher rate of success."

Gender Issues

Sex-discrimination lawsuits are on the rise. Is your company at risk?

JENNIFER GILL

For large corporations, the news has been grim: Last July, Boeing agreed to pay as much as $72.5 million to settle a class-action lawsuit by female employees. That same month, Morgan Stanley paid $54 million to settle a similar suit.

Sex-discrimination suits against small companies don't make headlines but they are just as common. In fact, nearly half of all sex-discrimination charges—running the gamut from sexual harassment to gender-related firing—filed with the Equal Employment Opportunity Commission last year were aimed at firms with 200 or fewer employees. And claims could surge in the years ahead as more women gain confidence from high-profile cases in the news, according to Cari Dominguez, chairperson of the EEOC. Many female baby boomers are entering their 50s and are "looking to leave a legacy," Dominguez says. "Women are taking on the role of whistleblower."

Smaller companies are particularly vulnerable because they tend to have less structured atmospheres and are less likely to have formal sex-discrimination policies in place, Dominguez adds. "A lack of infrastructure and awareness of the issues can lead a small business to run afoul of the law," she warns.

Donna Salyers, founder and president of Donna Salyers's Fabulous Furs, a faux-fur retailer based in Covington, Ky., learned that lesson three years ago. Back then, the retailer—which has 35 full-time employees, an online store, a retail shop in Covington, and celebrity clients such as longtime *Cosmopolitan* editor Helen Gurley Brown—was struggling to recover from the economic impact of the 9/11 terrorist attacks. Then Salyers received more shocking news: The EEOC was suing Fabulous Furs for sexual harassment on behalf of four temporary employees in the company's distribution center who claimed that their supervisor made offensive remarks to them. The women, who had been let go after the company's busy season, also claimed that they were fired in retaliation for their complaints. Salyers soon found herself consumed with the lawsuit, watching as her legal bills skyrocketed to $100,000. Finally, last fall, she decided to settle. Her company, which admitted no wrongdoing in the case, paid $45,000 in damages to the plaintiffs and agreed to implement a new sexual-harassment policy. "Small businesses like ours aren't equipped to handle these claims," says Guy van Rooyen, CEO of Fabulous Furs. "It's like a smack in the face."

Salyers, who founded Fabulous Furs in 1989, is determined that this never happen again. Before the lawsuit, her company's sex-discrimination policy consisted of little more than the standard guidelines in an employee handbook. After the suit was filed, however, she hired a full-time human resources director to develop and review her company's employee policies. As part of the settlement, she also created a complaint hot line for workers and began holding annual sex-discrimination seminars for managers. By being up-front about what is and is not permissible, Salyers hopes to limit her company's exposure to any future claims.

The EEOC's Dominguez wishes more privately owned companies would follow suit. Until recently, the commission's efforts have been focused on large corporations. But now, smaller companies are the top priority, says Dominguez, who has launched an aggressive outreach program to educate small and midsize businesses. "They're the brave new world for us," she says. "That's where the growth opportunities are for the country's economy, but I see liability potential, as well."

Federal antidiscrimination laws apply to businesses with 15 or more employees, and state or local statutes often cover even smaller ones. In Chicago, for instance, companies with just a single employee can be sued for discrimination. To find out where your company stands, call the small-business liaison at your local EEOC field office (see www. eeoc.gov for a list of offices). The liaison will explain the law, provide educational materials for your staff, and even make free presentations at your workplace.

Next, spell out your firm's antiharassment and equal-opportunity policies in an employee handbook. Most companies follow a standard template, which can be found on the website of the Employment Law Information Network (www.elinfonet.com). In the handbook, tell employees whom to contact in the event of a complaint. Be sure to name someone besides the employee's direct manager, in case the issue involves that person. Merely providing the information in a handbook may not be enough, so follow Salyers's lead by posting your policy in areas frequented by employees, such as the kitchen or the restroom.

Many female baby boomers are entering their 50s and are looking to leave a legacy. They're taking on the role of whistleblower.

Bear in mind that guidelines written in legalese can be difficult to understand. For instance, an employee may realize that telling a dirty joke is a no-no. But he may not be aware that asking a female subordinate about her childcare arrangements is a bad idea. One comment isn't an actionable offense, and federal law does not prohibit simple teasing, offhand comments, or isolated incidents that aren't extremely serious. But there could be trouble if the conduct is frequent and severe enough to create a hostile work environment or results in a tangible employment action, such as firing or demotion. To help clarify the law for your staff, hire an employment lawyer to hold annual sex-discrimination seminars. Some trade associations and chambers of commerce also offer workshops for members.

Finally, be sure to keep a written record of your employees' shortcomings, advises Susan Stahlfeld, a partner at law firm Miller Nash's Seattle office. In a surprising number of cases, managers criticize employees verbally during reviews but give them high marks on written evaluations. Such evaluations can be critical to your company's defense if, say, an employee claims she was fired based solely on her sex. "It comes down to what you have in that person's file," Stahlfeld says.

Of course, even if you take every precaution, sex-discrimination complaints may arise. To prevent them from snowballing into lawsuits, investigate each one immediately. "Putting your head in the sand is never a good idea," says Jill

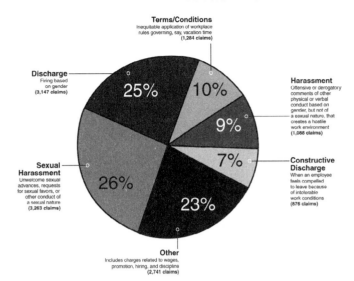

Figure 1 Discrimination Decoded. Last year, 12,399 sex-discrimination claims were filed against U.S. companies with between 15 and 100 workers. Here is a breakdown of the types of claims filed.

Schwartz, of Jill S. Schwartz & Associates, an employment law firm in Winter Park, Fla. For instance, if a female worker questions why she's being paid $10,000 less than her male counterpart, go over performance reviews and take her tenure into consideration. If there's a reason other than gender for the pay difference, explain it to her. If not, fix the discrepancy. As the recent spate of high-profile lawsuits has proved, granting a raise will cost much less than going to court.

Hiring Older Workers

Unique skills, values come through the experience of age.

STEPHEN BASTIEN

Wanted: Employees who are honest, responsible, dependable, loyal, focused, organized and mature. Is this too much to ask?

American employers spend millions of hours each year placing ads, prescreening, interviewing, hiring and training workers, only to find that many of the new hires work for only a few months and then decide they don't want to be "just a clerk" anymore or feel something better has come along as they work their way up the corporate ladder.

Where can American employers find dependable, steady employees who have no plans to move up and out? Employees who are dedicated to the job at hand and take pride in their work? Employees who cost less to hire, train and maintain?

The answer, I have found in many of my own business ventures, is senior citizens, or, for the purposes of this article, older workers.

Here are 10 advantages of hiring older workers that may solve managers' difficulties with maintaining a reliable, dedicated work-force and result in significant cost savings in both the short and long term.

1. Dedicated workers produce better quality work, which can result in significant savings. Stories abound of highly committed older workers finding others' potentially costly mistakes in everything from incorrect zip codes and misspelling of client names to pricing errors and accounting mistakes.

2. Punctuality seems to be a given for older workers. They look forward to going to work each day, so they arrive on time and ready to work.

3. Honesty is common among many older workers, whose values include personal integrity and a devotion to the truth.

4. Detail-oriented, focused and attentive workers add an intangible value that rubs off on all employees and can save thousands of dollars. One business owner described a case in which one of his older workers saved the company more than $50,000 on one large mailing job. His 75-year-old clerical worker recognized that all of the zip codes were off by one digit. Neither his mailing house nor his degreed and highly paid marketing manager had noticed it.

5. Pride in a job well done has become increasingly scarce among employees. Younger workers want to put in their time at work and leave, while older employees willingly stay later to get a job done because of their sense of pride in the final product.

6. Organizational skills among older workers mean employers who hire them are less likely to be a part of this startling statistic: More than a million staff hours are lost each year due to workplace disorganization.

7. Efficiency and the confidence to share their recommendations and ideas make older workers ideal employees. Their years of experience in the workplace give them superior understanding of how jobs can be done more efficiently, which saves companies money. Their confidence, built up over their years in the workforce, means they'll not hesitate to share their ideas with management.

8. Maturity comes from years of life and work experience and makes for workers who get less "rattled" when problems occur.

9. Setting an example for other employees is an intangible value many employers appreciate. Older workers make excellent mentors and role models, so training other employees is less difficult.

10. Reduced labor costs may be a benefit when hiring older workers. Most already have insurance plans from prior employers or have an additional source of income. They understand that working for a company can be about much more than just collecting a paycheck.

Employers who are hesitant to hire older workers should consider these benefits. Older workers' unique skills and values make hiring them a simple matter of rethinking the costs of high turnover in a more youthful workforce versus the benefits of experience and mature standards that older workers bring to the mix. So the next time you need to make a hiring decision, seriously consider older workers. Their contribution could positively impact the bottom line for years to come.

STEPHEN BASTIEN is an author and authority on entrepreneurship. His current venture, Bastien Financial Publications (www.usbj.biz), offers businesses the latest developments through daily newsletters. To contact him, call 1-800-407-9044 or send an e-mail to steve@creditnews.com.

The War Over Unconscious Bias

Wal-Mart and others are facing class actions for job discrimination. But the biggest problem isn't their policies, it's their managers' *unwitting* preferences. Can any company be immune?

Roger Parloff

Last February a federal appeals court panel in San Francisco decided, 2–1, to allow the largest class action employment discrimination case ever convened to go forward against Wal-Mart Stores. The class includes the more than two million women who have worked at any of the company's more than 4,000 retail stores nationwide since Dec. 26, 1998.

The case, known as *Dukes v. Wal-Mart,* accuses the retailer of discouraging the promotion of women store employees to managerial positions and of paying them less than men across all job positions. The suit seeks changes in the company's internal procedures, more than $1 billion in back pay, and punitive damages.

Wal-Mart denies any wrongdoing and asserts that it has put "enormous resources in seeking to have a diverse workplace and to make sure that women and minorities are having the best possible opportunities to succeed," as its lead lawyer, Theodore Boutrous Jr. of Gibson Dunn & Crutcher, puts it. (Boutrous has represented Time Inc., which publishes FORTUNE.) Wal-Mart has asked the full appeals court to reconsider the panel's approval of the class. ("Class certification" means the court believes that the claims by various employees share enough common elements to proceed as one combined suit rather than endless individual suits.) If Wal-Mart fails to win that, it will probably seek U.S. Supreme Court review.

Gender discrimination is always an incendiary accusation, and this case carries added emotional freight because Wal-Mart is Wal-Mart. It's not just the world's biggest private employer and the most admired company in this magazine's 2003 and 2004 surveys but also the most abhorred in other circles, particularly for its anti-union, penny-pinching labor practices.

But while the *Dukes* case does make some charges of intentional wrongdoing, it focuses mainly on three generic, almost abstract accusations that have become fixtures of nearly every contemporary employment discrimination dispute. These one-size-fits-all charges are less criticisms of Wal-Mart than of our society as a whole. It will be the rare large company that feels confident it could repel any of them.

Whether the defendant is Wal-Mart, Costco, Home Depot, FedEx, General Electric, MetLife, Merrill Lynch, Smith Barney, Morgan Stanley, Deloitte & Touche, or American Express—to name just a few that have been hit with such suits—the cases all stem from statistical evidence showing that the percentage of women or minority employees in portions of the workforce is markedly lower than in the available labor pool. The percentage of women or minorities in lower-level positions often far exceeds the percentage of those who are ever promoted to managerial positions, and their share keeps shrinking the higher up the corporate hierarchy one goes. (Sound like any companies you know?) Experts will often also present statistical analyses purporting to show that women or minorities are, on average, paid less than men or whites.

Once the statistical disparities have been established, the plaintiffs go on to make a second generic accusation: that "unconscious" bias is rife at the company. Supported by expert psychological testimony, the plaintiffs argue that managers in charge of promotion and pay decisions are unwittingly engaging in "spontaneous" and "automatic" stereotyping and "in-group favoritism" that results in the most desirable jobs at the company being filled by people who look like the incumbents, who are usually white males. (The companies' only defense is to challenge the admissibility of the expert testimony, which almost never works.)

Finally, the plaintiffs present the testimony of an expert organizational sociologist who explains that the company's promotion and pay procedures provide too much discretion to managers, allowing their unconscious biases to run rampant. (Know any companies where pay and promotion decisions have significant discretionary components?)

In case after case, these themes are debated by a regular cast of experts. Each side relies on a handful of statisticians, economists, psychologists, and sociologists, and the two teams go to battle in courtrooms around the country, much as the New England Patriots and Miami Dolphins play their scheduled rematches at least twice a year, sometimes at home and sometimes away. Usually the contests end with the class being certified and the defendant then settling for an eight-digit sum rather than risk facing a jury and the enormous exposure that a class action carries.

No scam is being perpetrated. What we are seeing is the clash of two sharply opposed philosophies of how active a company must become in the face of a phenomenon that is endemic and appropriately controversial in our country: workforce numbers that, when analyzed in certain plausible ways—though not in others—show discrepancies between how men and women, or blacks and whites, or the disabled and abled, are paid and promoted.

Such statistical disparities are not illegal per se, according to the Supreme Court, nor do they create any duty on the employer's part to ensure the numbers improve. But as we'll see, in practice employers are under precisely such pressure.

As maybe they should be. Whether you think forcing employers to monitor and increase their diversity is good or bad probably depends on your intuition as to whether existing statistical disparities generally reveal discrimination or whether they instead reflect a complex stew of social, historical, and cultural legacies that no company can or should be expected to correct. It also depends on how you feel about racial or gender quotas and preferences. Though such mechanisms are illegal, they will obviously be tempting to employers who want to avoid being hit with class-action employment discrimination lawsuits. For there is only one sure-fire way to inoculate oneself against such suits, and that is to have workforce numbers that look good even when analyzed by a plaintiffs' expert. And the cheapest and fastest way to get those is to use quotas or preferences.

> **"The rulings in the Wal-Mart case virtually guarantee that employers will be subjected to employment discrimination class actions with billions of dollars in potential damages."**
>
> —U.S. Chamber of Commerce

The Wal-Mart class action is no aberration; it's an epitome. It shares a common skeletal structure with almost every employment discrimination class action today and thus opens a telling window on a looming litigation threat to corporate America. The rulings in the Wal-Mart case "virtually guarantee that employers will be subjected to large-scale employment discrimination class actions with billions of dollars in

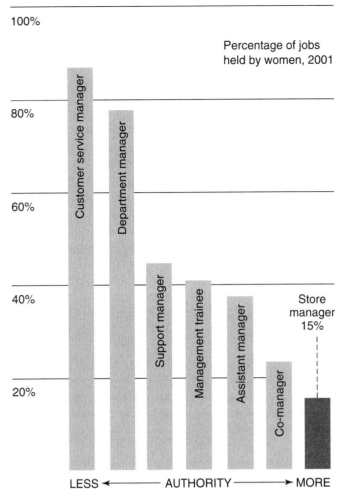

Percentage of jobs held by women, 2001

LESS ◄——— AUTHORITY ———► MORE

The plaintiffs' view. Discrimination in promotions at Wal-Mart is demonstrated by the numbers: As job authority increases, the percentage of women in those positions decreases.

Applicants for store manager positions, 2001

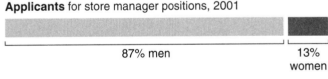

87% men   13% women

Offers for store manager positions, 2001

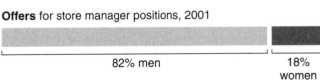

82% men   18% women

The defense's view. There's no gender discrimination at Wal-Mart: In fact, women were offered store manager positions at a higher rate than their rate of application.

Sources: Report of plaintiffs' expert Richard Drogin (plaintiff); report of Wal-Mart expert Joan G. Haworth (defendant).

potential damages, even . . . where only a few individuals complain of discrete instances of disparate treatment," the U.S. Chamber of Commerce asserted in an amicus brief.

The Wal-Mart rulings could end up representing a high-water mark, however. The underlying legal battles seem-destined for the Supreme Court. The urgent question is whether the current Court—with its staunchly conservative five-justice majority, sharp aversion to race-conscious remedies, and weak respect for prior precedent—will allow this situation to persist. The Wal-Mart suit may be the case that gives us the answer.

The federal employment discrimination laws, first enacted in 1964, prohibit two types of discrimination. The most easily understood variety is called disparate treatment: The plaintiff alleges that the employer treated him worse than some other employee because of race, color, religion, sex, or national origin.

Then there is "disparate impact." Here the plaintiff need not allege discriminatory intent. Instead he charges only that the defendant company is using some employment practice that, while possibly well intentioned, isn't essential to the job and acts in a way that systematically disadvantages a protected group. Employees have successfully challenged practices like requiring a high school diploma for certain blue-collar jobs (which put African Americans at a disadvantage in particular times and places); written tests (which put minorities at a disadvantage because of poor schools, language barriers, or cultural bias); and height requirements (which put Asian women seeking to become flight attendants at a disadvantage).

Though disparate treatment and disparate impact cases are both aimed at eradicating the same thing, there is potential tension between them. The goal of disparate treatment cases is to guarantee every worker equal opportunity, but not equal outcomes. The focus of disparate impact cases is on equal outcomes. If one pursues equal outcomes too single-mindedly, one can compromise the principle of equal opportunity by inducing the use of quotas.

In 1988 the Supreme Court faced what it recognized to be a momentous crossroads. A black bank teller who had been turned down for a promotion four times in favor of white applicants asked the Court to let her sue on a disparate impact theory, even though the only "employment practice" she challenged was the bank's policy of giving unbridled discretion to managers about whom to promote. It had long been recognized that unfettered discretion was vulnerable to *intentional* discrimination, and this bank employee was now arguing that it was also vulnerable to *subconscious* discrimination.

On the one hand, the Court's failure to allow such a suit might have permitted employment procedures that resulted in the functional equivalent of intentional discrimination. On the other, to permit it would come close to allowing plaintiffs to sue on the basis of statistical disparities alone. That in turn might force employers to adopt surreptitious quotas, even though courts have said they are illegal.

In the end, the Court let the case, known as *Watson v. Fort Worth Bank & Trust,* go forward, even while asserting that "an employer's policy of leaving promotion decisions to the unchecked discretion of lower-level supervisors should itself raise no inference of discriminatory conduct." Four of the eight justices participating, led by Justice Sandra Day O'Connor, stressed that statistical disparities alone were not suspect. She wrote, "It is completely unrealistic . . . to suppose that employers can eliminate, or discover and explain, the myriad of innocent causes that may lead to statistical imbalances in the composition of their workforces."

One of the first class actions to make use of the *Watson* precedent was *Stender v. Lucky Stores.* That case, brought in the late 1980s against a supermarket chain in Northern California, was handled by two men who would play key roles in employment discrimination litigation, including the Wal-Mart case. The first was a young but already accomplished employment lawyer, Brad Seligman. And the second was an organizational sociologist, William Bielby, who was an expert witness in the case. Bielby (pronounced BILL-by) had been studying gender segregation in the workplace since the 1960s and was then testifying in his first litigation. (Now 60, he is a professor at the University of Illinois in Chicago.)

Lucky Stores was a family-owned business, where store managers chose whom to place in which jobs without any job postings, written guidelines, or oversight. At Lucky Stores there was near total gender segregation: Almost all the cashiers were women, for instance, while almost all the managerial-track jobs were held by men. "So the issue there became, How do you get this extreme outcome when everything seems so fluid?" recalls Bielby.

The innocent possibility was that women sought out different jobs because of the responsibilities of raising children: They wanted lighter, more regular hours; no night shifts or weekends; and no geographic relocations. The illegal possibility was that male managers were, at least to some degree, *assuming* that these would be women's preferences, inadvertently blocking those who *did* want more responsibility from ever getting it. (Intentional discrimination was also possible, of course, but if that could be proved, one would not need a disparate impact theory.)

"There are studies that show that the strongest predictor of whether an opening is filled by a man or woman is whether the previous incumbent was man or woman."

—Plaintiffs expert William Bielby

In the *Lucky Stores* case Bielby testified both about the psychological literature concerning unconscious stereotypes and about the way the unfettered discretion given to managers at Lucky Stores allowed such stereotypes to run unchecked. "There are studies that show," Bielby says today, "that the strongest predictor of whether an opening is filled by a man or woman is whether the previous incumbent was a man or woman. . . . It's built into our understandings of what the work is about and who does the work, and it becomes the air you breathe."

In 1992, U.S. District Judge Marilyn Hall Patel ruled for the plaintiffs at trial, emphasizing Bielby's testimony in her opinion. (The case was settled for $107 million.) Judge Patel's ruling alerted other plaintiffs employment lawyers to the power of such testimony. Soon they were calling Bielby or a handful of other psychologists and sociologists to provide similar testimony in their cases.

In December 1999, Brad Seligman got a call from a New Mexico lawyer who had won several sex discrimination suits against Wal-Mart on behalf of individual women employees. The lawyer said he thought there was a much bigger problem and wanted Seligman's advice about bringing a class action.

Seligman, now 56, heads a nonprofit group called the Impact Fund. It operates from modest offices in the Berkeley marina. He founded the group in 1992—endowing it with $1.25 million of his own money—to mount, as its name suggests, high-impact employment discrimination cases. From his earlier days in private practice Seligman knew that while it was rewarding to win a nice recovery for an individual, a class action victory could "change a company." Given his political views, he says, that was much more gratifying.

Seligman, who dresses casually in a sweater, khakis, and sandals with white socks, is a child of the '60s. He started college at the University of California at Santa Cruz in 1969, became active in left-wing politics, dropped out, moved to Berkeley, and then moved again to a secluded cabin in Sonoma County. In late 1974, when he found himself unable to meet his $10-a-month rent, he applied to law school. "But my image of being a lawyer was strictly the white hat," he recalls. "I wanted it to have some meaning."

In 1980 he joined a private employment discrimination firm in San Francisco, excelled, became managing partner, and became rich. "Given my political background," he says, being wealthy "was fairly embarrassing at some level." In addition, he was becoming frustrated by "the imperatives of being in private practice"—i.e., staying profitable. "The market dynamics of these cases [puts an] emphasis on producing a large damages pot as quickly as possible," he explains, "and not so much on what I was interested in, which was systemic change."

In 1991, at age 40, he resigned his partnership, and the next year he started the Impact Fund. By the late 1990s, Seligman was looking to use the fund to broker partnerships between nonprofits and private class-action firms to launch significant cases. For-profit firms like 67-lawyer Cohen Milstein Hausfeld & Toll—which Seligman ultimately brought into the *Dukes* case as one of the Fund's five co-counsels—could provide the financial muscle and staff, while nonprofit partners lent the case credibility with the press and grass-roots groups, and made sure that the for-profits didn't grab a "cheap, early settlement," Seligman explains.

Upon getting the inquiry about Wal-Mart, Seligman called Marc Bendick, an economist who had then served as an expert in more than 75 employment cases. Bendick had a database of information compiled from forms, called EEO-1s, that large companies are required to file with the Equal Employment Opportunity Commission, breaking down their workforces by gender and race.

Bendick told Seligman that Wal-Mart's profile was skewed and that "compared to its major competitors, it stuck out like a sore thumb," as Seligman recalls. Bendick eventually computed that women composed 63.4% of Wal-Mart's hourly (nonmanagerial) workers yet just 33.6% of the store's salaried managers. More damning, the company's numbers were far below those of its 20 top competitors, which averaged 56.5% women at the store manager level.

Though these numbers are powerful, some caution is in order. Such "benchmark" or "comparator" studies—in which a company's EEO-1 data is compared to that of a group of purportedly similar companies—are a staple of class-action employment litigation, and the outcomes depend on how one defines the comparison group. Wal-Mart disputes Bendick's list of comparison companies and claims that when a broader group is used—reflecting Wal-Mart's wide geographic footprint and the variety of products and services it sells—it falls within the norm. It also claims that if Wal-Mart had counted its highest-level hourly-wage supervisors as "managers" on its EEO-1 forms, the way it believes several of Bendick's comparator firms do, the entire purported disparity vanishes.

Seligman filed the *Dukes* case in San Francisco federal court in June 2001. The mammoth discovery process then began, which, by mid-2003, had led to the taking of 200 depositions and the collection of millions of documents.

> **"This case represents Wal-Mart's worst nightmare, their policies are going to be judged by a San Francisco jury and a San Francisco judge."**
>
> —Plaintiffs lawyer Brad Seligman

Through that process, Seligman maintains that he unearthed evidence that "biased attitudes were at the very top of the company." Such evidence would support a disparate treatment claim—i.e., the charge that Wal-Mart intentionally discriminated—as well as a disparate impact claim. Seligman will produce proof, for instance, that at Monday morning meetings of high-level Sam's Club executives, female store employees were often referred to as "Janie Q's." A woman executive who found the term (of unknown origin) demeaning complained about it, but others continued to use it. While some in Bentonville, Ark., might have considered "Janie Q." endearing, it will likely sound condescending and offensive to a jury in San Francisco. (Wal-Mart tried to move the case to Arkansas, but U.S. District Judge Martin Jenkins denied the motion. "This case represents Wal-Mart's worst nightmare," Seligman says. "Their policies are going to be judged by a San Francisco jury and a San Francisco judge." San Francisco is in the Ninth Circuit, whose federal appeals court is regarded as the nation's most liberal.)

Through the discovery process Seligman also harvested more statistical data, in which his experts detected more gender disparities. The most important related to pay. According to computations performed by Richard Drogin, a statistician who by 2003 had served as a plaintiffs expert in about 30 cases, women store employees were paid less than men across all job positions (both hourly and managerial), even though women, on average, had more seniority and better performance evaluations. He calculated that women hourly workers were paid, on average, $1,100 less per year than men, while women managerial workers received $14,500 less. The compensation disparity claims became the most potent in the case, because they could potentially require back-pay reimbursements to every class member, not just the fraction who might have become managers.

The primary mechanism that was allegedly producing all these gaps was, once again, the granting of too much discretion to store managers, which predictably gave their unconscious bias free rein. To provide testimony on the literature relating to unconscious stereotyping and an analysis of why Wal-Mart's procedures failed to channel managerial discretion adequately, Seligman retained Bielby.

How can a court treat 4,000 Wal-Mart store managers as acting in exactly the same way when the plaintiffs' theory is that those store managers are granted too much autonomy?

Bielby would provide testimony on one additional critical issue. Seligman needed to finesse what defendants claim is an internal contradiction in all class actions that challenge a company's granting of "unfettered discretion" to managers. If each store's local manager is being granted unbridled discretion, one might expect to see significant differences in how each store treats men and women. Stores run by female store managers, for instance, might show less gender discrimination than those run by men.

Some male managers might also be better able to resist subconscious stereotyping than others. How can a court treat 4,000 store managers as acting identically for purposes of a class action when the plaintiffs' whole theory of the case is that those store managers are being granted too much autonomy?

In a rebuttal to that sort of argument, Bielby opined in his report that "a strong and widely shared organizational culture promotes uniformity of practices throughout an organization," and that Wal-Mart had such a culture. That could be inferred from such factors as Wal-Mart's "emphasis on the company's founder and its history, a mission statement defined by core values, frequent communication about the culture to employees," and so on. (None of those traits is unusual among big corporations, and Bielby has provided similar testimony in cases against, for instance, Home Depot, Brookshire Grocery Co., US Bancorp Piper Jaffray, and FedEx Express.)

To mount its statistical defense, Wal-Mart retained Joan Haworth, an economist who had, by then, served as an expert in more than 65 employment cases. As for the purported promotional disparities the plaintiffs experts had found—that women's presence in salaried managerial positions was far lower than their presence in the hourly workforce from which they were drawn—she found that the plaintiffs were simply failing to take into account employees' interest in such promotions. Her data showed that women were actually being offered store manager jobs in numbers that exceeded their percentage in the applicant pool. During the years 1999 to 2002, for instance, 12% of the applicants were women, while 17% of the offers went to women.

As for the plaintiffs' claims of pay disparity, defense expert Haworth likewise reached very different conclusions from plaintiffs' expert Drogin. She claimed that Drogin's analyses did not adequately take into account crucial factors, like the number of hours worked and whether they included night-shift work, which pays more. But her overarching criticism was that his approach amounted to pretending that a single person was making all promotion and pay decisions throughout Wal-Mart nationwide, when, according to depositions, most pay determinations were made at the store manager level or, in the case of certain specialty department employees, at the district manager level. When she performed statistical analyses at the store and district levels, reflecting Wal-Mart's claims about the way that decisions are made, she found that 92.8% of all the standard Wal-Mart and Supercenter stores showed no statistically significant pay disparities. Of the remainder, 5.2% showed disparities favoring men, while 2.0% showed disparities favoring women. In other words, more than 90% of class members worked at stores where women were statistically no worse off than men. Wal-Mart's argument, then, was that if a class action must be filed, it should be brought against the specific stores with disparities favoring men.

By September 2003, the case was ready for the all-important arguments on class certification, at which a judge considers whether to let the case proceed as a class action. This is often the decisive event in such a case, since disapproval of the class renders litigation impractical for most class members, while certification creates such large exposure for the defendant as to force settlement. In the Wal-Mart case an important part of the class certification proceeding was a challenge by Wal-Mart to the admissibility of psychological and sociological testimony on unconscious bias, which it challenged as junk science.

Such challenges have been routine features of class action employment cases since at least 1997, when one was brought by lawyers for Home Depot. (Home Depot lost its bid to exclude the testimony and eventually settled for $87.5 million.) The crux of the defense argument is always that the effects of unconscious stereotyping in the workplace are still too unproven to be the subject of helpful courtroom testimony. Defense experts argue that the plaintiffs' experts ignore or gloss over studies that cut against the plaintiffs' thesis, and that they overgeneralize from lab experiments that may have little bearing on real-world work settings. A typical stereotyping study, for instance, might involve college students who are asked to choose the more qualified applicant from among two fictional candidates—one male and one female, say—on the basis of résumés alone. Such experiments might not predict how real managers behave in work settings when choosing among employees that they've worked with closely for months. There's no question that a large body of scientific literature on unconscious stereotyping exists; the dispute is over what, if any, inferences can safely be drawn from it to particular workplace situations.

Wal-Mart lost its attempt to exclude the stereotyping testimony. Judge Jenkins ruled—as have most judges—that the defense experts' critiques went to the weight to be given the evidence, not its admissibility, and weight could be assessed by the jury.

Similarly, Judge Jenkins declined to resolve the numerous statistical disputes that had been presented to him. He ruled that at a class certification hearing he was not supposed to resolve such issues, which were to be deferred to a later stage of the litigation. The plaintiffs only had to present a theory that was plausible, which they had done. That's the ruling that was upheld by an appeals panel this past February, and which Wal-Mart is still appealing.

Meanwhile, the suits keep coming. In the 15 years since the *Lucky Stores* case, sociologist Bielby estimates that he has served as an expert witness for plaintiffs in "50 or 60" employment discrimination cases. (One of the cases is against a group of Hollywood film and TV studios, including entities owned by Time Warner, which also owns FORTUNE's publisher.) During that period he has obviously encountered many companies that were vastly more sophisticated than the family-run grocery chain he first critiqued. These have included FORTUNE 500 companies, many of which have written antidiscrimination policies, substantial human resources operations, and in-house legal departments counseling them on how to behave. Nevertheless, Bielby keeps finding failings in the companies' procedures. "The issues in the more sophisticated companies," he explains, "often have to do with, Are there specific vulnerabilities you can point to?"

In a race discrimination class action against FedEx, Bielby critiqued a performance review system that was based in part on objective factors spelled out in employee manuals. Bielby nevertheless found the process to be inadequate for a litany of reasons: "Judgments about the weights to be assigned to individual components of a performance dimension in order to obtain an overall rating . . . are left to the discretion of individual managers"; FedEx did no auditing to ensure that managers were adhering to the written guidelines; it didn't monitor whether there were racial disparities in the outcomes of these reviews; its training of the people performing the reviews lacked "hands-on rating exercises with instructor feedback" and was not "repeated at regular intervals"; and FedEx was not holding the raters accountable for how they performed the rating task, "with real consequences for inadequate performance." The class was certified in September 2005, and the parties announced a $53.5 million tentative settlement in April.

Just what sort of procedures would win Bielby's blessing? He concedes that no neutral procedural mechanism in itself will ever be sufficient; it must also be accompanied by auditing of the decision-making process, monitoring of the racial and gender outcomes, and holding decision-makers "accountable" for their "contributions" to diversity.

And therein lies the rub. To a pragmatic businessman, it may sound like Bielby is saying that companies should dock the pay of managers if they don't meet numerical diversity goals—creating a powerful incentive for managers to adopt surreptitious quotas and preferences. Bielby maintains that he's not recommending any such thing. The monitoring of outcomes that he's advocating is merely diagnostic testing, he insists. As for the "accountability" piece of it, he says, "make it part of the manager's job to contribute to the company's EEO goals. And by that I don't mean quotas or the number of men vs. women promoted. [Make clear] what the company's vision is of EEO and how that translates into specific responsibilities and duties for someone that has authority to make decisions about hiring, promotion, pay, and so on. And do that in a meaningful way—that's part of their performance evaluation—so they know that it's not just feel-good talk."

Since Wal-Mart filed its reconsideration motion in late February, both the appellate courts and the Supreme Court have issued a series of rulings that make Judge Jenkins's certification of the Wal-Mart class action appear ever more precarious. In its past term, for instance, the Court rendered two highly controversial, quite conservative 5–4 rulings in the area of antidiscrimination law.

"Neither case directly applies to our case," says Seligman, "but both cases say something deeply troubling about the direction of the U.S. Supreme Court." In the second of them, the Court struck down voluntary, race-conscious school-assignment programs adopted to achieve racial balance.

"Racial balancing is not permitted," Chief Justice John Roberts wrote.

If *Dukes v. Wal-Mart* does reach the Supreme Court, the suit will present a blockbuster test case, with potential to change the face of contemporary employment discrimination class actions. Given their near-universal exposure to such suits, FORTUNE 500 companies should be praying that it does.

Reflecting on Downsizing: What Have Managers Learned?

FRANCO GANDOLFI

Introduction

Organizational downsizing as a change management strategy has been adopted for more than two decades (Gandolfi, 2007). In the 1980s and early 1990s, it was implemented primarily by firms experiencing difficult economic times (Gandolfi, 2006). However, since the mid-1990s, downsizing has become a leading strategy of choice for a multitude of firms around the world (Mirabal and DeYoung, 2005). The prime impetus of most downsizing efforts is the desire for an immediate reduction of costs and increased levels of efficiency, productivity, profitability, and competitiveness (Farrell and Mavondo, 2004). Over the years, this strategy has generated a great deal of interest among scholars, managers, and the popular press. Some authors suggest that the research-based body of knowledge is still relatively underdeveloped (Macky, 2004), while others stress the confusion surrounding downsizing (Williams, 2004; Gandolfi, 2008). The adoption of strategic downsizing has remained popular (Maurer, 2005), yet significant empirical and anecdotal evidence suggests that the overall consequences are negative (Zyglidopoulos, 2003).

The primary objective of this article is to review the consequences of downsizing, focusing on the following questions: Does downsizing work? Have firms reaped the much anticipated benefits? In other words, what do we know about the effects and after-effects of downsizing? This paper draws out implications for executives and showcases five downsizing lessons that managers should consider. Finally, the paper suggests future research for this topic.

Downsizing: Background

Back in the mid-1970s, Charles Handy first predicted that the technological revolution would transform the lives of millions of individuals through a process he aptly termed 'down-sizing' (Appelbaum, Everard, and Hung, 1999). While few understood his prediction at the time, we now know that downsizing has been adopted as a management technique on a global scale (Macky, 2004). Firms have implemented downsizing as a "reactive response to organizational bankruptcy or recession" (Ryan and Macky, 1998) and proactively as a human resource (HR) strategy (Chadwick, Hunter, and Walston, 2004). Reflecting upon its pervasiveness, it is evident that downsizing has attained the status of a fully-fledged restructuring strategy (Cameron, 1994) with the intent of attaining a new level of competitiveness (Littler, 1998).

Admittedly, downsizing is not new. It came into prominence as a topic of both academic and practical concern in the 1980s and became a management mantra (Lecky, 1998) in the 1990s. The latter period subsequently became the "downsizing decade" (Dolan, Belout, and Balkin, 2000). Downsizing has transformed hundreds of thousands of firms and governmental agencies and the lives of tens of millions of employees around the world (Amundson, Borgen, Jordan, and Erlebach, 2004). The notion of downsizing has emerged from a number of disciplines and draws upon a wide range of management and organizational theories. The body of literature is extensive reflecting its prevalence in the U.S., the U.K., Canada, Western Europe, Australia, New Zealand, and Japan (Littler, 1998; Gandolfi and Neck, 2003; Farrell and Mavondo, 2004; Macky, 2004).

A single definition of downsizing does not exist across studies and disciplines. Still, it is clear that it means a contraction in the size of a firm's workforce. Cascio (1993) posits that downsizing is the planned elimination of positions or jobs whose primary purpose is to reduce the workforce, while Gandolfi (2006) adds that a myriad of terms have been used euphemistically in reference to downsizing, including "brightsizing" and "rightsizing."

Downsizing is ubiquitous. While manufacturing, retail, and service have accounted for the highest levels, downsizing has occurred in both the private and public sectors (Macky, 2004). Downsizing statistics show a sobering picture. The U.S. Bureau of Labor Statistics (BLS) reported that more than 4.3 million jobs were cut between 1985 and 1989 (Lee, 1992). The *New York Times* stated that more than 43 million jobs had been eliminated between 1979 and 1996 (Cascio, 2003). Cameron (1994) reported that 85% of the *Fortune 500* firms downsized between 1989 and 1994, and 100% had downsizing-related plans in the ensuing five years. Substantial evidence suggests that downsizing remains a popular restructuring strategy (Mirabal and DeYoung, 2005; Gandolfi, 2008).

Why do firms resort to downsizing? What are the driving forces? While downsizing is viewed as complicated and multifaceted (Gandolfi, 2006), it has generally been adopted either reactively or proactively (Macky, 2004). To put a single downsizing cause forward is problematic and underrates its inherent complexity. Each downsizing decision reflects a combination of company-specific, industry-specific, and macroeconomic factors (Drew, 1994). Downsizing firms frequently point to deregulation, globalization, mergers and acquisitions (M&A) activities, global competition, technological innovation, and a shift in business strategies to obtain and retain competitive advantages (Dolan, Belout, and Balkin, 2000; Sahdev, 2003; Gandolfi, 2008).

Downsizing Consequences

Downsizing has deep financial, organizational, and social consequences, covered extensively in the change management literature. A closer analysis of the overall effects presents a complex picture with the following questions emerging:

- Is downsizing an effective strategy?
- Does downsizing engender improved financial performance?
- Have firms reaped financial and organizational improvements?

The overall picture of the financial effects of downsizing is negative. While a few firms have reported financial improvements, the majority have failed to report increased levels of efficiency, effectiveness, productivity, and profitability (Cascio, 1993; Macky, 2004; Gandolfi, 2008). Table 1 presents a non-exhaustive overview of some of the findings.

In light of the available cross-sectional and longitudinal data, the following conclusions can be made:

- Most firms adopting downsizing strategies do not reap economic and organizational benefits;

- Non-downsized firms financially outperform downsized forms in the short-, medium-, and long-run;
- While some firms have shown positive financial outcomes, there is no empirical evidence to suggest a correlation between downsizing and improved financial performance;
- Some firms have reported positive financial indicators in the short term, yet the long-term financial consequences of downsizing have been shown to be consistently negative.

Downsizing also transcends financial consequences. A significant body of literature reports that downsizing has profound consequences on the workforce, the so-called "after," "side," or "secondary" downsizing effects (Littler, Dunford, Bramble, and Hede, 1997; Macky, 2004). At least three categories of people are directly affected by downsizing: survivors, victims, and executioners. A survivor remains with the firm, a victim is downsized out of a job involuntarily, while an executioner is entrusted with the downsizing implementation (Gandolfi, 2006). Table 2 presents the three categories of affected individuals with some of the major research findings.

While it could be presumed that it is better to be a downsizing survivor rather than a victim, does evidence support this? Determining and comparing the symptoms exhibited by victims and survivors, Devine and colleagues (2003) assert that surviving downsizing is difficult given the high levels of stress experienced by survivors compared to the victims (Devine, Reay, Stainton, and Collins-Nakai, 2003). The argument rests partly on the disparity in resources available to victims compared with those available to survivors. Victims commonly receive transition packages and outplacement services, while survivors receive very little, if any, resources and support. Devine et al. (2003) compared the outcomes for displaced and continuing employees, finding that the victims who found employment post-downsizing reported considerably more positive outcomes than did those who remained in the downsized environment. The victims felt lower levels of stress on the job, reported higher levels of perceived job control, and experienced fewer negative effects than the survivors. In light of that, the following conclusions can be made:

- Downsizing produces considerable human consequences;
- Downsizing affects the entire workforce, survivors, victims, and executioners, in a most profound manner;
- Survivors generally find themselves with increased workloads and job responsibilities while frequently receiving few or no resources, training, and support;

Table 1 Financial Effects of Downsizing

Researcher	Findings	Bottom-line
Zemke (1990)	A study conducted in 1989 and repeated in 1990 by the Philadelphia outplacement firm Right Associates. HR executives from 500 downsized firms said that the implementation of downsizing did not generate financial gains, but had in fact negative economic effects on the firm—25% in 1989 and 28% in 1990. Managers also reported significant "aftershocks" following downsizing.	• No financial gains reported • Negative economic effects • Significant "aftershocks"
Worrell, Davidson, and Sharma (1991)	Examined the impact of downsizing announcements on stock returns for a sample of 194 firms that announced layoffs during 1979–1987. They examined the stock returns of companies from 90 days prior to the announcement of the downsizing in the *Wall Street Journal* to 90 days after the announcement. There was a significantly negative market reaction to the announcements with the cumulative loss in stock value being about 2% of the value of the equity of the firms. For firms that provided restructuring and consolidation as the reason for the layoffs, there was a 3.6% increase in stock value over the 180-day test period, while stocks of firms citing financial distress as the reason for downsizing declined an average of 5.6% over the same period.	• Negative market reaction following downsizing announcements • Declining stock values post-downsizing
De Meuse, Vanderheiden, and Bergmann (1994).	Conducted a large downsizing study of *Fortune 100* companies measuring their financial performance over a five-year period, that is, two years prior to the announcement, the year of the announcement, and two years after the announcement. Statistical tests revealed no significant positive relationships for any of the financial variables. De Meuse et al. (1994) concluded that empirical evidence did not support the contention that downsizing leads to improved financial performance.	• No improved financial performance
Clark and Koonce (1995)	Carried out a U.S. study revealing that approximately 68% of all surveyed downsizing, restructuring, and reengineering efforts did not generate financial gains and benefits.	• 68% of firms failed to improve financial performance
Downs (1995)	Studied the financial implications following downsizing and reported that the severance pay expenses from downsizing, in particular, can be enormous. Downs (1995) cites Dow Chemical's experience with manager layoffs in the 1990s as "horribly expensive" and "destructive to shareholders' value" (Appelbaum et al., 1999).	• Severe negative financial implications following downsizing
Estok (1996)	Watson Wyatt Worldwide carried out a study of 148 major Canadian firms showing that 40% of downsizing efforts did not result in decreased expenses, and that more than 60% of firms did not experience an increase in profitability.	• 40% of firms failed to decrease expenses • 60% failed to increase profitability
Cascio, Young, and Morris (1997)	Studied data from the Standard and Poor (S&P) 500 between 1980 and 1994 examining 5,479 occurrences of changes in employment in terms of two dependent financial variables. They reported that firms engaging in downsizing did not show significantly higher returns than the average companies in their own industries.	• No higher financial returns after downsizing
Clark and Koonce (1995)	Reported that 68% of all downsizing activities were financially unsuccessful. Those that downsized and restructured specifically to become more profitable and efficient realized neither outcome. They concluded that downsizing outcomes were "tremendous disappointments" that fell well short of expectations (Williams, 2004).	• 68% of firms reported unsuccessful financial results after downsizing • Downsizing seen as disappointments
Cascio (1998)	Examined 311 S&P 500 firms that had downsized between 1981 and 1990 and concluded that downsizing *per se* did not lead to improved financial performance.	• Downsizing failed to produce positive financial results
Lecky (1998)	A major Australian study conducted by the Queensland University of Technology disclosed that a mere 40% of firms achieved an increase in productivity and only half accomplished a decrease in overall costs following downsizing.	• 60% of firms failed to improve productivity • 50% failed to decrease costs
Kirby (1999)	Reported that several longitudinal studies in Australia showed a consistently negative financial picture in that six out of ten downsized firms failed to cut overall costs or increase productivity.	• 60% of firms failed to cut costs • 60% of firms failed to increase productivity

(continued)

Table 1   Financial Effects of Downsizing *(continued)*

Researcher	Findings	Bottom-line
Appelbaum, Everard, and Hung (1999)	Cited a Mitchell & Co. study of 16 North American firms that had cut more than 10% of their respective workforces between 1982 and 1988. It was shown that two years after the initial stock price increase, 10 of the 16 stocks were quoting below market by 17–48% and 12 were below the comparable companies in their industries by 5–45%. Appelbaum et al. (1999) concluded that such results depicted the true financial impact of downsizing on firms.	• Firms cutting more than 10% of workforce underperformed non-cutters in terms of stock price
Morris, Cascio, and Young (1999)	Studied the financial performance of the S&P 500 Index subsequent to changes in employment from 1981 to 1992. The key indicators constituted overall profitability and the stock market performance. The tabulation showed that firms with stable employment consistently outperformed companies with employment downsizing. Also, firms that "upsized" (i.e., employment increases exceeded 5%) generated stock returns that were 50% higher than those of stable and downsized firms in the year that they upsized, and cumulative stock returns that were 20% higher over three years. Morris et al. (1999) concluded that a consistently positive correlation between downsizing and improved financial performance could not be established. Rather, empirical evidence suggested that downsizing was unlikely to lead to improvements in a firm's financial performance.	• Firms with stable employment outperformed firms with downsizing • Firms that upsized outperformed firms with stable and downsizing workforces • No correlation between downsizing and improved financial performance
Gandolfi (2001)	Conducted an extensive analysis of financial performance of large downsized banks in Australia. Empirical evidence suggested that the majority of downsized firms were unable to cut overall costs and to improve profitability. Only few study cases reported satisfactory financial improvements.	• Majority of firms failed to cut costs • Majority of firms failed to increase profitability
Griggs and Hyland (2003)	Watson Wyatt Worldwide conducted a study of 1,005 firms in 1991 and reported that widely anticipated economic and organizational benefits for downsized companies failed to materialize. Empirical evidence suggested that a mere 46% of downsized firms cut overall costs, fewer than 33% increased profitability, and only 21% reported satisfactory improvements in ROI.	• 54% of firms failed to cut costs • 66% failed to increase profitability • 9% failed to show satisfactory ROI
De Meuse, Bergmann, Vanderheiden, and Roraff (2004)	Conducted one of the most systematic longitudinal analyses of financial performance of downsized firms. The study examined the long-term relationships of downsizing on five measures of financial performance from 1987 until 1998. It was found that downsized firms performed significantly poorer up to two years following the announcement. Beginning with the third year, none of the differences reached statistical significance. When analyzing the magnitude of downsizing, the data revealed that firms that had downsized a small number of employees (i.e., up to 3%) performed significantly better in the announcement year, while firms that downsized more than 10% of the workforce significantly underperformed firms laying off less.	• Downsized firms underperformed others up to two years after announcement • Firms cutting more than 10% of workforce underperformed firms with less downsizing
Macky (2004)	Reported that a New Zealand study comprising 45 firms listed on the stock exchange and 110 nonlisted companies employing 50 or more people showed that firms that had downsized between 1997 and 1999 financially underperformed firms that had not engaged in downsizing. Macky (2004) concluded that despite the widespread use of downsizing, there was still little convincing research to show that downsizing produces the financial benefits expected by managers.	• Non-downsizers outperformed downsized firms financially • No correlation between downsizing and improved financial performance
Gandolfi (2008)	Conducted an extensive longitudinal study of financial performance of downsized firms in Australia and Switzerland. Empirical evidence suggested that the majority of downsized firms were unable to cut overall costs. Gandolfi (2008) concluded that downsizing *per se* did not lead to improved financial performance.	• Majority of firms failed to cut costs • Majority of firms failed to increase profitability

Source: Developed for this research.

Table 2 Downsizing Categories of Affected Individuals

Category	Findings	Bottom-line
Survivors	Display a number of symptoms during and after downsizing. The *first* sickness, the survivor syndrome, is a set of emotions, behaviors, and attitudes exhibited by surviving employees (Littler et al., 1997). Brockner (1988) asserts that downsizing engenders a variety of psychological states in survivors: guilt, positive inequity, anger, relief, and job insecurity. These mental states influence the survivors' work behaviors and attitudes, such as motivation, commitment, satisfaction, and job performance. Kinnie, Hutchinson, and Purcell (1998) identified survivor symptoms, including increased levels of stress, absenteeism, and distrust, as well as decreased levels of work quality, morale, and productivity. Cascio (1993) argues that the survivor syndrome is characterized by decreased levels of morale, employee involvement, work productivity, and trust towards management. Lecky (1998) reports that the survivor syndrome manifests itself in negative morale, decreased employee commitment, and increased concern about job security. Gettler (1998) observed similar symptoms among survivors in New Zealand, Australia, and South Africa suggesting a drop in productivity in line with data from the U.S. and Europe. The *second* sickness, survivor guilt, is a feeling of responsibility or remorse for some offence and is often expressed in terms of depression, fear, and anger (Noer, 1993). The reality of survivor guilt is comparable to the concept of combat syndrome, which refers to the feelings experienced by a soldier in combat upon the death of a fellow soldier. Feelings of relief for his own survival are often followed by feelings of immense guilt for his own survival (Allen, 1997). Cameron, Freeman, and Mishra (1993) assert that survivor guilt may occur when survivors work overtime or receive paychecks. Additionally, survivors may perceive that traditional attributes, such as loyalty, individual competence, and diligence are no longer valued since their co-workers, who had displayed such traits, were victims of downsizing. Littler et al. (1997) point out that survivor guilt arises when survivors perceive that their own performance merited no better treatment than that accorded the downsized victims. Schweiger, Ivancevich, and Power (1987) contend that it is not the terminations *per se* that create hostility, anger, bitterness, and survivor guilt but the manner in which the terminations were handled. Survivors expressed feelings of anger and disgust that their peers were downsized and felt guilt that they were not directly involved in the downsizing. The survivors also believed that their co-workers performed at least as well or even better than the survivors. Thus, the survivors' perceived feelings of bitterness, anger and disgust regarding the layoffs of co-workers may potentially result in survivor guilt (Appelbaum et al., 1999). The *third* sickness, survivor envy, reflects a survivor's feelings of envy towards the victims (Kinnie et al., 1998). Survivors presume that victims obtain special retirement packages and new jobs with more attractive compensation.	**Sickness 1: Survivor syndrome** • guilt • positive inequity • anger • relief • job insecurity **Mental states influence** • motivation • commitment • satisfaction • work performance **Symptoms include** • higher levels of stress • higher levels of absenteeism • higher levels of distrust • higher levels of job insecurity • decreased work quality • decreased morale • decreased productivity • decreased employee involvement • decreased trust toward management **Sickness 2: Survivor guilt** • depression • fear • anger **Sickness 3 Survivor envy** • feelings of envy toward victims
Victims	Strong evidence of adverse psychological effects resulting from job loss, including psychological stress, ill health, family problems, marital problems, reduced self-esteem, depression, psychiatric morbidity, helplessness, anxiety, and feelings of social isolation (Greenglass and Burke, 2001). There is some evidence suggesting that job loss caused by downsizing may generate permanent damage to the victims' careers (Dolan et al., 2000). Victims have reported a loss of earning power upon reemployment (Konovsky and Brockner, 1993). Studies suggest that victims have encountered feelings of cynicism, uncertainty, and decreased levels of commitment and loyalty that carry over to the next job (Macky, 2004). The focus in most downsized firms is on the victimized employees (Amundson et al., 2004) who are considered the primary victims of a downsizing and who need counseling, support, help, and re-training. Victims often receive generous outplacement services and financially attractive incentive packages (Gandolfi, 2006). These benefits generally include outplacement support, personal and family counseling, relocation expenses, retraining, and a variety of lucrative incentive packages, such as severance pay and benefits packages (Allen, 1997).	**Psychological effects** • psychological stress • ill health • family and problems • reduced self-esteem • psychiatric morbidity • depression • helplessness and anxiety • feelings of social isolation **Other effects** • damage to career • loss of earning power • feelings of cynicism, uncertainty, decreased levels of commitment and loyalty in future employment
Executioners	Likely to be an employee, manager, or consultant entrusted with the planning, execution, and evaluation of a downsizing activity (Downs, 1995). Little research has been documented on the emotional responses and reactions of the subjects implementing downsizing. Some evidence suggests that the implementers of downsizing suffer from similar psychological and emotional effects as the victims and survivors (Gandolfi, 2007) in that carrying downsizing responsibilities is emotionally taxing and professionally challenging (Clair and Dufresne, 2004).	**Psychological effects** • Similar effects as victims and survivors **Emotional effects** • Similar effects as victims and survivors

Source: Developed for this research.

- Victims commonly obtain outplacement services and financial packages when exiting the downsized firms;
- Survivors suffer from a range of downsizing-related sicknesses;
- Executioners suffer similar effects to those of victims and survivors.

Learning from the Past: What Have Executives Learned?

It is not presumptuous to state that organizations have failed to reap widely anticipated downsizing gains. Additionally, firms have been forced to contend with considerable human consequences. Still, there is sporadic evidence that a few firms have engaged in practices that generated positive effects. Considering the current findings, what have executives learned? What downsizing lessons can be deduced? Is it possible to determine best downsizing practice?

It must be understood that the reduction of workforces *per se* is not new. Workforces have always fluctuated, particularly in response to economic crises. This was the prevailing paradigm prior to the mid-1980s. However, the tide turned half way through the 1980s in that downsizing became decoupled from the business cycle (Gandolfi, 2005) and manifested itself as a fully-fledged, proactive HR strategy (Chadwick et al., 2004). As a result, downsizing attained the status of a restructuring strategy (Cameron, 1994). In the following decade, downsizing became a way of life (Filipowski, 1993) and a corporate panacea (Nelson, 1997). Paradoxically, this unprecedented development took place despite downsizing successes. The following are five downsizing lessons for executives contemplating a downsizing strategy:

Lesson 1: Downsizing Preparation

Research shows that organizations conduct downsizing without adequate HR plans, policies, and programs (Appelbaum, Delage, Labibb, and Gault, 1997; Gandolfi, 2001). Firms are also inadequately prepared for downsizing and severely neglect the survivors (Doherty and Horsted, 1995; Allen, 1997; Gandolfi and Neck, 2003). To some degree, this unpreparedness explains why firms have not been able to implement downsizing successfully. Why and how should managers prepare their firms for downsizing? Cameron (1994) draws attention to a U.S. firm that introduced a new HR system for all employees one year *prior to* the downsizing announcement. As a result of this proactive measure, the firm reported positive financial and organizational outcomes with minimal disruption and pain among the surviving and departing workforces. Similar findings were reported in a cross-sectional study in the Australian banking industry (Gandolfi, 2001). These examples demonstrate that proactive preparation for downsizing can positively contribute to a firm's preparedness for any major change. Therefore, the first implication for managers is to plan strategically and prepare proactively for downsizing. Executives will need to ensure that the firm's culture can and will embrace major change successfully. This will contribute to an organization's attaining change readiness (Gandolfi, 2006), which is a key requirement for successful downsizing and an indispensable factor of most change endeavors.

Lesson 2: Specific Downsizing Training

Firms are frequently ill-prepared for downsizing and fail to provide adequate training, support, and assistance to survivors. Gandolfi (2006) contends that while the workforce generally receives job-specific professional training and development, attention to personal development and growth during downsizing is confined to managers. Gandolfi (2006b) found that enhancing an employee's physical lifestyle, mental capacity, and emotional growth had the potential to proactively prepare the workforce for change and help individuals cape successfully with downsizing. Table 3 showcases the three categories of personal growth and development.

There is an increased awareness and understanding that survivors lack training, support, and assistance during and after the implementation of downsizing (Appelbaum et al., 1997; Macky, 2004; Gandolfi, 2006). This is remarkable given that survivors commonly face new job responsibilities (Mitchell, 1998), experience increased workloads (Dolan et al., 2000), and are driven to work harder after downsizing (Makawatsakul and Kleiner, 2003). Would it not make sense for the survivors to receive much needed training, support, and assistance in the wake of this new-found reality? Executives should ensure that firms invest in their workforces proactively and provide training, support, and assistance throughout the downsizing process. Without a doubt, a thoroughly prepared and adequately equipped workforce is more likely to be able to cope with and thrive in the wake of downsizing.

Lesson 3: Downsizing and the Survivor Syndrome

Downsizing survivor sicknesses have been referred to as "aftershocks" (Zemke, 1990) and the "aftermath" (Clark and Koonce, 1995) of downsizing. Clearly, the remaining

Table 3 Categories of Personal Development and Growth

Physical Lifestyle	Mental Capacity	Emotional Growth
Sports	Change management skills	Emotional reactions to change
Sauna	Stress management skills	The nature of change
Aerobics	Communication skills	The purpose of change
Massages	Interpersonal skills	The stages of change
Yoga classes	Presentation skills	Preparation for change
Fitness classes	Leadership skills	Self-awareness
Weightlifting classes	Teamwork skills	Counseling
Rock climbing	Mentoring and coaching skills	On-line emotional support
Table tennis	Conflict resolution skills	Emotional intelligence

Source: Adapted from Gandolfi (2006b).

employees play a significant role during downsizing in the sense that they either facilitate or impede the outcomes (Mishra and Spreitzer, 1998). This is a profound insight. Studies have shown that the lack of financial success following downsizing is frequently accompanied by the emergence of survivor illnesses. Scholars remain puzzled as to why firms ignore the survivors. Are those individuals not supposed to be the *cream of the crop* and, ultimately, the linchpins of future profitability? Did the survivors not endure because they are part of the solution rather than part of the problem? Downsizing experts have studied the survivor syndrome and the exhibited behaviors at the workplace extensively. To sum up the findings, many survivors exhibit work behaviors and attitudes that are dysfunctional to the firm and their own work performance (Beylerian and Kleiner, 2003). As a result, the impact of downsizing on the survivors is believed to be one of the major reasons for the failure of downsizing efforts and resulting long-term problems (Devine et al., 2003). Without a doubt, executives must pay considerable attention to survivors if they are serious about executing downsizing successfully. This includes a clear strategy on how to take care of the survivors during all downsizing phases (Gandolfi, 2001). Therefore, managers need to make sure that the survivors receive full access to counseling, support, help, and retraining (Allen, 1997) as well timely, honest, and unbiased information (Dolan et al., 2000).

Lesson 4: Counting the Downsizing Costs

Downsizing entails considerable financial cost. Research conducted by the University of Colorado reveals that the direct and indirect, or hidden, costs of downsizing are frequently underestimated (Gandolfi, 2001). There is even evidence suggesting that downsizing costs can minimize or negate any productivity gains (Littler et al.,

1997). Longitudinal data from Australian, South African, and New Zealand firms show that no gain would result if the extra costs associated with downsizing were factored in (Gettler, 1998). Table 4 presents the direct and indirect costs.

In 2006, the H. J. Heinz Company, one of the world's largest food producers, reported that earnings had slumped due to high costs related to downsizing (The Associated Press, 2007). A European firm reported an increase of 40% in recruitment and a 30% increase in training and development costs for new employees following its controversial downsizing. These unexpected expenses more than off-set the minimal productivity savings achieved through downsizing (Gandolfi, 2001).

Lesson 5: Downsizing as a Last Resort

A firm must carefully consider its options and assess the feasibility and applicability of cost reduction alternatives before deciding to downsize. Downsizing must be a last resort. While a substantial number of articles discussing the alternatives to downsizing have emerged, there is a lack of understanding of downsizing-related layoffs as they pertain to the actual cost-reduction stages. It is vital for an organization to recognize the cost-reduction stage that characterizes the firm's current business position and environment. Thus, a firm needs to determine the expected duration of the business downturn. Several HR practices are available as alternatives to downsizing to reduce costs. Some popular approaches include natural attrition, hiring freezes, mandatory vacations, reduced workweeks, limited overtime pay, salary reductions, facility shutdowns, and employee sabbaticals. Each technique has its own applicability, advantages, and disadvantages.

Table 4 Costs of Downsizing

Direct costs	Indirect (hidden) costs
• Severance pay, in lieu of notice	• Recruiting and employment costs of new hires
• Accrued holiday and sick pay	• Training and retraining
• Administrative processing costs	• Potential charges of discrimination
	• Survivor syndromes

Source: Adapted from Littler et al. (1997), Gettler (1998), Gandolfi (2001)

Future Research and Concluding Comments

Downsizing remains complex. While the body of literature is extensive and many valuable lessons have been learned over the past 30 years, the reactive and proactive practice of downsizing has continued unabated despite its dubious track record. In the 1990s, downsizing was declared the most understudied business phenomenon (Cameron, 1994; Freeman, 1994; Luthans and Sommer, 1999). The author of this paper would like to add that downsizing is probably also one of the most misunderstood and misinterpreted contemporary business phenomena. More research and, more important, a greater depth of understanding is required to establish and continue a meaningful dialogue between the business and academic communities. Some of the more pressing issues that need to be addressed and empirically examined include the following:

- What is the significance of the survivor syndrome?
- Is there a correlation between the survivor syndrome and the outcome of downsizing?
- What is the specific role of executioners during downsizing?
- What are the medium- and long-term personal and professional consequences for downsizing victims, survivors, and executioners?
- How and why should firms be prepared for downsizing? What is the best practice?
- What are the long-term financial consequences of downsizing?
- How do the frequency and magnitude of downsizing affect financial performance?
- How do alternatives to downsizing fare compared with downsizing-related layoffs?

This article reviewed the consequences of downsizing. While ample evidence suggests that downsizing produces negative outcomes, it is clear that downsizing-related permanent layoffs must be avoided at all costs. The paper presented five downsizing lessons that managers should consider before deciding to downsize.

References

Allen, R.K. (1997). Lean and mean: Workforce 2000 in America. *Journal of Workplace Learning, 9*(1). Retrieved from http://www.emerald-library.com/brev/08609ae1.html

Amundson, N., Borgen, W., Jordan, S., and Erlebach, A. (2004). Survivors of downsizing: Helpful and hindering experiences, *The Career Development Quarterly, 52,* 256–271.

Appelbaum, S.H., Delage, C., Labibb, N., and Gault, G. (1997). The survivor syndrome:Aftermath of down sizing. *Career Development International, 2*(6). Retrieved from http://www.emerald-library.com/brev/13702fd1.html

Appelbaum, S.H., Everard, A., and Hung, L. (1999). Strategic downsizing: Critical success factors. *Management Decision, 37*(7), 535–559.

Beylerian, M., and Kleiner, B. H. (2003). The downsized workplace. Management Research News, 26, 97–108.

Brockner, J. (1988). The effects of work layoffs in survivors: Research, theory and practice. *Research in Organizational Behavior, 10,* 213–255.

Cameron, K.S. (1994). Strategies for successful organizational downsizing, *Human Resource Management, 33*(2), 189–211.

Cameron, K.S., Freeman, S.J., and Mishra, A.K. (1993). Downsizing and redesigning organizations, In G. Huber and W. Glick (eds), *Organizational Change and Redesign* (pp 19–63) Oxford University Press, New York.

Cascio, W.F. (1993). Downsizing: What do we know? What have we learned? *Academy of Management Executive, 7*(1), 95–104.

Cascio, W.F., Young, C., and Morris, J. (1997). Financial consequences of employment change decisions in major U.S. corporations. *Academy of Management Journal, 40*(5), 1175–1189.

Cascio, W.F. (1998). *Applied psychology in human resource management,* 5th edition. Prentice Hall, Upper Saddle River, NJ.

Cascio, W.F. (2003, November). Responsible restructuring: Seeing employees as assets, not costs, *Ivey Business Journal Online.*

Chadwick, C., Hunter, L., and Walston, S. (2004). Effects of downsizing practices on the performance of hospitals. *Strategic Management Journal, 25*(5), 405–420.

Clair, J.A., and Dufresne, R.L. (2004). Playing the grim reaper: How employees experience carrying out a downsizing. *Human Relations, 57*(12), 1597–1625.

Clark, J., and Koonce, R. (1995). Engaging organizational survivors. *Training & Development, 49,* 8, 22–30

Crainer, S., and Obleng, E. (1995). Re-engineering: Overview. *The Financial Times Handbook of Management,* edited by Stuart Crainger, FT Pitman Publishing, 231–241.

De Meuse, K.P., Vanderheiden, P.A., and Bergmann, T.J. (1994). Announced layoffs: Their effect on corporate financial performance. *Human Resource Management, 33*(4), 509–530.

De Meuse, K.P., Bergmann, T.J., Vanderheiden, P.A., and Roraff, C.E. (2004). New evidence regarding organizational downsizing and a firm's financial performance: A long-term analysis. *Journal of Managerial Issues, 16,* 155–177.

Devine, K., Reay, T., Stainton, L., and Collins-Nakai, R. (2003). The stress of downsizing: Comparing survivors and victims. *Human Resource Management, 42,* 109–124.

Doherty, N., and Horsted, J. (1995, January 12). *Helping survivors to stay on board.* People Management, Personnel Publications Limited, London.

Dolan, S., Belout, A., and Balkin, D.B. (2000). Downsizing without downgrading: Learning how firms manage their survivors. *International Journal of Manpower, 21*(1), 34–46.

Downs, A. (1995). *Corporate executions.* Amacom, New York, NY.

Drew, S.A.W. (1994). Downsizing to improve strategic position. *MCB Management Decision, 32,* 1.

Estok, D. (1996). The high cost of dumbsizing. *Macleans's, 109*(23), 28–29.

Farrell, M., and Mavondo, F. (2004). The effect of downsizing strategy and reorientation strategy on a learning orientation. *Personnel Review, 33*(4), 383–402.

Filipowski, D. (1993, November). Don't rush downsizing: Plan, plan, plan. *Personnel Journal, 72*(11), 64–76.

Freeman, S.J. (1994). Organizational downsizing as convergence or reorientation: Implications for human resource management. *Human Resource Management, 33*(2), 213–238.

Gandolfi, F., and Neck, P. (2003). Organizational downsizing: A review of the background, its development, and current status, *The Australasian Journal of Business and Social Inquiry,* 1, 1.

Gandolfi, F. (2001). *How and why should training and development be implemented during the process of organizational downsizing?* Unpublished thesis for the award of Doctor of Business Administration (DBA), Southern Cross University, Australia.

Gandolfi, F. (2005). How do organizations implement downsizing? An Australian and New Zealand study. *Contemporary Management Research, 1*(1), 57–68.

Gandolfi, F. (2006). *Corporate downsizing demystified: A scholarly analysis of a business phenomenon.* The ICFAI University Press, Hyderabad, India.

Gandolfi, F. (2006b). Personal development and growth in a downsized banking organization: Summary of methodology and findings. *Journal of Human Resource Development International (HRDI), 9*(2), 207–226.

Gandolfi, F. (2007). How do large Australian and Swiss banks implement downsizing? *Journal of Management & Organization, 13*(2), 145–159.

Gandolfi, F. (2008). Learning from the past—Downsizing lessons for managers. *The Journal of Management Research, 8*(1), 1–14.

Gettler, L. (1998, June 16). Survey: Downsizing doesn't cut costs, *Sydney Morning Herald,* 27.

Greenglass, E.R., and Burke, R.J. (2001). Downsizing and restructuring, implications for stress and anxiety. *Anxiety, Stress, and Coping,* 14, 1–13.

Griggs, H.E., and Hyland, P. (2003). Strategic downsizing and learning organizations. *Journal of European Industrial Training, 24*(2–4), 177–187.

Kinnie, N., Hutchinson, S., and Purcell, J. (1998). Downsizing: Is it always lean and mean? *Personnel Review, 27*(4), 296–311.

Kirby, J. (1999, March 22). Downsizing gets the push. *Business Review Weekly.*

Konovsky, M.A., and Brockner, J. (1993). Managing victim and survivor layoff reactions: A procedural justice perspective, in R. Cropanzano (ed.), *Justice in the workplace: Approaching fairness in human resource management* (133–153), Lawrence Erlbaum, New Jersey.

Lecky, S. (1998, July 4). The failure of slash and earn. *Sydney Morning Herald,* 83–87.

Lee, C. (1992, July). After the cuts. *Training,* 17–23

Littler, C.R. (1998). Downsizing organizations: The dilemmas of change. *Human Resources Management Bulletin,* CCH Australia Limited, Sydney.

Littler, C.R., Dunford, R., Bramble, T., and Hede, A. (1997). The dynamics of downsizing in Australia and New Zealand. *Asia Pacific Journal of Human Resources, 35*(1), 65–79.

Luthans, B.C., and Sommer, S.M. (1999). The impact of downsizing on workplace attitudes, *Group and Organization Management, 24*(1), 46–70.

Macky, K. (2004). Organisational downsizing and redundancies: The New Zealand workers' experience. *New Zealand Journal of Employment Relations, 29*(1), 63–87.

Makawatsakul, N., and Kleiner, B.H. (2003). The effect of downsizing on morale and attrition. *Management Research News,* 26, 2–4.

Maurer, H. (2005, December 5). Downsizing in Detroit. *The Business Week.*

Mirabal, N., and DeYoung, R. (2005). Downsizing as a strategic intervention. *Journal of American Academy of Business, 6*(1), 39–45.

Mishra, A.K., and Spreitzer, G.M. (1998). Explaining how survivors respond to downsizing: The role of trust, empowerment, justice, and work redesign. *Academy of Management Review, 23*(3), 567–588

Mitchell, G. (1998). *The Trainer's Handbook: The AMA Guide to effective Training,* 3rd edition, AMACOM American Management Association, New York.

Morris, J.R., Cascio W.F., and Young, C.E. (1999, Winter). Downsizing after all these years: Questions and answers about who did it, how many did it, and who benefited from it. *Organizational Dynamics,* 78–87.

Nelson, B. (1997). The care of the un-downsized. *Training & Development, 51*(4), 40–43.

Noer, D. (1993). *Healing the wounds: Overcoming the trauma of layoffs and revitalizing downsized organizations.* Jossey-Bass, San Francisco, CA.

Ryan, L., and Macky K.A. (1998). Downsizing organizations: Uses, outcomes and strategies. *Asia Pacific Journal of Human Resources, 36*(2), 29–45.

Sahdev, K. (2003). Survivors' reactions to downsizing: The importance of contextual factors. *Human Resource Management Journal, 13*(4), 56–74.

Schweiger, D.M., Ivancevich, J.M., and Power, F.R. (1987). Executive actions for managing human resources before and after acquisition. *Academy of Management Executive, 1*(2), 127–138.

Smeltzer, L.R., and Zener, M.F. (1994). Minimizing the negative effect of employee layoffs through effective announcements. *Employee Counseling Today, 6*(4).

The Associated Press. (2007). *Heinz earnings fall on costs of downsizings.* Retrieved March 1, 2006 from http://www.nytimes.com/2006/03/01/business/01heinz.html?_r=1&oref=slogin

Williams, S.M. (2004). Downsizing—intellectual capital performance anorexia or enhancement? *The Learning Organization, 11*(4/5), 368–379.

Worrell, D.L., Davidson, W.N., and Sharma, V.M. (1991). Layoff announcements and stockholder wealth. *Academy of Management Journal, 34,* 662–678.

Zeffane, R., and Mayo, G. (1994). Rightsizing: The strategic human resources management challenge of the 1990s, *Management Decision, 32*(9).

Zemke, R. (1990, November). The ups and downs of downsizing. *Training,* 27–34.

Zyglidopoulos, S.C. (2003). The impact of downsizing on the corporate reputation for social performance. *Journal of Public Affairs, 4*(1), 11–25.

DR. FRANCO GANDOLFI, currently director of the MBA/EMBA programs at Regent University, specializes in human resource management and change management and regularly advises corporations in Australia and Switzerland. His published books include *Corporate Downsizing Demystified: A Scholarly Analysis of a Business Phenomenon.*

Fear of Firing

How the threat of litigation is making companies skittish about axing problem workers.

MICHAEL OREY

Would you have dared fire Hemant K. Mody? In February, 2003, the longtime engineer had returned to work at a General Electric Co. (GE) facility in Plainville, Conn., after a two-month medical leave. He was a very unhappy man. For much of the prior year, he and his superiors had been sparring over his performance and promotion prospects. According to court documents, Mody's bosses claimed he spoke disparagingly of his co-workers, refused an assignment as being beneath him, and was abruptly taking days off and coming to work late.

But Mody was also 49, Indian born, and even after returning from leave continued to suffer a major disability: chronic kidney failure that required him to receive daily dialysis. The run-ins resumed with his managers, whom he had accused flat out of discriminating against him because of his race and age. It doesn't take an advanced degree in human resources to recognize that the situation was a ticking time bomb. But Mody's bosses were fed up. They axed him in April, 2003.

The bomb exploded last July. Following a six-day trial, a federal court jury in Bridgeport, Conn., found GE's termination of Mody to be improper and awarded him $11.1 million, including $10 million in punitive damages. But the award wasn't for discrimination. The judge found those claims so weak that Mody wasn't allowed to present them. Instead, jurors concluded that Mody had been fired in retaliation for complaining about bias. GE is seeking to have the award overturned, and a spokesman said, "We feel strongly there is no basis for this claim." Through his attorney, Mody declined to discuss the case with *BusinessWeek*.

If this can happen to GE, a company famed for its rigorous performance reviews, with an HR operation that is studied worldwide, it can happen anywhere. It has never been easier for U.S. workers to go to court and allege that they've been sacked unfairly. Over the past 40 years federal, state, and local lawmakers have steadily expanded the categories of workers who enjoy special legal protection—a sprawling group that now includes women, minorities, gays, whistleblowers, the disabled, people over 40, employees who have filed workers' compensation claims, and workers who have been called away for jury duty or military service, among others. Factor in white men who believe that they are bias victims—so-called reverse-discrimination lawsuits—and

"it's difficult to find someone who doesn't have some capacity to claim protected status," observes Lisa H. Cassilly, an employment defense attorney at Alston & Bird in Atlanta.

These workers wield a potent weapon. They can force companies to prove in court that there was a legitimate business reason for their termination. And once a case is in court, it's expensive. A company can easily spend $100,000 to get a meritless lawsuit tossed out before trial. And if a case goes to a jury, the fees skyrocket to $300,000, and often much higher. The result: Many companies today are gripped by a fear of firing. Terrified of lawsuits, they let unproductive employees linger, lay off coveted workers while retaining less valuable ones, and pay severance to screwups and even crooks in exchange for promises that they won't sue. "I've seen us make decisions [about terminations] that in the absence of this litigious risk environment, you'd have a different result," acknowledges Johnny C. Taylor, Jr., head of HR at IAC/InterActiveCorp (IACI), the conglomerate that runs businesses such as Match.com and Ticketmaster.

Managers often fail to build a case for firing by shying away from regular and candid evaluations.

The fear of firing is particularly acute in the HR and legal departments. They don't directly suffer when an underperformer lingers in the corporate hierarchy, but they may endure unpleasant indirect consequences if that person files a lawsuit. Says Dick Grote, an Addison (Tex.) talent management consultant: "They don't get their bonuses based on the number of lawsuits they win. They get their bonuses based on the number of lawsuits they don't get involved in."

This set of divergent incentives puts line managers in a tough position. When they finally decide to get rid of the underperforming slob who plays PC solitaire all day in her cubicle, it can be surprisingly tough to do. And that, in turn, affects productive workers. "Few things demotivate an organization faster than tolerating and retaining low performers," says Grant Freeland, a regional leader in Boston Consulting Group's organization practice.

But it's often the supervisors themselves who bear much of the blame when HR says someone can't be shown the door. That's because most fail to give the kind of regular and candid evaluations that will allow a company to prove poor performance if a fired employee hauls them into court. Honest, if harsh, reviews not only offer legal cover, but they're also critical for organizations intent on developing top talent. "There were definitely a lot of situations where a supervisor got fed up with somebody and wanted to terminate them, but there's no paperwork," says Sara Anderson, who worked in HR at Perry Ellis International (PERY) and Kenneth Cole Productions Inc. (KCP) in New York. Frequently, the work that the manager suddenly claims is intolerable is accompanied by years of performance evaluations that say "meets expectations." Says Anderson: "You look in the file, and there's nothing there to prove [poor performance], so it's like it didn't happen."

Untouchable Nation

Fired workers who fall into a protected category have special legal status. These days, it's harder than you might imagine to find an American worker who wouldn't fall into one—or sometimes several—of these categories.

Total Labor Force: 151.4 million

- Minorities (31%)
- 40 and over (52%)
- Female (46%)
- Unprotected*: White males under 40 (16%)

*But not if the employee is: Disabled, gay, a whistle-blower, a veteran, foreign-born, called for jury duty, a workers' compensation claimant.

Data: U.S Bureau of Labor Statistics, 2006.

When Mody signed GE's job application in 1998, the form said his employment was "at will" and "the Company may terminate my employment at any time for any reason."

Well, not exactly.

The notion that American workers are employed "at will"— meaning, as one lawyer put it, you can be fired if your manager doesn't like the color of your socks—took root in the laissez-faire atmosphere of the late 19th century, and as an official matter is still the law of the land in every state, save Montana. The popular conception of at-will employment is exemplified by the television show *The Apprentice,* which features Donald Trump pointing a finger at an underling and ousting him or her on the spot. That dramatic gesture makes great television, but it isn't something that happens very frequently anymore in the American workplace.

The rise of unions was the first development to put a check on summary dismissal. Collective-bargaining agreements outlined the specific kinds of infractions that could lead to termination, and set up procedures for discipline and review that a company must follow before a worker can be fired. But unions generally didn't deal with the problem of discrimination, and in some cases perpetuated it.

For most American workers now, their status as at-will employees has been transformed by a succession of laws growing out of the civil rights movement in the 1960s that bar employers from making decisions based on such things as race, religion, sex, age, and national origin. This is hardly controversial. Even the legal system's harshest critics find little fault with rules aimed at assuring that personnel decisions are based on merit. And most freely acknowledge that it is much easier to fire people in the U.S. than it is in, say, most of Western Europe. Mass layoffs, in fact, are a recurring event on the American corporate scene. On Apr. 17, for example, Citigroup Inc. (C) announced it will shed some 17,000 workers.

Yet even in these situations, RIFs (for "reduction in force") are carefully vetted by attorneys to assess the impact on employees who are in a legally protected category. And these days the

majority of American workers fall into one or more such groups. Mody, for example, belonged to three because of who he was (age, race, and national origin) and two more because of things he had done (complained of discrimination and taken medical leave). That doesn't mean such people are immune from firing. But it does mean a company will have to show a legitimate, non-discriminatory business reason for the termination, should the matter ever land in court.

As it happens, the judge in Mody's case tossed out his discrimination claims. But the retaliation allegation did go to the jury—a development that is increasingly blindsiding businesses. Plaintiffs are winning large sums not because a company discriminated against them, but because the company retaliated when they complained about the unproven mistreatment.

The rules surrounding retaliation may sound crazy, but they are one of the big reasons why the fear of firing is so prevalent. Retaliation suits are a hot growth area in employment law. In 2005 and 2006, retaliation claims represented 30% of all charges individuals filed with the Equal Employment Opportunity Commission, a required first step before most discrimination cases can go to federal court. That's up from about 20% just 10 years ago. "Even if there isn't a good discrimination claim, the employee has a second bite at the apple," notes Martin W. Aron of defense firm Edwards Angell Palmer & Dodge in Short Hills, N.J. Last year the U.S. Supreme Court increased the legal risk to business by ruling that improper retaliation can involve acts far short of firing or demoting someone. So even excluding an employee from meetings, relocating his or her office, or other intangible slights could lead to liability.

Of course, prohibitions against retaliation exist for a good reason. Without them, many workers would find it too risky to come forward with even legitimate complaints. Yet defense attorneys are deeply suspicious that some workers abuse the protection. Fearing their jobs may be in jeopardy, they may quickly contact HR with an allegation of discrimination or call a corporate hotline to report misconduct, thereby cloaking themselves in the protection of anti-retaliation law. "That's a fairly common fact scenario," says Mike Delikat of Orrick Herrington & Sutcliffe in New York, a law firm that represents businesses. "The best defense is a good offense."

After 1991, when Congress allowed punitive damages and jury trials in job discrimination cases, litigation in the area exploded. In 2006, 14,353 employment cases were filed in federal court, up from 8,273 in 1990, though down from a peak of 20,955 in 2002. It should be noted that these statistics, which include both unlawful termination cases and other types of claims, dramatically understate the frequency with which companies deal with these issues. For every case that's filed in court, several more are quietly settled well beforehand.

Many of the lawsuits may seem ridiculous. IBM (IBM) is currently defending a case filed by James C. Pacenza, a plant worker it dismissed for visiting an adult Internet chat room while on the job. In his lawsuit, Pacenza claims that his propensity to such behavior stems from post-traumatic stress disorder, which he suffers as a result of military service in Vietnam, and that IBM violated the Americans with Disabilities Act. He also alleges that two other employees who had sex on an IBM desk were "merely transferred," so he was treated with undue harshness. Pacenza's attorney, Michael D. Diederich Jr., says his client "didn't violate any of IBM's policies regarding computer usage."

Even when employers beat back silly suits, it often doesn't feel like much of a victory. That's because meritless cases can still tie up companies in burdensome and expensive proceedings for years. In October, 2002, Southview Hospital in Dayton fired Karen Stephens, a nurse who worked in a unit for premature babies and other at-risk newborns. Six other nurses had reported that Stephens was abusive to infants, according to court filings, spanking them when they were fussy, wagging their noses until they screamed in pain, pinching their noses shut to force-feed them, and calling them "son of a bitch." Stephens, who was 60 at the time, sued Kettering Adventist Healthcare Network, which operates Southview, denying "inappropriate" conduct and alleging that the real reason she was let go was age discrimination.

Only after a year and a half of legal dueling did a federal district judge in Dayton toss out Stephens' claims in April, 2005. But then she appealed, and it took another year—and an additional round of legal briefing—before the U.S. Court of Appeals for the Sixth Circuit upheld the dismissal, noting that "Stephens has offered no evidence to indicate that she did not mistreat the infants," or that Kettering did not have a "legitimate, nondiscriminatory reason for discharging her." Kettering declined to comment on the case. "I never lost a baby in 25 years," Stephens said in an interview.

The cost and distraction of lawsuits lead many employers to engage in contortional, and at times perverse, litigation avoidance. Defense attorney Cassilly offers the story of one of her clients, a hospital in the Southeast forced to reduce its ranks because of budget cuts. The head of one department elected to let go a female employee in favor of keeping a more junior male, whom he had spent a great deal of effort to recruit and whom he felt was more valuable. But the hospital overrode that choice and laid off the man out of concern that it would be more exposed in a lawsuit by the woman.

Another of Cassilly's clients, a manufacturer, acquired a new facility and quickly identified one worker as having "a variety of performance problems." But the woman, an African American, had nothing in her personnel file indicating prior trouble, which made firing her a risky bet. So the company put her on a six-month "performance improvement program" to document her deficiencies—and to find out if she could mend her ways. She couldn't, and, Cassilly notes, her client "had to suffer through her poor performance during the whole period."

Early this year, Cassilly got a call from the client. They had just discovered that the woman, an office administrator, had stolen thousands of dollars from the company, and they promptly dismissed her. "It was almost a case where the company was delighted to find out they were the victim of theft," Cassilly says, as opposed to having to defend far more subjective performance evaluations.

Even in the face of theft, Revolution Partners, a small investment banking advisory firm in Boston, balked before showing one of its employees the door. The woman had used her company credit card for a personal shopping spree and plane ticket, but Revolution retained an employment attorney, got the woman to sign a form waiving her right to sue for wrongful dismissal, and after she was fired took no legal action to recover the amounts improperly charged. "We're a little firm, and the last thing I need is to spend a lot of time on a lawsuit, whether it's warranted or not," says Peter Falvey, one of Revolution's co-founders.

Falvey isn't alone. A number of defense attorneys and HR managers said companies they work for prefer to buy themselves peace of mind over facing the prospect of being sued. "They don't want the publicity or the expense," says Robert J. Nobile, an attorney at Seyfarth Shaw in New York. "Some of them say, Hey, we'll swallow our pride and pay 10 grand now rather than 100 grand later." That's an approach that makes IAC's Taylor shudder. "If that becomes your norm, then you train the plaintiffs' bar and your departing employees that they should expect something on the way out, no matter how poorly they perform," he says.

Many observers put much of the blame for fear of firing on HR. "The problem is much more with HR managers being nervous Nellies than it is a problem in actual legal exposure," says consultant Grote. The bigger risk is retaining poor performers, not terminating them, he says, provided the firing is done properly.

Indeed, at most companies HR is essentially a support function that gets called in only when a personnel problem has reached the crisis stage. At that point, the best they may be able to do is suggest the kind of risk-avoidance measures that drive managers crazy—such as requiring that an employee's deficiencies actually be documented in writing for an extended period before he or she is fired. This can be avoided, says Amy Rasner, a former HR manager in the fashion industry, if human resources personnel are teamed with line managers, working with them on an ongoing basis to develop and communicate specific, measurable performance objectives to employees.

In interview after interview, attorneys and HR execs say the biggest problem they confront in terminations is the failure of managers to have these kinds of conversations. In a 2005 Hewitt

For Every 10,000 Lawsuits, Few Losses, but High Cost

The maneuvering companies engage in to avoid wrongful-termination lawsuits is out of proportion to the risk of actually losing in court. One big reason: the high cost of litigating claims, even the ones that end up with the company winning.

Out of 10,000 Employment Suits	Stage of Lawsuit	Cumulative Cost for a Company to Defend a Single Lawsuit
	Filing	
7,000	Settle (most settlements are for nuisance value)	$10,000
	Summary Judgment	
2,400	Get resolved by summary judgment and other pretrial rulings	$100,000
	Start of Trial	
600	Go to trial	$175,000
	End of Trial	
186	Trials are won by plaintiffs	$250,000*
	Appeal	
13**	Plaintiffs victories survive appeal	$300,000

Sources: Cornell Law School; Hofstra Labor & Employment Law Journal; BW reporting.
*Assumes a five-day trial.
**Out of 22 trial losses typically appealed by companies.

Associates (HEW) survey of 129 major U.S. corporations, 72% said managers' ability to carry out performance management discussions and decisions effectively was the part of their personnel evaluation process most in need of improvement.

The reasons for this, of course, are varied. Some managers simply see the whole review process as a bureaucratic waste of time. It's also not easy to do. Many supervisors have been promoted into their jobs because they excelled in operations, not because they are skilled as managers. What's more, they've often spent a lot of time working alongside the very people they now oversee, so giving candid feedback to friends and former peers may be awkward. Managers in this position are "the biggest chickens on earth," says Fred Kiel, an executive-development consultant at KRW International Inc. in Minneapolis.

Ironically, when it came to handling personnel issues involving Mody, GE managers appear to have done most things right, offering regular and candid performance appraisals and involving HR and legal personnel at an early stage when matters began to sour. In trial exhibits and testimony, Mody's GE supervisors described him as a talented but prickly worker. Performance reviews and other documents faulted both his people and leadership skills.

But in the trial against GE, Mody's attorney, Scott R. Lucas of Stamford, Conn., laid out the details of what he labeled a campaign of retaliation against his client. Following a July, 2002, memo in which Mody accused the company of discrimination, Lucas told jurors, Mody's boss began complaining that he was absent and tardy too often. In a court filing, Lucas called this "a contrived performance issue," and says Mody was also "falsely criticized for lack of output."

What's more, just six weeks after having given Mody a "very favorable review," his boss gave Mody a "very poor and critical evaluation," according to the filing. Mody was excluded from various conferences and removed from "meaningful contribution" to projects. At one point, Mody's boss allegedly told him: "There are things I can ask you to do that if I asked you to do them, you would just quit." The last straw for Mody came when he returned from medical leave and was asked to do an assignment that he alleged was low-level and intentionally demeaning.

On July 18, jurors awarded Mody about $1.1 million in back pay and compensatory damages and—in one of several aspects of the case being challenged by GE—a tidy $10 million in punitive damages. Even for a company as big as GE, an $11.1 million verdict is plenty of cause to justify a fear of firing. But Mark S. Dichter, head of the employment practice at Morgan Lewis & Bockius in Philadelphia, thinks that's the wrong lesson to draw from the Mody case and other similar lawsuits. "I can design HR policies that can virtually eliminate your risk of facing employment claims, but you'll have a pretty lousy workforce," says Dichter. "At the end of the day, you have to run your business."

OREY is a senior writer for *BusinessWeek* in New York.

Protecting the Whistleblower

Companies should fine-tune internal probes to make investigation more asset than liability.

R. Scott Oswald and Jason Zuckerman

I
n litigating whistleblower retaliation claims, we have found that poorly conducted internal investigations can be extraordinarily helpful to plaintiffs and harmful to employers. In particular, investigations that are intended to discredit the concerned employee or cover up wrongdoing to protect the accused will, at a minimum, deprive the employer of an affirmative defense and can also provide circumstantial evidence of retaliatory intent.

Employers, however, can take fairly simple measures to prevent an investigation from becoming more of a liability than an asset. Following are five tips for conducting an effective internal investigation.

- **Keep the Concerned Employee Apprised of the Investigation.** For any employees, disclosing wrongdoing is a daunting experience. Therefore, a concerned employee likely will be anxious about potential retaliation and focused on achieving a prompt a resolution to the problem or wrongdoing that the employee disclosed.

If the concerned employee believes that the company is not taking the employee's concerns seriously or is failing to take necessary corrective actions, the employee likely will pursue other avenues to remedy the problem, such as contacting the media or a regulatory agency. Accordingly, it is essential for the investigator to keep the concerned employee apprised of the status of the investigation. The investigator should periodically update the concerned employee regarding the investigator's findings and give the concerned employee a chance to respond and provide additional information, documents or corroborating witnesses.

At the conclusion of the investigation, the concerned employee should be informed of corrective actions, such as strengthened internal controls to prevent the type of accounting fraud that the concerned employee brought to light.

- **Focus on the Concerned Employee's Allegation Rather than the Employee's Motive.** The surest sign that an investigation is pretextual is when the investigation focuses on the concerned employee's

motive for disclosing wrongdoing. As a matter of law, a whistleblower's motive is irrelevant. Accordingly, the investigation should focus on uncovering the veracity of the concerned employee's allegations, not on discrediting the source of the allegations.

- **Protect the Concerned Employee and Witnesses from Retaliation.** Not surprisingly, an employee accused of misconduct can be prone to resent the accuser and employees who assisted in an investigation. Accordingly, the employer should stay attuned to any retaliation resulting from an investigation, and should promptly respond to any retaliation.

If the concerned employee is harassed or subjected to pretextual discipline, co-workers would be chilled from disclosing wrongdoing. A chilled work environment is harmful to any organization because it will undermine management's ability to learn early on of future wrongdoing or misconduct. Moreover, a retaliatory investigation can result in liability for the employer.

For example, retaliating against a whistleblower by conducting a sham investigation and intentionally spreading false allegations of misconduct by the whistleblower gives rise to a claim of intentional infliction of emotional distress and other tort and employment actions.

Moreover, the Supreme Court recently clarified that a retaliation claim does not require proof of a tangible adverse job detriment, such as a termination or a demotion. Instead, the standard for retaliation is whether the conduct in question would dissuade an objective, reasonable person from making or supporting a charge of discrimination, or engaging in other forms of protected conduct.

Therefore, investigations must be conducted in a manner that will not discourage employees from reporting additional misconduct or wrongdoing.

- **Pay Heed to the Rights of the Accused.** Investigative findings based on uncorroborated allegations or dubious evidence can expose an employer to liability for a negligent investigation claim. Before taking any corrective actions based on the investigation's finding, such as terminating a manager accused of harassment, the investigative findings should be carefully scrutinized by at least one company official who was not involved in the investigation and has no stake in the outcome.

Factors to assess include whether the investigator failed to pursue leads, such as failing to interview a key witness; whether the investigator gave undue weight to hearsay; and whether the documentary evidence is consistent with the investigator's conclusions. Moreover, it is critical throughout an investigation to avoid defaming the accused.

- **Steer Clear of Unlawful Investigation Techniques and Preserve the Authenticity of Electronic Documents.** The Hewlett-Packard "pretexting" scandal, which resulted in a $14.5 million settlement and other sanctions, is a stark reminder of the importance of complying with state and federal privacy laws.

Throughout the investigation, consider whether any particular technique might run afoul of state wiretapping laws, the Electronic Communications Privacy Act, the Fair Credit Reporting Act or the Health Insurance Portability and Accountability Act.

Investigators should also take steps to avoid inadvertent corruption of electronic documents. As most documents are now created and transmitted electronically, an investigation will likely entail the gathering and review of various types of electronic documents. Merely opening or reading an electronic file, such as an email or a spreadsheet, alters the metadata of the file.

The metadata itself could contain critical evidence that might resolve conflicting accounts, such as when a document was transmitted, received or opened. To ensure that evidence uncovered in an investigation will retain its authenticity and be deemed reliable in potential litigation, create a "mirror image" or bit-by-bit copy of the source drive or database.

R. Scott Oswald and **Jason Zuckerman** are Principals at The Employment Law Group. They represent employees in whistleblower retaliation claims brought under the Sarbanes-Oxley Act and other protection provisions.

Learning to Love Whistleblowers

Some businesses that once feared whistleblowers are now giving workers new ways to report wrongdoing.

DARREN DAHL

Marvin windows and doors is a family-owned business in Warroad, Minnesota, and one of the world's largest custom manufacturers of wooden windows and doors. In 2005, the company grossed an estimated $500 million. As sales have increased, so has Marvin's work force, which now tops 5,500 employees spread among a dozen plants, including one in Honduras. To keep track of all these workers, the company recently implemented what software makers call a whistle-blowing system. It allows workers to anonymously submit tips, suggestions, and complaints to top executives in either English or Spanish about anything from safety conditions to bad managers to fraud and theft. "We want to demonstrate that we are serious about establishing an ethical culture," says senior vice president and general counsel Steve Tourek.

Marvin Windows is not alone in setting up a system that encourages whistle-blowing. An industry has sprung up to make it easy for employees to alert their bosses to trouble, and vendors report that clients include businesses of all sizes. One company with just nine workers recently signed up with EthicsPoint, a vendor that sets up toll-free 24-hour call centers and websites. Systems vary in price, but most start at about $12,000 per year, plus a sign-up fee.

The systems can also be used by companies to keep an eye on their top executives. Many systems will automatically route to a designated outside board member any tip that implicates a member of the management team like the CEO or the CFO.

The popularity of whistle-blowing systems is due in large part to the Sarbanes-Oxley Act of 2002, which compels public companies to establish procedures for identifying wrongdoing. Whistle-blowing software had been around for at least a decade, but after Congress passed the law, software firms created a lot of new applications, thinking that companies covered by the law would want them. To the surprise of many people in the industry, sales of whistle-blowing systems to private companies, which are not covered by Sarbanes-Oxley, are also on the rise. By using their employees as an early-warning system, employers seek to head off problems before they spiral out of control.

What Exactly Is an Internal Control?

The idea of companies soliciting whistleblowers would have seemed ridiculous a decade ago, when many executives viewed them as troublemakers and attention-seekers. Corporate scandals changed that. This year, 88 percent of respondents to a survey of public and private companies agreed that encouraging whistleblowers is good for business, according to Tatum Partners, a financial consulting firm based in Atlanta.

These results contrast with the conventional hatred of Sarbanes-Oxley, which has been blamed repeatedly for a range of corporate maladies from overzealous auditing to the torpid market for initial public offerings. One requirement in particular—that companies establish adequate "internal controls"—has been held up for criticism because the law doesn't spell out what an internal control is. Software companies have positioned whistleblower software as a suitable control.

To some extent, this sales pitch has worked. Many public companies have purchased whistleblower systems in the past few years. So have some privately held businesses that are compelled to adopt Sarbanes-Oxley-related policies by publicly held joint venture partners or customers or lenders. Then there are private firms that install these systems simply because they see real value in them. In a recent survey, PricewaterhouseCoopers found that 60 percent of private companies that have voluntarily adopted the regulations did so because they thought they were the "best business practices," while 59 percent felt that they would help a company address potential problems.

A Way to Avoid Jail Time

Some evidence suggests that it's wise for employers to implement any kind of system that encourages workers to speak up. In a 2004 study of 508 companies where occupational fraud occurred, the Association of Certified Fraud Examiners found that companies that uncovered troubling activity were more likely to find out about it from a co-worker's tip than from an internal or external audit. Moreover, organizations that had anonymous reporting systems in place suffered less than half

Table 1   Quiz: Name the Famous Whistleblowers

Many corporate and government truthtellers have enjoyed 15 minutes of fame, movie deals included.

1971	1974	1984	1993	2001	2002	2002	2003
a. This State Department officer slipped the **Pentagon Papers** to *The New York Times.*	**b.** This blue-collar worker raised **Plutonium plant safety concerns** before her untimely death.	**c.** She alleged **sexual harassment** at the "North Country" coal mine where she worked.	**d.** This ex-Brown & Williamson "insider" alleged that the **tobacco industry** made cigarettes more addictive.	**e.** He kicked off the most recent wave of corporate scandals when he alleged fraud at telecom **Global Crossing.**	**f.** One of *Time's* persons of the year, she detailed accounting irregularities at **Enron.**	**g.** This **WorldCom** auditor, another of *Time's* heroes, investigated $3.8 billion in accounting irregularities.	**h.** This Army Corps of Engineers official criticized **no-bid contracts** received by a Halliburton subsidiary in Iraq.

Quiz Answer Key

a. Daniel Ellsberg b. Karen Silkwood c. Lois Jensen d. Jeffrey Wigand e. Roy Olofson f. Sherron Watkins g. Cynthia Cooper h. Bunnatine H. Greenhouse

the financial losses from fraud sustained by companies without such systems.

There are other incentives for encouraging whistle-blowing. Sections 301 and 404 of Sarbanes-Oxley, which compel companies to maintain an ethical culture and a system of internal controls, have roots in the Federal Sentencing Guidelines for corporate crime and fraud that were established in 1991. These guidelines provide federal judges with a set of standards to use in doling out punishment for all companies, public or private, that are convicted of a crime. If a company can demonstrate that it has tried to develop an ethical culture, such as by adopting a whistleblower system, a judge may be lenient in handing out fines and jail time.

Fears of False Accusations

Nonetheless, there is one risk that most managers think long and hard about before they sign up. What happens if employees swamp the system with petty grievances? What if a worker fabricates an allegation? These were Gerald Massey's initial concerns. Massey is the CEO of Fios, a Portland, Oregon, company that lawyers hire to inspect computer equipment for information pertaining to a lawsuit. Because his firm was in the business of uncovering the misdeeds of companies involved in litigation or under investigation, Massey was predisposed to see the benefits of whistle-blowing software. And Fios had long since outgrown its trusty employee suggestion box, with 120 employees spread out among offices in four states. Even so, Massey says, "my board and I were worried that we would be opening a Pandora's box."

Massey's system went live in the fall of 2004, and some of his fears were certainly justified: Fios' 120 workers submitted more than 30 suggestions in the first 18 months. This usage was high. Most vendors say that the average annual volume of tips is a manageable four per every 100 employees. And, says Massey, all but two of these complaints were minor. This is typical. Vendors estimate that only about 3 percent of all tips involve a serious disclosure. For workers to trust the system to work, however, little gripes cannot be ignored, experts say. Every report must be taken seriously, and there can be no retaliation. Still, most managers are happy to field minor complaints about HR issues (which they should probably address anyway) in return for added vigilance about crucial legal and financial issues.

The enduring legacy of Sarbanes-Oxley and the recent scandals may be a change in the way companies look at employees who are unafraid to raise red flags. "We want the company to do the right thing," says Marvin Windows' Steve Tourek. "And we want to give our employees a place to tell us when we aren't."

DARREN DAHL can be e-mailed at DDahl@inc.com.

On Witnessing a Fraud

Saying no to the scam was easy, but deciding whether to report it was harder.

Don Soeken

Skiers in bright parkas swooshed by on the slopes as Joe pushed open the gleaming silver doors of the Highland Ski Club, ready to begin another day as computer technician. It was expensive living in the tourist town of Bastcliff, Colo., but Joe loved it. Little did he know, on this fine November morning, of the emotional storm that approached just inside the doors.

The nightmare began innocently enough, when a supervisor tapped Joe on the shoulder and murmured, "We've had an energy surge in the computer system. Will you check out the damage and report to the club manager?"

"Sure thing," said Joe. "I'll get right on it."

He found a relatively minor problem. The surge had fried a few underground wires and computer circuits, which would have to be replaced at a cost of about $15,000. When Joe reported this to the supervisor and the club manager, their response surprised him. They asked him to dig up nearly all the underground wire and cable, then dispose of it before the insurance adjuster arrived. If that were done, the cost of the repair job paid by the insurance company would come to $600,000.

"Wow, I don't think that's something I want to do," Joe told them. But his superiors assured him that if the scam were discovered, the company would be liable rather than him personally. They also noted the plan would allow the club to install a new computer system, which Joe had been asking for.

"I'm sorry," Joe said. "It's fraud, and I refuse to be part of it."

The club manager scowled angrily, and then shrugged as Joe left the room. Minutes later Joe was dismayed to learn that his fellow employee Todd was on his way to dig up the good wiring and stash it in a dumpster far removed from the clubhouse.

To clear his head, Joe stepped out into the cold bright air. Should he report the scam, he asked himself, or let it go? What should he do?

C. Fred Alford, Professor of Government and Politics, University of Maryland, College Park

Ever since my book on whistleblowing (Whistleblowers: Broken Lives and Organizational Power) was published, I've been contacted once a month from would-be whistleblowers asking what they should do. Usually the cases are complex, both factually and ethically. The first part of this case isn't. Joe is being asked to go along with felony fraud, and he has no choice but to say no. The second part is harder: Should he inform the insurance company and possibly get his friend Todd in trouble?

My advice is yes, he should make that phone call. You can't let something like this go—it's like seeing a traffic accident and not reporting it.

Joe will no doubt be fired, and will have to find new work. But he's in a field with a lot of jobs, unlike the field of nuclear engineering, for example, where whistleblowers have little chance to start over. I assume Joe has not been working at the ski club for years and years, since most of these jobs are staffed by young people looking for adventure.

If some or all of this is true, I recommend Joe move to another state, come up with a convincing explanation for the gap in his employment record, and get on with his life. Most whistleblowers want vindication—they want to fight a lawsuit for reinstatement. But it's enough to have done the right thing and move on.

Here my advice is practical rather than moral. Rather than explaining why he was fired, I'm suggesting Joe leave that job out of his resume and make something up to fill the gap. I recommend he lie. Not about having done something bad, but about having done something moral.

Don Soeken's Comments

Even at the risk of losing his job, Joe behaved with the ethical integrity he had been taught to value during childhood: he refused to be part of a fraud. Joe did what too many of us are afraid to do, in standing up for what's right.

As for reporting the fraud, I agree that Joe must call the insurance company. Prof. Alford introduces a surprising twist, in suggesting that when Joe loses his job, he should lie to smooth out his employment record. This is a question on which I think good people will disagree. I recommend that Joe keep the resume correct and list someone at the ski club who could help him get another job.

What Actually Happened

Joe reported the $600,000 attempted fraud to the insurance company, and admitted to his bosses he was the whistleblower. He was fired. The ski club received money from the insurance company, which was slow to investigate, and the outcome of that investigation is unknown. No negative consequences happened to Joe's coworker who dug up the cable. Joe later discovered the ski club had defrauded insurance companies on several occasions.

Joe found it hard to get another job, since his personnel file held a negative assessment of his job performance. Several evaluations said he had "problems with authority." Before the whistleblowing, similar evaluations had described Joe's work as superior. Soon, Joe was struggling with clinical depression.

He filed a lawsuit to seek various kinds of compensation—including lost wages. After years of legal wrangling, the judge ordered both mediation and settlement talks. Joe settled for an undisclosed payment. The company did not admit wrongdoing.

DON SOEKEN (helpline@tidal wave.net) is director of Integrity International, which provides counseling support and expert witness testimony for whistleblowers. See www.whistleblowing.us.

All cases in What Would You Do? are real, though disguised.

His Most Trusted Employee Was a Thief

Jane had taken $20,000 to pay for a child's medical care.

SHEL HOROWITZ

Jane had worked for Edward faithfully for four years, and he trusted her with all the intimate details of his business. She was the one he relied on to solve any problem, to handle his paper-work, to be his personal confidante. She didn't have an accounting background, but she exercised day-to-day oversight over his company's finances, including depositing all the checks and cash that came in. Edward considered Jane a close personal friend. And while she was well-compensated, he paid out-of-pocket for special medical treatment for one of her children, when it fell outside the employee health plan that covered her, but not her family.

Jane had earned Edward's complete trust—until the day he discovered that, over the course of years, she had embezzled $20,000. When Edward confronted her, Jane immediately admitted the theft. She apologized and explained it was to pay for her child's high medical expenses. She agreed to begin a repayment plan, but Edward knew she didn't have the financial resources to pay back the entire $20,000.

Logic would dictate that Edward immediately terminate Jane and begin the process of criminal prosecution—but this was a close friend. Cold logic wasn't the only thing working here; there was a history of so many years working side by side. If only Jane had asked him, Edward would have contributed further toward the child's treatment. Now, what would sending Jane to jail accomplish? It wouldn't repair his trust, and it would not bring back the lost dollars. And how could he leave those children with no parent to take care of them, to say nothing of the medical problems? At the same time, if he allowed Jane to escape responsibility for her actions, who is to say she wouldn't do it again?

Archie Carroll
Robert W. Scherer Chair of Management Terry College of Business, University of Georgia

Carroll presented this case to the Social Issues in Management on-line faculty discussion group, asking for advice on behalf of the business owner, who is a friend of his (names have been changed). Comments below reflect both Carroll's own thoughts, as well as input from 15 of his colleagues.

When I asked my faculty colleagues about this, their advice ranged the gamut. Some said keep Jane as an employee, since she'd feel enough guilt and shame that she would not repeat the bad behavior (and thus Edward could avoid the high cost of training a replacement). At the other extreme, some said Edward should consider criminal prosecution.

As much as a consensus existed, it was that criminal prosecution would not help the situation, especially as the business owner wanted to put the episode behind him. There was recognition that the employee had worked "above and beyond," and that it would not help her family to put them through the trial and possible imprisonment. There was, of course, strong agreement that the embezzlement was wrong and that the business should institute accounting controls to prevent a similar theft in the future.

Some of the more innovative suggestions included:

- Fire Jane, but have her demonstrate how she was able to circumvent his fraud controls so that a future employee couldn't repeat the theft.
- Show generosity and forgive the money, out of respect for Jane's difficult financial situation.
- Hire Jane back on a probationary basis, and either forgive the debt or have her pay it back in small increments.
- Have her sign a promissory note, treating the theft as a loan.

What Actually Happened

Edward fired Jane. He forgave half of the $20,000 taken, in recognition of the extra effort she had gone to on his behalf for four years. For the other $10,000, he had her execute a promissory note to repay $100 per month (eight years and four months to repay in full). He felt, however, that this money was tainted. Instead of keeping it, he plans to donate it to charity. Edward will also upgrade his accounting controls (which already involve five people), but also take a much more active role in monitoring his company's financial situation.

SHEL HOROWITZ, (shel@principledprofits.com) author of *Principled Profit: Marketing That Puts People First,* initiated the Business Ethics Pledge movement at www.principledprofits.com/25000influencers.html.

Erasing 'Un' from 'Unemployable'

Walgreen program trains the disabled to take on regular wage-paying jobs.

AMY MERRICK

Like many people with autism, Harrison Mullinax, a pale, redheaded 18-year-old with a serious expression, speaks in a monotonous, halting voice and sometimes struggles to concentrate on tasks. Unlike most who are autistic, he now has a real job.

Mr. Mullinax works eight hours a day at a new Walgreen Co. distribution center, where he wields a bar-code scanner, checking in boxes of merchandise bound for the company's drugstores. From his paycheck, he tithes to his church and sometimes treats his mother to dinner at Kenny's, a local buffet restaurant.

An innovative program at the distribution center is offering jobs to people with mental and physical disabilities of a nature that has frequently deemed them "unemployable," while saving Walgreen money through automation.

"It answered a prayer," says Mr. Mullinax's mother, Vikki, who gets him up for work at 5 each morning, before sending him off to the bus for work. "It's given us the hope that at some point Harrison can live with minimal assistance."

A number of large employers, such as McDonald's Corp. and Wal-Mart Stores Inc., recruit people with disabilities to be cashiers, maintenance workers or store greeters. At Home Depot Inc., developmentally disabled workers stock shelves, clean displays and help customers find items. Home Depot has been working with a nonprofit organization called Ken's Kids, which was formed a decade ago by a group of parents seeking employment opportunities for their young-adult children, and has placed more than 100 people in 54 stores. In addition, smaller businesses around the nation have made a goal of employing workers passed over by other companies.

Still, executives at Walgreen and the social-services agencies working with it believe the company's program has a larger number of disabled employees, doing more-sophisticated work, than is typically available to people with mental and physical challenges.

Mr. Mullinax, like many of Walgreen's employees with disabilities, learned his job in a large metal-clad shed 15 minutes down the road from the distribution center. There, trainees learn how to work in one of three departments: "case check-in," where workers initially receive merchandise; "de-trash," where they unpack the goods; and "picking," where they sort the products into tubs based on individual store orders.

The distribution center opened in January at a cost of $175 million. It currently employs 264 people, more than 40% of whom have various disabilities, and it is 20% more efficient than the company's older facilities. On some days, disabled employees are its most productive workers.

"One thing we found is they can all do the job," says Randy Lewis, a senior vice president of distribution and logistics at Walgreen, which is based in Deerfield, Ill. "What surprised us is the environment that it's created. It's a building where everybody helps each other out."

When they make the transition to the distribution center, disabled employees at first have a job coach. Those needing it learn social skills, from the importance of wearing deodorant to finding appropriate conversation topics.

The idea began four years ago, when Mr. Lewis was evaluating new technology that could make Walgreen's next round of distribution centers far more automated than in the past. Mr. Lewis asked: Could Walgreen make the work simple enough to employ people with cognitive disabilities?

For him, the question was personal. His 19-year-old son, Austin, has autism. "I'm keenly aware of the lack of opportunities for kids like that," he says. Among people with the disability, the unemployment rate can be as high as 95%, according to social-service agencies.

Because employing disabled people wasn't expected to affect the distribution center's costs or efficiency, it wasn't difficult for Mr. Lewis to persuade the Walgreen board and David Bernauer, then the company's chief executive and now its chairman, to try the project. "The fact that we can use disabled people for this was a great plus," Mr. Bernauer says. "It didn't move the needle on the business decision."

As part of the program, Walgreen converted its computer displays from lines of type to touch screens with a few icons. It persuaded vendors to include more information in bar codes on merchandise, so that employees wouldn't have to enter so much data themselves. It redesigned work stations so that people don't have to stretch as far, and it added help buttons to summon assistance. Instead of posting printed cards to remind workers about having their bags inspected, Walgreen shows a video of someone opening a bag.

Angela Campbell, the facility's career-outreach coordinator, suggested adding pictures to numbered work stations. In the "de-trash" area, where workers remove merchandise from boxes and prepare it to be sorted for individual stores, there are images of farm animals.

Ms. Campbell, who has cerebral palsy and carefully maneuvers the building's many flights of stairs, tells employees they should feel comfortable asking her awkward questions about why someone looks or behaves a certain way. "I know what it's like to fight your whole life to have an employer look past your disability," she says.

All workers are constantly monitored to track whether they're meeting productivity goals. One day, workers with disabilities topped the productivity list in three major departments, says Keith Scarbrough, the distribution center's manager.

Many trainees volunteer their time to learn, sometimes spending as much as a year without pay. Anderson County arranges transportation for many employees to get to work. Walgreen estimates that if it reaches its goal of employing 200 workers with disabilities, the value of the government benefits it receives will be about $3.5 million.

Starting pay at the distribution center is $10.85 an hour, climbing to $13.80 an hour after two years.

The disabilities of workers at the center run the gamut and present the supervisory staff with a variety of challenges. Desiree Neff, 43, struggles with her balance and uses a walker, her 26-year-old son and co-worker, Troy Mayben, is legally blind. Recently, Ms. Neff wanted to learn how to operate a forklift so she could expand her skills, but she didn't have a place to put her walker. An engineer devised a clamp that attaches the walker to the forklift.

In another case, managers didn't know what to do about a disruptive employee who screamed "Hello!" every morning. Some argued that the behavior was part of the worker's disability. But Deb Russell, the career-outreach manager for Walgreen, reasoned, "We don't allow anyone else to do that." She instructed workers to ignore his shouting. Within two days, she says, he stopped.

As for Vikki Mullinax, she says now that Harrison is working, she can spend more time with her husband and 16-year-old daughter. Harrison "has improved tremendously," she says.

Harrison Mullinax says he has made friends, and he likes being paid. Working at Walgreen, he says, has taught him how to offer help to others and "not to cuss anybody out."

From *The Wall Street Journal*, August 2, 2007, pp. B1+ (2 pages). Copyright © 2007 by Dow Jones & Company, Inc. Reprinted by permission via the Copyright Clearance Center.

The Parable of the Sadhu

**After encountering a dying pilgrim on a climbing trip
in the Himalayas, a businessman ponders the differences
between individual and corporate ethics.**

Bowen H. McCoy

Last year, as the first participant in the new six-month sabbatical program that Morgan Stanley has adopted, I enjoyed a rare opportunity to collect my thoughts as well as do some traveling. I spent the first three months in Nepal, walking 600 miles through 200 villages in the Himalayas and climbing some 120,000 vertical feet. My sole Western companion on the trip was an anthropologist who shed light on the cultural patterns of the villages that we passed through.

During the Nepal hike, something occurred that has had a powerful impact on my thinking about corporate ethics. Although some might argue that the experience has no relevance to business, it was a situation in which a basic ethical dilemma suddenly intruded into the lives of a group of individuals. How the group responded holds a lesson for all organizations, no matter how defined.

The Sadhu

The Nepal experience was more rugged than I had anticipated. Most commercial treks last two or three weeks and cover a quarter of the distance we traveled.

My friend Stephen, the anthropologist, and I were halfway through the 60-day Himalayan part of the trip when we reached the high point, an 18,000-foot pass over a crest that we'd have to traverse to reach the village of Muklinath, an ancient holy place for pilgrims.

Six years earlier, I had suffered pulmonary edema, an acute form of altitude sickness, at 16,500 feet in the vicinity of Everest base camp—so we were understandably concerned about what would happen at 18,000 feet. Moreover, the Himalayas were having their wettest spring in 20 years; hip-deep powder and ice had already driven us off one ridge. If we failed to cross the pass, I feared that the last half of our once-in-a-lifetime trip would be ruined.

The night before we would try the pass, we camped in a hut at 14,500 feet. In the photos taken at that camp, my face appears wan. The last village we'd passed through was a sturdy two-day walk below us, and I was tired.

During the late afternoon, four backpackers from New Zealand joined us, and we spent most of the night awake, anticipating the climb. Below, we could see the fires of two other parties, which turned out to be two Swiss couples and a Japanese hiking club.

To get over the steep part of the climb before the sun melted the steps cut in the ice, we departed at 3:30 A.M. The New Zealanders left first, followed by Stephen and myself, our porters and Sherpas, and then the Swiss. The Japanese lingered in their camp. The sky was clear, and we were confident that no spring storm would erupt that day to close the pass.

At 15,500 feet, it looked to me as if Stephen were shuffling and staggering a bit, which are symptoms of altitude sickness. (The initial stage of altitude sickness brings a headache and nausea. As the condition worsens, a climber may encounter difficult breathing, disorientation, aphasia, and paralysis.) I felt strong—my adrenaline was flowing—but I was very concerned about my ultimate ability to get across. A couple of our porters were also suffering from the height, and Pasang, our Sherpa sirdar (leader), was worried.

Just after daybreak, while we rested at 15,500 feet, one of the New Zealanders, who had gone ahead, came staggering down toward us with a body slung across his shoulders. He dumped the almost naked, barefoot body of an Indian holy man—a sadhu—at my feet. He had found the pilgrim lying on the ice, shivering and suffering from hypothermia. I cradled the sadhu's head and laid him out on the rocks. The New Zealander was angry. He wanted to get across the pass before the bright sun melted the snow. He said, "Look, I've done what I can. You have porters and Sherpa guides. You care for him. We're going on!" He turned and went back up the mountain to join his friends.

I took a carotid pulse and found that the sadhu was still alive. We figured he had probably visited the holy shrines at Muklinath and was on his way home. It was fruitless to question why he had chosen this desperately high route instead of the safe, heavily traveled caravan route through the Kali Gandaki gorge. Or why he was shoeless and almost naked, or how long he had been lying in the pass. The answers weren't going to solve our problem.

Stephen and the four Swiss began stripping off their outer clothing and opening their packs. The sadhu was soon clothed from head to foot. He was not able to walk, but he was very much alive. I looked down the mountain and spotted the Japanese climbers, marching up with a horse.

When I reached them, Stephen glared at me and said, "How do you feel about contributing to the death of a fellow man?"

Without a great deal of thought, I told Stephen and Pasang that I was concerned about withstanding the heights to come and wanted to get over the pass. I took off after several of our porters who had gone ahead.

On the steep part of the ascent where, if the ice steps had given way, I would have slid down about 3,000 feet, I felt vertigo. I stopped for a breather, allowing the Swiss to catch up with me. I inquired about the sadhu and Stephen. They said that the sadhu was fine and that Stephen was just behind them. I set off again for the summit.

Stephen arrived at the summit an hour after I did. Still exhilarated by victory, I ran down the slope to congratulate him. He was suffering from altitude sickness—walking 15 steps, then stopping, walking 15 steps, then stopping. Pasang accompanied him all the way up. When I reached them, Stephen glared at me and said: "How do you feel about contributing to the death of a fellow man?"

I did not completely comprehend what he meant. "Is the sadhu dead?" I inquired.

"No," replied Stephen, "but he surely will be!"

After I had gone, followed not long after by the Swiss, Stephen had remained with the sadhu. When the Japanese had arrived, Stephen had asked to use their horse to transport the sadhu down to the hut. They had refused. He had then asked Pasang to have a group of our porters carry the sadhu. Pasang had resisted the idea, saying that the porters would have to exert all their energy to get themselves over the pass. He believed they could not carry a man down 1,000 feet to the hut, reclimb the slope, and get across safely before the snow melted. Pasang had pressed Stephen not to delay any longer.

The Sherpas had carried the sadhu down to a rock in the sun at about 15,000 feet and pointed out the hut another 500 feet below. The Japanese had given him food and drink. When they had last seen him, he was listlessly throwing rocks at the Japanese party's dog, which had frightened him.

We do not know if the sadhu lived or died.

For many of the following days and evenings, Stephen and I discussed and debated our behavior toward the sadhu. Stephen is a committed Quaker with deep moral vision. He said, "I feel that what happened with the sadhu is a good example of the breakdown between the individual ethic and the corporate ethic. No one person was willing to assume ultimate responsibility for

the sadhu. Each was willing to do his bit just so long as it was not too inconvenient. When it got to be a bother, everyone just passed the buck to someone else and took off. Jesus was relevant to a more individualistic stage of society, but how do we interpret his teaching today in a world filled with large, impersonal organizations and groups?"

I defended the larger group, saying, "Look, we all cared. We all gave aid and comfort. Everyone did his bit. The New Zealander carried him down below the snow line. I took his pulse and suggested we treat him for hypothermia. You and the Swiss gave him clothing and got him warmed up. The Japanese gave him food and water. The Sherpas carried him down to the sun and pointed out the easy trail toward the hut. He was well enough to throw rocks at a dog. What more could we do?"

"You have just described the typical affluent Westerner's response to a problem. Throwing money—in this case, food and sweaters—at it, but not solving the fundamentals!" Stephen retorted.

I asked, "Where is the limit of our responsibility in a situation like this?"

"What would satisfy you?" I said. "Here we are, a group of New Zealanders, Swiss, Americans, and Japanese who have never met before and who are at the apex of one of the most powerful experiences of our lives. Some years the pass is so bad no one gets over it. What right does an almost naked pilgrim who chooses the wrong trail have to disrupt our lives? Even the Sherpas had no interest in risking the trip to help him beyond a certain point."

Stephen calmly rebutted, "I wonder what the Sherpas would have done if the sadhu had been a well-dressed Nepali, or what the Japanese would have done if the sadhu had been a well-dressed Asian, or what you would have done, Buzz, if the sadhu had been a well-dressed Western woman?"

"Where, in your opinion," I asked, "is the limit of our responsibility in a situation like this? We had our own well-being to worry about. Our Sherpa guides were unwilling to jeopardize us or the porters for the sadhu. No one else on the mountain was willing to commit himself beyond certain self-imposed limits."

Stephen said, "As individual Christians or people with a Western ethical tradition, we can fulfill our obligations in such a situation only if one, the sadhu dies in our care; two, the sadhu demonstrates to us that he can undertake the two-day walk down to the village; or three, we carry the sadhu for two days down to the village and persuade someone there to care for him."

"Leaving the sadhu in the sun with food and clothing—where he demonstrated hand-eye coordination by throwing a rock at a dog—comes close to fulfilling items one and two," I answered. "And it wouldn't have made sense to take him to the village where the people appeared to be far less caring than the Sherpas, so the third condition is impractical. Are you really saying that, no matter what the implications, we should, at the drop of a hat, have changed our entire plan?"

The Individual versus the Group Ethic

Despite my arguments, I felt and continue to feel guilt about the sadhu. I had literally walked through a classic moral dilemma without fully thinking through the consequences. My excuses for my actions include a high adrenaline flow, a superordinate goal, and a once-in-a-lifetime opportunity—common factors in corporate situations, especially stressful ones.

Real moral dilemmas are ambiguous, and many of us hike right through them, unaware that they exist. When, usually after the fact, someone makes an issue of one, we tend to resent his or her bringing it up. Often, when the full import of what we have done (or not done) hits us, we dig into a defensive position from which it is very difficult to emerge. In rare circumstances, we may contemplate what we have done from inside a prison.

Had we mountaineers been free of stress caused by the effort and the high altitude, we might have treated the sadhu differently. Yet isn't stress the real test of personal and corporate values? The instant decisions that executives make under pressure reveal the most about personal and corporate character.

> **As a group, we had no process for developing a consensus. We had no sense of purpose or plan.**

Among the many questions that occur to me when I ponder my experience with the sadhu are: What are the practical limits of moral imagination and vision? Is there a collective or institutional ethic that differs from the ethics of the individual? At what level of effort or commitment can one discharge one's ethical responsibilities?

Not every ethical dilemma has a right solution. Reasonable people often disagree; otherwise there would be no dilemma. In a business context, however, it is essential that managers agree on a process for dealing with dilemmas.

Our experience with the sadhu offers an interesting parallel to business situations. An immediate response was mandatory. Failure to act was a decision in itself. Up on the mountain we could not resign and submit our résumés to a headhunter. In contrast to philosophy, business involves action and implementation—getting things done. Managers must come up with answers based on what they see and what they allow to influence their decision-making processes. On the mountain, none of us but Stephen realized the true dimensions of the situation we were facing.

One of our problems was that as a group we had no process for developing a consensus. We had no sense of purpose or plan. The difficulties of dealing with the sadhu were so complex that no one person could handle them. Because the group did not have a set of preconditions that could guide its action to an acceptable resolution, we reacted instinctively as individuals. The cross-cultural nature of the group added a further layer of complexity. We had no leader with whom we could all identify and in whose purpose we believed. Only Stephen was willing to take charge, but he could not gain adequate support from the group to care for the sadhu.

Some organizations do have values that transcend the personal values of their managers. Such values, which go beyond profitability, are usually revealed when the organization is under stress. People throughout the organization generally accept its values, which, because they are not presented as a rigid list of commandments, may be somewhat ambiguous. The stories people tell, rather than printed materials, transmit the organization's conceptions of what is proper behavior.

For 20 years, I have been exposed at senior levels to a variety of corporations and organizations. It is amazing how quickly an outsider can sense the tone and style of an organization and, with that, the degree of tolerated openness and freedom to challenge management.

Organizations that do not have a heritage of mutually accepted, shared values tend to become unhinged during stress, with each individual bailing out for himself or herself. In the great takeover battles we have witnessed during past years, companies that had strong cultures drew the wagons around them and fought it out, while other companies saw executives—supported by golden parachutes—bail out of the struggles.

Because corporations and their members are interdependent, for the corporation to be strong the members need to share a preconceived notion of correct behavior, a "business ethic," and think of it as a positive force, not a constraint.

As an investment banker, I am continually warned by well-meaning lawyers, clients, and associates to be wary of conflicts of interest. Yet if I were to run away from every difficult situation, I wouldn't be an effective investment banker. I have to feel my way through conflicts. An effective manager can't run from risk either; he or she has to confront risk. To feel "safe" in doing that, managers need the guidelines of an agreed-upon process and set of values within the organization.

After my three months in Nepal, I spent three months as an executive-in-residence at both the Stanford Business School and the University of California at Berkeley's Center for Ethics and Social Policy of the Graduate Theological Union. Those six months away from my job gave me time to assimilate 20 years of business experience. My thoughts turned often to the meaning of the leadership role in any large organization. Students at the seminary thought of themselves as antibusiness. But when I questioned them, they agreed that they distrusted all large organizations, including the church. They perceived all large organizations as impersonal and opposed to individual values and needs. Yet we all know of organizations in which people's values and beliefs are respected and their expressions encouraged. What makes the difference? Can we identify the difference and, as a result, manage more effectively?

The word *ethics* turns off many and confuses more. Yet the notions of shared values and an agreed-upon process for dealing with adversity and change—what many people mean when they talk about corporate culture—seem to be at the heart of the ethical issue. People who are in touch with their own core beliefs and the beliefs of others and who are sustained by them can be more comfortable living on the cutting edge. At times, taking a tough line or a decisive stand in a muddle of ambiguity

When Do We Take a Stand?

I wrote about my experiences purposely to present an ambiguous situation. I never found out if the sadhu lived or died. I can attest, though, that the sadhu lives on in his story. He lives in the ethics classes I teach each year at business schools and churches. He lives in the classrooms of numerous business schools, where professors have taught the case to tens of thousands of students. He lives in several casebooks on ethics and on an educational video. And he lives in organizations such as the American Red Cross and AT&T, which use his story in their ethics training.

As I reflect on the sadhu now, 15 years after the fact, I first have to wonder, What actually happened on that Himalayan slope? When I first wrote about the event, I reported the experience in as much detail as I could remember, but I shaped it to the needs of a good classroom discussion. After years of reading my story, viewing it on video, and hearing others discuss it, I'm not sure I myself know what actually occurred on the mountainside that day!

I've also heard a wide variety of responses to the story. The sadhu, for example, may not have wanted our help at all—he may have been intentionally bringing on his own death as a way to holiness. Why had he taken the dangerous way over the pass instead of the caravan route through the gorge? Hindu businesspeople have told me that in trying to assist the sadhu, we were being typically arrogant Westerners imposing our cultural values on the world.

I've learned that each year along the pass, a few Nepali porters are left to freeze to death outside the tents of the unthinking tourists who hired them. A few years ago, a French group even left one of their own, a young French woman, to die there. The difficult pass seems to demonstrate a perverse version of Gresham's law of currency: The bad practices of previous travelers have driven out the values that new travelers might have followed if they were at home. Perhaps that helps to explain why our porters behaved as they did and why it was so difficult for Stephen or anyone else to establish a different approach on the spot.

Our Sherpa sirdar, Pasang, was focused on his responsibility for bringing us up the mountain safe and sound. (His livelihood and status in the Sherpa ethnic group depended on our safe return.) We were weak, our party was split, the porters were well on their way to the top with all our gear and food, and a storm would have separated us irrevocably from our logistical base.

The fact was, we had no plan for dealing with the contingency of the sadhu. There was nothing we could do to unite our multicultural group in the little time we had. An ethical dilemma had come upon us unexpectedly, an element of drama that may explain why the sadhu's story has continued to attract students.

I am often asked for help in teaching the story. I usually advise keeping the details as ambiguous as possible. A true ethical dilemma requires a decision between two hard choices. In the case of the sadhu, we had to decide how much to sacrifice ourselves to take care of a stranger. And given the constraints of our trek, we had to make a group decision, not an individual one. If a large majority of students in a class ends up thinking I'm a bad person because of my decision on the mountain, the instructor may not have given the case its due. The same is true if the majority sees no problem with the choices we made.

Any class's response depends on its setting, whether it's a business school, a church, or a corporation. I've found that younger students are more likely to see the issue as black-and-white, whereas older ones tend to see shades of gray. Some have seen a conflict between the different ethical approaches that we followed at the time. Stephen felt he had to do everything he could to save the sadhu's life, in accordance with his Christian ethic of compassion. I had a utilitarian response: do the greatest good for the greatest number. Give a burst of aid to minimize the sadhu's exposure, then continue on our way.

The basic question of the case remains, When do we take a stand? When do we allow a "sadhu" to intrude into our daily lives? Few of us can afford the time or effort to take care of every needy person we encounter. How much must we give of ourselves? And how do we prepare our organizations and institutions so they will respond appropriately in a crisis? How do we influence them if we do not agree with their points of view?

We cannot quit our jobs over every ethical dilemma, but if we continually ignore our sense of values, who do we become? As a journalist asked at a recent conference on ethics, "Which ditch are we willing to die in?" For each of us, the answer is a bit different. How we act in response to that question defines better than anything else who we are, just as, in a collective sense, our acts define our institutions. In effect, the sadhu is always there, ready to remind us of the tensions between our own goals and the claims of strangers.

is the only ethical thing to do. If a manager is indecisive about a problem and spends time trying to figure out the "good" thing to do, the enterprise may be lost.

Business ethics, then, has to do with the authenticity and integrity of the enterprise. To be ethical is to follow the business as well as the cultural goals of the corporation, its owners, its employees, and its customers. Those who cannot serve the corporate vision are not authentic businesspeople and, therefore, are not ethical in the business sense.

At this stage of my own business experience, I have a strong interest in organizational behavior. Sociologists are keenly studying what they call corporate stories, legends, and heroes as a way organizations have of transmitting value systems. Corporations such as Arco have even hired consultants to perform an audit of their corporate culture. In a company, a leader is a person who understands, interprets, and manages the corporate value system. Effective managers, therefore, are action-oriented people who resolve conflict, are tolerant of ambiguity, stress, and change, and have a strong sense of purpose for themselves and their organizations.

If all this is true, I wonder about the role of the professional manager who moves from company to company. How can he or she quickly absorb the values and culture of different organizations? Or is there, indeed, an art of management that is totally transportable? Assuming that such fungible managers do exist, is it proper for them to manipulate the values of others?

What would have happened had Stephen and I carried the sadhu for two days back to the village and become involved with the villagers in his care? In four trips to Nepal, my most interesting experience occurred in 1975 when I lived in a Sherpa home in the Khumbu for five days while recovering from altitude sickness. The high point of Stephen's trip was an invitation to participate in a family funeral ceremony in Manang. Neither experience had to do with climbing the high passes of the Himalayas. Why were we so reluctant to try the lower path, the ambiguous trail? Perhaps because we did not have a leader who could reveal the greater purpose of the trip to us.

Why didn't Stephen, with his moral vision, opt to take the sadhu under his personal care? The answer is partly because Stephen was hard-stressed physically himself and partly because, without some support system that encompassed our involuntary and episodic community on the mountain, it was beyond his individual capacity to do so.

I see the current interest in corporate culture and corporate value systems as a positive response to pessimism such as Stephen's about the decline of the role of the individual in large organizations. Individuals who operate from a thoughtful set of personal values provide the foundation for a corporate culture. A corporate tradition that encourages freedom of inquiry, supports personal values, and reinforces a focused sense of direction can fulfill the need to combine individuality with the prosperity and success of the group. Without such corporate support, the individual is lost.

That is the lesson of the sadhu. In a complex corporate situation, the individual requires and deserves the support of the group. When people cannot find such support in their organizations, they don't know how to act. If such support is forthcoming, a person has a stake in the success of the group and can add much to the process of establishing and maintaining a corporate culture. Management's challenge is to be sensitive to individual needs, to shape them, and to direct and focus them for the benefit of the group as a whole.

For each of us the sadhu lives. Should we stop what we are doing and comfort him; or should we keep trudging up toward the high pass? Should I pause to help the derelict I pass on the street each night as I walk by the Yale Club en route to Grand Central Station? Am I his brother? What is the nature of our responsibility if we consider ourselves to be ethical persons? Perhaps it is to change the values of the group so that it can, with all its resources, take the other road.

BOWEN H. McCOY retired from Morgan Stanley in 1990 after 28 years of service. He is now a real estate and business counselor, a teacher and a philanthropist.

Editor's Note—This article was originally published in the September–October 1983 issue of *HBR*. For its republication as an HBR Classic, Bowen H. McCoy has written the commentary "When Do We Take a Stand?" to update his observations.

The Ethics of Edits
When a Crook Changes the Contract

SHEL HOROWITZ

When Richard fired Susan for insubordination, she was a department head who had worked her way up from an entry-level finance job. Richard asked Susan to sign a document that released the company from any claims related to her termination. She signed without protest and left the company. Once Susan was gone, things got weird. Something wasn't right with the audits, previously handled by Susan. A thorough investigation led to the discovery that Susan had embezzled more than $800,000 from Richard's company. Richard also learned she had been prosecuted for stealing thousands of dollars from a previous employer and was sentenced to three years' probation.

And when Richard sued her to regain the money, he received another shock: Susan had edited the termination contract, adding a clause that eliminated the company's ability to recover any claims against her. She had not told the company about the changes she made, which were not initialed on the document. But she freely admitted that she had doctored it. Richard had prepared the original document and did not realize Susan had changed it. And, because he was not aware of her previous conviction for large-scale fraud, he signed it without re-reading it—and without catching the alteration.

It is unfortunate that Richard did not exercise due diligence and check the document for unilateral changes before signing it. Software exists that would have surfaced these changes instantly.

Richard was clearly negligent and erred in not thoroughly reading the version of the document Susan signed. But it seems reasonable to conclude that the more grievous offense, likely to reach to fraud, is the cloaked change made by Susan, which protected her against any claims against her. Richard should consult counsel to explore ways to seek a legal remedy.

In the meantime, this case offers an interesting moment in which civil and moral law coincide. At its core is the principle of disclosure. Often at the heart of legal breaches, such as accounting irregularities, is the absence of disclosure. Similarly, a lack of disclosure is often the hallmark of moral and ethical lapses. Even a two-year-old child recognizes Randall as the villain in the film Monsters, Inc. Why? Because Randall operates in darkness and often appears in a slithering fashion, unannounced. The bottom line: If an issue is "on the table," it is more likely to be ethical; if it is "under the table" and cloaked, there is more likelihood of a legal and/or ethical lapse.

What Actually Happened

This case is still in the courts, and the laws in Richard's state are, unfortunately, ambiguous. Richard's lawyers argue that the document he signed was not the document he had prepared, and because he was not made aware of the changes, his signature was fraudulently obtained. Susan's lawyers say that he should have read the entire contract through again, and that the signature is binding.

All of this begs the question: How did Susan gain so much trust that she was able to embezzle that much money so easily? Here's Richard's analysis: "She was easy to manage. I got lulled to sleep. She always took direction, never complained, was compliant with all requests, and was very good at being a friend to everyone. She invited her department to her home each year, treated them well and in a nurturing way, and was their trusted advisor. When it came to tenure, this department, finance, had the best. It is very hard to figure this out when you are being manipulated by a master. Her every move was calculated and I was dealing from the perspective of trust and reasonableness."

Lessons Learned

Susan's betrayal caused a major wake-up call for Richard and for his company. Richard accepts responsibility for both failing to require adequate back-ground checks as Susan worked her way up to positions of greater authority, and for neglecting to re-read the contract after Susan returned it. These days, everyone who works for Richard, even a model employee (as Susan had appeared to be) undergoes rigorous screening before hiring or promotion. "We do credit checks, criminal checks, call every reference and check every previous employer."

SHEL HOROWITZ, author of *Principled Profit: Marketing That Puts People First,* initiated the Business Ethics Pledge movement at www.business-ethics-pledge.org.

UNIT 3

Business and Society: Contemporary Ethical, Social, and Environmental Issues

Unit Selections

Key Points to Consider

- How well are organizations responding to issues of work and family schedules, day care, and telecommuting?

- Should corporations and executives face criminal charges for unsafe products, dangerous working conditions, and industrial pollution?

- What ethical dilemmas are managements likely to face when conducting business in foreign environments?

Student Web Site

www.mhcls.com

Internet References

National Immigrant Forum
http://www.immigrationforum.org
Workopolis.com
http://sympatico.workopolis.com
United Nations Environment Programme (UNEP)
http://www.unep.ch
United States Trade Representative (USTR)
http://www.ustr.gov

© BananaStock/PunchStock

Both at home and abroad, there are social and environmental issues that have potential ethical consequences for management. Incidents of insider trading, deaths resulting from unsafe products or work environments, AIDS in the workplace, and the adoption of policies for involvement in the global market are a few of the issues that need to be seriously addressed by the management.

This unit investigates the nature and ramifications of prominent ethical, social, and environmental issues facing management today. The unit's articles are grouped into three sections. The first article scrutinizes the importance of companies gaining and maintaining trust in the marketplace. The last three articles in this subsection provide some thoughtful insight on ways companies are embracing customer service practices, how executives and their Human Resource teams are attempting to find better ways to deal with workplace romances, and how Starbucks is reaching out to both employees and customers with disabilities.

The first article in the second subsection explains why women aren't making it to the C-suite. The second article scrutinizes how companies can avoid green marketing myopia and improve consumer appeal for environmentally preferable products. The last article in this subsection probes deeply into rising attacks on America's most sensitive computer networks.

The subsection *Global Ethics* concludes this unit with readings that provide helpful insight on ethical issues and dilemmas inherent in multinational operations. They describe adapting ethical decisions to a global marketplace and offer guidelines for helping management deal with product quality and ethical issues in international markets as well as examining the complex social issues faced by professional women in South Korea.

Trust in the Marketplace

JOHN E. RICHARDSON AND LINNEA BERNARD MCCORD

Traditionally, ethics is defined as a set of moral values or principles or a code of conduct.

. . . Ethics, as an expression of reality, is predicated upon the assumption that there are right and wrong motives, attitudes, traits of character, and actions that are exhibited in interpersonal relationships. Respectful social interaction is considered a norm by almost everyone.

. . . the overwhelming majority of people perceive others to be ethical when they observe what is considered to be their genuine kindness, consideration, politeness, empathy, and fairness in their interpersonal relationships. When these are absent, and unkindness, inconsideration, rudeness, hardness, and injustice are present, the people exhibiting such conduct are considered unethical. A genuine consideration of others is essential to an ethical life. (Chewning, pp. 175–176).

An essential concomitant of ethics is of trust. Webster's Dictionary defines trust as "assured reliance on the character, ability, strength or truth of someone or something." Businesses are built on a foundation of trust in our free-enterprise system. When there are violations of this trust between competitors, between employer and employees, or between businesses and consumers, our economic system ceases to run smoothly. From a moral viewpoint, ethical behavior should not exist because of economic pragmatism, governmental edict, or contemporary fashionability—it should exist because it is morally appropriate and right. From an economic point of view, ethical behavior should exist because it just makes good business sense to be ethical and operate in a manner that demonstrates trustworthiness.

Robert Bruce Shaw, in *Trust in the Balance*, makes some thoughtful observations about trust within an organization. Paraphrasing his observations and applying his ideas to the marketplace as a whole:

1. Trust requires consumers have confidence in organizational promises or claims made to them. This means that a consumer should be able to believe that a commitment made will be met.
2. Trust requires integrity and consistency in following a known set of values, beliefs, and practices.
3. Trust requires concern for the well-being of others. This does not mean that organizational needs are not given

appropriate emphasis—but it suggests the importance of understanding the impact of decisions and actions on others—i.e. consumers. (Shaw, pp. 39–40)

Companies can lose the trust of their customers by portraying their products in a deceptive or inaccurate manner. In one recent example, a Nike advertisement exhorted golfers to buy the same golf balls used by Tiger Woods. However, since Tiger Woods was using custom-made Nike golf balls not yet available to the general golfing public, the ad was, in fact, deceptive. In one of its ads, Volvo represented that Volvo cars could withstand a physical impact that, in fact, was not possible. Once a company is "caught" giving inaccurate information, even if done innocently, trust in that company is eroded.

Companies can also lose the trust of their customers when they fail to act promptly and notify their customers of problems that the company has discovered, especially where deaths may be involved. This occurred when Chrysler dragged its feet in replacing a safety latch on its Minivan (Geyelin, pp. A1, A10). More recently, Firestone and Ford had been publicly brought to task for failing to expeditiously notify American consumers of tire defects in SUVs even though the problem had occurred years earlier in other countries. In cases like these, trust might not just be eroded, it might be destroyed. It could take years of painstaking effort to rebuild trust under these circumstances, and some companies might not have the economic ability to withstand such a rebuilding process with their consumers.

A *20/20* and *New York Times* investigation on a recent *ABC 20/20* program, entitled "The Car Dealer's Secret" revealed a sad example of the violation of trust in the marketplace. The investigation divulged that many unsuspecting consumers have had hidden charges tacked on by some car dealers when purchasing a new car. According to consumer attorney Gary Klein, "It's a dirty little secret that the auto lending industry has not owned up to." (*ABC News 20/20*)

The scheme worked in the following manner. Car dealers would send a prospective buyer's application to a number of lenders, who would report to the car dealer what interest rate the lender would give to the buyer for his or her car loan. This interest rate is referred to as the "buy rate." Legally a car dealer is not required to tell the buyer what the "buy rate" is or how much the dealer is marking up the loan. If dealers did most of the loans at the buy rate, they only get a small fee. However, if they were able to convince the buyer to pay a higher rate, they made considerably more money. Lenders encouraged car dealers to charge the buyer a higher rate than the "buy rate" by agreeing to split the extra income with the dealer.

David Robertson, head of the Association of Finance and Insurance Professionals—a trade group representing finance managers—defended the practice, reflecting that it was akin to a retail markup on loans. "The dealership provides a valuable service on behalf of the customer in negotiating these loans," he said. "Because of that, the dealership should be compensated for that work." (*ABC News 20/20*)

Careful examination of the entire report, however, makes one seriously question this apologetic. Even if this practice is deemed to be legal, the critical issue is what happens to trust when the buyers discover that they have been charged an additional 1–3% of the loan without their knowledge? In some cases, consumers were led to believe that they were getting the dealer's bank rate, and in other cases, they were told that the dealer had shopped around at several banks to secure the best loan rate they could get for the buyer. While this practice may be questionable from a legal standpoint, it is clearly in ethical breach of trust with the consumer. Once discovered, the companies doing this will have the same credibility and trustworthiness problems as the other examples mentioned above.

The untrustworthiness problems of the car companies was compounded by the fact that the investigation appeared to reveal statistics showing that black customers were twice as likely as whites to have their rate marked up—and at a higher level. That evidence—included in thousands of pages of confidential documents which *20/20* and *The New York Times* obtained from a Tennessee court—revealed that some Nissan and GM dealers in Tennessee routinely marked up rates for blacks, forcing them to pay between $300 and $400 more than whites. (*ABC News 20/20*)

This is a tragic example for everyone who was affected by this markup and was the victim of this secret policy. Not only is trust destroyed, there is a huge economic cost to the general public. It is estimated that in the last four years or so, Texas car dealers have received approximately $9 billion of kickbacks from lenders, affecting 5.2 million consumers. (*ABC News 20/20*)

Let's compare these unfortunate examples of untrustworthy corporate behavior with the landmark example of Johnson & Johnson which ultimately increased its trustworthiness with consumers by the way it handled the Tylenol incident. After seven individuals, who had consumed Tylenol capsules contaminated by a third party died, Johnson & Johnson instituted a total product recall within a week costing an estimated $50 million after taxes. The company did this, not because it was responsible for causing the problem, but because it was the right thing to do. In addition, Johnson & Johnson spearheaded the development of more effective tamper-proof containers for their industry. Because of the company's swift response, consumers once again were able to trust in the Johnson & Johnson name. Although Johnson & Johnson suffered a decrease in market share at the time because of the scare, over the long term it has maintained its profitability in a highly competitive market.

Certainly part of this profit success is attributable to consumers believing that Johnson & Johnson is a trustworthy company. (Robin and Reidenbach)

The e-commerce arena presents another example of the importance of marketers building a mutually valuable relationship with customers through a trust-based collaboration process. Recent research with 50 e-businesses reflects that companies which create and nurture trust find customers return to their sites repeatedly. (Dayal . . . . p. 64)

In the e-commerce world, six components of trust were found to be critical in developing trusting, satisfied customers:

- State-of-art reliable security measures on one's site
- Merchant legitimacy (e.g., ally one's product or service with an established brand)
- Order fulfillment (i.e. placing orders and getting merchandise efficiently and with minimal hassles)
- Tone and ambiance—handling consumers' personal information with sensitivity and iron-clad confidentiality
- Customers feeling that they are in control of the buying process
- Consumer collaboration—e.g., having chat groups to let consumers query each other about their purchases and experiences (Dayal . . . , pp. 64–67)

Additionally, one author noted recently that in the e-commerce world we've moved beyond brands and trademarks to "trustmarks." This author defined a trustmark as a

. . . (D)istinctive name or symbol that emotionally binds a company with the desires and aspirations of its customers. It's an emotional connection—and it's much bigger and more powerful than the uses that we traditionally associate with a trademark. . . . (Webber, p. 214)

Certainly if this is the case, trust—being an emotional link—is of supreme importance for a company that wants to succeed in doing business on the Internet.

It's unfortunate that while a plethora of examples of violation of trust easily come to mind, a paucity of examples "pop up" as noteworthy paradigms of organizational courage and trust in their relationship with consumers.

In conclusion, some key areas for companies to scrutinize and practice with regard to decisions that may affect trustworthiness in the marketplace might include:

- Does a company practice the Golden Rule with its customers? As a company insider, knowing what you know about the product, how willing would you be to purchase it for yourself or for a family member?
- How proud would you be if your marketing practices were made public. . . . shared with your friends. . . . or family? (Blanchard and Peale, p. 27)
- Are bottom-line concerns the sole component of your organizational decision-making process? What about human rights, the ecological/environmental impact, and other areas of social responsibility?
- Can a firm which engages in unethical business practices with customers be trusted to deal with its

employees any differently? Unfortunately, frequently a willingness to violate standards of ethics is not an isolated phenomenon but permeates the culture. The result is erosion of integrity throughout a company. In such cases, trust is elusive at best. (Shaw, p. 75)

- Is your organization not only market driven, but also value-oriented? (Peters and Levering, Moskowitz, and Katz)
- Is there a strong commitment to a positive corporate culture and a clearly defined mission which is frequently and unambiguously voiced by upper-management?
- Does your organization exemplify trust by practicing a genuine relationship partnership with your customers— *before, during, and after* the initial purchase? (Strout, p. 69)

Companies which exemplify treating customers ethically are founded on a covenant of trust. There is a shared belief, confidence, and faith that the company and its people will be fair, reliable, and ethical in all its dealings. ***Total trust is the belief that a company and its people will never take opportunistic advantage of customer vulnerabilities***. (Hart and Johnson, pp. 11–13)

References

ABC News 20/20, "The Car Dealer's Secret," October 27, 2000.

Blanchard, Kenneth, and Norman Vincent Peale, *The Power of Ethical Management*, New York: William Morrow and Company, Inc., 1988.

Chewning, Richard C., *Business Ethics in a Changing Culture* (Reston, Virginia: Reston Publishing, 1984).

Dayal, Sandeep, Landesberg, Helen, and Michael Zeissner, "How to Build Trust Online," *Marketing Management*, Fall 1999, pp. 64–69.

Geyelin, Milo, "Why One Jury Dealt a Big Blow to Chrysler in Minivan-Latch Case," *Wall Street Journal*, November 19, 1997, pp. A1, A10.

Hart, Christopher W. and Michael D. Johnson, "Growing the Trust Relationship," *Marketing Management*, Spring 1999, pp. 9–19.

Hosmer, La Rue Tone, *The Ethics of Management*, second edition (Homewood, Illinois: Irwin, 1991).

Kaydo, Chad, "A Position of Power," *Sales & Marketing Management*, June 2000, pp. 104–106, 108ff.

Levering, Robert; Moskowitz, Milton; and Michael Katz, *The 100 Best Companies to Work for in America* (Reading, Mass.: Addison-Wesley, 1984).

Magnet, Myron, "Meet the New Revolutionaries," *Fortune*, February 24, 1992, pp. 94–101.

Muoio, Anna, "The Experienced Customer," *Net Company*, Fall 1999, pp. 025–027.

Peters, Thomas J. and Robert H. Waterman Jr., *In Search of Excellence* (New York: Harper & Row, 1982).

Richardson, John (ed.), *Annual Editions: Business Ethics 00/01* (Guilford, CT: McGraw-Hill/Dushkin, 2000).

_____, *Annual Editions: Marketing 00/01* (Guilford, CT: McGraw-Hill/Dushkin, 2000).

Robin, Donald P., and Erich Reidenbach, "Social Responsibility, Ethics, and Marketing Strategy: Closing the Gap Between Concept and Application," *Journal of Marketing*, Vol. 51 (January 1987), pp. 44–58.

Shaw, Robert Bruce, *Trust in the Balance*, (San Francisco: Jossey-Bass Publishers, 1997).

Strout, Erin, "Tough Customers," *Sales Marketing Management*, January 2000, pp. 63–69.

Webber, Alan M., "Trust in the Future," *Fast Company*, September 2000, pp. 209–212ff.

DR. JOHN E. RICHARDSON is Professor of Marketing in the Graziadio School of Business and Management at Pepperdine University, Malibu, California. **DR. LINNEA BERNARD MCCORD** is Associate Professor of Business Law in the Graziadio School of Business and Management at Pepperdine University, Malibu, California.

Survey: Unethical Behavior Unreported

Second poll finds many teens think cheating, lying or violent behavior an acceptable means to an end.

JAMES C. HYATT

nethical behavior persists, and is even condoned under some circumstances, according to two separate surveys of workplace behavior and of teenage attitudes.

In the workplace over the past year, "more than half (56 percent) of employees surveyed had personally observed violations of company ethics standards, policy or the law," according to the Ethics Resource Center's (ERC) 2007 National Business Ethics Survey. Many saw multiple violations.

More than two of five employees (42 percent) who witnessed misconduct did not report it through any company channels, the survey found. The findings reflected interviews with almost 2,000 employees at U.S. public and private companies of all sizes.

"Despite new regulation and significant efforts to reduce misconduct and increase reporting when it does occur, the ethics risk landscape in American business is as treacherous as it was before implementation of the Sarbanes-Oxley Act of 2002," said ERC President Patricia Harned.

And among teenagers who consider themselves "ethically prepared," nearly 40 percent say it is sometimes necessary to cheat, plagiarize, lie or even behave violently to succeed, reported the fifth annual "Junior Achievement/Deloitte Teen Ethics Survey."

Pressure to succeed in school seems to be driving many teens' opinions that unethical behavior is an acceptable means to an end, the report summary said. "Of the teens who think plagiarism is acceptable on some level, 37 percent think a personal desire to succeed is justification. And that number climbs to 51 percent among students who feel overwhelming pressure to succeed.

Both studies, in general, concluded that more needs to be done to emphasize the consequences of unethical behavior.

According to Harned, "There is a strong sense of futility and fear among employees when it comes to reporting ethical misconduct, and that increases the danger to business. More than half (54 percent) of employees who witnessed but did not report misconduct believed that reporting would not lead to corrective action. More than a third (36 percent) of non-reporters feared retaliation from at least one source; but our research shows that having a strong ethical culture virtually eliminates retaliation."

She added: "Employees at all levels have not increased their 'ethical courage' in recent years. The rate of observed misconduct has crept back above where it was in 2000. And employees' willingness to report misconduct has not improved, either.

"The good news is that the rate of misconduct is cut by three-fourths at companies with strong ethical cultures, and reporting is doubled at companies with comprehensive ethics programs."

ERC helps organizations design and measure the strength of their culture and the effectiveness of ethics programs.

The study found less than 40 percent of employees are aware of comprehensive ethics and compliance programs at their companies. The programs are largely driven by legal and regulatory compliance, and designed in reaction to past mistakes. "The fact is, only about 25 percent of companies actually have a well-implemented ethics and compliance program in place, despite their transformative impact," Harned said.

The NBES also found most employees prefer to report misconduct to a person, especially someone with whom they already have a relationship, rather than to a company "hotline." Only three percent of misconduct reports were made to company hotlines.

Among other findings:

- Conflicts of interest (employees putting their own interest above their company's), lying to employees and abusive or intimidating behavior posed severe risk to companies in 2007.
- Companies faced high risk in several areas, including: Internet abuse; misreporting work time; lying to customers, vendors and the public; and discrimination.
- In general, the risks associated with abusive behavior and lying to stakeholders appear to rise with the number of company employees.

The Junior Achievement survey found "particularly alarming" its finding that 23 percent of teens surveyed think violence toward another person is acceptable on some level, including for settling an argument and revenge.

"The high percentages of teenagers who freely admit that unethical behavior can be justified is alarming," said David Miller, Ph.D., Executive Director of the Yale Center for Faith and Culture and Assistant Professor (Adjunct) of Business Ethics, who reviewed the findings. "It suggests an attitude of ethical relativism and rationalization of whatever actions serve one's immediate needs and purposes.

"This way of thinking will inevitably lead to unethical if not illegal actions that will damage individual lives and ruin corporate reputations," he said.

The survey also found that teens have difficulty in understanding that unethical behavior transcends the boundaries between private life, school or work life, and online behavior. More than a quarter (27 percent) of all teens surveyed said it is not fair for an employer to suspend or fire employees for unethical behavior outside of their jobs and another quarter (26 percent) said they weren't sure if it was fair or not.

CRO Trends is written by **James C. Hyatt** (JCHyatt@yahoo.com) a N.J.-based freelance writer formerly with *The Wall Street Journal*.

Congress Stops Playing Games with Toy Safety

David Lazarus

Enrique Barajas was poking around the little shops of the Toy District in downtown Los Angeles the other day with his 4-year-old daughter and 1-year-old son. The store shelves were packed with inexpensive imports, mostly from China.

Barajas, 27, said he liked buying toys for his kids, but he found it hard to know what was safe and what potentially could harm them.

"The government should be doing more," he said. "It's never enough, what they do."

That's about to change.

After months of wrangling, congressional leaders finally came to terms last week on landmark legislation that represents the most sweeping overhaul of U.S. product-safety rules in decades.

The Senate approved the bill Thursday after a similar vote by the House of Representatives a day earlier. President Bush is expected to sign the legislation into law.

"This is a huge deal," said Rachel Weintraub, director of product safety for the Consumer Federation of America. "It's going to change the products in the marketplace."

Not immediately, though. The various provisions of the bill would be enacted at different times over the coming months. That means shoppers will have to remain vigilant when buying toys and other goods this holiday season.

By next year at this time, though, the product-safety landscape could be very different. Among other things, the legislation would:

- Beef up the Consumer Product Safety Commission with new funding and resources. The commission is responsible for overseeing the safety of 15,000 product categories, including items as varied as toys, cribs, power tools and kitchen appliances.
- Require mandatory third-party testing of products for kids age 12 and under. Most such products are now subject to a mix of regulatory standards and frequently make it to store shelves without being tested in advance.
- Ban the sale of children's products containing lead and certain types of phthalates, which are chemicals used to soften plastic that have been linked to long-term health problems.

- Provide safeguards for whistle-blowers who alert authorities to unsafe products and industry practices.
- Establish a searchable database of all reports of deaths, injuries or illnesses related to consumer products.

The legislation would increase the penalty cap for civil fines to $100,000 from $5,000 for individual penalties and up to $15 million for violations involving multiple products. It also would require tracking labels that would allow officials to trace a product back to its factory in the event of a recall.

More than 45 million kids' products—mostly produced in Chinese factories—were recalled last year.

El Segundo's Mattel Inc., the world's largest toy maker, was responsible for about 20 million recalled toys. Some, like a die-cast vehicle depicting the Sarge character from "Cars," were found to have lead in the paint. Others had small magnets that posed a risk of internal injuries if swallowed.

Then there was Hasbro Inc.'s Easy-Bake Oven, nearly a million of which had to be recalled after dozens of little girls were burned or had their hands caught in the oven's door. One 5-year-old had to have a finger partially amputated.

Even though manufacturers and retailers vowed to crack down on defective products, the number of recalls of toys and children's products increased 22% in the nine months ended June 30 from a year earlier, according to government data.

"The 22% increase suggests strongly that what the toy industry called 'last year's problem' remains very much today's problem," said Ami Gadhia, policy counsel for Consumers Union.

Jim Neill, a spokesman for the National Assn. of Manufacturers, said businesses generally supported strengthening the Consumer Product Safety Commission but were wary of other aspects of the legislation.

He said his organization was particularly concerned about the whistle-blower provision and the database of potentially unsafe products, both of which, he said, could lead to "unintended consequences."

Neill also said a provision authorizing state attorneys general to help enforce federal safety laws "may blur the lines on national uniform standards."

At this point, consumers need all the help they can get. The Consumer Product Safety Commission has been a decidedly low priority for the Bush administration.

The three-person commission has been without a chair since July 2006, when Bush appointee Hal Stratton left to take a job with a law firm that specializes in shooting down class-action lawsuits filed by consumers.

In March 2007, Bush nominated Michael Baroody, a leading manufacturing industry lobbyist, to head the commission. Baroody withdrew from consideration after lawmakers demanded copies of his severance agreement with the National Assn. of Manufacturers.

It now appears likely that no one will be appointed to the long-vacant post until after a new president is sworn in.

Meanwhile, consumers' distrust of imported toys and the sour economy have taken a severe toll on many Toy District merchants. A number of shops have closed in recent months. Others are barely hanging on.

"There's no business," said Michael Chang, a salesman at W.T. Toys on 4th Street. "Many stores are closing."

He led me outside his shop and pointed to the adjacent toy stores. One went out of business a few months ago, Chang said. The other closed in July.

"Maybe we'll be closed by Christmas," Chang said of his own shop.

At nearby A-Mart Toys, salesman Michael La said the owner of his shop had already decided to pull the plug. "We're finished selling toys," he said.

In the coming months, La said, the shop will be restocked with some other product—bicycles, maybe.

What will be done with all the toys now filling the shelves, the Chinese-made dolls, action figures and remote-control cars?

La smiled. "We will sell them cheap to another company," he said.

The new product-safety legislation won't make those toys any safer. But it would go a long way toward ensuring that future toy shipments meet much higher standards.

Does It Pay to Be Good?

Yes, say advocates of corporate citizenship, who believe their time has come—finally.

A. J. VOGL

Corporate citizenship: For believers, the words speak of the dawning of a new era of capitalism, when business, government, and citizen groups join forces for the greater good, to jointly tackle such problems as water shortages and air pollution, to do something about the 1.2 billion people who live on less than a dollar a day.

Corporate citizenship: For critics of today's capitalism, the words smack of hypocrisy, big business' cynical response to charges of greed and corruption in high places, intended to mollify those who say corporations have too much power and that they wield it shamelessly. Critics charge that corporate citizenship is a placebo to the enemies of globalization, a public-relations smoke screen, capitalism's last-ditch attempt to preserve itself by co-opting its opposition.

Corporate citizenship: For many, it remains a diffuse concept, but generally it speaks to companies voluntarily adopting a triple bottom line, one that takes into account social, economic, and environmental considerations as well as financial results. Though some associate corporate citizenship with charity and philanthropy, the concept goes further—it embraces a corporate *conscience* above and beyond profits and markets. David Vidal, who directs research in global corporate citizenship at The Conference Board, comments, "Citizenship is not, as some critics charge, window dressing for the corporation. It deals with primary business relationships that are part of a company's strategic vision, and a good business case can be made for corporate citizenship."

Whether you are a critic or believer, however, there is no question that corporate citizenship—a term that embraces corporate social responsibility (CSR) and sustainability—is no longer a concept fostered by idealists on the fringe. It has entered the mainstream.

But why *now*? Though the era of corporate citizenship was ushered in with the fall of the Berlin Wall and the rise of market capitalism worldwide, current sentiment against big business has given new weight to the cause. Virtually every opinion survey shows that people think corporations have too much power, and that they will do anything in the pursuit of profits. And now, to add to public distrust, we have a flagging economy, a shambolic stock market, and what have been called "pornographic" CEO salaries. These circumstances have given citizenship's champions new planks for their platform, such as accounting and compensation practices. At the same time, attacks on the very nature of business have sent corporate leaders searching for a bright spot, and that spot may very well be the concept of corporate citizenship.

But that makes corporate enthusiasm for citizenship sound like a calculated, even cynical stance that is likely to last only as long as the environment remains hostile. There are grounds for believing that it is more than that, that it speaks to deeper changes in the greater world that make it *necessary* for large corporations to do good. Some of these changes include:

Tightening regulatory pressures. France, for instance, requires all companies listed on the Paris Stock Exchange to include information about their social and environmental performance within their financial statements; the Johannesburg Stock Exchange requires compliance with a CSR-based code of conduct; and the United Kingdom (the first nation with a minister for corporate social responsibility) requires pension-fund managers to disclose the degree to which social and environmental criteria are part of their investment decisions.

Will there be more national legislation? "If you had asked me that three or four years ago, I would have answered, 'Unclear, or probably not,'" says Allen White. White is acting chief executive of Global Reporting Initiative, an Amsterdam-based organization that has developed uniform guidelines for CSR reporting. "But in 2002 we've seen developments that could not have been anticipated several years ago, developments that have challenged companies to reconstruct or restore credibility, challenges to markets to demonstrate to investors that available information is accurate. Governments have taken note and are considering legislative and regulatory action."

Changing demographics. A socially engaged and better-educated population demands that the companies with which they do business—as consumers, employees, or investors—conform to higher standards. Both consumers and employees tell researchers that they prefer to purchase from and work for a company that is a good corporate citizen. On the investor front,

Investors Are Listening

For companies in sectors not considered exemplars of corporate citizenship—munitions, pornography, gambling, and tobacco (yes); liquor (probably); and oil (maybe)—there's good news: The market hasn't penalized them for their supposed lack of citizenship. For companies at the opposite end of the spectrum, there's also good news: Investors haven't penalized them for their expenditures on social causes.

On balance, the better news is for the socially responsible companies, who have long labored under the assumption that the investor automatically pays a price for investing in a socially responsible company or mutual fund—the price, of course, being a company or fund that doesn't perform as well as its peers that don't fly the socially-responsible banner.

Investors appear to be listening. According to Financial Research Corp., investors added $1.29 billion of new money into socially responsible funds during the first half of 2002, compared to $847.1 million added during all of 2001. Over the year ending July 31, the average mutual fund—including stock, bond, and balanced funds—was down 13 percent, while comparable socially responsible funds were down 19 percent. But advocates point out that different indices—particularly the Domini Social Index, a capitalization-weighted market index of 400 common stocks screened according to social and environmental criteria, and the Citizen's Index, a market-weighted portfolio of common stocks representing ownership in 300 of the most socially responsible U.S. companies, have outperformed the S&P 500 over the last one, three, and five years.

While the $13 billion invested in socially responsible funds (according to Morningstar) comprises only about 2 percent of total fund assets, advocates expect this percentage to climb to 10 percent by 2012, says Barbara Krumsiek, chief executive of the Bethesda, Md.-based Calvert Group, a mutual-fund complex specializing in socially responsible investing. And others' tallies are far higher: The nonprofit Social Investment Forum counts more than $2 trillion in total assets under management in portfolios screened for socially concerned investors, including socially screened mutual funds and separate accounts managed for socially conscious institutions and individual investors.

Plus, recent corporate scandals may have raised many investors' consciousness: In the first half of 2002, socially responsible mutual funds saw their assets increase by 3 percent, while conventional diversified funds lost 9.5 percent in total assets. People may have decided that if their mutual-fund investments were going to lose money, it might as well be for a good cause.

—A.J.V.

activists—including individuals, socially responsible mutual funds, public pension funds, and religious groups—submitted 800 resolutions in 2002, according to Meg Voorhes, director of the social-issues department at Investor Responsibility Research Center, a Washington, D.C.-based organization that tracks proxies.

More opportunity for investors to back their convictions with money. Socially aware investors can choose among some 230 mutual funds, and, according to Steven J. Schueth of the nonprofit Social Investment Forum, more than 800 independent asset managers identify themselves as managers of socially responsible portfolios for institutional investors and high-net-worth individuals. (See "Investors Are Listening.") Indexes of social and environmental performance—like the Dow Jones Sustainability World Indexes and FTSE4Good—are becoming significant market factors in screening for good citizenship. These indexes have teeth in them: They will and do drop companies that fail to meet social-responsibility standards.

Pressure from nongovernmental organizations. Not only are international NGOs growing in number—at last count, there were 28,000 worldwide—their visibility and credibility are on the rise. Last year, PR executive Richard Edelman told the World Economic Forum, "NGOs are now the Fifth Estate in global governance—the true credible source on issues related to the environment and social justice." While Americans generally trust corporations more than NGO "brands," the opposite is true in Europe. A study conducted by Edelman's firm found that Amnesty International, the World Wildlife Fund, and Greenpeace outstripped by a margin of nearly two to one the four highest-rated corporations in Europe: Microsoft, Bayer, Shell, and Ford. As in other areas, it appears, European public opinion affirming social responsibility is ahead of that of the United States.

The most prominent corporate citizens rarely receive commensurate rewards.

Greater transparency. If good news travels fast, bad news moves faster. The Internet has given a platform to critics who, if they existed before, could be ignored; now they will be heard. There is the by-now-classic story of MIT graduate student Jonah Peretti, who submitted the word *sweatshop* to Nike's personalize-your-shoes iD program. Nike refused the order, terming the word "inappropriate slang." Peretti replied, "I have decided to order the shoes with a different iD, but I would like to make one small request. Could you please send me a color snapshot of the ten-year-old Vietnamese girl who makes my shoes?" His e-mail correspondence was forwarded around the world and picked up by the mass media. Nike, in its first annual "corporate responsibility report," responded convincingly to charges that it exploited workers—indeed, the company is generally known as a CSR innovator—but inevitably sounded defensive.

Bringing Standards up to Code

In May 2000, the International Chamber of Commerce counted more than 40 codes, existing or in preparation, intended to govern the activities of global corporations; among the most prominent are those of the OECD, the U.N. Global Compact, and the International Labor Organization.

Companies may be forgiven for having been confused over which set of guidelines to follow.

That confusion appears to be on the way to being lifted through the "2002 Sustainability Reporting Guidelines," introduced at the World Summit in Johannesburg by the Global Reporting Initiative. The guidelines are not another code. Rather, they are an attempt to create a generally accepted reporting framework for social responsibility. The outcome of two years of work by GRI, the guidelines are a rejoinder to the "deep scepticism" that "the creation of new wealth . . . will do anything to decrease social inequities," as the document's introduction states. In nearly 100 pages, the guidelines cover such issues as transparency, sustainability, auditability, and comparability.

The last of these issues is critical, argues Eric Israel, a partner at BearingPoint, the consultancy formerly known as KPMG Consulting. "The meaning of citizenship for one particular company can be completely different than for another," he says. "So how do you benchmark an organization and compare it to others in the same industry? Up to now, there's been no equivalent of GAAP for social responsibility. That's where GRI comes in with its guidelines."

How does one verify that GRI guidelines have been met? Since the advent of CSR codes, companies have hired organizations, ranging from consultancies like BearingPoint to single-issue nonprofits, to verify their compliance for onlookers' eyes. Some monitor the companies themselves and attest that standards are being met—for instance, Chiquita Brands International has partnered with the Rainforest Alliance, which sends inspectors to each farm and offers its Better Bananas seal of approval to products from those farms that pass muster.

Other firms simply verify companies' CSR reports, the public face of compliance with codes. Considering the many codes in circulation and the range of organizations hired to verify compliance, it's not easy to put any particular report in broader context. That's where another organization, London-based AccountAbility, enters the picture.

Last June, AccountAbility issued something called the AA1000S Assurance Standard, which outlines principles around verification and CSR auditing—and which the firm hopes will become the gold standard of CSR verification standards. AccountAbility has credibility because of its governing constituencies—businesses, nonprofits, accountancies, researchers and academics, and consultancies—and its endorsement of GRI's reporting guidelines will likely give a boost to acceptance of both. "What we do is entirely complementary to what GRI does," says AccountAbility COO Mike Peirce. "It's a marriage made in heaven." In future, then, expect to see more annual reports that cite GRI guidelines verified by accountants using AccountAbility standards.

But the existence of these codes and organizations is only a first step; there's still a long way to go. According to a recent OECD survey, only one in five companies with codes of conduct share compliance information with the public, and third-party auditing remains the exception rather than the rule.

—A.J.V.

All of these factors have led to increasing corporate acceptance of the importance of citizenship. Every three years, BearingPoint, the consultancy formerly known as KPMG Consulting, surveys global *Fortune* 250 companies on corporate-responsibility issues. The latest survey found that 45 percent of the 250 companies surveyed issued environmental, social, and/or sustainability reports in 2001, up from 35 percent in 1998, and the number of U.S. companies that issued such reports increased 14 percent over the same period. Today, too, two-thirds of the world's largest companies use their Websites to trumpet their social and environmental activities.

Which is not to say that all these corporations have become true believers. "[W]e have to acknowledge," writes Steve Hilton, a British CSR consultant, "that fear of exposure and the need for compliance are the most powerful forces galvanizing the majority of active corporate citizens."

No Good Deed Goes Unpunished

As necessary as corporate citizenship may be, it still faces challenges from both inside and outside the corner office. Perhaps the most disheartening of these hurdles is that the most prominent corporate citizens rarely receive rewards commensurate with their prominence. As Hilton and Giles Gibbons, co-authors of the pro-CSR *Good Business: Your World Needs You*, point out, "Curiously, the companies whose hearts are most visibly fixed to their pinstriped sleeves tend to be the ones that attract the most frequent and venomous attacks from anti-business critics." Is this because critics feel that devious agendas lie behind the enlightened policies? Noreena Hertz, a British critic of corporate citizenship, wonders whether Microsoft, by putting computers in schools today, will determine how children learn tomorrow.

Is it that corporations haven't gotten their stories across properly, or that they *have*—and are still being vilified? The experience of McDonald's in this arena is revealing. Last April, the fast-food chain published its first social-responsibility report, composed of 46 pages summarizing its efforts in four categories: community, environment, people, and marketplace. Those efforts have been rewarded in some courts of public opinion: In 2000 and 2001 *Financial Times*/PricewaterhouseCoopers surveys of media and NGOs, McDonald's placed 14th among the world's most respected companies for environmental performance.

At the same time, few corporations have been attacked as savagely as McDonald's for its "citizenship." It has been portrayed as an omnivorous monster that destroys local businesses and culture, promotes obesity, treats its employees badly, and despoils the environment. McDonald's goes to great lengths to answer these charges in its social-responsibility report—which was itself widely criticized—but, like Nike, it can't help looking defensive. It will take a great deal more than a report of its good works to diminish the Golden Arches as a symbol of "capitalist imperialism" in the eyes of antiglobalists or to stanch the vitriol on such Websites as Mcspotlight.

There's no question that the bar is set exceedingly high in the arena of corporate social involvement. Philip Morris Cos. spends more than $100 million a year, most conspicuously in a series of TV commercials, on measures to discourage underage smoking—and still critics charge that the Philip Morris campaign is a cynical PR stunt that actually *encourages* kids to smoke. The company has been accused of having "a profound conflict of interest that cannot be overcome."

Another tobacco company, BAT, the world's second-largest, put some members of the social-responsibility establishment in an uncomfortable position when, last July, it became the industry's first company to publish a social-responsibility report. Few knew what to think upon reading the tobacco company's blunt rhetoric—"[T]here is no such thing as a 'safe' cigarette. . . . We openly state that, put simply, smoking is a cause of certain serious diseases"—and the 18 pages devoted to the risks of smoking. BAT even had its report audited by an independent verifier. All this wasn't nearly enough to satisfy antismoking groups, of course—they continue to view the company with deep suspicion. Would anyone have predicted otherwise?

When accused of being overly suspicious, critics point to one company that, over the last six years, won numerous awards for its environmental, human rights, anti-corruption, anti-bribery, and climate-change policies; a company prominent on "most admired" and "best companies to work for" lists; a company that issued a report on the good deeds that supported its claim to be a top corporate citizen. That company was Enron.

No one would argue that Enron is typical, yet its debacle has tainted other companies. It also raises a difficult question about CSR: What is the link between how a company is managed—corporate governance—and corporate citizenship? Steve Hilton, speaking from London, says that the link is not really understood in the United Kingdom: "People here have not made the connection between the corporate-governance, executive-compensation, and accounting-fraud issues in the United States and operational issues that come under the heading of corporate citizenship. I would argue they're all part of the same thing."

So would Transparency International's Frank Vogl, co-founder of the anti-corruption NGO. He believes that CSR has been undermined because it has been disconnected from corporate-conduct issues. "Foreign public trust in Corporate America has been diminished," he said, "and there is scant evidence that U.S. business leaders recognize the global impact of the U.S. scandals."

Vogl says that, for most countries in the world, corruption is much more of a social-responsibility issue than either the environment or labor rights. "What U.S. businesspeople see as a facilitating payment may be seen in developing countries as a bribe," he comments, "and I think that provides some insight into why the United States ranks behind 12 other countries on the Transparency International Bribe Payers Index. To me, corporate citizenship means you don't bribe foreign officials. That's the worst kind of hypocrisy."

Will They Be Good in Bad Times?

The specter of hypocrisy raises its head in another quarter as well: Do employees of companies claiming to be good corporate citizens see their employer's citizenship activities as a diversion or cover-up to charges of bad leadership and poor management practices? Certainly, if recent surveys are a guide, top management needs to restore its credibility with employees. In a recent Mercer Human Resource Consulting study, only a third of the 2,600 workers surveyed agreed with the statement, "I can trust management in my organization to always communicate honestly." And a Walker Information survey of employees found that only 49 percent believe their senior leaders to be "people of high personal integrity." If CSR is perceived by employees merely as puffery to make top management look good, it will not get under an organization's cultural skin.

Businesses needn't apologize for making products that other Americans want to buy.

Even if there is a genuine management commitment, corporations have other obligations that may take precedence, begging the question: Will corporations be good citizens in bad times as well as good? The experience of Ford Motor Co. brings the question to earth. In August, Ford issued its third annual corporate-citizenship report. Previous reports had drawn plaudits from environmentalists, but this one, coming at a time when the automaker faced financial difficulties, was attacked by the same environmentalists for failing to set aggressive goals for reducing greenhouse-gas emissions or improving gas mileage. Sierra Club's executive director called it "a giant step in the wrong direction for Ford Motor Co., for American consumers, and for the environment."

Lingering tough economic conditions may impel other companies to take their own "giant steps" backward. An old business saw has it that when times get tough and cuts have to be made, certain budgets are at the top of the list for cutbacks—advertising for one, public relations for another. For companies in which corporate citizenship is seen as an extension of public relations, of "image building" or "reputation management," it may suffer this fate.

Which is as it should be, say some critics. As *The Wall Street Journal* lectured CEO William Ford on its editorial page: "We also hope Mr. Ford has learned from his mistake of ceding the moral and political high ground to environmentalists. . . .

Businesses needn't apologize for making products that other Americans want to buy. Their first obligation is to their shareholders and employees and that means above all making an honest profit."

Attacked from All Sides

While many skeptics criticize the ways in which corporate social responsibility is enacted, some take matters a step further by asking if the concept should exist at all. Who would object to the idea of a company doing good, of moving beyond the traditional and literal bottom line, to take a larger view of the reason for its existence? You may be surprised: There are many critics, and they come from various and sometimes unpredictable directions.

First is a group that says corporate social responsibility is flawed at its heart because it's doing the right thing for the wrong reason. The right thing, they believe, is doing the right thing because it is right, as a matter of principle—not because it advances the firm's business interests. The rejoinder, of course, is that if a larger social or environmental good is met, we should not quibble about motivation. As corporate-governance activist Robert A.G. Monks points out: "You can get backing from institutional investors only if you talk a commercial idiom."

Next is a group of dissimilar critics who believe that, in attempting to pursue goals of corporate citizenship, companies are doing things that are none of their business. Paradoxically, these critics come from both the right and the left.

The right feels that the business of business should be business: As Michael Prowse argues in the *Financial Times*, the role of the corporation "is to provide individuals with the means to be socially responsible. Rather than trying to play the role of social worker, senior executives should concentrate on their statutory obligations. We should not expect benevolence of them, but we should demand probity: the socially responsible chief executive is the one who turns a profit without lying, cheating, robbing or defrauding anyone."

The left, on the other hand, feels that corporations are usurping the powers of government, to the detriment of the citizenry and democracy itself. Noreena Hertz, the British academic and broadcaster who wrote of *The Silent Takeover: Global Capitalism and the Death of Democracy,* is not only dubious about business taking over responsibilities that she feels properly belong to government—she is skeptical about business' ability to handle them: "[M]anagers of multinationals operating in the third world are often overwhelmed by the social problems they encounter, and understandably find it difficult to know which causes to prioritize. . . . Their contributions can be squandered, or diverted through corruption."

And what happens, she asks, when a corporation decides to pull out, if government has allowed private industry to take over its role? Worse still, she worries about situations in which a socially responsible corporation could use its position "to exact a stream of IOUs and quid pro quos, to demand ever more favorable terms and concessions from host governments."

Then there is a group of critics who see corporate citizenship as a diversionary ploy to placate a public outraged at dubious corporate practices. They will concede that Enron, WorldCom, and Tyco are egregious exceptions, but are other companies exemplars of probity? Hardly. Can companies be considered good corporate citizens when they move their headquarters to Bermuda to avoid taxes (and enrich their CEOs in the process)? Can companies like General Electric, Monsanto, Merck, SmithKline Beecham, and Chiquita Brands International claim the moral high ground when they have cut employee benefits in connection with mergers and spinoffs? And what of such companies as Wyeth, Wal-Mart, McKesson, and Merrill Lynch? Can they, ask the critics, be considered high-minded citizens when the top executives accumulate pots of money in their deferred-compensation accounts? This may be why PR *eminence grise* John Budd says, "For at least the next 18 post-Enron months, I certainly would not counsel any CEO to magically appear publicly as an enlightened champion of social responsibility. The circumstances make it automatic that it would be perceived as spinning."

Last, there is a group of critics that says that simply doing more good than we're doing now is not enough, that we have to rethink the nature of the beast—capitalism itself. Steven Piersanti, president of Berrett-Koehler Publishers, is in the thick of this intellectual contretemps. Last fall, his firm published two books that took divergent views on the issue. The first, *Walking the Talk*, was written by Swiss industrialist Stephan Schmidheiny, along with two colleagues at the World Business Council for Sustainable Development, Chad Holliday of DuPont and Philip Watts of Royal Dutch/Shell. "It advances a reformist view that major changes are needed in our business world," says Piersanti, "but that these changes can best be achieved by reforms within our existing economic structures, institutions, and systems." The second book, *Alternatives to Economic Globalization: A Better World Is Possible*, presents "an activist view that existing economic structures are insufficient and that new structures, institutions, and systems are needed in the world."

It's likely that doubts about the nature and purpose of corporate citizenship will continue to be raised from all quarters. But with social-responsibility reporting and verification initiatives in place and likely government regulation down the road, there's reason to think that their voices will become more isolated.

—A.J.V.

Does the "Business Case" Really Have a Case?

But hold on: What about the so-called business case for corporate citizenship—that it contributes to making "an honest profit"? Unfortunately, it's difficult to quantify in cost-benefit terms what that contribution is. Not something to be concerned about, says Simon Zadek, CEO of AccountAbility, a London-based institute that has established CSR verification standards. (See "Bringing Standards Up to Code.") "It is a fact that the vast majority of day-to-day business decisions are taken without any explicit cost-benefit analysis," he says, pointing to employee training as an example of a corporate expenditure that is difficult to quantify in cost-benefit terms. What he doesn't mention is that, when business is suffering, training is usually among the expenditures to be cut back or eliminated.

Ultimately, Zadek concedes that, in strictly quantifiable terms, one cannot make a cost-benefit case for corporate citizenship. "Although the question 'Does corporate citizenship pay?' is technically right, it is misleading in practice," he says. "Rephrasing the core question as 'In what ways does corporate citizenship contribute to achieving the core business strategy?' is far preferable."

To some hardheaded corporate types, Zadek's reasoning may seem disingenuous, but even the hardheads can't be dismissive—at least publicly. Moreover, they would probably acknowledge that corporate citizenship, in concept and practice, has come too far to be ignored. In the future, it may well become what Steve Hilton calls a "hygiene factor," a condition of doing business. Hilton's firm, Good Business, consults with firms on citizenship issues. "I think business leaders are coming to realize CSR's potential to go beyond a compliance/risk-management issue into a genuine business tool," he says. "That's been the rhetoric all along, but the reality has been that it's been a slightly marginal issue. With few exceptions, it's been seen as an add-on, without being incorporated into core business decision-making."

This is Zadek's point when he argues the case for what he calls "third-generation corporate citizenship." The first generation is defined by cause-related marketing and short-term reputation management. The second occurs when social and environmental objectives become a core part of long-term business strategy; as an example, he points to automakers competing in the arena of emission controls. The third generation is based on collective action, where corporations join with competitors, NGOs, and government "to change the underlying rules of the game to ensure that business delivers adequate social and environmental results."

Changing the rules means, for one thing, a more level playing field. "In CSR," says AccountAbility COO Mike Peirce, "companies that are leaders might suffer a penalty if there's a big gap between themselves and laggards in the field, so they'd like

everybody ticking along at at least a basic level." In other words, a socially responsible company does not want to be penalized financially for being socially responsible. Of course, a cynic might reply that if CSR indeed provides the competitive advantage that its proponents insist it does, then it is the laggards that should suffer the severest financial penalty.

Expect citizenship proponents to make corporate governance itself the issue.

To convince doubters, efforts are being made to schematically quantify corporate social responsibility. In a recent *Harvard Business Review* article titled "The Virtue Matrix: Calculating the Return on Corporate Responsibility," Roger L. Martin makes a point of treating corporate responsibility as a product or service like any other. According to Martin, who is dean of the University of Toronto's Rotman School of Management, his matrix can help companies sort out such questions as whether a citizenship initiative will erode a company's competitive position.

Even if Martin's formula seems overly clinical, it supports the trend toward closer analysis of what social responsibility means and what it brings to corporations practicing it. But analysis will take you only so far. "[I]t is impossible to prove the direction of the flow of causality," writes Chad Holliday, chairman and CEO of DuPont and co-author of *Walking the Talk: The Business Case for Sustainable Development.* "Does a company become profitable and thus enjoy the luxury of being able to worry about environmental and social issues or does the pursuit of sustainability make a company more profitable?"

But for large public companies, the question of whether it truly pays to be good will be asked less and less; for them, it will be *necessary* to be good, if only to avoid appearing Neanderthal. That means that corporate social responsibility, itself nothing less than a growth industry today, will become "normalized" into corporate cultures.

Yes, there will be an effort to level the playing field in CSR, but, further, expect citizenship proponents to attempt to raise the field to a higher level by making corporate governance itself the issue. "Unless we make basic structural changes," says Marjorie Kelly, the editor of *Business Ethics* magazine and a frequent critic of CSR, "it'll be nothing but window dressing. The corporate scandals have given a real-world demonstration that business without ethics collapses, and that has given us an extraordinary opportunity to change the way we do business."

A. J. VOGL is editor of *Across the Board.* He wrote "Worry About the Details" in the Sept/Oct issue.

Women and the Labyrinth *of* Leadership

When you put all the pieces together, a new picture emerges for why women don't make it into the C-suite. It's not the glass ceiling, but the sum of many obstacles along the way.

ALICE H. EAGLY AND LINDA L. CARLI

If one has misdiagnosed a problem, then one is unlikely to prescribe an effective cure. This is the situation regarding the scarcity of women in top leadership. Because people with the best of intentions have misread the symptoms, the solutions that managers are investing in are not making enough of a difference.

That there is a problem is not in doubt. Despite years of progress by women in the workforce (they now occupy more than 40% of all managerial positions in the United States), within the C-suite they remain as rare as hens' teeth. Consider the most highly paid executives of *Fortune 500* companies—those with titles such as chairman, president, chief executive officer, and chief operating officer. Of this group, only 6% are women. Most notably, only 2% of the CEOs are women, and only 15% of the seats on the boards of directors are held by women. The situation is not much different in other industrialized countries. In the 50 largest publicly traded corporations in each nation of the European Union, women make up, on average, 11% of the top executives and 4% of the CEOs and heads of boards. Just seven companies, or 1%, of *Fortune* magazine's Global 500 have female CEOs. What is to blame for the pronounced lack of women in positions of power and authority?

In 1986 the *Wall Street Journal's* Carol Hymowitz and Timothy Schellhardt gave the world an answer: "Even those few women who rose steadily through the ranks eventually crashed into an invisible barrier. The executive suite seemed within their grasp, but they just couldn't break through the glass ceiling." The metaphor, driven home by the article's accompanying illustration, resonated; it captured the frustration of a goal within sight but somehow unattainable. To be sure, there was a time when the barriers were absolute. Even within the career spans of 1980s-era executives, access to top posts had been explicitly denied. Consider comments made by President Richard Nixon, recorded on White House audiotapes and made public through the Freedom of Information Act. When explaining why he

would not appoint a woman to the U.S. Supreme Court, Nixon said, "I don't think a woman should be in any government job whatsoever . . . mainly because they are erratic. And emotional. Men are erratic and emotional, too, but the point is a woman is more likely to be." In a culture where such opinions were widely held, women had virtually no chance of attaining influential leadership roles.

Times have changed, however, and the glass ceiling metaphor is now more wrong than right. For one thing, it describes an absolute barrier at a specific high level in organizations. The fact that there have been female chief executives, university presidents, state governors, and presidents of nations gives the lie to that charge. At the same time, the metaphor implies that women and men have equal access to entry- and mid-level positions. They do not. The image of a transparent obstruction also suggests that women are being misled about their opportunities, because the impediment is not easy for them to see from a distance. But some impediments are not subtle. Worst of all, by depicting a single, unvarying obstacle, the glass ceiling fails to incorporate the complexity and variety of challenges that women can face in their leadership journeys. In truth, women are not turned away only as they reach the penultimate stage of a distinguished career. They disappear in various numbers at many points leading up to that stage.

Metaphors matter because they are part of the storytelling that can compel change. Believing in the existence of a glass ceiling, people emphasize certain kinds of interventions: top-to-top networking, mentoring to increase board memberships, requirements for diverse candidates in high-profile succession horse races, litigation aimed at punishing discrimination in the C-suite. None of these is counterproductive; all have a role to play. The danger arises when they draw attention and resources away from other kinds of interventions that might attack the problem more potently. If we want to make better progress, it's time to rename the challenge.

Walls All Around

A better metaphor for what confronts women in their professional endeavors is the labyrinth. It's an image with a long and varied history in ancient Greece, India, Nepal, native North and South America, medieval Europe, and elsewhere. As a contemporary symbol, it conveys the idea of a complex journey toward a goal worth striving for. Passage through a labyrinth is not simple or direct, but requires persistence, awareness of one's progress, and a careful analysis of the puzzles that lie ahead. It is this meaning that we intend to convey. For women who aspire to top leadership, routes exist but are full of twists and turns, both unexpected and expected. Because all labyrinths have a viable route to the center, it is understood that goals are attainable. The metaphor acknowledges obstacles but is not ultimately discouraging.

If we can understand the various barriers that make up this labyrinth, and how some women find their way around them, we can work more effectively to improve the situation. What are the obstructions that women run up against? Let's explore them in turn.

Vestiges of prejudice. It is a well-established fact that men as a group still have the benefit of higher wages and faster promotions. In the United States in 2005, for example, women employed full-time earned 81 cents for every dollar that men earned. Is this true because of discrimination or simply because, with fewer family demands placed on them and longer careers on average, men are able to gain superior qualifications? Literally hundreds of correlational studies by economists and sociologists have attempted to find the answer.

One of the most comprehensive of these studies was conducted by the U.S. Government Accountability Office. The study was based on survey data from 1983 through 2000 from a representative sample of Americans. Because the same people responded to the survey repeatedly over the years, the study provided accurate estimates of past work experience, which is important for explaining later wages.

The GAO researchers tested whether individuals' total wages could be predicted by sex and other characteristics. They included part-time and full-time employees in the surveys and took into account all the factors that they could estimate and that might affect earnings, such as education and work experience. Without controls for these variables, the data showed that women earned about 44% less than men, averaged over the entire period from 1983 to 2000. With these controls in place, the gap was only about half as large, but still substantial. The control factors that reduced the wage gap most were the different employment patterns of men and women: Men undertook more hours of paid labor per year than women and had more years of job experience.

Marriage and parenthood are associated with higher wages for men but not for women.

Although most variables affected the wages of men and women similarly, there were exceptions. Marriage and parenthood, for instance, were associated with higher wages for men but not for women. In contrast, other characteristics, especially years of education, had a more positive effect on women's wages than on men's. Even after adjusting wages for all of the ways men and women differ, the GAO study, like similar studies, showed that women's wages remained lower than men's. The unexplained gender gap is consistent with the presence of wage discrimination.

Similar methods have been applied to the question of whether discrimination affects promotions. Evidently it does. Promotions come more slowly for women than for men with equivalent qualifications. One illustrative national study followed workers from 1980 to 1992 and found that white men were more likely to attain managerial positions than white women, black men, and black women. Controlling for other characteristics, such as education and hours worked per year, the study showed that white men were ahead of the other groups when entering the labor market and that their advantage in attaining managerial positions grew throughout their careers. Other research has underscored these findings. Even in culturally feminine settings such as nursing, librarianship, elementary education, and social work (all specifically studied by sociologist Christine Williams), men ascend to supervisory and administrative positions more quickly than women.

The findings of correlational studies are supported by experimental research, in which subjects are asked to evaluate hypothetical individuals as managers or job candidates, and all characteristics of these individuals are held constant except for their sex. Such efforts continue the tradition of the Goldberg paradigm, named for a 1968 experiment by Philip Goldberg. His simple, elegant study had student participants evaluate written essays that were identical except for the attached male or female name. The students were unaware that other students had received identical material ascribed to a writer of the other sex. This initial experiment demonstrated an overall gender bias: Women received lower evaluations unless the essay was on a feminine topic. Some 40 years later, unfortunately, experiments continue to reveal the same kind of bias in work settings. Men are advantaged over equivalent women as candidates for jobs traditionally held by men as well as for more gender-integrated jobs. Similarly, male leaders receive somewhat more favorable evaluations than equivalent female leaders, especially in roles usually occupied by men.

Interestingly, however, there is little evidence from either the correlational or the experimental studies that the odds are stacked higher against women with each step up the ladder—that is, that women's promotions become progressively less likely than men's at higher levels within organizations. Instead, a general bias against women appears to operate with approximately equal strength at all levels. The scarcity of female corporate officers is the sum of discrimination that has operated at all ranks, not evidence of a particular obstacle to advancement as women approach the top. The problem, in other words, is not a glass ceiling.

Resistance to women's leadership. What's behind the discrimination we've been describing? Essentially, a set of widely shared conscious and unconscious mental associations about women, men, and leaders. Study after study has affirmed that people associate women and men with different traits and link men with more of the traits that connote leadership. Kim Campbell, who briefly served as the prime minister of Canada in 1993, described the tension that results:

> I don't have a traditionally female way of speaking. . . . I'm quite assertive. If I didn't speak the way I do, I wouldn't have been seen as a leader. But my way of speaking may have grated on people who were not used to hearing it from a woman. It was the right way for a leader to speak, but it wasn't the right way for a woman to speak. It goes against type.

In the language of psychologists, the clash is between two sets of associations: communal and agentic. Women are associated with communal qualities, which convey a concern for the compassionate treatment of others. They include being especially affectionate, helpful, friendly, kind, and sympathetic, as well as interpersonally sensitive, gentle, and soft-spoken. In contrast, men are associated with agentic qualities, which convey assertion and control. They include being especially aggressive, ambitious, dominant, self-confident, and forceful, as well as self-reliant and individualistic. The agentic traits are also associated in most people's minds with effective leadership—perhaps because a long history of male domination of leadership roles has made it difficult to separate the leader associations from the male associations.

As a result, women leaders find themselves in a double bind. If they are highly communal, they may be criticized for not being agentic enough. But if they are highly agentic, they may be criticized for lacking communion. Either way, they may leave the impression that they don't have "the right stuff" for powerful jobs.

Given this double bind, it is hardly surprising that people are more resistant to women's influence than to men's. For example, in meetings at a global retail company, people responded more favorably to men's overt attempts at influence than to women's. In the words of one of this company's female executives, "People often had to speak up to defend their turf, but when women did so, they were vilified. They were labeled 'control freaks'; men acting the same way were called 'passionate.' "

Verbally intimidating others can undermine a woman's influence, and assertive behavior can reduce her chances of getting a job or advancing in her career.

Studies have gauged reactions to men and women engaging in various types of dominant behavior. The findings are quite consistent. Nonverbal dominance, such as staring at others while speaking to them or pointing at people, is a more damaging behavior for women than for men. Verbally intimidating others can undermine a woman's influence, and assertive behavior can

reduce her chances of getting a job or advancing in her career. Simply disagreeing can sometimes get women into trouble. Men who disagree or otherwise act dominant get away with it more often than women do.

Self-promotion is similarly risky for women. Although it can convey status and competence, it is not at all communal. So while men can use bluster to get themselves noticed, modesty is expected even of highly accomplished women. Linguistics professor Deborah Tannen tells a story from her experience: "This [need for modesty] was evident, for example, at a faculty meeting devoted to promotions, at which a woman professor's success was described: She was extremely well published and well known in the field. A man commented with approval, 'She wears it well.' In other words, she was praised for not acting as successful as she was."

Another way the double bind penalizes women is by denying them the full benefits of being warm and considerate. Because people expect it of women, nice behavior that seems noteworthy in men seems unimpressive in women. For example, in one study, helpful men reaped a lot of approval, but helpful women did not. Likewise, men got away with being unhelpful, but women did not. A different study found that male employees received more promotions when they reported higher levels of helpfulness to coworkers. But female employees' promotions were not related to such altruism.

While one might suppose that men would have a double bind of their own, they in fact have more freedom. Several experiments and organizational studies have assessed reactions to behavior that is warm and friendly versus dominant and assertive. The findings show that men can communicate in a warm or a dominant manner, with no penalty either way. People like men equally well and are equally influenced by them regardless of their warmth.

It all amounts to a clash of assumptions when the average person confronts a woman in management. Perhaps this is why respondents in one study characterized the group "successful female managers" as more deceitful, pushy, selfish, and abrasive than "successful male managers." In the absence of any evidence to the contrary, people suspect that such highly effective women must not be very likable or nice.

Issues of leadership style. In response to the challenges presented by the double bind, female leaders often struggle to cultivate an appropriate and effective leadership style—one that reconciles the communal qualities people prefer in women with the agentic qualities people think leaders need to succeed. Here, for instance, is how Marietta Nien-hwa Cheng described her transition to the role of symphony conductor:

> I used to speak more softly, with a higher pitch. Sometimes my vocal cadences went up instead of down. I realized that these mannerisms lack the sense of authority. I strengthened my voice. The pitch has dropped. . . . I have stopped trying to be everyone's friend. Leadership is not synonymous with socializing.

It's difficult to pull off such a transformation while maintaining a sense of authenticity as a leader. Sometimes the whole effort can backfire. In the words of another female leader, "I think that there is a real penalty for a woman who behaves like a man. The men don't like her and the women don't either." Women leaders worry a lot about these things, complicating the labyrinth that they negotiate. For example, Catalyst's study of *Fortune* 1000 female executives found that 96% of them rated as critical or fairly important that they develop "a style with which male managers are comfortable."

Does a distinct "female" leadership style exist? There seems to be a popular consensus that it does. Consider, for example, journalist Michael Sokolove's profile of Mike Krzyzewski, head coach of the highly successful Duke University men's basketball team. As Sokolove put it, "So what is the secret to Krzyzewski's success? For starters, he coaches the way a woman would. Really." Sokolove proceeded to describe Krzyzewski's mentoring, interpersonally sensitive, and highly effective coaching style.

More scientifically, a recent meta-analysis integrated the results of 45 studies addressing the question. To compare leadership skills, the researchers adopted a framework introduced by leadership scholar James MacGregor Burns that distinguishes between transformational leadership and transactional leadership. Transformational leaders establish themselves as role models by gaining followers' trust and confidence. They state future goals, develop plans to achieve those goals, and innovate, even when their organizations are generally successful. Such leaders mentor and empower followers, encouraging them to develop their full potential and thus to contribute more effectively to their organizations. By contrast, transactional leaders establish give-and-take relationships that appeal to subordinates' self-interest. Such leaders manage in the conventional manner of clarifying subordinates' responsibilities, rewarding them for meeting objectives, and correcting them for failing to meet objectives. Although transformational and transactional leadership styles are different, most leaders adopt at least some behaviors of both types. The researchers also allowed for a third category, called the laissez-faire style—a sort of non-leadership that concerns itself with none of the above, despite rank authority.

The meta-analysis found that, in general, female leaders were somewhat more transformational than male leaders, especially when it came to giving support and encouragement to subordinates. They also engaged in more of the rewarding behaviors that are one aspect of transactional leadership. Meanwhile, men exceeded women on the aspects of transactional leadership involving corrective and disciplinary actions that are either active (timely) or passive (belated). Men were also more likely than women to be laissez-faire leaders, who take little responsibility for managing. These findings add up to a startling conclusion, given that most leadership research has found the transformational style (along with the rewards and positive incentives associated with the transactional style) to be more suited to leading the modern organization. The research tells us not only that men and women do have somewhat different leadership styles, but also that women's approaches are the more generally effective—while men's often are only somewhat effective or actually hinder effectiveness.

Is It Only a Question of Time?

It is a common perception that women will steadily gain greater access to leadership roles, including elite positions. For example, university students who are queried about the future power of men and women say that women's power will increase. Polls have shown that most Americans expect a woman to be elected president or vice president within their lifetimes. Both groups are extrapolating women's recent gains into the future, as if our society were on a continuous march toward gender equality.

But social change does not proceed without struggle and conflict. As women gain greater equality, a portion of people react against it. They long for traditional roles. In fact, signs of a pause in progress toward gender equality have appeared on many fronts. A review of longitudinal studies reveals several areas in which a sharp upward trend in the 1970s and 1980s has been followed by a slowing and flattening in recent years (for instance, in the percentage of managers who are women). The pause is also evident in some attitudinal data—like the percentage of people who approve of female bosses and who believe that women are at least as well suited as men for politics.

Social scientists have proposed various theories to explain this pause. Some, such as social psychologist Cecilia Ridgeway, believe that social change is activating "people's deep seated interests in maintaining clear cultural understandings of gender difference." Others believe progress has reached its limit given the continuing organization of family life by gender, coupled with employer policies that favor those who are not hampered by primary responsibility for child rearing.

It may simply be that women are collectively catching their breath before pressing for more change. In the past century, feminist activism arose when women came to view themselves as collectively subjected to illegitimate and unfair treatment. But recent polls show less conviction about the presence of discrimination, and feminism does not have the cultural relevance it once had. The lessening of activism on behalf of all women puts pressure on each woman to find her own way.

Another part of this picture, based on a separate meta-analysis, is that women adopt a more participative and collaborative style than men typically favor. The reason for this difference is unlikely to be genetic. Rather, it may be that collaboration can get results without seeming particularly masculine. As women navigate their way through the double bind, they seek ways to project authority without relying on the autocratic behaviors that people find so jarring in women. A viable path is to bring others into decision making and to lead as an encouraging teacher and positive role model. (However, if there is not a critical mass of other women to affirm the legitimacy of a participative style, female leaders usually conform to whatever style is typical of the men—and that is sometimes autocratic.)

Demands of family life. For many women, the most fateful turns in the labyrinth are the ones taken under pressure of family responsibilities. Women continue to be the ones who interrupt their careers, take more days off, and work part time. As a result, they have fewer years of job experience and fewer hours of employment per year, which slows their career progress and reduces their earnings.

In one study of Chicago lawyers, researchers sought to understand why women were much less likely than men to hold the leadership positions in large law firms—the positions that are most highly paid and that confer (arguably) the highest prestige. They found that women were no less likely than men to begin their careers at such firms but were more likely to leave them for positions in the public sector or corporate positions. The reasons for their departures were concentrated in work/family trade-offs. Among the relatively few women who did become partners in a firm, 60% had no children, and the minority who had children generally had delayed childbearing until attaining partner status.

There is no question that, while men increasingly share housework and child rearing, the bulk of domestic work still falls on women's shoulders. We know this from time-diary studies, in which people record what they are doing during each hour of a 24-hour day. So, for example, in the United States married women devoted 19 hours per week on average to housework in 2005, while married men contributed 11 hours. That's a huge improvement over 1965 numbers, when women spent a whopping 34 hours per week to men's five, but it is still a major inequity. And the situation looks worse when child care hours are added.

Mothers provide more child care hours than they did in earlier generations—despite the fact that fathers are putting in a lot more time than in the past.

Although it is common knowledge that mothers provide more child care than fathers, few people realize that mothers provide more than they did in earlier generations—despite the fact that fathers are putting in a lot more time than in the past. National studies have compared mothers and fathers on the amount of their primary child care, which consists of close interaction not combined with housekeeping or other activities. Married mothers increased their hours per week from 10.6 in 1965 to 12.9 in 2000, and married fathers increased theirs from 2.6 to 6.5. Thus, though husbands have taken on more domestic work, the work/family conflict has not eased for women; the gain has been offset by escalating pressures for intensive parenting and the increasing time demands of most high-level careers.

Even women who have found a way to relieve pressures from the home front by sharing child care with husbands, other family members, or paid workers may not enjoy the full workplace benefit of having done so. Decision makers often assume that mothers have domestic responsibilities that make it inappropriate to promote them to demanding positions. As one participant in a study of the federal workforce explained, "I mean, there were 2 or 3 names [of women] in the hat, and they said, 'I don't want to talk about her because she has children who are still home in these [evening] hours.' Now they don't pose that thing about men on the list, many of whom also have children in that age group."

One study suggests that social capital is even more necessary to managers' advancement than skillful performance of traditional managerial tasks.

Underinvestment in social capital. Perhaps the most destructive result of the work/family balancing act so many women must perform is that it leaves very little time for socializing with colleagues and building professional networks. The social capital that accrues from such "nonessential" parts of work turns out to be quite essential indeed. One study yielded the following description of managers who advanced rapidly in hierarchies: Fast-track managers "spent relatively more time and effort socializing, politicking, and interacting with outsiders than did their less successful counterparts . . . [and] did not give much time or attention to the traditional management activities of planning, decision making, and controlling or to the human resource management activities of motivating/reinforcing, staffing, training/developing, and managing conflict." This suggests that social capital is even more necessary to managers' advancement than skillful performance of traditional managerial tasks.

Even given sufficient time, women can find it difficult to engage in and benefit from informal networking if they are a small minority. In such settings, the influential networks are composed entirely or almost entirely of men. Breaking into those male networks can be hard, especially when men center their networks on masculine activities. The recent gender discrimination lawsuit against Wal-Mart provides examples of this. For instance, an executive retreat took the form of a quail-hunting expedition at Sam Walton's ranch in Texas. Middle managers' meetings included visits to strip clubs and Hooters restaurants, and a sales conference attended by thousands of store managers featured a football theme. One executive received feedback that she probably would not advance in the company because she didn't hunt or fish.

Management Interventions That Work

Taking the measure of the labyrinth that confronts women leaders, we see that it begins with prejudices that benefit men and penalize women, continues with particular resistance to women's leadership, includes questions of leadership style and authenticity, and—most dramatically for many women—features the challenge of balancing work and family responsibilities. It becomes clear that a woman's situation as she reaches her peak career years is the result of many turns at many challenging junctures. Only a few individual women have made the right combination of moves to land at the center of power—but as for the rest, there is usually no single turning point where their progress was diverted and the prize was lost.

What's to be done in the face of such a multifaceted problem? A solution that is often proposed is for governments to implement and enforce antidiscrimination legislation and thereby require organizations to eliminate inequitable practices. However, analysis of discrimination cases that have gone to court has shown that legal remedies can be elusive when gender inequality results from norms embedded in organizational structure and culture. The more effective approach is for organizations to appreciate the subtlety and complexity of the problem and to attack its many roots simultaneously. More specifically, if a company wants to see more women arrive in its executive suite, it should do the following:

Increase people's awareness of the psychological drivers of prejudice toward female leaders, and work to dispel those perceptions. Raising awareness of ingrained bias has been the aim of many diversity-training initiatives, and no doubt they have been more helpful than harmful. There is the danger they will be undermined, however, if their lessons are not underscored by what managers say and do in the course of day-to-day work.

Change the long-hours norm. Especially in the context of knowledge work, it can be hard to assess individuals' relative contributions, and managers may resort to "hours spent at work" as the prime indicator of someone's worth to the organization. To the extent an organization can shift the focus to objective measures of productivity, women with family demands on their time but highly productive work habits will receive the rewards and encouragement they deserve.

Reduce the subjectivity of performance evaluation. Greater objectivity in evaluations also combats the effects of lingering prejudice in both hiring and promotion. To ensure fairness, criteria should be explicit and evaluation processes designed to limit the influence of decision makers' conscious and unconscious biases.

Use open-recruitment tools, such as advertising and employment agencies, rather than relying on informal social networks and referrals to fill positions. Recruitment from within organizations also should be transparent, with postings of open positions in appropriate venues. Research has shown that such personnel practices increase the numbers of women in managerial roles.

Ensure a critical mass of women in executive positions—not just one or two women—to head off the problems that come with tokenism. Token women tend to be pegged into narrow stereotypical roles such as "seductress," "mother," "pet," or "iron maiden." (Or more colorfully, as one woman banker put it, "When you start out in banking, you are a slut or a geisha.") Pigeonholing like this limits women's options and makes it difficult for them to rise to positions of responsibility. When women are not a small minority, their identities as women become less salient, and colleagues are more likely to react to them in terms of their individual competencies.

Avoid having a sole female member of any team. Top management tends to divide its small population of women managers among many projects in the interests of introducing diversity to them all. But several studies have found that, so outnumbered, the women tend to be ignored by the men. A female vice president of a manufacturing company described how, when she or another woman ventures an idea in a meeting, it tends to be overlooked: "It immediately gets lost in the conversation. Then two minutes later, a man makes the same suggestion, and it's 'Wow! What a great idea!' And you sit there and think, 'What just happened?'" As women reach positions of higher power and authority, they increasingly find themselves in gender-imbalanced groups—and some find themselves, for the first time, seriously marginalized. This is part of the reason that the glass ceiling metaphor resonates with so many. But in fact, the problem can be present at any level.

Help shore up social capital. As we've discussed, the call of family responsibilities is mainly to blame for women's underinvestment in networking. When time is scarce, this social activity is the first thing to go by the wayside. Organizations can help women appreciate why it deserves more attention. In particular, women gain from strong and supportive mentoring relationships and connections with powerful networks. When a well-placed individual who possesses greater legitimacy (often a man) takes an interest in a woman's career, her efforts to build social capital can proceed far more efficiently.

Prepare women for line management with appropriately demanding assignments. Women, like men, must have the benefit of developmental job experiences if they are to qualify for promotions. But, as one woman executive wrote, "Women have been shunted off into support areas for the last 30 years, rather than being in the business of doing business, so the pool of women trained to assume leadership positions in any large company is very small." Her point was that women should be taught in business school to insist on line jobs when they enter the workforce. One company that has taken up the challenge has been Procter & Gamble. According to a report by Claudia Deutsch in the *New York Times,* the company was experiencing an executive attrition rate that was twice as high for women as for men. Some of the women reported having to change companies to land jobs that provided challenging work. P&G's subsequent efforts to bring more women into line management both improved its overall retention of women and increased the number of women in senior management.

Establish family-friendly human resources practices. These may include flextime, job sharing, telecommuting, elder care provisions, adoption benefits, dependent child care options, and employee-sponsored on-site child care. Such support can allow women to stay in their jobs during the most demanding years of child rearing, build social capital, keep up to date in their fields, and eventually compete for higher positions. A study of 72 large U.S. firms showed (controlling for other variables) that family-friendly HR practices in place in 1994 increased the proportion of women in senior management over the subsequent five years.

Allow employees who have significant parental responsibility more time to prove themselves worthy of promotion. This recommendation is particularly directed to organizations, many of them professional services firms, that have established "up or out" career progressions. People not ready for promotion at the same time as the top performers in their cohort aren't simply left in place—they're asked to leave. But many parents (most often mothers), while fully capable of reaching that level of achievement, need extra time—perhaps a year or two—to get there. Forcing them off the promotion path not only reduces the number of women reaching top management positions, but also constitutes a failure by the firm to capitalize on its early investment in them.

Welcome women back. It makes sense to give high-performing women who step away from the workforce an opportunity to return to responsible positions when their circumstances change. Some companies have established "alumni" programs, often because they see former employees as potential sources of new business. A few companies have gone further to activate these networks for other purposes, as well. (Procter & Gamble taps alumni for innovation purposes; Booz Allen sees its alumni ranks as a source of subcontractors.) Keeping lines of communication open can convey the message that a return may be possible.

Encourage male participation in family-friendly benefits. Dangers lurk in family-friendly benefits that are used only by women. Exercising options such as generous parental leave and part-time work slows down women's careers. More profoundly, having many more women than men take such benefits can harm the careers of women in general because of the expectation that they may well exercise those options. Any effort toward greater family friendliness should actively recruit male participation to avoid inadvertently making it harder for women to gain access to essential managerial roles.

Managers can be forgiven if they find the foregoing list a tall order. It's a wide-ranging set of interventions and still far from exhaustive. The point, however, is just that: Organizations will succeed in filling half their top management slots with women—and women who are the true performance equals of their male counterparts—only by attacking all the reasons they are absent today. Glass ceiling-inspired programs and projects can do just so much if the leakage of talented women is happening on every lower floor of the building. Individually, each of these interventions has been shown to make a difference. Collectively, we believe, they can make all the difference.

The View from Above

Imagine visiting a formal garden and finding within it a high hedgerow. At a point along its vertical face, you spot a rectangle—a neatly pruned and inviting doorway. Are you aware as you step through that you are entering a labyrinth? And, three doorways later, as the reality of the puzzle settles in, do you have any idea how to proceed? This is the situation in which many women find themselves in their career endeavors. Ground-level perplexity and frustration make every move uncertain.

When the eye can take in the whole of the puzzle—the starting position, the goal, and the maze of walls—solutions begin to suggest themselves.

Labyrinths become infinitely more tractable when seen from above. When the eye can take in the whole of the puzzle—the starting position, the goal, and the maze of walls—solutions begin to suggest themselves. This has been the goal of our research. Our hope is that women, equipped with a map of the barriers they will confront on their path to professional achievement, will make more informed choices. We hope that managers, too, will understand where their efforts can facilitate the progress of women. If women are to achieve equality, women and men will have to share leadership equally. With a greater understanding of what stands in the way of gender-balanced leadership, we draw nearer to attaining it in our time.

ALICE H. EAGLY (eagly@northwestern.edu) is a professor of psychology and holds the James Padilla Chair of Arts and Sciences at Northwestern University, in Evanston, Illinois; she is also a faculty fellow at Northwestern's Institute for Policy Research. **LINDA L. CARLI** (lcarli@wellesley.edu) is an associate professor of psychology at Wellesley College, in Massachusetts; her current research focus is on gender discrimination and other challenges faced by professional women. The two are coauthors of *Through the Labyrinth: The Truth about How Women Become Leaders* (Harvard Business School Press, forthcoming in October), from which this article is adapted.

Avoiding Green Marketing Myopia

Ways to Improve Consumer Appeal for Environmentally Preferable Products

JACQUELYN A. OTTMAN, EDWIN R. STAFFORD, AND CATHY L. HARTMAN

In 1994, Philips launched the "EarthLight," a super energy-efficient compact fluorescent light (CFL) bulb designed to be an environmentally preferable substitute for the traditional energy-intensive incandescent bulb. The CFL's clumsy shape, however, was incompatible with most conventional lamps, and sales languished. After studying consumer response, Philips reintroduced the product in 2000 under the name "Marathon," to emphasize the bulb's five-year life. New designs offered the look and versatility of conventional incandescent light bulbs and the promise of more than $20 in energy savings over the product's life span compared to incandescent bulbs. The new bulbs were also certified by the U.S. Environmental Protection Agency's (EPA) Energy Star label. Repositioning CFL bulbs' features into advantages that resonated with consumer values—convenience, ease-of-use, and credible cost savings—ultimately sparked an annual sales growth of 12 percent in a mature product market.[1]

Philips' experience provides a valuable lesson on how to avoid the common pitfall of "green marketing myopia." Philips called its original entry "EarthLight" to communicate the CFL bulbs' environmental advantage. While noble, the benefit appealed to only the deepest green niche of consumers. The vast majority of consumers, however, will ask, "If I use 'green' products, what's in it for me?" In practice, green appeals are not likely to attract mainstream consumers unless they also offer a desirable benefit, such as cost-savings or improved product performance.[2] To avoid green marketing myopia, marketers must fulfill consumer needs and interests beyond what is good for the environment.

Although no consumer product has a zero impact on the environment, in business, the terms "green product" and "environmental product" are used commonly to describe those that strive to protect or enhance the natural environment by conserving energy and/or resources and reducing or eliminating use of toxic agents, pollution, and waste.[3] Paul Hawken, Amory Lovins, and L. Hunter Lovins write in their book *Natural Capitalism: Creating the Next Industrial Revolution* that greener, more sustainable products need to dramatically increase the productivity of natural resources, follow biological/cyclical production models, encourage dematerialization, and reinvest in and contribute to the planet's "natural" capital.[4] Escalating energy prices, concerns over foreign oil dependency, and calls for energy conservation are creating business opportunities for energy-efficient products, clean energy, and other environmentally-sensitive innovations and products—collectively known as "cleantech"[5] (see the box on page 116). For example, Pulitzer Prize–winning author and *New York Times* columnist Thomas L. Friedman argues that government policy and industry should engage in a "geo-green" strategy to promote energy efficiency, renewable energy, and other cleantech innovations to help alleviate the nation's

dependency on oil from politically conflicted regions of the world.[6] Friedman asserts that such innovations can spark economic opportunity and address the converging global challenges of rising energy prices, terrorism, climate change, and the environmental consequences of the rapid economic development of China and India.

To exploit these economic opportunities to steer global commerce onto a more sustainable path, however, green products must appeal to consumers outside the traditional green niche.[7] Looking at sustainability from a green engineering perspective, Arnulf Grubler recently wrote in *Environment,* "To minimize environmental impacts by significant orders of magnitude requires the blending of good engineering with good economics as well as changing consumer preferences."[8] The marketing discipline has long argued that innovation must consider an intimate understanding of the customer,[9] and a close look at green marketing practices over time reveals that green products must be positioned on a consumer value sought by targeted consumers.

Drawing from past research and an analysis of the marketing appeals and strategies of green products that have either succeeded or failed in the marketplace over the past decade, some important lessons emerge for crafting effective green marketing and product strategies.[10] Based on the evidence, successful green products are able to appeal to mainstream consumers or lucrative market niches and frequently command price premiums by offering "non-green" consumer value (such as convenience and performance).

Green Marketing Myopia Defined

Green marketing must satisfy two objectives: improved environmental quality and customer satisfaction. Misjudging either or overemphasizing the former at the expense of the latter can be termed "green marketing myopia." In 1960, Harvard business professor Theodore Levitt introduced the concept of "marketing myopia" in a now-famous and influential article in the *Harvard Business Review.*[11] In it, he characterized the common pitfall of companies' tunnel vision, which focused on "managing products" (that is, product features, functions, and efficient production) instead of "meeting customers' needs" (that is, adapting to consumer expectations and anticipation of future desires). Levitt warned that a corporate preoccupation on products rather than consumer needs was doomed to failure because consumers select products and new innovations that offer benefits they desire. Research indicates that many green products have failed because of green marketing myopia—marketers' myopic focus on their products' "greenness" over the broader expectations of consumers or other market players (such as regulators or activists).

Green marketing must satisfy two objectives: improved environmental quality and customer satisfaction.

For example, partially in response to the 1987 Montreal Protocol, in which signatory countries (including the United States) agreed to phase out ozone-depleting chlorofluorocarbons (CFCs) by 2000, Whirlpool (in 1994) launched the "Energy Wise" refrigerator, the first CFC-free cooler and one that was 30 percent more efficient than the U.S. Department of Energy's highest standard.[12] For its innovation, Whirlpool won the "Golden Carrot," a $30 million award package of consumer rebates from the Super-Efficient Refrigerator Program, sponsored by the Natural Resources Defense Council and funded by 24 electric utilities. Unfortunately, Energy Wise's sales languished because the CFC-free benefit and energy-savings did not offset its $100 to $150 price premium, particularly in markets outside the rebate program, and the refrigerators did not offer additional features or new styles that consumers desired.[13] General Motors (GM) and Ford encountered similar problems when they launched their highly publicized EV-1 and Think Mobility electric vehicles, respectively, in the late 1990s to early 2000s in response to the 1990 zero-emission vehicle (ZEV) regulations adopted in California.[14] Both automakers believed their novel two-seater cars would be market successes (GM offered the EV-1 in a lease program, and Ford offered Think Mobility vehicles as rentals via the Hertz car-rental chain). Consumers, however, found electric vehicles' need for constant recharging with few recharging locations too inconvenient. Critics charged that the automakers made only token efforts to make electric cars a success, but a GM spokesperson recently explained, "We spent more than $1 billion to produce and market the vehicle, [but] fewer than 800 were leased."[15] Most drivers were not willing to drastically change their driving habits and expectations to accommodate electric cars, and the products ultimately were taken off the market.[16]

Aside from offering environmental benefits that do not meet consumer preferences, green marketing myopia can also occur when green products fail to provide credible, substantive environmental benefits. Mobil's Hefty photodegradable plastic trash bag is a case in point. Introduced in 1989, Hefty packages prominently displayed the term "degradable" with the explanation that a special ingredient promoted its decomposition into harmless particles in landfills "activated by exposure to the elements" such as sun, wind, and rain. Because most garbage is buried in landfills that allow limited exposure to the elements, making degradation virtually impossible, the claim enraged environmentalists. Ultimately, seven state attorneys general sued Mobil on charges of deceptive advertising and consumer fraud. Mobil removed the claim from its packaging and vowed to use extreme caution in making environmental claims in the future.[17]

Other fiascos have convinced many companies and consumers to reject green products. Roper ASW's 2002 "Green Gauge Report" finds that the top reasons consumers do not buy green products included beliefs that they require sacrifices—inconvenience, higher costs, lower performance—without significant environmental benefits.[18] Ironically, despite what consumers think, a plethora of green products available in the marketplace are in fact desirable because they deliver convenience, lower operating costs, and/or better performance. Often these are not marketed along with their green benefits, so consumers do not immediately recognize them as green and form misperceptions about their benefits. For instance, the appeal of premium-priced Marathon and other brands of CFL bulbs can be attributed to their energy savings and long life, qualities that make them convenient and economical over time. When consumers are convinced of the desirable "non-green" benefits of environmental products, they are more inclined to adopt them.

Other environmental products have also scored market successes by either serving profitable niche markets or offering mainstream appeal. Consider the Toyota Prius, the gas-electric hybrid vehicle that achieves about 44 miles per gallon of gasoline.[19] In recent years, Toyota's production has hardly kept pace with the growing demand, with buyers enduring long waits and paying thousands above the car's sticker price.[20] Consequently, other carmakers have scrambled to launch their own hybrids.[21] However, despite higher gas prices, analysts assert that it can take 5 to 20 years for lower gas expenses to offset many hybrid cars' higher prices. Thus, economics alone cannot explain their growing popularity.

Analysts offer several reasons for the Prius' market demand. Initially, the buzz over the Prius got a boost at the 2003 Academy Awards when celebrities such as Cameron Diaz, Harrison Ford, Susan Sarandon, and Robin Williams abandoned stretch limousines and oversized sport utility vehicles, arriving in Priuses to symbolize support for reducing America's dependence on foreign oil.[22] Since then, the quirky-looking Prius' badge of "conspicuous conservation" has satisfied many drivers' desires to turn heads and make a statement about their social responsibility, among them Google founders Larry Page and Sergey Brin, columnist Arianna Huffington, comic Bill Maher, and Charles, Prince of Wales.[23] The Prius ultimately was named *Motor Trend's* Car of the Year in 2004. The trendy appeal of the Prius illustrates that some green products can leverage consumer desires for being distinctive. Others say the Prius is just fun to drive—the dazzling digital dashboard that offers continuous feedback on fuel efficiency and other car operations provides an entertaining driving experience. More recently, however, the Prius has garnered fans for more practical reasons. A 2006 Maritz Poll finds that owners purchased hybrids because of the convenience of fewer fill-ups, better performance, and the enjoyment of driving the latest technology.[24] In some states, the Prius and other high-mileage hybrid vehicles, such as Honda's Insight, are granted free parking and solo-occupancy access to high occupancy vehicle (HOV) lanes.[25] In sum, hybrid vehicles offer consumers several desirable benefits that are not necessarily "green" benefits.

Many environmental products have become so common and widely distributed that many consumers may no longer recognize them as green because they buy them for non-green reasons. Green household products, for instance, are widely available at supermarkets and discount retailers, ranging from energy-saving Tide Coldwater laundry detergent to non-toxic Method and Simple Green cleaning products. Use of recycled or biodegradable paper products (such as plates, towels, napkins, coffee filters, computer paper, and other goods) is also widespread. Organic and rainforest-protective "shade grown" coffees are available at Starbucks and other specialty stores and supermarkets. Organic baby food is expected to command 12 percent market share in 2006 as parents strive to protect their children's mental and physical development.[26] Indeed, the organic food market segment has increased 20 percent annually since 1990, five times faster than the conventional food market, spurring the growth of specialty retailers such as Whole Foods Market and Wild Oats. Wal-Mart, too, has joined this extensive distribution of organic products.[27] Indeed, Wal-Mart has recently declared that in North American stores, its non-farm-raised fresh fish will be certified by the Marine Stewardship Council as sustainably harvested.[28]

Super energy-efficient appliances and fixtures are also becoming popular. Chic, front-loading washing machines, for example, accounted for 25 percent of the market in 2004, up from 9 percent in 2001.[29] EPA's Energy Star label, which certifies that products consume up to 30 percent less energy than comparable alternatives, is found on products ranging from major appliances to light fixtures to entire buildings (minimum efficiency standards vary from product to product). The construction industry is becoming increasingly green as government and industry demand office buildings that are "high

Emerging Age of Cleantech

In a 1960 *Harvard Business Review* article, Harvard professor Theodore Levitt introduced the classic concept of "marketing myopia" to characterize businesses' narrow vision on product features rather than consumer benefits.[1] The consequence is that businesses focus on making better mousetraps rather than seeking better alternatives for controlling pests. To avoid marketing myopia, businesses must engage in "creative destruction," described by economist Joseph Schumpeter as destroying existing products, production methods, market structures and consumption patterns, and replacing them with ways that better meet ever-changing consumer desires.[2] The dynamic pattern in which innovative upstart companies unseat established corporations and industries by capitalizing on new and improved innovations is illustrated by history. That is, the destruction of Coal Age technologies by Oil Age innovations, which are being destroyed by Information Age advances and the emerging Age of Cleantech—clean, energy- and resource-efficient energy technologies, such as those involving low/zero-emissions, wind, solar, biomass, hydrogen, recycling, and closed-loop processes.[3]

Business management researchers Stuart Hart and Mark Milstein argue that the emerging challenge of global sustainability is catalyzing a new round of creative destruction that offers "unprecedented opportunities" for new environmentally sensitive innovations, markets, and products.[4] Throughout the twentieth century, many technologies and business practices have contributed to the destruction of the very ecological systems on which the economy and life itself depends, including toxic contamination, depletion of fisheries and forests, soil erosion, and biodiversity loss. Recent news reports indicate, however, that many companies and consumers are beginning to respond to programs to help conserve the Earth's natural resources, and green marketing is making a comeback.[5] The need for sustainability has become more acute economically as soaring demand, dwindling supplies, and rising prices for oil, gas, coal, water, and other natural resources are being driven by the industrialization of populous countries, such as China and India. Politically, America's significant reliance on foreign oil has become increasingly recognized as a security threat. Global concerns over climate change have led 141 countries to ratify the Kyoto Protocol, the international treaty requiring the reduction of global warming gases created through the burning of fossil fuels. Although the United States has not signed the treaty, most multinational corporations conducting business in signatory nations are compelled to reduce their greenhouse gas emissions, and many states (such as California) and cities (such as Chicago and Seattle) have or are initiating their own global warming gas emission reduction programs.[6] State and city-level policy incentives and mandates, such as "renewable portfolio standards," requiring utilities to provide increasing amounts of electricity from clean, renewable sources such as wind and solar power, are also driving cleaner technology markets.

While some firms have responded grudgingly to such pressures for more efficient and cleaner business practices, others are seizing the cleantech innovation opportunities for new twenty-first-century green products and technologies for competitive advantage. Toyota, for instance, plans to offer an all-hybrid fleet in the near future to challenge competitors on both performance and fuel economy.[7] Further, Toyota is licensing its technology to its competitors to gain profit from their hybrid sales as well. General Electric's highly publicized "Ecomagination" initiative promises a greener world with a plan to double its investments (to $1.5 billion annually) and revenues (to $20 billion) from fuel-efficient diesel locomotives, wind power, "clean" coal, and other cleaner innovations by 2010.[8] Cleantech is attracting investors looking for the "Next Big Thing," including Goldman Sachs and Kleiner Perkins Caufield & Byers.[9] Wal-Mart, too, is testing a sustainable 206,000-square foot store design in Texas that deploys 26 energy-saving and renewable-materials experiments that could set new standards in future retail store construction.[10] In sum, economic, political, and environmental pressures are coalescing to drive cleaner and greener technological innovation in the twenty-first century, and companies that fail to adapt their products and processes accordingly are destined to suffer from the consequences of marketing myopia and creative destruction.

1. T. Levitt, "Marketing Myopia," *Harvard Business Review* 28, July–August (1960): 24–47.
2. See J. Schumpeter, *The Theory of Economic Development* (Cambridge: Harvard University Press, 1934); and J. Schumpeter, *Capitalism, Socialism and Democracy* (New York: Harper Torchbooks, 1942).
3. "Alternate Power: A Change Is in the Wind," *Business Week,* 4 July 2005, 36–37.
4. S. L. Hart and M. B. Milstein, "Global Sustainability and the Creative Destruction of Industries," *MIT Sloan Management Review* 41, Fall (1999): 23–33.
5. See for example T. Howard, "Being Eco-Friendly Can Pay Economically; 'Green Marketing' Sees Growth in Sales, Ads," *USA Today,* 15 August 2005; and E. R. Stafford, "Energy Efficiency and the New Green Marketing," *Environment,* March 2003, 8–10.
6. J. Ball, "California Sets Emission Goals That Are Stiffer than U.S. Plan," *Wall Street Journal,* 2 June 2005; and J. Marglis, "Paving the Way for U.S. Emissions Trading," *Grist Magazine,* 14 June 2005, www.climatebiz.com/sections/news_print .dfm?NewsID=28255.
7. Bloomberg News, "Toyota Says It Plans Eventually to Offer an All-Hybrid Fleet," 14 September 2005, http://www.nytimes.com/2005/09/14/automobiles/14toyota.html.
8. J. Erickson, "U.S. Business and Climate Change: Siding with the Marketing?" *Sustainability Radar,* June, www.climatebiz.com/sections/new_ print .cfm?NewsID=28204.
9. *BusinessWeek,* note 3 above.
10. Howard, note 5 above.

performance" (for example, super energy- and resource-efficient and cost-effective) and "healthy" for occupants (for example, well-ventilated; constructed with materials with low or no volatile organic compounds [VOC]). The U.S. Green Building Council's "Leadership in Energy and Environmental Design" (LEED) provides a rigorous rating system and green building checklist that are rapidly becoming the standard for environmentally sensitive construction.[30]

Home buyers are recognizing the practical long-term cost savings and comfort of natural lighting, passive solar heating, and heat-reflective windows, and a 2006 study sponsored by home improvement retailer Lowe's found nine out of ten builders surveyed are incorporating energy-saving features into new homes.[31] Additionally, a proliferation of "green" building materials to serve the growing demand has emerged.[32] Lowe's competitor The Home Depot is testing an 'EcoOptions' product line featuring natural fertilizers and mold-resistant drywall in its Canadian stores that may filter into the U.S. market.[33] In short, energy efficiency and green construction have become mainstream.

The diversity and availability of green products indicate that consumers are not indifferent to the value offered by environmental benefits. Consumers are buying green—but not necessarily for environmental reasons. The market growth of organic foods and energy-efficient appliances is because consumers desire their perceived safety and money savings, respectively.[34] Thus, the apparent paradox between what consumers say and their purchases may be explained, in part, by green marketing myopia—a narrow focus on the greenness of products that blinds companies from considering the broader consumer and societal desires. A fixation on products' environmental merits has resulted frequently in inferior green products (for example, the original EarthLight and GM's EV-1 electric car) and unsatisfying consumer experiences. By contrast, the analysis of past research and marketing strategies finds that successful green products have avoided green marketing myopia by following three important principles: "The Three Cs" of consumer value positioning, calibration of consumer knowledge, and credibility of product claims.

Consumer Value Positioning

The marketing of successfully established green products showcases non-green consumer value, and there are at least five desirable benefits commonly associated with green products: efficiency and cost effectiveness; health and safety; performance; symbolism and status; and convenience. Additionally, when these five consumer value propositions are not inherent in the green product, successful green marketing programs bundle (that is, add to the product design or market offering) desirable consumer value to broaden the green product's appeal. In practice, the implication is that product designers and marketers need to align environmental products' consumer value (such as money savings) to relevant consumer market segments (for example, cost-conscious consumers).

Efficiency and Cost Effectiveness

As exemplified by the Marathon CFL bulbs, the common inherent benefit of many green products is their potential energy and resource efficiency. Given sky-rocketing energy prices and tax incentives for fuel-efficient cars and energy-saving home improvements and appliances, long-term savings have convinced cost-conscious consumers to buy green.

Recently, the home appliance industry made great strides in developing energy-efficient products to achieve EPA's Energy Star rating. For example, Energy Star refrigerators use at least 15 percent less energy and dishwashers use at least 25 percent less energy than do traditional models.[35] Consequently, an Energy Star product often commands a price premium. Whirlpool's popular Duet front-loading washer and dryer, for example, cost more than $2,000, about double the price of conventional units; however, the washers can save up to 12,000 gallons of water and $110 on electricity annually compared to standard models (Energy Star does not rate dryers).[36]

Laundry detergents are also touting energy savings. Procter & Gamble's (P&G) newest market entry, Tide Coldwater, is designed to clean clothes effectively in cold water. About 80 to 85 percent of the energy used to wash clothes comes from heating water. Working with utility companies, P&G found that consumers could save an average of $63 per year by using cold rather than warm water.[37] Adopting Tide Coldwater gives added confidence to consumers already washing in cold water. As energy and resource prices continue to soar, opportunities for products offering efficiency and savings are destined for market growth.

Health and Safety

Concerns over exposure to toxic chemicals, hormones, or drugs in everyday products have made health and safety important choice considerations, especially among vulnerable consumers, such as pregnant women, children, and the elderly.[38] Because most environmental products are grown or designed to minimize or eliminate the use of toxic agents and adulterating processes, market positioning on consumer safety and health can achieve broad appeal among health-conscious consumers. Sales of organic foods, for example, have grown considerably in the wake of public fear over "mad cow" disease, antibiotic-laced meats, mercury in fish, and genetically modified foods.[39] Mainstream appeal of organics is not derived from marketers promoting the advantages of free-range animal ranching and pesticide-free soil. Rather, market positioning of organics as flavorful, healthy alternatives to factory-farm foods has convinced consumers to pay a premium for them.

A study conducted by the Alliance for Environmental Innovation and household products-maker S.C. Johnson found that consumers are most likely to act on green messages that strongly connect to their personal environments.[40] Specifically, findings suggest that the majority of consumers prefer such environmental household product benefits as "safe to use around children," "no toxic ingredients," "no chemical residues," and "no strong fumes" over such benefits as "packaging can be recycled" or "not tested on animals." Seventh Generation, a brand of non-toxic and environmentally-safe household products, derived its name from the Iroquois belief that, "In our every deliberation, we must consider the impact of our decisions on the next seven generations." Accordingly, its products promote the family-oriented value of making the world a safer place for the next seven generations.

Indoor air quality is also a growing concern. Fumes from paints, carpets, furniture, and other décor in poorly ventilated "sick buildings" have been linked to headaches, eye, nose, and throat irritation, dizziness, and fatigue among occupants. Consequently, many manufacturers have launched green products to reduce indoor air pollution. Sherwin Williams, for example, offers "Harmony," a line of interior paints that is low-odor, zero-VOC, and silica-free. And Mohawk sells EverSet Fibers, a carpet that virtually eliminates the need for harsh chemical cleaners because its design allows most stains to be removed with water. Aside from energy efficiency, health and safety have been key motivators driving the green building movement.

Performance

The conventional wisdom is that green products don't work as well as "non-green" ones. This is a legacy from the first generation of environmentally sensitive products that clearly were inferior. Consumer perception of green cleaning agents introduced in health food stores in the 1960s and 1970s, for example, was that "they cost twice as much to remove half the grime."[41] Today, however, many green products are designed to perform better than conventional ones and can command a price premium. For example, in addition to energy efficiency, front-loading washers clean better and are gentler on clothes compared to conventional top-loading machines because they spin clothes in a motion similar to clothes driers and use centrifugal force to pull dirt and water away from clothes. By contrast, most top-loading washers use agitators to pull clothes through tanks of water, reducing cleaning and increasing wear on clothes. Consequently, the efficiency and high performance benefits of top-loading washers justify their premium prices.

Market positioning on consumer safety and health can achieve broad appeal among health-conscious consumers.

Homeowners commonly build decks with cedar, redwood, or pressure-treated pine (which historically was treated with toxic agents such as arsenic). Wood requires stain or paint and periodic applications of chemical preservatives for maintenance. Increasingly, however, composite deck material made from recycled milk jugs and wood fiber, such as Weyerhaeuser's ChoiceDek, is marketed as the smarter alternative. Composites are attractive, durable, and low maintenance. They do not contain toxic chemicals and never need staining or chemical preservatives. Accordingly, they command a price premium—as much as two to three times the cost of pressure-treated pine and 15 percent more than cedar or redwood.[42]

Likewise, Milgard Windows' low emissivity SunCoat Low-E windows filter the sun in the summer and reduce heat loss in the winter. While the windows can reduce a building's overall energy use, their more significant benefit comes from helping to create a comfortable indoor radiant temperature climate and protecting carpets and furniture from harmful ultraviolet rays. Consequently, Milgard promotes the improved comfort and performance of its SunCoat Low-E windows over conventional windows. In sum, "high performance" positioning can broaden green product appeal.

Symbolism and Status

As mentioned earlier, the Prius, Toyota's gas-electric hybrid, has come to epitomize "green chic." According to many automobile analysts, the cool-kid cachet that comes with being an early adopter of the quirky-looking hybrid vehicle trend continues to partly motivate sales.[43] Establishing a green chic appeal, however, isn't easy. According to popular culture experts, green marketing must appear grass-roots driven and humorous without sounding preachy. To appeal to young people, conservation and green consumption need the unsolicited endorsement of high-profile celebrities and connection to cool technology.[44] Prius has capitalized on its evangelical following and high-tech image with some satirical ads, including a television commercial comparing the hybrid with Neil Armstrong's moon landing ("That's one small step on the accelerator, one giant leap for mankind.") and product placements in popular Hollywood films and sitcoms (such as *Curb Your Enthusiasm*). More recently, Toyota has striven to position its "hybrid synergy drive" system as a cut above other car makers' hybrid technologies with witty slogans such as, "Commute with Nature," "mpg:)," and "There's Nothing Like That New Planet Smell."[45] During the 2006

Super Bowl XL game, Ford launched a similarly humorous commercial featuring Kermit the Frog encountering a hybrid Escape sports utility vehicle in the forest, and in a twist, changing his tune with "I guess it *is* easy being green!"[46]

In business, where office furniture symbolizes the cachet of corporate image and status, the ergonomically designed "Think" chair is marketed as the chair "with a brain and a conscience." Produced by Steelcase, the world's largest office furniture manufacturer, the Think chair embodies the latest in "cradle to cradle" (C2C) design and manufacturing. C2C, which describes products that can be ultimately returned to technical or biological nutrients, encourages industrial designers to create products free of harmful agents and processes that can be recycled easily into new products (such as metals and plastics) or safely returned to the earth (such as plant-based materials).[47] Made without any known carcinogens, the Think chair is 99 percent recyclable; it disassembles with basic hand tools in about five minutes, and parts are stamped with icons showing recycling options.[48] Leveraging its award-winning design and sleek comfort, the Think chair is positioned as symbolizing the smart, socially responsible office. In sum, green products can be positioned as status symbols.

Convenience

Many energy-efficient products offer inherent convenience benefits that can be showcased for competitive advantage. CFL bulbs, for example, need infrequent replacement and gas-electric hybrid cars require fewer refueling stops—benefits that are highlighted in their marketing communications. Another efficient alternative to incandescent bulbs are light-emitting diodes (LEDs): They are even more efficient and longer-lasting than CFL bulbs; emit a clearer, brighter light; and are virtually unbreakable even in cold and hot weather. LEDs are used in traffic lights due to their high-performance convenience. Recently, a city in Idaho became a pioneer by adopting LEDs for its annual holiday Festival of Lights. "We spent so much time replacing strings of lights and bulbs," noted one city official, "[using LEDs] is going to reduce two-thirds of the work for us."[49]

To encourage hybrid vehicle adoption, some states and cities are granting their drivers the convenience of free parking and solo-occupant access to HOV lanes. A Toyota spokesperson recently told the *Los Angeles Times,* "Many customers are telling us the carpool lane is the main reason for buying now."[50] Toyota highlights the carpool benefit on its Prius Web site, and convenience has become an incentive to drive efficient hybrid cars in traffic-congested states like California and Virginia. Critics have charged, however, that such incentives clog carpool lanes and reinforce a "one car, one person" lifestyle over alternative transportation. In response, the Virginia legislature has more recently enacted curbs on hybrid drivers' use of HOV lanes during peak hours, requiring three or more people per vehicle, except for those that have been grandfathered in.[51]

Solar power was once used only for supplying electricity in remote areas (for example, while camping in the wilderness or boating or in homes situated off the power grid). That convenience, however, is being exploited for other applications. In landscaping, for example, self-contained solar-powered outdoor evening lights that recharge automatically during the day eliminate the need for electrical hookups and offer flexibility for reconfiguration. With society's increasing mobility and reliance on electronics, solar power's convenience is also manifest in solar-powered calculators, wrist watches, and other gadgets, eliminating worries over dying batteries. Reware's solar-powered "Juice Bag" backpack is a popular portable re-charger for students, professionals, and outdoor enthusiasts on the go. The Juice Bag's flexible, waterproof solar panel has a 16.6-volt capacity to generate 6.3 watts to recharge PDAs, cell phones, iPods, and other gadgets in about 2 to 4 hours.[52]

Bundling

Some green products do not offer any of the inherent five consumer-desired benefits noted above. This was the case when energy-efficient and CFC-free refrigerators were introduced in China in the 1990s. While Chinese consumers preferred and were willing to pay about 15 percent more for refrigerators that were "energy-efficient," they did not connect the environmental advantage of "CFC-free" with either energy efficiency or savings. Consequently, the "CFC-free" feature had little impact on purchase decisions.[53] To encourage demand, the CFC-free feature was bundled with attributes desired by Chinese consumers, which included energy efficiency, savings, brand/quality, and outstanding after-sales service.

According to popular culture experts, green marketing must appear grass-roots driven and humorous without sounding preachy.

Given consumer demand for convenience, incorporating time-saving or ease-of-use features into green products can further expand their mainstream acceptance. Ford's hybrid Escape SUV comes with an optional 110-volt AC power outlet suitable for work, tailgating, or camping. Convenience has also enhanced the appeal of Interface's recyclable FLOR carpeting, which is marketed as "practical, goof-proof, and versatile." FLOR comes in modular square tiles with four peel-and-stick dots on the back for easy installation (and pull up for altering, recycling, or washing with water in the sink). Modularity offers versatility to assemble tiles for a custom look. Interface promotes the idea that its carpet tiles can be changed and reconfigured in minutes to dress up a room for any occasion. The tiles come in pizza-style boxes for storage, and ease of use is FLOR's primary consumer appeal.

Finally, Austin (Texas) Energy's "Green Choice" program has led the nation in renewable energy sales for the past three years.[54] In 2006, demand for wind energy outpaced supply so that the utility resorted to selecting new "Green Choice" subscribers by lottery.[55] While most utilities find it challenging to sell green electricity at a premium price on its environmental merit, Austin Energy's success comes from bundling three benefits that appeal to commercial power users: First, Green Choice customers are recognized in broadcast media for their corporate responsibility; second, the green power is marketed as "home grown," appealing to Texan loyalties; and third, the program offers a fixed price that is locked in for 10 years. Because wind power's cost is derived primarily from the construction of wind farms and is not subject to volatile fossil fuel costs, Austin Energy passes its inherent price stability onto its Green Choice customers. Thus, companies participating in Green Choice enjoy the predictability of their future energy costs in an otherwise volatile energy market.

In summary, the analysis suggests that successful green marketing programs have broadened the consumer appeal of green products by convincing consumers of their "non-green" consumer value. The lesson for crafting effective green marketing strategies is that planners need to identify the inherent consumer value of green product attributes (for example, energy efficiency's inherent long-term money savings) or bundle desired consumer value into green products (such as fixed pricing of wind power) and to draw marketing attention to this consumer value.

Calibration of Consumer Knowledge

Many of the successful green products in the analysis described here employ compelling, educational marketing messages and slogans that connect green product attributes with desired consumer value. That is, the marketing programs successfully calibrated consumer knowledge to recognize the green product's consumer benefits. In many instances, the environmental benefit was positioned as secondary, if mentioned at all. Changes made in EPA's Energy Star logo provide an example, illustrating the program's improved message calibration over the years. One of Energy Star's early marketing messages, "EPA Pollution Preventer," was not only ambiguous but myopically focused on pollution rather than a more mainstream consumer benefit. A later promotional message, "Saving The Earth. Saving Your Money." better associated energy efficiency with consumer value, and one of its more recent slogans, "Money Isn't All You're Saving," touts economic savings as the chief benefit. This newest slogan also encourages consumers to think implicitly about what else they are "saving"—the logo's illustration of the Earth suggests the answer, educating consumers that "saving the Earth" can also meet consumer self-interest.

The connection between environmental benefit and consumer value is evident in Earthbound Farm Organic's slogan, "Delicious produce is our business, but health is our bottom line," which communicates that pesticide-free produce is flavorful and healthy. Likewise, Tide Coldwater's "Deep Clean. Save Green." slogan not only assures consumers of the detergent's cleaning performance, but the term "green" offers a double meaning, connecting Tide's cost saving with its environmental benefit. Citizen's solar-powered Eco-Drive watch's slogan, "Unstoppable Caliber," communicates the product's convenience and performance (that is, the battery will not die) as well as prestige. Table 1 on page 120 shows other successful marketing messages that educate consumers of the inherent consumer value of green.

Some compelling marketing communications educate consumers to recognize green products as "solutions" for their personal needs *and* the environment.[56] When introducing its Renewal brand, Rayovac positioned the reusable alkaline batteries as a solution for heavy battery users and the environment with concurrent ads touting "How to save $150 on a CD player that costs $100" and "How to save 147 batteries from going to landfills." Complementing the money savings and landfill angles, another ad in the campaign featured sports star Michael Jordan proclaiming, "More Power. More Music. And More Game Time." to connect Renewal batteries' performance to convenience.[57] In practice, the analysis conducted here suggests that advertising that draws attention to how the environmental product benefit can deliver desired personal value can broaden consumer acceptance of green products.

Credibility of Product Claims

Credibility is the foundation of effective green marketing. Green products must meet or exceed consumer expectations by delivering their promised consumer value and providing substantive environmental benefits. Often, consumers don't have the expertise or ability to verify green products' environmental and consumer values, creating misperceptions and skepticism. As exemplified in the case of Mobil's Hefty photodegradable plastic trash bag described earlier, green marketing that touts a product's or a company's environmental credentials can spark the scrutiny of advocacy groups or regulators. For example, although it was approved by the U.S. Food and Drug Administration, sugar substitute

Splenda's "Made from sugar, so it tastes like sugar" slogan and claim of being "natural" have been challenged by the Sugar Association and Generation Green, a health advocacy group, as misleading given that its processing results in a product that is "unrecognizable as sugar."[58]

To be persuasive, past research suggests that green claims should be specific and meaningful.[59] Toyota recognizes the ambiguity of the term "green" and discourages its use in its marketing of its gas-electric hybrid cars. One proposed slogan, "Drive green, breathe blue" was dismissed in favor of specific claims about fuel efficiency, such as "Less gas in. Less gasses out."[60] Further, environmental claims must be humble and not over-promise. When Ford Motor Company publicized in *National*

Table 1 Marketing Messages Connecting Green Products with Desired Consumer Value

Value	Message and Business/Product
Efficiency and cost effectiveness	"The only thing our washer will shrink is your water bill." —ASKO "Did you know that between 80 and 85 percent of the energy used to wash clothes comes from heating the water? Tide Coldwater—The Coolest Way to Clean." —Tide Coldwater Laundry Detergent "mpg:)" —Toyota Prius
Health and safety	"20 years of refusing to farm with toxic pesticides. Stubborn, perhaps. Healthy, most definitely." —Earthbound Farm Organic "Safer for You and the Environment." —Seventh Generation Household Cleaners
Performance	"Environmentally friendly stain removal. It's as simple as H_2O." —Mohawk EverSet Fibers Carpet "Fueled by light so it runs forever. It's unstoppable. Just like the people who wear it." —Citizen Eco-Drive Sport Watch
Symbolism	"Think is the chair with a brain and a conscience." —Steelcase's Think Chair "Make up your mind, not just your face." —The Body Shop
Convenience	"Long life for hard-to-reach places." —General Electric's CFL Flood Lights
Bundling	"Performance and luxury fueled by innovative technology." —Lexus RX400h Hybrid Sports Utility Vehicle

Source: Compiled by J.A. Ottman, E.R. Stafford, and C.L. Hartman, 2006.

Geographic and other magazines its new eco-designed Rouge River Plant that incorporated the world's largest living roof of plants, critics questioned the authenticity of Ford's environmental commitment given the poor fuel economy of the automaker's best-selling SUVs.[61] Even the Prius has garnered some criticism for achieving considerably less mileage (approximately 26 percent less according to *Consumer Reports*) than its government sticker rating claims, although the actual reduced mileage does not appear to be hampering sales.[62] Nonetheless, green product attributes need to be communicated honestly and qualified for believability (in other words, consumer benefits and environmental effectiveness claims need to be compared with comparable alternatives or likely usage scenarios). For example, Toyota includes an "actual mileage may vary" disclaimer in Prius advertising. When Ford's hybrid Escape SUV owners complained that they were not achieving expected mileage ratings, Ford launched the "Fuel-Economy School" campaign to educate drivers about ways to maximize fuel efficiency.[63] Further, EPA is reconsidering how it estimates hybrid mileage ratings to better reflect realistic driving conditions (such as heavy acceleration and air conditioner usage).[64]

Third Party Endorsements and Eco-Certifications

Expert third parties with respected standards for environmental testing (such as independent laboratories, government agencies, private consultants, or nonprofit advocacy organizations) can provide green product endorsements and/or "seals of approval" to help clarify and bolster the believability of product claims.[65] The "Energy Star" label, discussed earlier, is a common certification that distinguishes certain electronic products as consuming up to 30 percent less energy than comparable alternatives. The U.S. Department of Agriculture's "USDA Organic" certifies the production and handling of organic produce and dairy products.

Green Seal and Scientific Certification Systems emblems certify a broad spectrum of green products. Green Seal sets specific criteria for various categories of products, ranging from paints to cleaning agents to hotel properties, and for a fee, companies can have their products evaluated and monitored annually for certification. Green Seal-certified products include Zero-VOC Olympic Premium interior paint and Johnson Wax professional cleaners. Green Seal has also certified the Hyatt Regency in Washington, DC, for the hotel's comprehensive energy and water conservation, recycling programs, and environmental practices. By contrast, Scientific Certification Systems (SCS) certifies specific product claims or provides a detailed "eco-profile" for a product's environmental impact for display on product labels for a broad array of products, from agricultural products to fisheries to construction. For example, Armstrong hard surface flooring holds SCS certification, and SCS works with retailers like The Home Depot to monitor its vendors' environmental claims.[66]

Although eco-certifications differentiate products and aid in consumer decisionmaking, they are not without controversy. The science behind eco-seals can appear subjective and/or complex, and critics may take issue with certification criteria.[67] For example, GreenOrder, a New York-based environmental consulting firm, has devised a scorecard to evaluate cleantech products marketed in General Electric's "Ecomagination" initiative, which range from fuel-efficient aircraft engines to wind turbines to water treatment technologies. Only those passing GreenOrder's criteria are marketed as Ecomagination products, but critics have questioned GE's inclusion of "cleaner coal" (that is, coal gasification for cleaner burning and sequestration of carbon dioxide emissions) as an "Ecomagination" product.[68]

Although eco-certifications differentiate products and aid in consumer decisionmaking, they are not without controversy.

Consequently, when seeking endorsements and eco-certifications, marketers should consider the environmental tradeoffs and complexity of their products and the third parties behind endorsements and/or certifications: Is the third party respected? Are its certification methodologies accepted by leading environmentalists, industry experts, government regulators, and other key stakeholders? Marketers should educate their customers about the meaning behind an endorsement or an eco-seal's criteria. GE recognizes that its cleaner coal technology is controversial but hopes that robust marketing and educational outreach will convince society about cleaner coal's environmental benefits.[69] On its Web site, GE references U.S. Energy Information Administration's statistics that coal accounts for about 24 percent of the world's total energy consumption, arguing that coal will continue to be a dominant source of energy due to its abundance and the increasing electrification of populous nations such as China and India.[70] In response to GE's commitment to clean coal, Jonathan Lash, president of the World Resources Institute, said, "Five years ago, I had to struggle to suppress my gag response to terms like 'clean coal,' but I've since faced the sobering reality that every two weeks China opens a new coal-fired plant. India is moving at almost the same pace. There is huge environmental value in developing ways to mitigate these plants' emissions."[71]

Word-of-Mouth Evangelism and the Internet

Increasingly, consumers have grown skeptical of commercial messages, and they're turning to the collective wisdom and experience of their friends and peers about products.[72] Word-of-mouth or "buzz" is perceived to be very credible, especially as consumers consider and try to comprehend complex product innovations. The Internet, through e-mail and its vast, accessible repository of information, Web sites, search engines, blogs, product ratings sites, podcasts, and other digital platforms, has opened significant opportunities for tapping consumers' social and communication networks to diffuse credible "word-of-mouse" (buzz facilitated by the Internet) about green products. This is exemplified by one of the most spectacular product introductions on the Web: Tide Coldwater.

In 2005, Procter & Gamble partnered with the non-profit organization, the Alliance to Save Energy (ASE), in a "viral marketing" campaign to spread news about the money-saving benefits of laundering clothes in cold water with specially formulated Tide Coldwater.[73] ASE provided credibility for the detergent by auditing and backing P&G's claims that consumers could save an average of $63 a year if they switched from warm to cold water washes. ASE sent e-mail promotions encouraging consumers to visit Tide.com's interactive Web site and take the "Coldwater Challenge" by registering to receive a free sample. Visitors could calculate how much money they would save by using the detergent, learn other energy-saving laundry tips, and refer e-mail addresses of their friends to take the challenge as well. Tide.com offered an engaging map of the United States where, over time, visitors could track and watch their personal networks grow across the country when their friends logged onto the site to request a free sample.

Given the immediacy of e-mail and the Internet, word-of-mouse is fast becoming an important vehicle for spreading credible news about new products. According to the Pew Internet & American Life Project, 44 percent of online U.S. adults (about 50 million Americans) are "content creators," meaning that they contribute to the Internet via blogs, product recommendations, and reviews.[74] To facilitate buzz, however, marketers need to create credible messages, stories, and Web sites about their products that are so compelling, interesting, and/or entertaining that consumers will seek the information out and forward it to their friends and family.[75] The fact that P&G was able to achieve this for a low-involvement product is quite remarkable.

International online marketing consultant Hitwise reported that ASE's e-mail campaign increased traffic at the Tide Coldwater Web site by 900 percent in the first week, and then tripled that level in week two.[76] Within a few months, more than one million Americans accepted the "Coldwater Challenge," and word-of-mouse cascaded through ten degrees of separation across all 50 states and more than 33,000 zip codes.[77] In October 2005, Hitwise reported that Tide.com ranked as the twelfth most popular site by market share of visits in the "Lifestyle—House and Garden" category.[78] No other laundry detergent brand's Web site has gained a significant Web presence in terms of the number of visits.

P&G's savvy implementation of "The Three Cs"—consumer value positioning on money savings, calibration of consumer knowledge about cold wash effectiveness via an engaging Web site, and credible product messages dispatched by a respected non-profit group and consumers' Internet networks—set the stage for Tide Coldwater's successful launch.

The Future of Green Marketing

Clearly, there are many lessons to be learned to avoid green marketing myopia (see the box)—the short version of all this is that effective green marketing requires applying good marketing principles to make green products desirable for consumers. The question that remains, however, is, what is green marketing's future? Historically, green marketing has been a misunderstood concept. Business scholars have viewed it as a "fringe" topic, given that environmentalism's acceptance of limits and conservation does not mesh well with marketing's traditional axioms of "give customers what they want" and "sell as much as you can." In practice, green marketing myopia has led to ineffective products and consumer reluctance. Sustainability, however, is destined to dominate twenty-first century commerce. Rising energy prices, growing pollution and resource consumption in Asia, and political pressures to address climate change are driving innovation toward healthier, more-efficient, high-performance products. In short, all marketing will incorporate elements of green marketing.

As the authors of *Natural Capitalism* argue, a more sustainable business model requires "product dematerialization"—that is, commerce will shift from the "sale of goods" to the "sale of services" (for example, providing illumination rather than selling light bulbs).[79] This model is illustrated, if unintentionally, by arguably the twenty-first century's hottest product—Apple's iPod. The iPod gives consumers the convenience to download, store, and play tens of thousands of songs without the environmental impact of manufacturing and distributing CDs, plastic jewel cases, and packaging.

Innovations that transform material goods into efficient streams of services could proliferate if consumers see them as desirable. To encourage energy and water efficiency, Electrolux piloted a "pay-per-wash" service in Sweden in 1999 where consumers were given new efficient washing machines for a small home installation fee and then were charged 10 Swedish kronor (about $1) per use. The machines were connected via the Internet to a central database to monitor use, and Electrolux maintained ownership and servicing of the washers. When the machines had served their duty, Electrolux took them

Summary of Guideposts for the "Three Cs"

Evidence indicates that successful green products have avoided green marketing myopia by following three important principles: consumer value positioning, calibration of consumer knowledge, and the credibility of product claims.

Consumer Value Positioning

- Design environmental products to perform as well as (or better than) alternatives.
- Promote and deliver the consumer-desired value of environmental products and target relevant consumer market segments (such as market health benefits among health-conscious consumers).
- Broaden mainstream appeal by bundling (or adding) consumer-desired value into environmental products (such as fixed pricing for subscribers of renewable energy).

Calibration of Consumer Knowledge

- Educate consumers with marketing messages that connect environmental product attributes with desired consumer value (for example, "pesticide-free produce is healthier"; "energy-efficiency saves money"; or "solar power is convenient").

- Frame environmental product attributes as "solutions" for consumer needs (for example, "rechargeable batteries offer longer performance").
- Create engaging and educational Internet sites about environmental products' desired consumer value (for example, Tide Coldwater's interactive Web site allows visitors to calculate their likely annual money savings based on their laundry habits, utility source (gas or electricity), and zip code location).

Credibility of Product Claims

- Employ environmental product and consumer benefit claims that are specific, meaningful, unpretentious, and qualified (that is, compared with comparable alternatives or likely usage scenarios).
- Procure product endorsements or eco-certifications from trustworthy third parties, and educate consumers about the meaning behind those endorsements and eco-certifications.
- Encourage consumer evangelism via consumers' social and Internet communication networks with compelling, interesting, and/or entertaining information about environmental products (for example, Tide's "Coldwater Challenge" Web site included a map of the United States so visitors could track and watch their personal influence spread when their friends requested a free sample).

---

back for remanufacturing. Pay-per-wash failed, however, because consumers were not convinced of its benefits over traditional ownership of washing machines.[80] Had Electrolux better marketed pay-per-wash's convenience (for example, virtually no upfront costs for obtaining a top-of-the-line washer, free servicing, and easy trade-ins for upgrades) or bundled pay-per-wash with more desirable features, consumers might have accepted the green service. To avoid green marketing myopia, the future success of product dematerialization and more sustainable services will depend on credibly communicating and delivering consumer-desired value in the marketplace. Only then will product dematerialization steer business onto a more sustainable path.

Notes

1. G. Fowler, "'Green Sales Pitch Isn't Moving Many Products," *Wall Street Journal,* 6 March 2002.

2. See, for example, K. Alston and J. P. Roberts, "Partners in New Product Development: S.C. Johnson and the Alliance for Environmental Innovation," *Corporate Environmental Strategy* 6, no. 2: 111–28.

3. See, for example, J. Ottman, *Green Marketing: Opportunity for Innovation* (Lincolnwood [Chicago]: NTC Business Books, 1997).

4. P. Hawken, A. Lovins, and L. H. Lovins, *Natural Capitalism: Creating the Next Industrial Revolution* (Boston: Little, Brown, and Company, 1999).

5. See, for example, *Business Week,* "Alternate Power: A Change in the Wind," 4 July 2005, 36–37.

6. See T. L. Friedman, "Geo-Greening by Example," *New York Times,* 27 March 2005; and T. L. Friedman, "The New 'Sputnik' Challenges: They All Run on Oil," *New York Times,* 20 January 2006.

7. There is some debate as to how to define a "green consumer." Roper ASW's most recent research segments American consumers by their propensity to purchase environmentally sensitive products into five categories, ranging from "True Blue Greens," who are most inclined to seek out and buy green on a regular basis (representing 9 percent of the population), to "Basic Browns," who are the least involved group and believe environmental indifference is mainstream (representing 33 percent of the population); see Roper ASW "Green Gauge Report 2002: Americans Perspective on Environmental Issues—Yes . . . But," November 2002, http://www.industry. com/conferences/november2002/nov2002_proceedings/ plenary/greenguage2002.pdf (accessed 7 February 2006). Alternatively, however, some marketers view green consumers as falling into three broad segments concerned with preserving the planet, health consequences of environmental problems, and animal welfare; see Ottman, note 3 above, pages 19–44. Because environmental concerns are varied, ranging from resource/energy conservation to wildlife protection to air quality, marketing research suggests that responses to green advertising appeals vary by consumer segments. For example, in one study, young college-educated students were found to be drawn to health-oriented green appeals, whereas working adults were more responsive toward health, waste, and energy

appeals; see M. R. Stafford, T. F. Stafford, and J. Chowdhury, "Predispositions Toward Green Issues: The Potential Efficacy of Advertising Appeals," *Journal of Current Issues and Research in Advertising* 18, no. 2 (1996): 67–79. One of the lessons from the study presented here is that green products must be positioned on the consumer value sought by targeted consumers.

8. A. Grubler, "Doing More with Less: Improving the Environment through Green Engineering," *Environment 48,* no. 2 (March 2006): 22–37.

9. See, for example, L. A. Crosby and S. L. Johnson, "Customer-Centric Innovation," *Marketing Management* 15, no. 2 (2006): 12–13.

10. The methodology for this article involved reviewing case descriptions of green products discussed in the academic and business literature to identify factors contributing to consumer acceptance or resistance. Product failure was defined as situations in which the green product experienced very limited sales and ultimately was either removed from the marketplace (such as General Motor's EV1 electric car and Electrolux's "pay-per-wash" service) or re-positioned in the marketplace (such as Philips' "EarthLight"). Product success was defined as situations in which the green product attained consumer acceptance and was widely available at the time of the analysis. Particular attention centered on the market strategies and external market forces of green products experiencing significant growth (such as gas-electric hybrid cars and organic foods), and the study examined their market context, pricing, targeted consumers, product design, and marketing appeals and messages.

11. See T. Levitt, "Marketing Myopia," *Harvard Business Review* 28, July–August (1960): 24–47.

12. A. D. Lee and R. Conger, "Market Transformation: Does it Work? The Super Energy Efficient Refrigerator Program," *ACEEE Proceedings,* 1996, 3.69–3.80.

13. Ibid.

14. The California Air Resources Board (CARB) adopted the Low-Emission Vehicle (LEV) regulations in 1990. The original LEV regulations required the introduction of zero-emission vehicles (ZEVs) in 1998 as 2 percent of all vehicles produced for sale in California, and increased the percentage of ZEVs from 2 percent to 10 percent in 2003. By 1998, significant flexibility was introduced through partial ZEV credits for very-low-emission vehicles. For a review, see S. Shaheen, "California's Zero-Emission Vehicle Mandate," *Institute of Transportation Studies,* Paper UCD-ITS-RP-04-14, 2 September 2004.

15. C. Palmeri, "Unplugged," *Business Week,* 20 March 2006, 12.

16. "Think Tanks," *Automotive News,* 6 March 2006, 42; J. Ottman, "Lessons from the Green Graveyard," *Green@Work,* April 2003, 62–63.

17. J. Lawrence, "The Green Revolution: Case Study," *Advertising Age,* 29 January 1991, 12.

18. See Roper ASW, note 7 above.

19. "Fuel Economy: Why You're Not Getting the MPG You Expect," *Consumer Reports,* October 2005, 20–23.

20. J. O'Dell, "Prices Soar for Hybrids with Rights to Fast Lane," *Los Angeles Times,* 27 August 2005.

21. M. Landler and K. Bradsher, "VW to Build Hybrid Minivan with Chinese," *New York Times,* 9 September 2005.

22. K. Carter, "'Hybrid' Cars Were Oscars' Politically Correct Ride," *USA Today,* 31 March 2003.

23. See, for example, H. W. Jenkins, "Dear Valued Hybrid Customer . . . ," *Wall Street Journal,* 30 November 2005; E. R. Stafford, "Conspicuous Conservation," *Green@Work,* Winter 2004, 30–32. A recent Civil Society Institute poll found that 66 percent of survey participants agreed that driving fuel efficient vehicles was "patriotic"; see Reuters, "Americans See Fuel Efficient Cars as 'Patriotic,'" 18 March 2005, http://www.planetark.com/avantgo/dailynewsstory.cfm?newsid=29988.

24. "Rising Consumer Interest in Hybrid Technology Confirmed by Maritz Research," PRNewswire, 5 January 2006.

25. O'Dell, note 20 above.

26. J. Fetto, "The Baby Business," *American Demographics,* May 2003, 40.

27. See D. McGinn, "The Green Machine," *Newsweek,* 21 March 2005, E8–E12; and J. Weber, "A Super-Natural Investing Opportunity," *Business 2.0,* March 2005, 34.

28. A. Murray, "Can Wal-Mart Sustain a Softer Edge?" *Wall Street Journal,* 8 February 2006.

29. C. Tan, "New Incentives for Being Green," *Wall Street Journal,* 4 August 2005.

30. For an overview of the Leadership in Energy and Environmental Design Green Building Rating System, see http://www.usgbc. org. The 69-point LEED rating system addresses energy and water use, indoor air quality, materials, siting, and innovation and design. Buildings can earn basic certification or a silver, gold, or platinum designation depending on the number of credits awarded by external reviewers. Critics charge, however, that the costly and confusing administration of the LEED system is inhibiting adoption of the program and impeding the program's environmental objectives; see A. Schendler and R. Udall, "LEED is Broken; Let's Fix It," *Grist Magazine,* 16 October 2005, http://www.grist.com/comments/soapbox/2005/10/26/leed/index1.html.

31. GreenBiz.com, "Survey: Home Builders Name Energy Efficiency as Biggest Industry Trend," 26 January 2006, http://www.greenerbuildings.com/news_details.cfm?NewsID=30221.

32. D. Smith, "Conservation: Building Grows Greener in Bay Area," *San Francisco Chronicle,* 1 June 2005.

33. E. Beck, "Earth-Friendly Materials Go Mainstream," *New York Times,* 5 January 2006, 8.

34. J. M. Ginsberg and P. N. Bloom, "Choosing the Right Green Marketing Strategy," *MIT Sloan Management Journal,* Fall 2004: 79–84.

35. Tan, note 29 above.

36. Tan, note 29, above.

37. C. C. Berk, "P&G Will Promote 'Green' Detergent," *Wall Street Journal,* 19 January 2005.

38. K. McLaughlin, "Has Your Chicken Been Drugged?" *Wall Street Journal,* 2 August 2005; and E. Weise, "Are Our Products Our Enemy?" *USA Today,* 13 August 2005.

39. McLaughlin, ibid.

40. Alston and Roberts, note 2 above.

41. R. Leiber, "The Dirt on Green Housecleaners," *Wall Street Journal,* 29 December 2005.

42. M. Alexander, "Home Improved," *Readers Digest,* April 2004, 77–80.

43. For example, see D. Leonhardt, "Buy a Hybrid, and Save a Guzzler," *New York Times,* 8 February 2006.

44. See, for example, D. Cave, "It's Not Sexy Being Green (Yet)," *New York Times,* 2 October 2005.

45. G. Chon, "Toyota Goes After Copycat Hybrids; Buyers are Asked to Believe Branded HSD Technology is Worth the Extra Cost," *Wall Street Journal,* 22 September 2005.

46. B. G. Hoffman, "Ford: Now It's Easy Being Green," *Detroit News,* 31 January 2006.

47. See W. McDonough and M. Braungart, *Cradle to Cradle: Remaking the Way We Make Things* (New York: North Point Press, 2002).

48. R. Smith, "Beyond Recycling: Manufacturers Embrace 'C2C' Design," *Wall Street Journal,* 3 March 2005.

49. K. Hafen, "Preston Festival Goes LED," *Logan Herald Journal,* 21 September 2005.

50. O'Dell, note 20 above.

51. A. Covarrubias, "In Carpool Lanes, Hybrids Find Cold Shoulders," *Los Angeles Times,* 10 April 2006.

52. M. Clayton, "Hot Stuff for a Cool Earth," *Christian Science Monitor,* 21 April 2005.

53. See Ogilvy & Mather Topline Report, *China Energy-Efficient CFC-Free Refrigerator Study* (Beijing: Ogilvy & Mather, August 1997); E. R. Stafford, C. L. Hartman, and Y. Liang, "Forces Driving Environmental Innovation Diffusion in China: The Case of Green-freeze," *Business Horizons* 9, no. 2 (2003): 122–35.

54. J. Baker, Jr., K. Denby, and J. E. Jerrett, "Market-based Government Activities in Texas," *Texas Business Review,* August 2005, 1–5.

55. T. Harris, "Austinites Apply to Save With Wind Power," *KVUE News,* 13 February 2006.

56. J. Ottman, note 3 above.

57. J. Ottman, note 3 above.

58. Generation Green, "Splenda Letter to Federal Trade Commission," 13 January 2005, http://www.generationgreen.org/2005_01-FTC-letter.htm (accessed 7 February 2006).

59. J. Davis, "Strategies for Environmental Advertising," *Journal of Consumer Marketing* 10, no. 2 (1993): 23–25.

60. S. Farah, "The Thin Green Line," *CMO Magazine,* 1 December 2005, http://www.cmomagazine.com/read/120105/green_line.html (accessed 9 February 2006).

61. Ibid.

62. See Jenkins, note 23 above.

63. See Farah, note 60 above.

64. M. Maynard, "E.P.A. Revision is Likely to Cut Mileage Ratings," *New York Times,* 11 January 2006.

65. For a more comprehensive overview of eco-certifications and labeling, see L. H. Gulbrandsen, "Mark of Sustainability? Challenges for Fishery and Forestry Eco-labeling," *Environment* 47, no. 5 (2005): 8–23.

66. For a comprehensive overview of other eco-certifications, see Consumers Union's Web site at http://www.eco-labels.org/home.cfm.

67. Gulbrandsen, note 65 above, pages 17–19.

68. Farah, note 60 above.

69. Farah, note 60 above.

70. See GE Global Research, *Clean Coal,* http://ge.com/research/grc_2_1_3.html (accessed 16 April 2006).

71. A. Griscom Little, "It Was Just My Ecomagination," *Grist Magazine,* 10 May 2005, http://grist.org/news/muck/2005/05/10/little-ge/index.html.

72. E. Rosen, *The Anatomy of Buzz: How to Create Word-of-Mouth Marketing* (New York: Doubleday, 2000).

73. Viral marketing is a form of "word-of-mouse" buzz marketing defined as "the process of encouraging honest communication among consumer networks, and it focuses on email as the channel." See J. E. Phelps, R. Lewis, L. Mobilio, D. Perry, and N. Raman, "Viral Marketing or Electronic Word-of-Mouth Advertising: Examining Consumer Responses and Motivation to Pass Along Email," *Journal of Advertising Research* 44, no. 4 (2004): 333–48.

74. G. Ramsey, "Ten Reasons Why Word-of-Mouth Marketing Works," Online Media Daily, 23 September 2005, http://publications.mediapost.com/index.cfm?fuseaction=Articles.san&s=34339&Nid=15643&p=114739 (accessed 16 February 2006).

75. See Rosen, note 72 above.

76. Ramsey, note 74 above.

77. Tide press release, "ColdWater Challenge Reaches One Million," http://www.tide.com/tidecoldwater/challenge.html (accessed 13 September 2005).

78. L. Prescott, "Case Study: Tide Boosts Traffic 9-fold," iMedia Connection, 30 November 2005, http://www.imdiaconnection.com/content/7406.asp.

79. Hawken, Lovins, and Lovins, note 4 above; see also A. B. Lovins, L. H. Lovins, and P. Hawken, "A Road Map for Natural Capitalism," *Harvard Business Review,* May–June 1999, 145–58.

80. J. Makower, "Green Marketing: Lessons from the Leaders," Two Steps Forward, September 2005, http://makower.typepad.com/joel_makower/2005/09/green_marketing.html.

JACQUELYN A. OTTMAN is president of J. Ottman Consulting, Inc. in New York and author of *Green Marketing: Opportunity for Innovation,* 2nd edition (NTC Business Books, 1997). She can be reached at jaottman@greenmarketing.com. EDWIN R. STAFFORD is an associate professor of marketing at Utah State University, Logan. He researches the strategic marketing and policy implications of clean technology (also known as "cleantech") and is the co-principal investigator for a $1 million research grant from the U.S. Department of Energy on the diffusion of wind power in Utah. He may be reached at ed.stafford@usu.edu. CATHY L. HARTMAN is a professor of marketing at Utah State University, Logan. Her research centers on how interpersonal influence and social systems affect the diffusion of ideas and clean products and technology. She is principal investigator on a $1 million U.S. Department of Energy grant for developing wind power in the state of Utah. She can be contacted at cathy.hartman@usu.edu.

The New E-spionage Threat

A *BusinessWeek* probe of rising attacks on America's most sensitive computer networks uncovers startling security gaps.

BRIAN GROW, KEITH EPSTEIN, AND CHI-CHU TSCHANG

The e-mail message addressed to a Booz Allen Hamilton executive was mundane—a shopping list sent over by the Pentagon of weaponry India wanted to buy. But the missive turned out to be a brilliant fake. Lurking beneath the description of aircraft, engines, and radar equipment was an insidious piece of computer code known as "Poison Ivy" designed to suck sensitive data out of the $4 billion consulting firm's computer network.

The Pentagon hadn't sent the e-mail at all. Its origin is unknown, but the message traveled through Korea on its way to Booz Allen. Its authors knew enough about the "sender" and "recipient" to craft a message unlikely to arouse suspicion. Had the Booz Allen executive clicked on the attachment, his every keystroke would have been reported back to a mysterious master at the Internet address cybersyndrome.3322.org, which is registered through an obscure company headquartered on the banks of China's Yangtze River.

The U.S. government, and its sprawl of defense contractors, have been the victims of an unprecedented rash of similar cyber attacks over the last two years, say current and former U.S. government officials. "It's espionage on a massive scale," says Paul B. Kurtz, a former high-ranking national security official. Government agencies reported 12,986 cyber security incidents to the U.S. Homeland Security Dept. last fiscal year, triple the number from two years earlier. Incursions on the military's networks were up 55% last year, says Lieutenant General Charles E. Croom, head of the Pentagon's Joint Task Force for Global Network Operations. Private targets like Booz Allen are just as vulnerable and pose just as much potential security risk. "They have our information on their networks. They're building our weapon systems. You wouldn't want that in enemy hands," Croom says. Cyber attackers "are not denying, disrupting, or destroying operations—yet. But that doesn't mean they don't have the capability."

A Monster

When the deluge began in 2006, officials scurried to come up with software "patches," "wraps," and other bits of triage. The effort got serious last summer when top military brass discreetly summoned the chief executives or their representatives from the 20 largest U.S. defense contractors to the Pentagon for a "threat briefing." *BusinessWeek* has learned the U.S. government has launched a classified operation called Byzantine Foothold to detect, track, and disarm intrusions on the government's most critical networks. And President George W. Bush on Jan. 8 quietly signed an order known as the Cyber Initiative to overhaul U.S. cyber defenses, at an eventual cost in the tens of billions of dollars, and establishing 12 distinct goals, according to people briefed on its contents. One goal in particular illustrates the urgency and scope of the problem: By June all government agencies must cut the number of communication channels, or ports, through which their networks connect to the Internet from more than 4,000 to fewer than 100. On Apr. 8, Homeland Security Dept. Secretary Michael Chertoff called the President's order a cyber security "Manhattan Project."

But many security experts worry the Internet has become too unwieldy to be tamed. New exploits appear every day, each seemingly more sophisticated than the previous one. The Defense Dept., whose Advanced Research Projects Agency (DARPA) developed the Internet in the 1960s, is beginning to think it created a monster. "You don't need an Army, a Navy, an Air Force to beat the U.S.," says General William T. Lord, commander of the Air Force Cyber Command, a unit formed in November, 2006, to upgrade Air Force computer defenses. "You can be a peer force for the price of the PC on my desk." Military officials have long believed that "it's cheaper, and we kill stuff faster, when we use the Internet to enable high-tech warfare," says a top adviser to the U.S. military on the overhaul of its computer security strategy. "Now they're saying, Oh, shit."

Adding to Washington's anxiety, current and former U.S. government officials say many of the new attackers are trained professionals backed by foreign governments. "The new breed of threat that has evolved is nation-state-sponsored stuff," says Amit Yoran, a former director of Homeland Security's National Cyber Security Div. Adds one of the nation's most senior military officers: "We've got to figure out how to get at it before our regrets exceed our ability to react."

The military and intelligence communities have alleged that the People's Republic of China is the U.S.'s biggest cyber menace. "In the past year, numerous computer networks around the world,

An Evolving Crisis

Major attacks on the U.S. government and defense industry—and their code names.

Solar Sunrise

February, 1998. Air Force and Navy computers are hit by malicious code that sniffed out a hole in a popular enterprise software operating system, patched its own entry point—then did nothing. Some attacks are routed through the United Arab Emirates while the U.S. is preparing for military action in Iraq. Turns out the attacks were launched by two teenagers in Cloverdale, Calif., and an Israeli accomplice who called himself the "Analyzer."

Moonlight Maze

March, 1998, through 1999. Attackers use special code to gain access to Web sites at the Defense Dept., NASA, the Energy Dept., and weapons labs across the country. Large packets of unclassified data are stolen. "At times, the end point [for the data] was inside Russia," says a source familiar with the investigation. The sponsor of the attack has never been identified. The Russian government denied any involvement.

Titan Rain

2004. Hackers believed to be in China access classified data stored on computer networks of defense contractor Lockheed Martin, Sandia National Labs, and NASA. The intrusions are identified by Shawn Carpenter, a cyber security analyst at Sandia Labs. After he reports the breaches to the U.S. Army and FBI, Sandia fires him. Carpenter later sues Sandia for wrongful termination. In February, 2007, a jury awards him $4.7 million.

Byzantine Foothold

2007. A new form of attack, using sophisticated technology, deluges outfits from the State Dept. to Boeing. Military cyber security specialists find the "resources of a nation-state behind it" and call the type of attack an "advanced persistent threat." The breaches are detailed in a classified document known as an Intelligence Community Assessment. The source of many of the attacks, allege U.S. officials, is China. China denies the charge.

including those owned by the U.S. government, were subject to intrusions that appear to have originated within the PRC," reads the Pentagon's annual report to Congress on Chinese military power, released on Mar. 3. The preamble of Bush's Cyber Initiative focuses attention on China as well.

Wang Baodong, a spokesman for the Chinese government at its embassy in Washington, says "anti-China forces" are behind the allegations. Assertions by U.S. officials and others of cyber intrusions sponsored or encouraged by China are unwarranted, he wrote in an Apr. 9 e-mail response to questions from *BusinessWeek*. "The Chinese government always opposes and forbids any cyber crimes including 'hacking' that undermine the security of computer networks," says Wang. China itself, he adds, is a victim, "frequently intruded and attacked by hackers from certain countries."

Because the Web allows digital spies and thieves to mask their identities, conceal their physical locations, and bounce malicious code to and fro, it's frequently impossible to pinpoint specific attackers. Network security professionals call this digital masquerade ball "the attribution problem."

A Credible Message

In written responses to questions from *BusinessWeek*, officials in the office of National Intelligence Director J. Michael McConnell, a leading proponent of boosting government cyber security, would not comment "on specific code-word programs" such as Byzantine Foothold, nor on "specific intrusions or possible victims." But the department says that "computer intrusions have been successful against a wide range of government and corporate networks across the critical infrastructure and defense industrial base." The White House declined to address the contents of the Cyber Initiative, citing its classified nature.

The e-mail aimed at Booz Allen, obtained by *BusinessWeek* and traced back to an Internet address in China, paints a vivid picture of the alarming new capabilities of America's cyber enemies. On Sept. 5, 2007, at 08:22:21 Eastern time, an e-mail message appeared to be sent to John F. "Jack" Mulhern, vice-president for international military assistance programs at Booz Allen. In the high-tech world of weapons sales, Mulhern's specialty, the e-mail looked authentic enough. "Integrate U.S., Russian, and Indian weapons and avionics," the e-mail noted, describing the Indian government's expectations for its fighter jets. "Source code given to India for indigenous computer upgrade capability." Such lingo could easily be understood by Mulhern. The 62-year-old former U.S. Naval officer and 33-year veteran of Booz Allen's military consulting business is an expert in helping to sell U.S. weapons to foreign governments.

The e-mail was more convincing because of its apparent sender: Stephen J. Moree, a civilian who works for a group that reports to the office of Air Force Secretary Michael W. Wynne. Among its duties, Moree's unit evaluates the security of selling U.S. military aircraft to other countries. There would be little reason to suspect anything seriously amiss in Moree's passing along the highly technical document with "India MRCA Request for Proposal" in the subject line. The Indian government had just released the request a week earlier, on Aug. 28, and the language in the e-mail closely tracked the request. Making the message appear more credible still: It referred to upcoming Air Force communiqués and a "Teaming Meeting" to discuss the deal.

But the missive from Moree to Jack Mulhern was a fake. An analysis of the e-mail's path and attachment, conducted for *BusinessWeek* by three cyber security specialists, shows it was sent by an unknown attacker, bounced through an Internet address in South Korea, was relayed through a Yahoo! server in New York, and finally made its way toward Mulhern's Booz Allen in-box. The analysis also shows the code—known as "malware," for malicious software—tracks keystrokes on the computers of people who open it. A separate program disables security measures such as password protection on Microsoft Access database files, a program often used by large organizations such as the U.S. defense industry to manage big batches of data.

An E-mail's Journey

While hardly the most sophisticated technique used by electronic thieves these days, "if you have any kind of sensitive documents on Access databases, this [code] is getting in there and getting them out," says a senior executive at a leading cyber security firm that analyzed the e-mail. (The person requested anonymity because his firm provides security consulting to U.S. military departments, defense contractors, and financial institutions.) Commercial computer security firms have dubbed the malicious code "Poison Ivy."

But the malware attached to the fake Air Force e-mail has a more devious—and worrisome—capability. Known as a remote administration tool, or RAT, it gives the attacker control over the "host" PC, capturing screen shots and perusing files. It lurks in the background of Microsoft Internet Explorer browsers while users surf the Web. Then it phones home to its "master" at an Internet address currently registered under the name cybersyndrome.3322.org.

The digital trail to cybersyndrome.3322.org, followed by analysts at *BusinessWeek*'s request, leads to one of China's largest free domain-name-registration and e-mail services. Called 3322.org, it is registered to a company called Bentium in the city of Changzhou, an industry hub outside Shanghai. A range of security experts say that 3322.org provides names for computers and servers that act as the command and control centers for more than 10,000 pieces of malicious code launched at government and corporate networks in recent years. Many of those PCs are in China; the rest could be anywhere.

The founder of 3322.org, a 37-year-old technology entrepreneur named Peng Yong, says his company merely allows users to register domain names. "As for what our users do, we cannot completely control it," says Peng. The bottom line: If Poison Ivy infected Jack Mulhern's computer at Booz Allen, any secrets inside could be seen in China. And if it spread to other computers, as malware often does, the infection opens windows on potentially sensitive information there, too.

It's not clear whether Mulhern received the e-mail, but the address was accurate. Informed by *BusinessWeek* on Mar. 20 of the fake message, Booz Allen spokesman George Farrar says the company launched a search to find it. As of Apr. 9, says Farrar, the company had not discovered the e-mail or Poison Ivy in Booz Allen's networks. Farrar says Booz Allen computer security executives examined the PCs of Mulhern and an assistant who received his e-mail. "We take this very seriously," says Farrar. (Mulhern, who retired in March, did not respond to e-mailed requests for comment and declined a request, through Booz Allen, for an interview.)

Air Force officials referred requests for comment to U.S. Defense Secretary Robert M. Gates' office. In an e-mailed response to *BusinessWeek,* Gates' office acknowledges being the target of cyber attacks from "a variety of state and non-state-sponsored organizations to gain unauthorized access to, or otherwise degrade, [Defense Dept.] information systems." But the Pentagon declined to discuss the attempted Booz Allen break-in. The Air Force, meanwhile, would not make Stephen Moree available for comment.

The bogus e-mail, however, seemed to cause a stir inside the Air Force, correspondence reviewed by *BusinessWeek* shows.

On Sept. 4, defense analyst James Mulvenon also received the message with Moree and Mulhern's names on it. Security experts believe Mulvenon's e-mail address was secretly included in the "blind copy" line of a version of the message. Mulvenon is director of the Center for Intelligence Research & Analysis and a leading consultant to U.S. defense and intelligence agencies on China's military and cyber strategy. He maintains an Excel spreadsheet of suspect e-mails, malicious code, and hacker groups and passes them along to the authorities. Suspicious of the note when he received it, Mulvenon replied to Moree the next day. Was the e-mail "India spam?" Mulvenon asked.

"I apologize—this e-mail was sent in error—please delete," Moree responded a few hours later.

"No worries," typed Mulvenon. "I have been getting a lot of trojaned Access databases from China lately and just wanted to make sure."

"Interesting—our network folks are looking into some kind of malicious intent behind this e-mail snafu," wrote Moree. Neither the Air Force nor the Defense Dept. would confirm to *BusinessWeek* whether an investigation was conducted. A Pentagon spokesman says that its procedure is to refer attacks to law enforcement or counterintelligence agencies. He would not disclose which, if any, is investigating the Air Force e-mail.

Digital Intruders

By itself, the bid to steal digital secrets from Booz Allen might not be deeply troubling. But Poison Ivy is part of a new type of digital intruder rendering traditional defenses—firewalls and updated antivirus software—virtually useless. Sophisticated hackers, say Pentagon officials, are developing new ways to creep into computer networks sometimes before those vulnerabilities are known. "The offense has a big advantage over the defense right now," says Colonel Ward E. Heinke, director of the Air Force Network Operations Center at Barksdale Air Force Base. Only 11 of the top 34 antivirus software programs identified Poison Ivy when it was first tested on behalf of *BusinessWeek* in February. Malware-sniffing software from several top security firms found "no virus" in the India fighter-jet e-mail, the analysis showed.

"Poison ivy" is part of a new type of digital intruder rendering traditional perimeter defenses like firewalls virtually useless.

Over the past two years thousands of highly customized e-mails akin to Stephen Moree's have landed in the laptops and PCs of U.S. government workers and defense contracting executives. According to sources familiar with the matter, the attacks targeted sensitive information on the networks of at least seven agencies—the Defense, State, Energy, Commerce, Health & Human Services, Agriculture, and Treasury departments—and also defense contractors Boeing, Lockheed Martin, General Electric, Raytheon, and General Dynamics, say current and former government network security experts. Laura Keehner, a spokeswoman for the Homeland Security Dept., which coordinates protection of government computers, declined to comment on specific intrusions. In written responses to questions from

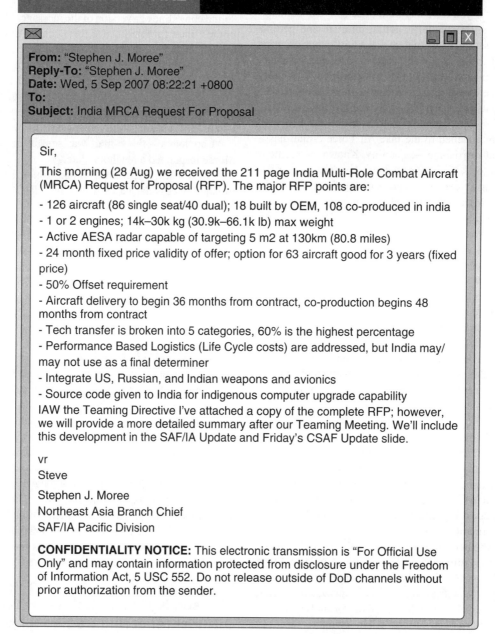

A BRILLIANT FAKE   The bogus e-mail aimed at Booz Allen Hamilton

From: "Stephen J. Moree"
Reply-To: "Stephen J. Moree"
Date: Wed, 5 Sep 2007 08:22:21 +0800
To:
Subject: India MRCA Request For Proposal

Sir,

This morning (28 Aug) we received the 211 page India Multi-Role Combat Aircraft (MRCA) Request for Proposal (RFP). The major RFP points are:

- 126 aircraft (86 single seat/40 dual); 18 built by OEM, 108 co-produced in india
- 1 or 2 engines; 14k–30k kg (30.9k–66.1k lb) max weight
- Active AESA radar capable of targeting 5 m2 at 130km (80.8 miles)
- 24 month fixed price validity of offer; option for 63 aircraft good for 3 years (fixed price)
- 50% Offset requirement
- Aircraft delivery to begin 36 months from contract, co-production begins 48 months from contract
- Tech transfer is broken into 5 categories, 60% is the highest percentage
- Performance Based Logistics (Life Cycle costs) are addressed, but India may/may not use as a final determiner
- Integrate US, Russian, and Indian weapons and avionics
- Source code given to India for indigenous computer upgrade capability

IAW the Teaming Directive I've attached a copy of the complete RFP; however, we will provide a more detailed summary after our Teaming Meeting. We'll include this development in the SAF/IA Update and Friday's CSAF Update slide.

vr
Steve

Stephen J. Moree
Northeast Asia Branch Chief
SAF/IA Pacific Division

CONFIDENTIALITY NOTICE: This electronic transmission is "For Official Use Only" and may contain information protected from disclosure under the Freedom of Information Act, 5 USC 552. Do not release outside of DoD channels without prior authorization from the sender.

BusinessWeek, Keehner says: "We are aware of and have defended against malicious cyber activity directed at the U.S. Government over the past few years. We take these threats seriously and continue to remain concerned that this activity is growing more sophisticated, more targeted, and more prevalent." Spokesmen for Lockheed Martin, Boeing, Raytheon, General Dynamics, and General Electric declined to comment. Several cited policies of not discussing security-related matters.

The rash of computer infections is the subject of Byzantine Foothold, the classified operation designed to root out the perpetrators and protect systems in the future, according to three people familiar with the matter. In some cases, the government's own cyber security experts are engaged in "hack-backs"—following the malicious code to peer into the hackers' own computer systems. *BusinessWeek* has learned that a classified document called an intelligence community assessment, or ICA, details the Byzantine intrusions and assigns each a unique Byzantine-related name. The ICA has circulated in recent months among selected officials at U.S. intelligence agencies, the Pentagon, and cyber security consultants acting as outside reviewers. Until December, details of the ICA's contents had not even been shared with congressional intelligence committees.

Now, Senate Intelligence Committee Chairman John D. Rockefeller (D-W. Va.) is said to be discreetly informing fellow senators of the Byzantine operation, in part to win their support for needed appropriations, many of which are part of classified "black" budgets kept off official government books. Rockefeller declined to comment. In January a Senate Intelligence Committee staffer urged his boss, Missouri Republican Christopher "Kit"

Anatomy of a Spear-Phish

The three stages of a successful spear-phishing attack.

Net Reconnaissance

Online cunning need not start with insiders or illegally obtained information. Attackers can scour the Web—studying public documents, chat rooms, and blogs—to build digital dossiers about the jobs, responsibilities, and personal networks of targets.

Constructing the "Spear-Phish"

Attackers build an e-mail with a Web link or attachment on a subject likely to trick the victim into clicking on it. Common spear-phish topics include news events, earnings results, and Word and PowerPoint documents containing real info. The e-mail address is made to look like it comes from a logical sender.

Harvesting the Data

When the victim opens the attachment or clicks on the Web link, malicious code hidden inside combs document files, steals passwords, and sends the data to a "command and control" server, often in a foreign country, which collects the data for study.

Bond, the committee's vice-chairman, to supplement closed-door testimony and classified documents with a viewing of the movie *Die Hard 4* on a flight the senator made to New Zealand. In the film, cyber terrorists breach FBI networks, purloin financial data, and bring car traffic to a halt in Washington. Hollywood, says Bond, doesn't exaggerate as much as people might think. "I can't discuss classified matters," he cautions. "But the movie illustrates the potential impact of a cyber conflict. Except for a few things, let me just tell you: It's credible."

"Phishing," one technique used in many attacks, allows cyber spies to steal information by posing as a trustworthy entity in an online communication. The term was coined in the mid-1990s when hackers began "fishing" for information (and tweaked the spelling). The e-mail attacks on government agencies and defense contractors, called "spear-phish" because they target specific individuals, are the Web version of laser-guided missiles. Spear-phish creators gather information about people's jobs and social networks, often from publicly available information and data stolen from other infected computers, and then trick them into opening an e-mail.

Devious Script

Spear-phish tap into a cyber espionage tactic that security experts call "Net reconnaissance." In the attempted attack on Booz Allen, attackers had plenty of information about Moree: his full name, title (Northeast Asia Branch Chief), job responsibilities, and e-mail address. Net reconnaissance can be surprisingly simple, often starting with a Google search. (A lookup of the Air Force's Pentagon e-mail address on Apr. 9, for instance, retrieved 8,680 e-mail addresses for current or former Air Force personnel and departments.) The information is woven into a fake e-mail with a link to an infected Web site or containing an attached document. All attackers have to do is hit their send button. Once the e-mail is opened, intruders are automatically ushered inside the walled perimeter of computer networks—and malicious code such as Poison Ivy can take over.

By mid-2007 analysts at the National Security Agency began to discern a pattern: personalized e-mails with corrupted attachments such as PowerPoint presentations, Word documents, and Access database files had been turning up on computers connected to the networks of numerous agencies and defense contractors.

A previously undisclosed breach in the autumn of 2005 at the American Enterprise Institute—a conservative think tank whose former officials and corporate executive board members are closely connected to the Bush Administration—proved so nettlesome that the White House shut off aides' access to the Web site for more than six months, says a cyber security specialist familiar with the incident. The Defense Dept. shut the door for even longer. Computer security investigators, one of whom spoke with *BusinessWeek,* identified the culprit: a few lines of Java script buried in AEI's home page, www.aei.org, that activated as soon as someone visited the site. The script secretly redirected the user's computer to another server that attempted to load malware. The malware, in turn, sent information from the visitor's hard drive to a server in China. But the security specialist says cyber sleuths couldn't get rid of the intruder. After each deletion, the furtive code would reappear. AEI says otherwise—except for a brief accidental recurrence caused by its own network personnel in August, 2007, the devious Java script did not return and was not difficult to eradicate.

The breach of a highly sensitive State Dept. Bureau posed a risk to CIA operatives in embassies around the globe.

The government has yet to disclose the breaches related to Byzantine Foothold. *BusinessWeek* has learned that intruders managed to worm into the State Dept.'s highly sensitive Bureau of Intelligence & Research, a key channel between the work of intelligence agencies and the rest of the government. The breach posed a risk to CIA operatives in embassies around the globe, say several network security specialists familiar with the effort to cope with what became seen as an internal crisis. Teams worked around-the-clock in search of malware, they say, calling the White House regularly with updates.

The attack began in May, 2006, when an unwitting employee in the State Dept.'s East Asia Pacific region clicked on an attachment in a seemingly authentic e-mail. Malicious code was embedded in the Word document, a congressional speech, and opened a Trojan "back door" for the code's creators to peer inside the State Dept.'s innermost networks. Soon, cyber security engineers began spotting more intrusions in State Dept. computers across the globe. The malware took advantage of previously unknown vulnerabilities in the Microsoft operating system. Unable to develop a patch quickly enough, engineers watched helplessly as streams of State Dept. data slipped through the back door and into the Internet ether. Although they were unable to fix the vulnerability, specialists came up with a temporary scheme to block further infections. They also yanked connections to the Internet.

One member of the emergency team summoned to the scene recalls that each time cyber security professionals thought they had eliminated the source of a "beacon" reporting back to its master, another popped up. He compared the effort to the arcade game Whack-A-Mole. The State Dept. says it eradicated the infection, but only after sanitizing scores of infected computers and servers and changing passwords. Microsoft's own patch, meanwhile, was not deployed until August, 2006, three months after the infection. A Microsoft spokeswoman declined to comment on the episode, but said: "Microsoft has, for several years, taken a comprehensive approach to help protect people online."

There is little doubt among senior U.S. officials about where the trail of the recent wave of attacks leads. "The Byzantine series tracks back to China," says Air Force Colonel Heinke. More than a dozen current and former U.S. military, cyber security, and intelligence officials interviewed by *BusinessWeek* say China is the biggest emerging adversary—and not just clubs of rogue or enterprising hackers who happen to be Chinese. O. Sami Saydjari, a former National Security Agency executive and now president of computer security firm Cyber Defense Agency, says the Chinese People's Liberation Army, one of the world's largest military forces, with an annual budget of $57 billion, has "tens of thousands" of trainees launching attacks on U.S. computer networks. Those figures could not be independently confirmed by *Business-Week*. Other experts provide lower estimates and note that even one hacker can do a lot of damage. Says Saydjari: "We have to look at this as equivalent to the launch of a Chinese Sputnik." China vigorously disputes the spying allegation and says its military posture is purely defensive.

Hints of the perils perceived within America's corridors of power have been slipping out in recent months. In Feb. 27 testimony before the U.S. Senate Armed Services Committee, National Intelligence Director McConnell echoed the view that the threat comes from China. He told Congress he worries less about people capturing information than altering it. "If someone has the ability to enter information in systems, they can destroy data. And the destroyed data could be something like money supply, electric-power distribution, transportation sequencing, and that sort of thing." His conclusion: "The federal government is not well-protected and the private sector is not well-protected."

Worries about China-sponsored Internet attacks spread last year to Germany, France, and Britain. British domestic intelligence agency MI5 had seen enough evidence of intrusion and theft of corporate secrets by allegedly state-sponsored Chinese hackers by November, 2007, that the agency's director general, Jonathan Evans, sent an unusual letter of warning to 300 corporations, accounting firms, and law firms—and a list of network security specialists to help block computer intrusions. Some recipients of the MI5 letter hired Peter Yapp, a leading security consultant with London-based Control Risks. "People treat this like it's just another hacker story, and it is almost unbelievable," says Yapp. "There's a James Bond element to it. Too many people think, 'It's not going to happen to me.' But it has."

Identifying the thieves slipping their malware through the digital gates can be tricky. Some computer security specialists doubt China's government is involved in cyber attacks on U.S. defense

The Government's Response

Key elements of the U.S. "Cyber Initiative," signed on Jan. 8.

Cut Connections
Aims to cut the number of portals between government networks and the Internet from more than 4,000 to fewer than 100.

Passive Intrusion Prevention
Requires a plan to identify when unauthorized entities have gained access to computer networks.

Active Intrusion Prevention
Requires a program to trace cyber intrusions back to their source, both countries and people.

Counterintelligence Strategy
Requires a plan to deter and prevent future computer network breaches.

Counterintelligence Tools
Launches a program to develop the technology for cyber forensic analysis.

Education
Creates training programs to develop technical skills to improve cyber security.

Fusing Operations
Combines the computer command posts known as "network operations centers" of an unknown number of agencies.

Cyber R&D
Launches a plan to develop offensive and defensive cyber capabilities, including those developed by contractors.

Leap-Ahead Technologies
Aims to invent "killer apps" to win the cyber arms race.

Critical Infrastructure Protection
Calls for a plan to work with the private sector, which owns and operates most of the Internet.

Revisit Project Solarium
Like the Eisenhower project to deter nuclear war, aims to prevent a cyber war.

Improve Federal Acquisitions
Starts program to ensure government IT products and services are secure.

targets. Peter Sommer, an information systems security specialist at the London School of Economics who helps companies secure networks, says: "I suspect if it's an official part of the Chinese government, you wouldn't be spotting it."

A range of attacks in the past two years on U.S. and foreign government entities, defense contractors, and corporate networks have been traced to Internet addresses registered through Chinese domain name services such as 3322.org, run by Peng Yong. In late March, *BusinessWeek* interviewed Peng in an apartment on the 14th floor of the gray-tiled residential building that houses the five-person office for 3322.org in Changzhou. Peng says he started 3322.org in 2001 with $14,000 of his own money so the growing ranks of China's Net surfers could register Web sites and distribute data. "We felt that this business would be very popular, especially as broadband, fiber-optic cables, [data transmission technology] ADSL, these ways of getting on the Internet took off," says Peng (translated by *BusinessWeek* from Mandarin), who drives a black Lexus IS300 bought last year.

His 3322.org has indeed become a hit. Peng says the service has registered more than 1 million domain names, charging $14 per year for "top-level" names ending in .com, .org, or .net. But cyber security experts and the Homeland Security Dept.'s U.S. Computer Emergency Readiness Team (CERT) say that 3322.org is a hit with another group: hackers. That's because 3322.org and five sister sites controlled by Peng are dynamic DNS providers. Like an Internet phone book, dynamic DNS assigns names for the digits that mark a computer's location on the Web. For example, 3322.org is the registrar for the name cybersyndrome.3322 .org at Internet address 61.234.4.28, the China-based computer that was contacted by the malicious code in the attempted Booz Allen attack, according to analyses reviewed by *BusinessWeek*. "Hackers started using sites like 3322.org so that the malware phones home to the specific name. The reason? It is relatively difficult to have [Internet addresses] taken down in China," says Maarten van Horenbeeck, a Belgium-based intrusion analyst for the SANS Internet Storm Center, a cyber threat monitoring group.

Target: Private Sector

Peng's 3322.org and sister sites have become a source of concern to the U.S. government and private firms. Cyber security firm Team Cymru sent a confidential report, reviewed by *Business-Week*, to clients on Mar. 7 that illustrates how 3322.org has enabled many recent attacks. In early March, the report says, Team Cymru received "a spoofed e-mail message from a U.S. military entity, and the PowerPoint attachment had a malware widget embedded in it." The e-mail was a spear-phish. The computer that controlled the malicious code in the PowerPoint? Cybersyndrome.3322 .org—the same China-registered computer in the attempted attack on Booz Allen. Although the cybersyndrome Internet address may not be located in China, the top five computers communicating directly with it were—and four were registered with a large state-owned Internet service provider, according to the report.

A person familiar with Team Cymru's research says the company has 10,710 distinct malware samples that communicate to masters registered through 3322.org. Other groups reporting attacks from computers hosted by 3322.org include activist group Students for a Free Tibet, the European Parliament, and U.S.

Bancorp according to security reports. Team Cymru declined to comment. The U.S. government has pinpointed Peng's services as a problem, too. In a Nov. 28, 2007, confidential report from Homeland Security's U.S. CERT obtained by *BusinessWeek*, "Cyber Incidents Suspected of Impacting Private Sector Networks," the federal cyber watchdog warned U.S. corporate information technology staff to update security software to block Internet traffic from a dozen Web addresses after spear-phishing attacks. "The level of sophistication and scope of these cyber security incidents indicates they are coordinated and targeted at private-sector systems," says the report. Among the sites named: Peng's 3322.org, as well as his 8800.org, 9966.org, and 8866.org. Homeland Security and U.S. CERT declined to discuss the report.

Peng says he has no idea hackers are using his service to send and control malicious code. "Are there a lot?" he says when asked why so many hackers use 3322.org. He says his business is not responsible for cyber attacks on U.S. computers. "It's like we have paved a road and what sort of car [users] drive on it is their own business," says Peng, who adds that he spends most of his time these days developing Internet telephony for his new software firm, Bitcomm Software Tech Co. Peng says he was not aware that several of his Web sites and Internet addresses registered through them were named in the U.S. CERT report. On Apr. 7, he said he planned to shut the sites down and contact the U.S. agency. Asked by *BusinessWeek* to check his database for the person who registered the computer at the domain name cybersyndrome.3322.org, Peng says it is registered to Gansu Railway Communications, a regional telecom subsidiary of China's Railways Ministry. Peng declined to provide the name of the registrant, citing a confidentiality agreement. "You can go through the police to find out the user information," says Peng.

U.S. cyber security experts say it's doubtful that the Chinese government would allow the high volume of attacks on U.S. entities from China-based computers if it didn't want them to happen. "China has one of the best-controlled Internets in the world. Anything that happens on their Internet requires permission," says Cyber Defense Group's Saydjari. The Chinese government spokesman declined to answer specific questions from *Business-Week* about 3322.org.

Britain's MI5 intelligence agency sent a warning in 2007 to 300 companies about thefts of corporate secrets by Chinese hackers.

But Peng says he can do little if hackers exploit his goodwill—and there hasn't been much incentive from the Chinese government for him to get tough. "Normally, we take care of these problems by shutting them down," says Peng. "Because our laws do not have an extremely clear method to handle this problem, sometimes we are helpless to stop their services." And so, it seems thus far, is the U.S. government.

Global Diversity: The Next Frontier

PETER ORTIZ

C orporate America faces a challenging enough task understanding the increasingly diverse United States, but to remain competitive, companies must address what happens on a larger playing field.

Embracing diversity globally requires an appreciation of distinctive societal, governmental and cultural values, including a lack of metrics that U.S. diversity leaders rely upon as benchmarking tools.

For example, while racial and ethnic demographics serve Rohini Anand as valuable measures for evaluating work-force diversity at Sodexho in the United States, the senior vice president and chief diversity officer doesn't always have that type of ready information in other countries.

"In France . . . you can't identity people by ethnicity or race," says Anand, whose company, Sodexho, is No. 14 on The 2006 DiversityInc Top 50 Companies for Diversity list. "All you can do is collect gender information, so it becomes extremely challenging if you don't know what the numbers and percentages are in your work force to establish any target."

So how does Sodexho handle this challenge? Inclusively. Anand relies on the viewpoints of a 12-person global task force from South America, Australia, Asia and Europe. The group meets virtually once a month to discuss the company's action plan and to share and report on best practices as well as understand the cultural nuances that define diversity in their respective societies.

Sodexho, which has operations in more than 70 countries, started its diversity initiative in North America four years ago when Anand came on board and found a champion in then-Sodexho CEO of North America, Michel Landel. Now as CEO of Sodexho Alliance, Landel advocates for diversity on a global scale. About 10 percent to 15 percent of managers' total bonuses are linked to diversity objectives for recruiting, retention and promotion of women and people of color in the United States, she says.

"That's his commitment, his passion, his realization of the need for cultural competence, and the success of our business is what really took it to [another] level," she says. "He has taken the same tenor and tone to the global arena as well where he is making it very much a part of his legacy and his strategy." With the global initiative 1.5 years old, Sodexho is beginning to address the diversity challenges in France. "One of the first things we're doing is to develop some training programs for our managers,

particularly around recruiting to make sure that there is unbiased recruiting as well as to allow managers the opportunity to recognize talent," Anand says.

The Greater Global Challenge

Deeply embedded customs and values in countries can make it difficult for U.S. corporations to carry out even the most basic equality measures. In South Korea, for example, there still is a cultural expectation that women stay home and take care of their children, leading many companies, both South Korean and foreign, to ignore investment in training women, says Michalle E. Mor Barak, a professor at the University of Southern California's School of Social Work and Marshall School of Business.

"It's not just that you are not utilizing half of the potential work force to its fullest, but you're also not addressing the expectations of your potential [women] customers," Mor Barak says. "To some extent you need diversity to address the varying expectations of your potential customers. Different viewpoints can greatly enrich the company's vision."

Mor Barak, who has published articles on global work force diversity and inclusion, including a book, *Managing Diversity: Toward a Globally Inclusive Workplace,* says many U.S. companies don't know how to address diversity issues in other countries. This results in a disparity between diversity initiatives at home and abroad. A good first step is working with people who are familiar with the foreign and U.S. culture.

"You create a bridge between the two and come up with initiatives that will promote diversity while being respectful of the local culture," Mor Barak says.

In France, the principle behind not identifying residents by race and ethnicity is meant to promote equality by identifying every French citizen, regardless of skin color or ethnicity, as French. A potential drawback is a lack of data companies can use to learn about diversity in French society, but this shouldn't limit a proactive company from learning about its own work-force diversity. Mor Barak suggests distributing surveys that ask employees how they identify themselves and how included they feel in the organization.

"On the advantage side, any accommodation for diversity in the long run benefits the organizational mission because it introduces a variety of ideas and thinking that can help the company be more creative and cater to different groups of customers," she says.

American Express' global team is divided into a U.S. and international council and was created in 2003. The international council consists of four regions: Europe-Middle East-Africa; Latin America and Caribbean; Japan, Asia-Pacific, Australia; and Canada. American Express is No. 30 on The 2006 DiversityInc Top 50 Companies for Diversity list.

Henry Hernandez, vice president and chief diversity officer, says the company has "to be sensitive to the fact that we may have to differentiate between what might be able to be done or approached from a U.S. perspective versus international." Where American Express may be similar to other corporations that are proactive on diversity initiatives in the United States, the financial-services giant must be cognizant on a global scale as well. Nearly half of the company's more than 66,000 employees live outside the United States.

"It really does have to span across the globe," Hernandez says.

The company must remain sensitive to the knowledge, awareness, skill sets and competencies that will differ from region to region.

Different Historic Perspectives

The United States has had a head start in corporate diversity that can be traced back to the Civil Rights Movement and the fight for equality and rights.

"It wasn't even referred to then as diversity, but when you think of the evolution, it's been a long one, whereas outside the United States, it may not have even been addressed that way," Hernandez says.

Bernard Anderson, an assistant secretary in the U.S. Department of Labor under former President Clinton, points out that progressive diversity initiatives by U.S. corporations are rooted in the Civil Rights Movement. Only when the U.S. government made employment discrimination illegal and created opportunities through the Civil Rights Act of 1964 and Affirmative Action did opportunities start to really filter down through corporate America.

"Before 1964, it was perfectly legal to deny employment to minority groups and women without explaining why," Anderson says.

Anderson, who today is a professor of management at the Wharton School of Business at the University of Pennsylvania, says that during Clinton's term, critics unfairly linked affirmative action with taking away opportunities for white men. This led many corporations to instead adapt the term "diversity," which gave broader meaning.

"Affirmative action for the most part is limited to employment, and diversity goes beyond employment . . . Diversity deals with work and family life and a lot of things that affirmative action never touched," Anderson says. "Diversity is now the mechanism that, in addition to broadening opportunities to groups previously excluded, also helps the firms be more financially successful."

Anderson notes—and DiversityInc Top 50 research supports—that more than 80 percent of U.S. corporations don't have diversity initiatives, but most of those that do are Fortune 500 companies. At the same time, Anderson, a self-described "voracious" critic of U.S. corporations, says "there is not a country in this world" that offers the same opportunities for people of color and women as the United States. But Anderson is doubtful that many large corporations that also operate globally can ensure their proactive diversity practices are followed outside the United States.

"What they do overseas will depend entirely upon national policies of countries they are operating in regarding equal-employment opportunities," he says.

With the exception of a few countries, including South Africa and some Scandinavian countries, most foreign governments have not mandated laws that create a solid foundation for diversity initiatives to thrive. U.S. corporations with strong diversity programs that give them a competitive advantage at home may not see the same results overseas.

Anderson also advised the Rev. Leon Sullivan on the Sullivan Principles he developed in 1977. These principles pushed for companies operating in South Africa under apartheid to honor human rights and equal opportunity in their businesses. While a number of U.S. companies signed on during apartheid, Sullivan could not find any Western European company that would do the same, Anderson says.

That lack of comprehension of the value of diversity remains. In France today, he notes it is difficult for women to gain employment in certain occupations, such as construction and manufacturing.

"Unless the cultural and moralistic values of that country support equal employment . . . an American company attempting to operate diversity programs overseas might operate at a competitive disadvantage in that market," Anderson says.

The Global Success Stories

Global diversity at HSBC is embodied in its description as the "The World's Local Bank," encompassing 284,000 employees in 76 countries and territories. These employees also serve more than 125 million customers. HSBC's U.S. operation is No. 13 on The 2006 DiversityInc Top 50 Companies for Diversity list.

In 2005, the London-based financial-services organization counted one-third of its pretax profits from North America, another third from Europe and one-third from the Asia Pacific region, according to Michael Shearer, senior manager, global diversity. On a global level, diversity is not just about "visible difference such as gender, ethnicity, disability or age," Shearer says. "It is also about different perspectives on working and leadership style, problem solving, managing relationships, creativity and business growth. Put simply, we see this as [an] important and growing focus because, by drawing on local knowledge and different perspectives of colleagues around the world, [it] enables us [to] serve our customers better."

In Australia, Sodexho partners with organizations in developing strategies to better recruit and retain employees from the indigenous aboriginal population. But learning best practices goes both ways and any leading role the United States plays should not be interpreted as a "here we are to show you how it's done" attitude, Anand says.

"In Scandinavian countries, as far as gender was concerned, there were some big surprises around policies for me," she says. "Women get 12 months of maternity leave and men have to use one month of that leave."

Failure of fathers to use that one month results in forfeiture of the entire 12-months' leave, Anand says. In Norway, a law requires that at least one woman sit on corporate boards, she says.

"Many countries are much better than the United States in terms of work/life balance issues, and that has been a big learning [experience] for me," Anand says.

Companies in countries that fail to address shortcomings in best practices could hurt their operations as they increasingly find themselves competing for talent globally. As its global task force continues to exchange diversity practices, Sodexho hopes to draw talent worldwide.

"It's going to be another differentiator for us," Anand says. "It will position us to manage our work force better and position us to take advantage of emerging markets."

American Express utilizes a training module for managers, Valuing Diversity and Practicing Inclusion, to maintain a consistency with its world operations. But inherent in that consistency is the understanding that adjustments may be made to adapt to local cultures. The company piloted the training module in Latin America in 2004.

"We actually identify facilitators who are sensitive to and knowledgeable about those particular markets," Hernandez says. "We always allow them a period of time to be able to adapt, modify and customize some materials so that it resonates well with employees."

While many of the managers worldwide speak English, the company also finds that managers from outside the United States are more engaged during the training when it is done in their native languages. One training example, titled Alejandro's Dilemma, educates managers about missed opportunities during a virtual telephone conference call. An employee may come from a culture where it is impolite to interrupt and be reluctant to offer ideas during the conference call.

"You have to be cognizant of the fact that someone who is at a meeting might be sitting quietly and has an incredible amount to contribute but isn't given the opportunity, or when the call is over, might not know the way to express themselves," Hernandez says.

The company has diversity goals linked to compensation for vice presidents and higher.

The objective is "to equip our leaders with being able to address cultural differences and being able to manage across borders," Hernandez says. Another program, Cultures at Work, combines classroom learning and an online tool, "cultural navigator," for managers.

Through its Group Diversity Management Committee, HSBC shares best-practice approaches from different regions by using an employee-diversity intranet system. The company also offers in-depth cultural training that includes intensive language training for employees sent to other countries and 400 permanently expatriated, globally mobile international managers.

"We can see two benefits to cross-cultural competence," Shearer says. "It helps us understand the diversity—and needs—of customer markets . . . [and] it helps employees to think differently and openly, to see beyond established parameters."

Trouble in Toyland

Lawmakers, Wal-Mart vow action amid recalls; Lead-tainted products and other hazards spur plans for hearings and better oversight.

ABIGAIL GOLDMAN

Amid a fresh spate of toy recalls, members of Congress said Thursday that they would hold hearings about product safety and Wal-Mart Stores Inc. vowed to increase testing and oversight of the playthings it sold.

But neither of those actions will guarantee a trouble-free toy aisle any time soon, according to activists who contend that legislation is needed to mandate stricter standards.

"The government agencies and the quality control operations in the companies that are supposed to prevent these problems are not working," said Jean Halloran, a food and product safety expert for Consumers Union, the publisher of Consumer Reports. "You need to start from the point of view that to a large degree, you're on your own. You are the one who has to protect yourself and your family."

In Washington, a House subcommittee requested information from 19 companies responsible for recent recalls of more than 9 million lead-tainted children's products imported from China.

The subcommittee on commerce, trade and consumer protection also said it would hold a hearing on the issue next month.

"I am outraged that in 2007 lead-tainted products continue to endanger the health of our children," said Rep. Bobby L. Rush (D-Ill.). "Children put everything into their mouths—if they swallow trinkets made with high quantities of lead, it can kill them."

Meanwhile Wal-Mart—the nation's largest retailer and No. 1 toy seller—said it would ask toy manufacturers to resubmit safety test results for toys already on shelves or on their way to Wal-Mart or Sam's Club stores.

Wal-Mart said it was increasing its third-party testing, adding an average of 200 more toy safety tests a day.

The retailer, which said it would share its test results with the toy industry and other retailers, identified a priority list of about 5,000 toys that are targeted at children younger than 3 and which are made with either paint or magnets—two hazards identified in recent recalls, company executives said.

The retailer also said it was in discussions with manufacturers and an industry trade group about a children's product seal of approval, which would certify that a product passed independent safety tests. In addition to toy problems, the retailer this year recalled children's bibs because the vinyl material on them could contain lead.

"We have heard from customers that they are still concerned," said Laura Phillips, Wal-Mart's merchandise manager for toys. "We are trying to play a role here to alleviate their concerns and reassure them about the safety of the products that they are going to be buying."

Some consumer activists, however, were unimpressed.

"These are things they should have been doing already—the manufacturers, the distributors and the retailers," said Edmund Mierzwinski, who handles toy safety issues for U.S. Public Interest Research Group. "The toy manufacturers and the department stores have worried too much about price and not enough about quality. So they're responsible for this mess."

Halloran, of Consumers Union, said the best advice her group and others have are common-sense ways to protect children. A list of ways to prevent lead poisoning, on the ConsumerReports.org blog, includes such steps as checking toys against the government's recall list.

The group also recommends discarding toys with chipped paint, deteriorated plastic or other worn parts. The group suggests avoiding all toy jewelry for young children, because those playthings are often imported and have in the past been associated with lead charms or paint—a serious problem because small children often suck on the metal decorations they wear.

Consumers Union also suggests that all toddlers be tested for lead exposure by their pediatricians.

More important, Halloran said, the government needs to take more responsibility for ensuring product safety. The group supports proposed legislation that would require third-party safety certification for children's products and expand the authority and funding of the agency that ensures product safety.

The toy industry's biggest trade group said its members had a good system of safety standards and compliance and that the group was working toward a "uniform safety program."

A safety seal is another possibility, said an executive with the Toy Industry Assn., whose members make up about 80% of the $22 billion in annual domestic toy sales.

"The first step for us is enhancing the system and making sure the system works," said Joan Lawrence, the group's vice president of standards and regulatory affairs. "I don't know if hearings are necessary because we have long been in conversations with individual members and we plan to continue those conversations."

Although officials with the federal agency that oversees toy safety stress that they have recalled fewer toys this year than in 2006, a series of high-profile toy problems has heightened consumer attention, particularly with lead contamination of children's products.

Earlier this week, four toy companies recalled more than 340,000 Chinese-made toys with popular characters such as Curious George and SpongeBob SquarePants because of potential contamination from lead.

Those recalls followed a series of Chinese-made toy recalls from the nation's biggest toy maker, El Segundo-based Mattel Inc., which early this month warned about possible lead paint problems on 1.5 million Fisher-Price infant and preschool toys then, two weeks later, recalled more than 400,000 die-cast vehicles for the same reason.

And in June, toy maker RC2 Corp. recalled 1.5 million Thomas & Friends wooden train toys, also imported from China, because of possible lead paint.

Cracks in a Particularly Thick Glass Ceiling

Women in South Korea are slowly changing a corporate culture that lags behind the rest of the country.

MOON IHLWAN

South Koreans are a bit conflicted about career women. Gender wasn't much of an issue in the selection of a female astronaut to fly this month on the country's first space mission. But when women are seeking workaday corporate jobs, some South Korean men still resist change. Outer space is one thing, but a woman in the next cubicle is something else.

For years, most educated women in South Korea who wanted to work could follow but one career path, which began and ended with teaching. The situation started to change after the 1998 Asian financial crisis. Thousands of men lost their jobs or took salary cuts, and their wives had to pick up the slack by starting businesses in their homes or seeking part-time work. A couple of years later, the government banned gender discrimination in the workplace and required businesses with more than 500 employees to set up child-care facilities. It also created a Gender Equality Ministry.

These days the government hires thousands of women (42% of its new employees last year), many for senior positions in the judiciary, international trade administration, and foreign service. Startups and foreign companies also employ (and promote) increasing numbers of Korean women.

One of the Guys

But at the top 400 companies, many of which are family-run conglomerates, it's hard for women to reach the upper ranks. In all, about 8% of working women hold managerial positions. (In the U.S. nearly 51% do.) "We have a long way to go," says Cho Jin Woo, director of the Gender Equality Ministry.

South Koreans are grappling with traditional attitudes about women, a hierarchical business culture, and the need to open up the workplace to compete globally. A senior manager at SK Holdings, which controls the giant mobile phone carrier SK Telecom (SKM), says he avoids hiring women because he believes they lack tenacity. When deadlines are tight, he says, "you need people prepared to put in long hours at the office." Park Myung Soon, a 39-year-old woman who is in charge of business development at the carrier, says, "Many men are preoccupied with the notion that women are a different species." To get ahead, Park says she had to achieve 120% of what her male colleagues did—as well as play basketball and drink with them after work. "Luckily, I like sports, and I like to drink," she says.

When Choi Dong Hee joined SK's research arm in 2005, she was the only woman there and had no major assignment until she created one. After conducting a yearlong study, Choi, 30, proposed changing the company's policy to allow subscribers to use any wireless portal. Her managers ignored her. She persisted. Finally, they agreed to let her brief the division head, who agreed to let her make her case to the company chairman. Choi worked on the presentation for three weeks straight, sometimes alone in the office overnight (to her boss's horror). In the end, the company did adopt the open policy she advocated. Now her managers are quick to say that women's perspectives can help SK better serve its customers.

Sonia Kim, who is in charge of TV marketing at Samsung Electronics, says her male colleagues rarely argue with the boss, even if they think he's wrong. Kim, though, persuaded her manager to let her develop a promotional campaign rather than rely on an ad agency she thought had lost its creative edge. Kim also says some of the men used to overturn decisions made during the day while out drinking after hours. Since she and other women at Samsung complained, Kim says, the practice has mostly stopped.

How Barbie Is Making Business a Little Better

Corporations such as Mattel, Nike and Home Depot are using their clout to improve working conditions around the world.

EDWARD IWATA

The sewing factory in Tepeji del Rio, Mexico, made cute Barbie costumes under a Mattel license, but its workplace allegedly was horrendous.

According to a complaint filed last fall with the U.S. Labor Department by a Mexican union, the Rubie's de Mexico factory: employed underage workers, forced employees to work overtime and take pregnancy tests, and subjected workers to chemical smells that caused vomiting and fainting. A Mattel inspection of the plant found violations of Mattel's global-manufacturing codes of conduct. One violation was workers could not choose which union to join, contrary to Mattel's "right to free association" policy, says Mattel and Stephen Coats, head of the U.S./Labor Education in the Americas Project, a labor rights group.

Mattel says it recently severed ties with Rubie's after it missed a Jan. 31 deadline to fix that violation. Attorneys for Rubie's de Mexico, a contractor for Mattel licensee Rubie's Costume in New York, deny the allegations in the labor complaint, calling Rubie's "a responsible corporate citizen . . . that hopes to work with Mattel again."

Since launching its codes in 1997, Mattel has cut off several dozen suppliers and licensees whose factories fell short of Mattel's standards—a model for codes adopted recently by the International Council of Toy Industries.

"We call it zero tolerance," says Mattel Senior Vice President Jim Walter. "If we find evidence of systematic violations, we're not going to do business with you."

> **"We call it zero tolerance. If we find evidence of systematic violations, we're not going to do business with you."**
> **—Jim Walter, Mattel senior vice president**

Mattel is one of many U.S. corporations taking social responsibilities more seriously in foreign markets, from the rain forests of Asia to civil-war-torn Africa. As Yahoo, Google and other Internet giants face harsh criticism for their business practices in China, more companies realize it's smart business to be good corporate citizens in the exploding global economy.

Companies have come a long way since the 1980s, when public outrage against apartheid forced many to withdraw their investments in South Africa, and the 1990s, when apparel and footwear companies were attacked for sweatshop labor conditions in suppliers' plants.

In earlier decades, businesses viewed such issues—known as corporate social responsibility, or CSR—as annoyances. Corporations closed ranks when attacked by labor and human rights activists and environmentalists.

Now CSR practices play a key role in business strategy. Companies are closely monitoring their supply chains. They're teaming with activists and government officials to tackle problems. Manufacturers such as General Electric and Ford Motor are investing billions of dollars in energy-saving products and plants.

"Ten years ago, only a handful of companies looked seriously at this," says Bennett Freeman, a former State Department official who is managing director at the Burson-Marsteller public relations firm. "Now, every major company has to act on the issue. It's a business imperative."

Harsh Realities

The global economy is forcing U.S. multinationals to deal with harsher social and political realities, from civil violence in Nigeria to the dictatorship in China. Activists continue to pressure companies to conduct business with a conscience.

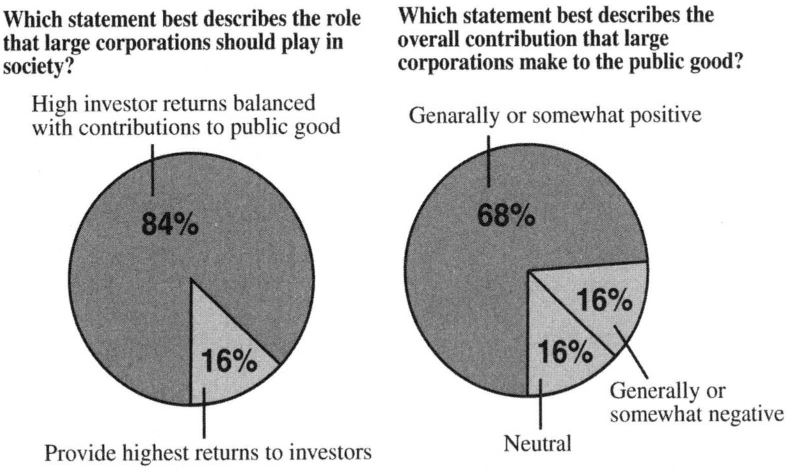

Which statement best describes the role
that large corporations should play in
society?

High investor returns balanced
with contributions to public good

84%

16%

Provide highest returns to investors

Which statement best describes the
overall contribution that large
corporations make to the public good?

Genarally or somewhat positive

68%

16%

16%

Generally or
somewhat negative

Neutral

Figure 1 Businesses accept social responsibility. Business executives around
the world say that corporations need to be responsive to shareholders and contribute to the public good. These are the questions asked and their responses.

Companies also fear bad publicity and legal woes, such as
lawsuits filed by labor lawyers against Coca-Cola, Exxon-
Mobil and other companies, accusing them of complicity in
human rights abuses abroad.

Not all executives, though, think that corporate social
responsibility is a business priority. Companies can do little
when faced with civil wars and authoritarian regimes, and
it's near-impossible to police the many thousands of contractors in worldwide supply chains.

But corporations clearly are moving on the issue by
adopting:

Codes of conduct. About 2,000 companies have joined
the United Nations Global Compact, which urges businesses
to embrace labor, human rights and environmental practices,
from banning child and forced labor to using environmentally sound technologies.

Hundreds of company and voluntary industry codes also
have sprung up in apparel and toy manufacturing, electronics, jewelry, the coal, nuclear and chemical industries and
other sectors.

Critics say companies have little incentive to obey the
codes. Manufacturers, for instance, didn't lessen pollution
until they faced stiffer environmental laws and criminal
prosecution.

"Most companies are getting a free pass with these codes
of conduct," says Terry Collingsworth, an attorney at the
International Labor Rights Fund.

But supporters say the codes—such as the electronic
industry's backed by Intel and other high-tech titans—give
U.S. companies standard manufacturing and workplace rules
amid conflicting international laws.

"They're a good first step," says Aron Cramer, president
of Business for Social Responsibility, a non-profit group of

corporations. "Now an army of people around the world are
reviewing factories and improving work conditions."

Home Depot polices itself. Since the late-1990s, the
company—which sells 8,000 wood products—has stopped
buying from suppliers who get wood from endangered trees
and rain forests.

The company spends more than $400 million a year on
so-called certified wood approved by industry environmental
standards, says Home Depot Vice President Ron Jarvis.

Social goals that boost business. In 2004, business
professors Frank Schmidt and Sara Rynes at the University
of Iowa looked at 52 studies on corporate social responsibility over 30 years. They found that well-run, profitable businesses also boasted solid social and environmental records.

"Socially aware companies add value to their products
and services," says CEO Jeffrey Hollender of Seventh Generation, a natural home-products firm.

Companies are setting benchmarks for performance on
social issues. Like Seventh Generation, Mattel and Cisco
Systems, they're putting out "corporate responsibility"
reports similar to annual financial reports.

Hoping to spark local economies in countries where they
do business, Cisco and other firms are investing heavily in
education and job training in Africa, Asia, Latin America and
the Middle East.

Over the past decade, Cisco has poured $250 million into
computer-network training programs with 220,000 graduates
in developing nations, says Tae Yoo, a Cisco vice president.

FedEx, working with non-profit Environmental Defense
and industrial manufacturer Eaton, is betting good environmental practices will pay off.

Two years ago, the delivery company launched a pilot project using 20 hybrid electric trucks in New York, Sacramento,

137

Accepting Responsibility

Business executives around the world say that corporations need to be responsive to shareholders and contribute to the public good. Responses to the following questions:

- Which statement best describes the role that large corporations should play in society?
- High investor returns balanced with contributions to public good 84%
- Provide highest returns to investors 16%

Which statement best describes the overall contribution that large corporations make to the public good?

- Generally or somewhat positive 68%
- Generally or somewhat negative 16%
- Neutral 16%

Source: *McKinsey Quarterly* survey of 4,238 global business executives in 116 nations conducted in December 2005.

Washington and Tampa. The goal: to slash smog-causing emissions by 75% and get 50% more travel on the same amount of diesel fuel.

If all goes well, FedEx will use hybrid trucks to replace aging vehicles in its fleet of 30,000 delivery trucks in the USA and Canada, says FedEx environmental head Mitch Jackson.

"Companies come into this with a lot of cynicism," says Gwen Ruta at Environmental Defense. "Once they study the issues, they see it's a huge business benefit and the right thing to do."

Critics such as David Vogel, a University of California, Berkeley, business professor and author of *The Market for Virtue,* says corporate social responsibility is overrated. Investors don't care, and consumers won't pay higher prices for environmentally safe goods.

"Companies will make the world a better place as long as it doesn't cost too much," he says. "That's the limit of corporate responsibility."

Better monitoring. A decade ago, U.S. companies had few people to inspect thousands of manufacturing sites. Their superficial audits "didn't get at the root causes of problems," says Auret van Heerden, executive director of the non-profit Fair Labor Association.

Today, Van Heerden says, more corporations are strengthening their monitoring and teaching suppliers how to better run their plants and manage workers.

The Fair Labor Association estimates that 30 or 40 companies—including Reebok, Patagonia, Liz Claiborne and Phillips-Van Heusen—now have rigorous, first-class audit programs.

Mattel sends inspection teams to some of its 300 suppliers' sites in China, Indonesia and other countries. Armed with a 50-page checklist, they eyeball safety conditions, interview workers and ensure employees are treated well.

The audits—by Mattel and Prakash Sethi, a business professor at Baruch College and founder of the International Center for Corporate Accountability—praise some plants but warn others to shape up or lose Mattel's business.

"It's not empty rhetoric," Sethi says. "Vendors have a financial incentive to comply with Mattel's codes."

Nike also is a seasoned veteran of audits. In the 1990s, the company was a favorite target of activists because of foreign sweatshops run by its suppliers.

Now Nike inspects many of its 1,000 suppliers' factories worldwide. It grades them from A to D and warns poorly run sites to improve or get dropped, says Nike Vice President Dusty Kidd.

"Beyond the policing," Kidd says, "factories need to manage their work and manage it well."

That's no easy task—especially in countries with authoritarian regimes. Look at the problem facing Yahoo, Google, Microsoft and Cisco Systems, which were blasted last month by Congress and human rights groups for their Internet and sales practices in China.

Critics accuse the companies of compromising their values so the Chinese authorities will let them operate in the huge market. Despite the growing number of U.S. companies there, labor conditions and violence against workers have worsened, charges Sharon Hom, executive director of Human Rights in China. "Their presence alone will not lead to improvements," Hom says.

A Fundamental Purpose

The Internet companies disagree.

"We take our ethical and moral issues super-seriously," says Andrew McLaughlin, senior policy counsel at Google. "As an information company, freedom of speech and expression are fundamental to our purpose."

Google protects the confidentiality of users from the Chinese government and also tells users when a search result on google.cn.com, the company's Chinese website, is being censored.

The Internet companies also are consulting with human rights groups, U.S. government officials and scholars to draw up business guidelines for China.

Companies are doing the right thing by staying in China, says Edward Ahnert, a business professor at Southern

Methodist University and former president of the Exxon-Mobil Foundation. "Engaging the Chinese is better than shunning them," he says.

Reebok, for instance, is trying to improve the lot of Chinese workers. The company runs democratic-style elections in seven factories, with employees enthusiastically joining committees that work with management.

Reebok Vice President Doug Cahn says the company has shown "that workers' voices could be heard in China." The long-run goal: more worker-management collaboration in all of Reebok's 160 supplier factories in China.

As the China debate heats up, it's clear that companies' social responsibilities will loom larger everywhere as international trade grows.

"We're drafting rules of the road in the new global economy," says Michael Posner, executive director of Human Rights First. "We've made progress, but there's still a long way to go."

UNIT 4

Ethics and Social Responsibility in the Marketplace

Unit Selections

Key Points to Consider

• What responsibility does an organization have to reveal product defects to consumers?

• Given the competitiveness of the business arena, is it possible for marketing personnel to behave ethically and also survive and prosper? Explain. Give suggestions that could be incorporated into the marketing strategy for firms that want to be both ethical and successful.

• Name some organizations that make you feel genuinely valued as a customer. What are the characteristics of these organizations that distinguish them from their competitors? Explain.

• Which area of marketing strategy is most subject to public scrutiny in regard to ethics—product, pricing, place, or promotion? Why? Give some examples of unethical techniques or strategies involving each of these four areas.

Student Web Site

www.mhcls.com

Internet References

Business for Social Responsibility (BSR)
http://www.bsr.org/
Total Quality Management Sites
http://www.nku.edu/~lindsay/qualhttp.html
U.S. Navy
http://www.navy.mil

© Masterfile (Royalty-Free Division)

From a consumer viewpoint, the marketplace is the "proof of the pudding" or the place where the "rubber meets the road" for business ethics. In other words, what the company has promulgated about the virtues of its product or service has little meaning if the company's actual marketing practices and its treatment of the consumer contradict its claims.

At its core, marketing has a very noble and moral purpose: to satisfy human needs and wants and to help people through the exchange process. Marketing involves the coordination of the variables of product, price, place, and promotion to effectively and efficiently address the needs of consumers. Unfortunately, at times the unethical marketing practices of some firms have cast a shadow of suspicion over marketing in general. Since marketing is the aspect of business that is most visible to the public, it has perhaps taken a disproportionate share of the criticism directed toward the free-enterprise system.

This unit takes a careful look at the strategic process and practice of incorporating ethics into the marketplace. The first subsection, *Marketing Strategy and Ethics,* contains articles describing how marketing strategy and ethics can be integrated in the marketplace. The first article wrestles with the question: "Is Marketing Ethics an Oxymoron?" The last four articles in this subsection reveal the use of direct-to-consumer (DTC) advertising of prescription drugs, the significant impact of technology on marketing and ethics, how rude and blatantly unjust customers should be treated, and the culpability of the participants in the mortgage market meltdown.

In the next subsection, *Ethical Practices in the Marketplace,* the first two articles delineate the importance of having an organizational culture that encourages and supports sound ethical behavior and socially responsible business practices. The last article in this subsection describes how the proliferation of swag may have undercut the integrity of the press.

Is Marketing Ethics an Oxymoron?

PHILIP KOTLER

Every profession and business has to wrestle with ethical questions. The recent wave of business scandals over inaccurate reporting of sales and profits and excessive pay and privileges for top executives has brought questions of business ethics to the fore. And lawyers have been continuously accused of "ambulance chasing," jury manipulation, and inflated fees, leaving the plaintiffs with much less than called for in the judgment. Physicians have been known to recommend certain drugs as more effective while receiving support from pharmaceutical companies.

Marketers are not immune from facing a whole set of ethical issues. For evidence, look to Howard Bowen's classic questions from his 1953 book, *Social Responsibilities of the Businessman:*

"Should he conduct selling in ways that intrude on the privacy of people, for example, by door-to-door selling? Should he use methods involving ballyhoo, chances, prizes, hawking, and other tactics which are at least of doubtful good taste? Should he employ 'high pressure' tactics in persuading people to buy? Should he try to hasten the obsolescence of goods by bringing out an endless succession of new models and new styles? Should he appeal to and attempt to strengthen the motives of materialism, invidious consumption, and keeping up with the Joneses?" (Also see Smith, N. Craig and Elizabeth Cooper-Martin [1997], "Ethics and Target Marketing: The Role of Product Harm and Consumer Vulnerability," *Journal of Marketing,* July, 1–20.)

The issues raised are complicated. Drawing a clear line between normal marketing practice and unethical behavior isn't easy. Yet it's important for marketing scholars and those interested in public policy to raise questions about practices that they may normally endorse but which may not coincide with the public interest.

We will examine the central axiom of marketing: Companies that satisfy their target customers will perform better than those that don't. Companies that satisfy customers can expect repeat business; those that don't will get only one-time sales. Steady profits come from holding onto customers, satisfying them, and selling them more goods and services.

This axiom is the essence of the well-known marketing concept. It reduces to the formula "Give the customer what he wants." This sounds reasonable on the surface. But notice that it carries an implied corollary: "Don't judge what the customer wants."

Marketers have been, or should be, a little uneasy about this corollary. It raises two public interest concerns: (1) What if the customer wants something that isn't good for him or her? (2) What if the product or service, while good for the customer, isn't good for society or other groups?

When it comes to the first question, what are some products that some customers desire that might not be good for them? These would be products that can potentially harm their health, safety, or well-being. Tobacco and hard drugs such as cocaine, LSD, or ecstasy immediately come to mind.

As for the second question, examples of products or services that some customers desire that may not be in the public's best interest include using asbestos as a building material or using lead paint indiscriminately. Other products and services where debates continue to rage as to whether they are in the public's interest include the right to own guns and other weapons, the right to have an abortion, the right to distribute hate literature, and the right to buy large gas guzzling and polluting automobiles.

EXECUTIVE briefing

Marketers should be proud of their field. They have encouraged and promoted the development of many products and services that have benefited people worldwide. But this is all the more reason that they should carefully and thoughtfully consider where they stand on the ethical issues confronting them today and into the future. Marketers are able to take a stand and must make the effort to do so in order to help resolve these issues.

We now turn to three questions of interest to marketers, businesses, and the public:

1. Given that expanding consumption is at the core of most businesses, what are the interests and behaviors of companies that make these products?
2. To what extent do these companies care about reducing the negative side effects of these products?
3. What steps can be taken to reduce the consumption of products that have questionable effects and is limited intervention warranted?

Expanding Consumption

Most companies will strive to enlarge their market as much as possible. A tobacco company, if unchecked, will try to get everyone who comes of age to start smoking cigarettes. Given that cigarettes are addictive, this promises the cigarette company "customers for life." Each new customer will create a 50-year profit stream for the cigarette company if the consumer continues to favor the same brand—and live long enough. Suppose a new smoker starts at the age of 13, smokes for 50 years, and dies at 63 from lung cancer. If he spends $500 a year on cigarettes, he will spend $25,000 over his lifetime. If the company's profit rate is 20%, that new customer is worth $5,000 to the company (undiscounted). It is hard to imagine a company that doesn't want to attract a customer who contributes $5,000 to its profits.

The same story describes the hard drug industry, whose products are addictive and even more expensive. The difference is that cigarette companies can operate legally but hard drug companies must operate illegally.

Other products, such as hamburgers, candy, soft drinks, and beer, are less harmful when consumed in moderation, but are addictive for some people. We hear a person saying she has a "sweet tooth." One person drinks three Coca-Colas a day, and another drinks five beers a day. Still another consumer is found who eats most of his meals at McDonald's. These are the "heavy users." Each company treasures the heavy users who account for a high proportion of the company's profits.

All said, every company has a natural drive to expand consumption of its products, leaving any negative consequences to be the result of the "free choice" of consumers. A high-level official working for Coca-Cola in Sweden said that her aim is to get people to start drinking Coca-Cola for breakfast (instead of orange juice). And McDonald's encourages customers to choose a larger hamburger, a larger order of French fries, and a larger cola drink. And these companies have some of the best marketers in the world working for them.

Reducing Side Effects

It would not be a natural act on the part of these companies to try to reduce or restrain consumption of their products. What company wants to reduce its profits? Usually some form of public pressure must bear on these companies before they will act.

The government has passed laws banning tobacco companies from advertising and glamorizing smoking on TV. But Philip Morris' Marlboro brand still will put out posters showing its mythical cowboy. And Marlboro will make sure that its name is mentioned in sports stadiums, art exhibits, and in labels for other products.

Tobacco companies today are treading carefully not to openly try to create smokers out of young people. They have stopped distributing free cigarettes to young people in the United States as they move their operations increasingly into China.

Beer companies have adopted a socially responsible attitude by telling people not to over-drink or drive during or after drinking. They cooperate with efforts to prevent underage people from buying beer. They are trying to behave in a socially responsible manner. They also know that, at the margin, the sales loss resulting from their "cooperation" is very slight.

McDonald's has struggled to find a way to reduce the ill effects (obesity, heart disease) of too much consumption of their products. It tried to offer a reduced-fat hamburger only to find consumers rejecting it. It has offered salads, but they weren't of good quality when originally introduced and they failed. Now it's making a second and better attempt.

Limited Intervention

Do public interest groups or the government have the right to intervene in the free choices of individuals? This question has been endlessly debated. On one side are people who resent any intervention in their choices of products and services. In the extreme, they go by such names as libertarians, vigilantes, and "freedom lovers." They have a legitimate concern about government power and its potential abuse. Some of their views include:

- The marketer's job is to "sell more stuff." It isn't the marketer's job to save the world or make society a better place.
- The marketer's job is to produce profits for the shareholders in any legally sanctioned way.
- A high-minded socially conscious person should not be in marketing. A company shouldn't hire such a person.

On the other side are people concerned with the personal and societal costs of "unregulated consumption." They are considered do-gooders and will document that Coca-Cola delivers six teaspoons of sugar in every bottle or can. They will cite statistics on the heavy health costs of obesity, heart disease, and liver damage that are caused by failing to reduce the consumption of some of these products. These costs fall on everyone through higher medical costs and taxes. Thus, those who don't consume questionable products are still harmed through the unenlightened behavior of others.

Ultimately, the problem is one of conflict among different ethical systems. Consider the following five:

Ethical egoism. Your only obligation is to take care of yourself (Protagoras and Ayn Rand).
Government requirements. The law represents the minimal moral standards of a society (Thomas Hobbes and John Locke).
Personal virtues. Be honest, good, and caring (Plato and Aristotle).
Utilitarianism. Create the greatest good for the greatest number (Jeremy Bentham and John Stuart Mill).
Universal rules. "Act only on that maxim through which you can at the same time will that it should become a universal law" (Immanuel Kant's categorical imperative).

Clearly, people embrace different ethical viewpoints, making marketing ethics and other business issues more complex to resolve.

Let's consider the last two ethical systems insofar as they imply that some interventions are warranted. Aside from the weak gestures of companies toward self-regulation and appearing concerned, there are a range of measures that can be taken by those wishing to push their view of the public interest. They include the following six approaches:

1. Encouraging these companies to make products safer. Many companies have responded to public concern or social pressure to make their products safer. Tobacco companies developed filters that would reduce the chance of contracting emphysema or lung cancer. If a leaf without nicotine could give smokers the same satisfaction, they would be happy to replace the tobacco leaf. Some tobacco companies have even offered information or aids to help smokers limit their appetite for tobacco or curb it entirely.

Every company has a natural drive to expand consumption of its products, leaving any negative consequences to be the result of the "free choice" of consumers.

Food and soft drink companies have reformulated many of their products to be "light," "nonfat," or "low in calories." Some beer companies have introduced non-alcoholic beer. These companies still offer their standard products but provide concerned consumers with alternatives that present less risk to their weight or health.

Auto companies have reluctantly incorporated devices designed to reduce pollution output into their automobiles. Some are even producing cars with hybrid fuel systems to further reduce harmful emissions to the air. But the auto companies still insist on putting out larger automobiles (such as Hummers) because the "public demands them."

What can we suggest to Coca-Cola and other soft drink competitors that are already offering "light" versions of their drinks? First, they should focus more on developing the bottled water side of their businesses because bottled water is healthier than sugared soft drinks. Further, they should be encouraged to add nutrients and vitamins in standard drinks so these drinks can at least deliver more health benefits, especially to those in undeveloped countries who are deprived of these nutrients and vitamins. (Coca-Cola has some brands doing this now.)

What can we suggest to McDonald's and its fast food competitors? The basic suggestion is to offer more variety in its menu. McDonald's seems to forget that, while parents bring their children to McDonald's, they themselves usually prefer to eat healthier food, not to mention want their children eating healthier foods. How about a first-class salad bar? How about moving more into the healthy sandwich business? Today more Americans are buying their meals at Subway and other sandwich shops where they feel they are getting healthier and tastier food for their dollar.

There seems to be a correlation between the amount of charity given by companies in some categories and the category's degree of "sin." Thus, McDonald's knows that over-consumption of its products can be harmful, but the company is very charitable. A cynic would say that McDonald's wants to build a bank of public goodwill to diffuse potential public criticism.

2. Banning or restricting the sale or use of the product or service. A community or nation will ban certain products where there is strong public support. Hard drugs are banned, although there is some debate about whether the ban should include marijuana and lighter hard drugs. There are even advocates who oppose banning hard drugs, believing that the cost of policing and criminality far exceed the cost of a moderate increase that might take place in hard drug usage. Many people today believe that the "war on drugs" can never be won and is creating more serious consequences than simply dropping the ban or helping drug addicts, as Holland and Switzerland have done.

Some products carry restrictions on their purchase or use. This is particularly true of drugs that require a doctor's prescription and certain poisons that can't be purchased without authorization. Persons buying guns must be free of a criminal record and register their gun ownership. And certain types of guns, such as machine guns, are banned or restricted.

3. Banning or limiting advertising or promotion of the product. Even when a product isn't banned or its purchase restricted, laws may be passed to prevent producers from advertising or promoting the product. Gun, alcohol, and tobacco manufacturers can't advertise on TV, although they can advertise in print media such as magazines and newspapers. They can also inform and possibly promote their products online.

Manufacturers get around this by mentioning their brand name in every possible venue: sports stadiums, music concerts, and feature articles. They don't want to be forgotten in the face of a ban on promoting their products overtly.

4. Increasing "sin" taxes to discourage consumption. One reasonable alternative to banning a product or its promotion is to place a "sin" tax on its consumption. Thus, smokers pay hefty government taxes for cigarettes. This is supposed to have three effects when done right. First, the higher price should discourage consumption. Second, the tax revenue could be used to finance the social costs to health and safety caused by the consumption of the product. Third, some of the tax revenue could be used to counter-advertise the use of the product or support public education against its use. The last effect was enacted by California when it taxed tobacco companies and used the money to "unsell" tobacco smoking.

5. Public education campaigns. In the 1960s, Sweden developed a social policy to use public education to raise a nation of non-smokers and non-drinkers. Children from the first grade up were educated to understand the ill effects of tobacco and alcohol. Other countries are doing this on a less systematic and intensive basis. U.S. public schools devote parts of occasional courses to educate students against certain temptations with mixed success. Girls, not boys, in the United States seem to be more prone to taking up smoking. The reason often given by girls is that smoking curbs their appetite for food and consequently helps them avoid becoming overweight, a problem they consider more serious than lung cancer taking place 40 years later.

Sex education has become a controversial issue, when it comes to public education campaigns. The ultra-conservative camp wants to encourage total abstinence until marriage. The more liberal camp believes that students should be taught the risks of early sex and have the necessary knowledge to protect themselves. The effectiveness of both types of sex education is under debate.

6. Social marketing campaigns. These campaigns describe a wide variety of efforts to communicate the ill effects of certain behaviors that can harm the person, other persons, or society as a whole. These campaigns use techniques of public education, advertising and promotion, incentives, and channel development to make it as easy and attractive as possible for people to change their behavior for the better. (See Kotler, Philip, Eduardo Roberto, and Nancy Lee (2002), *Social Marketing: Improving the Quality of Life,* 2nd ed. London: Sage Publications.) Social marketing uses the tools of commercial marketing—segmentation, targeting, and positioning, and the four Ps (product, price, place, and promotion)—to achieve voluntary compliance with publicly endorsed goals. Some social marketing campaigns, such as family planning and anti-littering, have achieved moderate to high success. Other campaigns including anti-smoking, anti-drugs ("say no to drugs"), and seat belt promotion have worked well when supplemented with legal action.

Social Responsibility and Profits

Each year *Business Ethics* magazine publishes the 100 best American companies out of 1,000 evaluated. The publication examines the degree to which the companies serve seven stakeholder groups: shareholders, communities, minorities and women, employees, environment, non-U.S. stakeholders, and customers. Information is gathered on lawsuits, regulatory problems, pollution emissions, charitable contributions, staff diversity counts, union relations, employee benefits, and awards. Companies are removed from the list if there are significant scandals or improprieties. The research is done by Kinder, Lydenberg, Domini (KLD), an independent rating service. (For more details see the Spring 2003 issue of *Business Ethics.*)

The 20 best-rated companies in 2003 were (in order): General Mills, Cummins Engine, Intel, Procter & Gamble, IBM, Hewlett-Packard, Avon Products, Green Mountain Coffee, John Nuveen Co., St. Paul Companies, AT&T, Fannie Mae, Bank of America, Motorola, Herman Miller, Expedia, Autodesk, Cisco Systems, Wild Oats Markets, and Deluxe.

The earmarks of a socially responsible company include:

- Living out a deep set of company values that drive company purpose, goals, strategies, and tactics
- Treating customers with fairness, openness, and quick response to inquiries and complaints
- Treating employees, suppliers, and distributors fairly
- Caring about the environmental impact of its activities and supply chain
- Behaving in a consistently ethical fashion

The intriguing question is whether socially responsible companies are more profitable. Unfortunately, different research studies have come up with different results. The correlations between financial performance (FP) and social performance (SP) are sometimes positive, sometimes negative, and sometimes neutral, depending on the study. Even when FP and SP are positively related, which causes which? The most probable finding is that high FP firms invest slack resources in SP and then discover the SP leads to better FP, in a viscious circle. (See Waddock, Sandra A. and Samuel B. Graves [1997], "The Corporate Social Performance-Financial Performance Link," *Strategic Management Journal,* 18 (4), 303–319.)

Marketers' Responsibilities

As professional marketers, we are hired by some of the aforementioned companies to use our marketing toolkit to help them sell more of their products and services. Through our research, we can discover which consumer groups are the most susceptible to increasing their consumption. We can use the research to assemble the best 30-second TV commercials, print ads, and sales incentives to persuade them that these products will deliver great satisfaction. And we can create price discounts to tempt them to consume even more of the product than would normally be healthy or safe to consume.

But, as professional marketers, we should have the same ambivalence as nuclear scientists who help build nuclear bombs or pilots who spray DDT over crops from the airplane. Some of us, in fact, are independent enough to tell these clients that we will not work for them to find ways to sell more of what hurts people. We can tell them that we're willing to use our marketing toolkit to help them build new businesses around substitute products that are much healthier and safer.

But, even if these companies moved toward these healthier and safer products, they'll probably continue to push their current "cash cows." At that point, marketers will have to decide whether to work for these companies, help them reshape their offerings, avoid these companies altogether, or even work to oppose these company offerings.

Remember Marketing's Contributions

Nothing said here should detract from the major contributions that marketing has made to raise the material standards of living around the world. One doesn't want to go back to the kitchen where the housewife cooked five hours a day, washed dishes by hand, put fresh ice in the ice box, and washed and dried clothes in the open air. We value refrigerators, electric stoves, dishwashers, washing machines, and dryers. We value the invention and diffusion of the radio, the television set, the computer, the Internet, the cellular phone, the automobile, the movies, and even frozen food. Marketing has played a major role in their instigation and diffusion. Granted, any of these are capable of abuse (bad movies or TV shows), but they promise and deliver much that is good and valued in modern life.

Marketers have a right to be proud of their field. They search for unmet needs, encourage the development of products and services addressing these needs, manage communications to inform people of these products and services, arrange for easy accessibility and availability, and price the goods in a way that represents superior value delivered vis-à-vis competitors' offerings. This is the true work of marketing.

PHILIP KOTLER is S.C. Johnson and Son Distinguished Professor of International Marketing, Kellogg School of Management, Northwestern University. He may be reached at pkotler@nwu.edu.

Author's Note—The author wishes to thank Professor Evert Gummesson of the School of Business, Stockholm University, for earlier discussion of these issues.

Truth in Advertising
Rx Drug Ads Come of Age

CAROL RADOS

You may have seen the advertisement: A melodrama of crime and corruption, conflict and emotion, centering on indoor hit men like dust and dander, and outdoor hit men such as pollen and ragweed, all threatening to offend a young and very beautiful woman's nose. The 45-second broadcast ad covers everything from talking to your doctor to the possible side effects that people can expect. Then the narrator mentions "Flonase."

According to the U.S. General Accounting Office . . . pharmaceutical manufacturers spent $2.7 billion on DTC advertising in 2001 alone.

Entertaining though it may be, the Food and Drug Administration says this promotional piece about nasal allergy relief also has all the elements of a well-crafted, easy-to-understand prescription drug advertisement directed at consumers, and it meets agency requirements for these ads.

Direct-to-consumer (DTC) advertising of prescription drugs in its varied forms—TV, radio, magazines, newspapers—is widely used throughout the United States. DTC advertising is a category of promotional information about specific drug treatments provided directly to consumers by or on behalf of drug companies. According to the U.S. General Accounting Office—the investigational arm of Congress—pharmaceutical manufacturers spent $2.7 billion on DTC advertising in 2001 alone.

The Controversy

Whether it's a 1940s, detective-style film noir of unusual allergy suspects or a middle-aged man throwing a football through a tire swing announcing that he's "back in the game," the DTC approach to advertising prescription drugs has been controversial. Some say that DTC promotion provides useful information to consumers that results in better health outcomes. Others argue that it encourages overuse of prescription drugs and use of the most costly treatments, instead of less expensive treatments that would be just as satisfactory.

There seems to be little doubt that DTC advertising can help advance the public health by encouraging more people to talk with health care professionals about health problems, particularly undertreated conditions such as high blood pressure and high cholesterol.

DTC advertising also can help remove the stigma that accompanies diseases that in the past were rarely openly discussed, such as erectile dysfunction or depression. DTC ads also can remind patients to get their prescriptions refilled and help them adhere to their medication regimens.

On the other hand, ads that are false or misleading do not advance—and may even threaten—the public health. While the FDA encourage DTC advertisements that contain accurate information, the agency also has the job of making sure that consumers are not misled or deceived by advertisements that violate the law.

"The goal here is getting truthful, non-misleading information to consumers about safe and effective therapeutic products so they can be partners in their own health care" says Peter Pitts, the FDA's associate commissioner for external relations. "Better-informed consumers are empowered to choose and use the products we regulate to improve their health."

How Ads Affect Consumers

The FDA surveyed both patients and physicians about their attitudes and experiences with DTC advertising between 1999 and 2002. The agency summarized the findings of these surveys in January 2003 in the report, *Assessment of Physician and Patient Attitudes Toward Direct-to-Consumer Promotion of Prescription Drugs.*

DTC advertising appears to influence certain types of behavior. For example, the FDA surveys found that among patients who visited doctors and asked about a prescription drug by brand name because of an ad they saw, 88 percent actually had the condition the drug treats. This is important, Pitts says, because physician visits that result in earlier detection of a disease, combined with appropriate treatment, could mean that more people

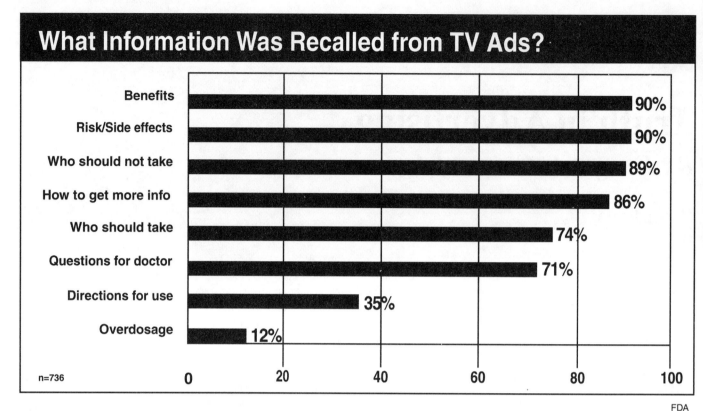

Figure 1 In three FDA surveys conducted in 1999 and 2002, patients reported recalling this information from TV ads.

will live longer, healthier, more productive lives without the risk of future costly medical interventions.

With the number of ailments Patricia A. Sigler lives with—diabetes, fibromyalgia, high blood pressure, high cholesterol, nerve damage, and a heart defect called mitral valve prolapse—the 64-year-old small business owner in Jefferson, Md., says that she's always on the lookout for medicines that might improve her quality of life, and that she pays attention to DTC ads for prescription drugs.

Some Doctors Don't Agree

Michael S. Wilkes, M.D., vice dean of the medical school at the University of California, Davis, says that two reasons he doesn't like DTC advertising are that patients may withhold information from their doctors or try to treat themselves. Aiming prescription drug ads at consumers can affect the "dynamics of the patient-provider relationship," and ultimately, the patient's quality of care, Wilkes says. DTC advertising can motivate consumers to seek more information about a product or disease, but physicians need to help patients evaluate health-related information they obtain from DTC advertising, he says.

"DTC advertising may cultivate the belief among the public that there is a pill for every ill and contribute to the medicalization of trivial ailments, leading to an even more overmedicated society," Wilkes says. "Patients need to trust that I've got their best interest in mind."

Others who favor DTC ads say that consumer-directed information can be an important educational tool in a time when

more patients want to be involved in their own health care. Carol Salzman, M.D., Ph.D., an internist in Chevy Chase, Md., emphasizes, however, that physicians still need to remain in control of prescribing medications.

"Doctors shouldn't feel threatened by their patients asking for a medicine by name," she says, "but at the same time, patients shouldn't come in expecting that a drug will be dispensed just because they asked for it."

Salzman says she finds it time-consuming "trying to talk people out of something they have their hearts set on." Wilkes agrees. Discussions motivated by ads that focus on specific drugs or trivial complaints, he says, could take time away from subjects such as a patient's symptoms, the range of available treatments, and specific details about a patient's illness.

Education or Promotion?

At least one patient advocacy group is concerned about what it says are the downsides of advertising prescription drugs directly to consumers, claiming that DTC ads often masquerade as educational tools, but provide more promotion than education. The ads, they say, provide little access to unbiased information.

"People need to be careful with ads that it isn't just hype that they're going to feel better, with no objectivity of the downsides," says Linda Golodner, president of the National Consumers League in Washington, D.C. Although all DTC advertisements must disclose risk information, she says what is typically communicated is a brand name, a reason to use the product, and an impression of the product. Golodner wants all

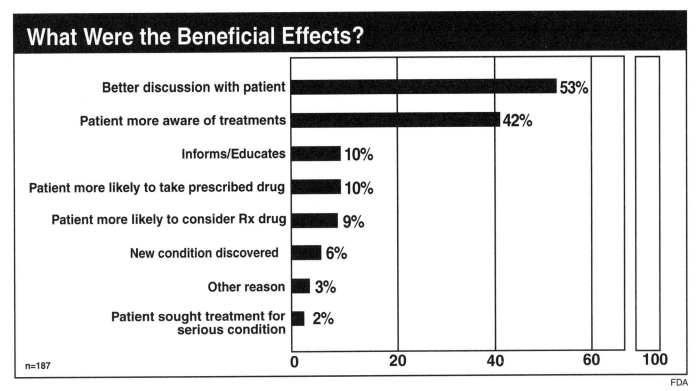

What Were the Beneficial Effects?

Better discussion with patient — 53%
Patient more aware of treatments — 42%
Informs/Educates — 10%
Patient more likely to take prescribed drug — 10%
Patient more likely to consider Rx drug — 9%
New condition discovered — 6%
Other reason — 3%
Patient sought treatment for serious condition — 2%

n=187

0   20   40   60   100

FDA

Figure 2 Physicians reported that DTC ads had these beneficial effects for patients.

offices within the FDA that have a responsibility for any aspect of DTC advertising to work together. "There's a lot of the same information out there, so why not bring it all together so that consumers can understand it better?"

Truth in Advertising

The FDA has regulated the advertising of prescription drugs since 1962, under the Federal Food, Drug, and Cosmetic Act and related regulations. The regulations establish detailed requirements for ad content. Most other advertising, including that of over-the-counter drugs, is regulated by the Federal Trade Commission under a different set of rules.

The FDA's Division of Drug Marketing, Advertising, and Communications (DDMAC) oversees two types of promotion for prescription drugs: promotional labeling and advertising. Advertising includes commercial messages broadcast on television or radio, communicated over the telephone, or printed in magazines and newspapers. Prescription drug ads must contain information in a "brief summary" relating to both risks and benefits. Recognizing the time constraints of broadcast ads, FDA regulations provide that a broadcast advertisement may include, instead of a brief summary information relating to the major risks. The ad must also make "adequate provision" for distributing the FDA-approved labeling in connection with the broadcast ad. This refers to the concept of providing ways for consumers to find more complete information about the drug.

Most ads fulfill this requirement by including a toll-free telephone number, a Web site address, or a link to a concurrently running print ad. They also encourage consumers to talk to their health care providers. Both print and broadcast ads directed at consumers may only make claims that are supported by scientific evidence.

DDMAC oversight helps ensure that pharmaceutical companies accurately communicate the benefits and risks of an advertised drug. The regulations require that advertising for prescription drugs must disclose certain information about the product's uses and risks.

In addition, advertisements cannot be false or misleading and cannot omit material facts. FDA regulations also call for "fair balance" in product claim ads. This means that the risks and benefits must be presented with comparable scope, depth, and detail, and that information relating to the product's effectiveness must be fairly balanced by risk information.

The FDA does not generally require prior approval of DTC ads, although companies are required to submit their ads to the FDA at the time they begin running. The agency, therefore, routinely examines these commercials and published DTC ads after they become available to the public. FDA, however, also is happy to review proposed ads if a drug company makes a request.

"We look at a lot of DTC ads before they run," says Kathryn J. Aikin, Ph.D., a social scientist in DDMAC. "Manufacturers typically want to be sure they're getting started on the right foot."

The Trouble with Ads

Of the three types of DTC advertisements, the first and most common—product-claim ads—mention a drug's name and the condition it is intended to treat, and describe the risks and

DTC Ads at a Glance

Product-claim ads:

- mention a drug by name
- make representations about the drug, such as its safety and effectiveness
- must have fair balance of information about effectiveness and risks
- are required to disclose risks in a "brief summary" of benefits and risks (for print ads)
- are required to give a "major statement" of risks and "adequate provision" for finding out more, such as a toll-free number (for broadcast ads).

Reminder ads:

- provide the name of the medication
- may provide other minimal information, such as cost and dosage form
- do not make a representation about the drug, such as the drug's use, effectiveness, or safety
- are not required to provide risk information.

Help-seeking ads:

- educate consumers about a disease or medical condition
- let people know that treatments exist for a medical condition
- don't name a specific drug
- are not required to provide risk information.

benefits associated with taking the drug. Some manufacturers have decided not to present this much information and instead, have made use of two other kinds of ads. "Reminder" ads give only the name of the product, but not what it is used for, and "help-seeking" ads contain information about a disease, but do not mention a specific drug. These help-seeking—or disease-awareness—ads can be extremely informative and, because they name no drug, they are not regulated by the FDA. Examples of help-seeking ads are those that mention high cholesterol or diabetes, and then direct you to ask your doctor about treatments. Reminder ads call attention to a drug's name, but say nothing about the condition it is used to treat, its effectiveness, or safety information. A reminder ad is not required to include risk information.

There has been a great deal of discussion about the brief summary that accompanies DTC print ads. The typical brief summary is not brief and uses technical language. This is because it reprints all of the risk information from the physician labeling. People have complained that the brief summary cannot be understood by consumers. Aikin says, "Patients do not typically read the brief summary in DTC print ads unless

they're interested in the product." Even then, she says, much information is likely glanced at, rather than fully read.

Public input and the FDA's own experiences with DTC promotion prompted the agency to publish two new draft guidances in February 2004: one on the brief summary, and one on help-seeking ads. These guidances are designed to encourage more informative, understandable ads.

Advertising Guidance

The draft guidance on the brief summary encourages companies to use consumer-friendly language and formats to convey prescription drug risk information—through a "less is more" approach. This approach focuses on the most serious and the most common risks of a drug, rather than listing every risk from the physician labeling. "Even though the information currently in the brief summary is complete, accurate, and in compliance," says Pitts, "it does not mean that patients are deriving the maximum benefit from it."

Sometimes marketers combine help-seeking ads with perceptually similar reminder ads in a way that causes the audience to perceive the two pieces as one advertisement. Appearing individually, these ads are exempted by regulation from the risk disclosure requirement. Combined, however, both ads can, in some cases, make a product-claim advertisement that requires risk disclosure.

The agency's recent draft guidance on help-seeking ads explains that help-seeking and reminder ads must appear distinct to avoid coming under the regulations for a product-claim ad. The draft guidance also address's the separation needed between the two types of ads—in space for print ads, and in time for TV ads.

Those in Violation

For companies that don't follow the rules, DDMAC's possible actions include two types of letters—"untitled" and "warning." These letters address advertisements that make misleading claims about a drug's effectiveness—violations such as overstating the effectiveness of the drug, suggesting a broader range of indicated uses than the drug has been approved for, and lack of risk information. In both types of letters, DDMAC asks that the advertisement be withdrawn.

Warning letters, which are sent to companies that have violated the law repeatedly or that have committed serious regulatory violations in their advertising, typically request corrective advertisements to assure that the audience that received the original false or misleading information also receives truthful and accurate information.

Untitled letters are usually, but not always, sent to companies for first-time offenses or for less serious violations.

For example, the 60-second DTC broadcast television ad featuring "Digger," the well-known animated dermatophyte microorganism touting Lamisil (terbinafine), a treatment for nail fungus, was initially found to be false or misleading. The FDA sent an untitled letter to the makers of Lamisil for overstating the drug's effectiveness, minimizing its risk information, and making an unsubstantiated superiority claim. As a result, the manufacturer, Novartis Pharmaceuticals Corp., stopped running that ad.

DDMAC recently sent a warning letter to Bristol-Myers Squibb Co. about false or misleading promotional materials for Pravachol (pravastatin sodium), a drug approved to lower cholesterol in people with high cholesterol, to help prevent heart attacks in people with high cholesterol or heart disease, and to help prevent stroke in people with heart disease. One of the company's ads misleadingly suggested that the drug had been proven to help prevent stroke in all people worried about having a stroke, regardless of whether or not they had heart disease.

Another ad, directed at diabetes patients, misleadingly suggested that Pravachol had been proven to help prevent heart attacks and stroke in people with diabetes. Following the warning letter, the company created a corrective ad campaign acknowledging that Pravachol had not been approved for these indications.

Assessing DTC advertising is an on-going process for the FDA. As more research surfaces, the agency will continue to evaluate DTC drug promotion and will take additional measures as appropriate to protect the public health.

From *FDA Consumer*, July/August 2004, pp. 21–24, 26–27. Published 2004 by U.S. Food and Drug Administration. www.fda.gov

Marketing, Consumers and Technology
Perspectives for Enhancing Ethical Transactions

The advance of technology has influenced marketing in a number of ways that have ethical implications. Growth in use of the Internet and e-commerce has placed electronic "cookies," spyware, spam, RFIDs, and data mining at the forefront of the ethical debate. Some marketers have minimized the significance of these trends. This overview paper examines these issues and introduces the two articles that follow. It is hoped that these entries will further the important "marketing and technology" ethical debate.

GENE R. LACZNIAK AND PATRICK E. MURPHY

Any casual survey of the twenty-first-century marketplace reveals an economic landscape of robust e-commerce and numerous emergent forms of technologically assisted marketing. An observer of this scene might assert for good reason that marketers are increasingly leveraging their new technology to erode the consumers' right to autonomy (Kelly and Rowland 2000). A number of these current technology aided practices are problematic in terms of their potential invasiveness (Marshall 1999), their violations of consumer privacy rights (Hemphill 2002) or simply their added disadvantage to consumers (Gordon 2002).

Consider just the following illustrations:

- **E-Commerce Cookies and Spyware.** When consumers log on to a website to seek purchase information or to conduct an online transaction, a "cookie" might be placed on their personal computers, allowing sellers to track movements on that and perhaps other Internet sites visited (Linn 2004). When consumers download software, part of the usage agreement (which often consumers fail to read due to its intentional length and complexity) sometimes includes the acceptance of shadow software that records site surfs and targets pop-up ads at these users. In these ways, marketers gather considerable information about how consumers traverse the web and in what specific sequence their purchase decision unfolds. A recent development regarding cookies is that more companies are only using first party cookies (put on by the site visited) and resisting third party cookies (placed by an outside company) to increase consumer trust (Kesmodel 2005).

- **Spam.** One of the least satisfying dimensions of the growing e-commerce environment is spam—unsolicited e-mail that typically attempts to sell products and services to Internet users. The most irritating forms of such spam include advertisements for easy (high cost) financing, gambling sites, pornographic material and diet supplements. Worse, sometimes as consumers open spam message attachments to ascertain their nature, instructions are introduced to the computer "page jacking" users to a seller's website and possibly "mouse trapping" them so that efforts to electronically escape from that site dump them to a related site or a revised form of the original solicitation. Worse still, buyers receive faux messages from purportedly known business partners (a practice known as "phishing") asking the receiver to verify personal information that if rendered will aid identity theft (Borzo 2004). It is estimated that approximately 50 percent of all e-mails received can be categorized as spam (Swartz 2004). The Controlling the Assault of Non-Solicited Pornography and Marketing Act of 2003 (CAN-SPAM) went into effect in January 2004 and required companies to conspicuously label their commercial e-mails and provide clear methods to opt out of future ads (Chang 2004). Despite this legislation, consumer frustration with spam, along with lost personal and organizational productivity, has grown to alarming proportions (Davidson 2004; Friel 2005).

- **RFIDs.** Another technology on the ascendance involves RFIDs or radio frequency identification tags. Diffusion of this technology could also engender significant consumer privacy concerns and raise ethical questions (Covert 2004; Peslak 2005). RFIDs are millimeter-wide microchips (about the size of a match head) that can contain a substantial amount of data about the product in which it is imbedded. The microchip has the capacity to send out that information via wireless signal to a radio scanner. This is the same technology currently used for some drive-by toll booth passes as well as for quick gasoline purchases via electronic "key chain fob" rather than credit card swipe. Currently, RFIDs are used mainly for internal inventory tracking and control. For example, Wal-Mart uses this technology in its distribution centers and is requiring that it be incorporated by all its suppliers in the next couple of years (Feder 2003). Wal-Mart is getting some "push back" on this demand from suppliers primarily due to cost considerations (Hays 2004). And Pfizer is utilizing RFIDs to guarantee that certain of its drug products (e.g., Viagra) have not been counterfeited (Appleby 2004). However, as RFID technology becomes more widely applied and refined, it could potentially provide marketing researchers with the capability to "enter" a consumer's home or garage and, given the proper scanner-receivers, identify the nature, amount, and source of many of the products contained therein (Hajewski 2003).

- **Data Mining.** Market researchers are also accumulating, via computerized files, an increasing amount of information about their customers. Given the compiling capabilities of database software, much of the information is aggregated from disparate buying situations. Made easier by widespread consumer acceptance of preferred buyer cards and credit purchasing, such information is combined using personal identifiers such as phone number, household address, driver's license registration or even social security number (Loveman 2003). Then using "data mining" techniques—sophisticated multi-variable statistical models that can extract scattered information from large consumer data pools—marketers are able to construct individual consumer profiles for millions of shoppers (Berson, et al. 2000; Murphy, et al. 2005). Disturbingly, these profiles are then copied and sold to other marketers who use it to predict likely purchase prospects for their goods and services. As a result, a growing and permanent record exists of what individual consumers buy, where they bought it, the price paid and the incentives that motivated the transaction. Amazingly, some marketers use this information to try to drive away consumers who they project will not be particularly profitable (McWilliams 2004).

Taking all of this into account, it is understandable that many consumers are troubled by certain technology aided marketing practices that might be construed as prying, irritating and exploitive. In fact, a 2003 Harris interactive poll of over one thousand U.S. adults found that 69 percent of respondents agreed that consumers have lost all control over how their personal information is collected and used (Loyle 2003). Some social observers have gone so far as to opine that privacy rights will be to the twenty-first century what civil rights and women's equality were to the twentieth.

It was with such concerns in mind that in the summer of 2003 the *Business Ethics Quarterly* issued a call for papers addressing ethical issues stemming from the technology and marketing nexus. While privacy questions are the most obvious issue, erosion of other consumer rights such as *access* (e.g., the so-called digital divide), *property* (e.g., electronic copyrights), *security* (e.g., protection of sensitive consumer data by sellers), and *redress* (e.g., the ability to verify personal records) are increasingly being challenged by marketing approaches that rely heavily on the latest technologies. The ultimate economic and social ramifications of emergent marketing technology are uncertain, but it seems clear that many new ethical questions will arise. Thus, academic scholars were invited to provide their research-based or analytic perspectives on any important dimension of such issues.

Marketers' Defense of Ethical Criticism

A perusal of the business and popular press suggests that marketing practitioners have already been mounting a defense to the perceived ethical criticisms of their new technologies. To illustrate this point, a few of the more common marketing apologetics are noted below.

- **Marketing practitioners assert that when the effects of a marketing technology or its application become socially troubling, the existing regulatory framework responds by outlawing or suppressing the most annoying and harmful transgressions.** They point to the 2003 institution of the federally administered *national no call* list that restricts telemarketers from contacting consumers that are signatories (Davidson 2003). If households listed on this roll are called (certain exceptions apply), telemarketers are subject to an $11,000 fine per violation. It is estimated that this legislation, in conjunction with existing state programs, will eliminate up to 90 percent of all telemarketing calls. Marketers also highlight the thirty-three states that have laws regulating spam (Mangalindan 2003) as well as the federal 2004 "Can Spam" Act, which mandates that e-sellers cannot hide behind false addresses, thus making their identities more traceable. Consumer groups, however, characterize the Act's provisions as ineffective because among other things it does nothing to control the flow of spam from non-domestic e-sellers (Davidson 2004). Finally, marketers underscore the Children's Online Privacy Protection Act of 2002 as a model example of how well the current oversight system works (Lans-Retsky 2004). Known as COPPA, this legislation safeguards a particularly vulnerable group, children, from most forms of online marketing research. For example, COPPA makes it a violation for any marketer to knowingly gather online personal information from children younger than thirteen years of age without specific parental consent. Already two major companies, Mrs. Fields Cookies and Hershey's (candy) Direct have incurred significant fines for COPPA violations (Loyle 2003). To date, COPPA is the only anti-privacy statute that has been passed in the United States.

- **Marketers contend that the problems attributed to new selling technologies are overstated, not really novel and represent only slightly different forms of old practices that are already well tolerated by consumers.** They observe that junk mail has long clogged household mailboxes; some consumers dislike it, others look forward to it. Marketers question how spam is any different than junk mail and recommend that consumers simply use the delete button more liberally (Goldman 2003). Furthermore, justifying their opinions with national survey data, marketers suggest there is great variability among consumers in their tolerance for direct selling (Milne and Rohm 2000). Marketers also argue that concerns about the privacy dimensions of RFID tagged products are widely overblown (Ody 2004). Yet in Texas, this technology is being used to track the movement of hundreds of young school children in order to provide a record that they entered or exited school buses and as an early warning sign of possible kidnapping (Richtel 2004).

- **Marketers emphasize that some aspects of the much discussed consumer privacy debate may be exaggerated because many consumers are willing to give away personal information quite readily.** For instance, the majority of consumers volunteer detailed demographic information on product warranty forms although only the most basic information (name and address) is required to activate the coverage for most products. Consumer acceptance of preferred shopper cards, used in exchange for various discounts and rewards at the sponsoring retailer, has never been stronger as buyers sign up in droves surely knowing that their every purchase is tracked in detail. And digital cable TV, tethered to interactive capability, is steadily increasing its subscriber base with customers presumably knowing that their viewing selections can be logged and classified. In short, many marketers believe that it is difficult to defend or even establish a scrupulous buyers' right to privacy when so many consumers signal by their actions that they simply don't mind sharing their personal information with vendors or at least are willing to hand it over in exchange for minimal perks. Business philosophers have observed as much (De George 1999). As one privacy director remarked in response to privacy statutes: "Forget laws and standards—you need to send the right message to the right person at the right time" (Lager 2005: 35).

Emerging Issues in Marketing and Technology

Of course, blanket defenses for widely varying applications of marketing technology are not particularly useful. As is necessary when significant new technologies impact the economy, numerous questions arise, some of an ethical nature, that need to be systematically investigated. With this special issue on marketing and technology, *Business Ethics Quarterly* hopes to advance the conversation about some of these questions in an analytic and reasoned fashion. The articles contained in this issue build on some already existing foundational work. A partial list of such writing includes Caudill and Murphy 2000, Donaldson 2001, and Peace et al. 2002, as well as Kracher and Corritore 2004. This last paper makes a particularly significant point about e-commerce, suggesting that it requires not so much a new ethics but a dedicated evaluation of the new manifestations of economic exchange from various traditional ethical frameworks. Kracher and Corritore also make a particularly strong case for the centrality of *trust* as a solution to many of the emerging problems of the electronic marketplace. Such advocacy adds to the themes previously expressed by Grabner-Kraeuter (2002), Hemphill (2002) and Koehn (2003).

The first paper in this special issue addresses "Privacy Rights on the Internet: Self Regulation or Government Regulation?" Norman E. Bowie and Karim Jamal (2006) review an earlier empirical study (Jamal, Maier, and Sunder 2003) and combine it with information gathered in the U.K. to examine whether high traffic websites are honoring their promises to consumers regarding privacy. This is a critical ethical and economic question because privacy concerns have been shown to be a major factor in depressing the growth rate of Internet shopping (Tedeschi 2000). Moreover, the extent of keeping privacy promises by Internet sellers will help determine whether the U.S. government needs to supplement current industry self regulation, presently implemented through various "assurance seals" and privacy policies that specify the subsequent usage of any buyer information that has been gathered. Some consumer advocates have called for European style restrictions prohibiting any secondary use of information provided by consumers (Scheibal and Gladstone 2000). The authors use Kantian reasoning to establish the centrality of a consumer's right to privacy. However, based on the significantly high compliance rates by U.S. sellers in apparently honoring buyer privacy (as demonstrated by their empirical test), government mandated regulation of privacy policies are *not* recommended at this time. Bowie and Jamal observe, however, that an explicit "opt-in" provision for any further usage of consumer information, beyond the original transaction, is the approach most aligned with the basic right of consumer autonomy.

In the second paper, "Online Brands and Trademark Conflicts: A Hegelian Perspective," Richard A. Spinello (2006) draws on the philosophy of George Hegel, particularly his conception of property rights, to clarify and somewhat limit the legal claims of corporations to Internet domain names that incorporate their trademarks. As Internet commerce has mushroomed, various external parties have tried to incorporate famous names into their own domain addresses in order to create confusion, divert traffic to their own sites or extract ransom from the trademarked name owners. A widely reported incident of such usurpation in a non-commercial setting was whitehouse.com (a porn site) as contrasted with whitehouse.gov, the e-mail contact address for staff serving the U.S. President. Spinello argues that Hegel's view of property appears to usefully balance the marketer's rights to trademark protection with competing consumer claims more fairly than other philosophies. For example, a reasonable person attempting to shop Wal-Mart online might well confuse Wal-Mart.org (a potentially bogus address) with Wal-Mart.com. And so, if there is a dispute about domain address rights, the trademark claims of Wal-Mart should prevail. However, using Hegelian reasoning, Spinello contends that Wal-Martsucks.com (a website likely critical of the firm) would *not* be confused by a reasonable person as the home page of the real Wal-Mart. So, in this latter case, private property rights to the disputed ether space—a legitimate forum for social criticism—ought not to be available to the corporation.

To be sure, these *BEQ* papers are just the opening round in what should be an on-going dialog about ethical issues emanating from the marketing and technology interface. We encourage interested scholars to further address the ethical implications of questions such as:

- Is it fair for marketers to use electronic customer profiles to actively *discourage* transactions from customers that are projected to be unprofitable to serve?

- Is it proper for online marketers to utilize targeted *price discrimination* based on the past online behaviors of individual consumers without acknowledging the protocol behind the practice?

- What can be done about *consumer abuses* caused by international e-marketers not subject to local or national marketing regulations?

This last question raises one of the more poignant issues about the borderless world of Internet marketing. Since cyberspace is global, how can it ever be effectively regulated by governmental authorities that are geographically bound? It would seem that the universality of the web marketing world makes it critically imperative that prevailing ethical norms and values be established among citizens in order to reduce buyer exploitation and enhance transactional trust. In other words, the future fairness and justice of Internet marketing will depend far more on ethics than law. Finally, the discussion contained in this special issue of *BEQ* does not specifically address the ethical implications involved in the use of new marketing technologies not directly connected to a web selling environment. For example, the increased sophistication, miniaturization, and lower cost of surveillance capability has added to the arsenal of marketing researchers interested in doing covert observational consumer studies (Hagerty and Berman 2003). Who will watch these consumer watchers? Ethical evaluations of these offline applications of marketing technology are needed.

In the end, marketing practitioners adopt new technology because it promises to increase the efficiency or effectiveness of exchange. Such applications imply lower costs or greater convenience for consumers. In this manner, the use of new technology has always been a driver of the material abundance available in the marketplace. But typically, new technologies bring with them some questionable and often unintended side effects. One critical role for those in the Academy interested in ethics is to identify and evaluate those side effects in terms of how they must be balanced to promote greater economic fairness and justice.

A continuation of discussions contained in this issue of *BEQ* is welcomed, encouraged and anticipated.

References

Appleby, J. 2004. "FDA Guidelines Call for Radio Technology to Control Counterfeit Drugs." *USA Today* (November 16): 7B.

Berson, A., S. Smith, and K. Thurling. 2000. *Building Data Mining Applications for CRM* (Columbus: McGraw-Hill).

Borzo, J. 2004. "Something's Phishy." *The Wall Street Journal* (November 15): R8, R11.

Bowie, N., and K. Jamal. 2006. "Privacy Rights on the Internet: Self Regulation or Government Regulation?" *Business Ethics Quarterly* 16:3 (July): 323–42.

Caudill, E. M., and P. E. Murphy. 2000. "Consumer Online Privacy: Legal and Ethical Issues." *Journal of Public Policy & Marketing* 19(1): 7–19.

Chang, J. 2004. "Private Property." *Sale and Marketing Management* (December): 22–26.

Covert, J. 2004. "Down, but Far from Out." *The Wall Street Journal* (January 12): R5, R8.

Davidson, P. 2003. "FTC Told to Enforce Do-Not-Call List." *USA Today* (October 8): 1B.

_____. 2004. "Do-Not-Spam Registry Could Result in More Spam, FTC Says." *USA Today* (June 16): B1.

De George, R. T. 1999. "Business Ethics and the Information Age." *Bentley College Center for Business Ethics/Bell Atlantic Lecture Series* (March 22): 1–20.

Donaldson, T. 2001. "Ethics in Cyberspace: Have We Seen this Movie Before?" *Business and Society Review* 106(4): 273.

Feder, B. J. 2003. "Wal-Mart Plan Could Cost Suppliers Millions." *The New York Times* (November 10): 1–2, http://www.nytimes.com.

Friel, A. L. 2005. "The Spam Spat: How Will Marketers Be Affected by the Fight Against Spam?" *Marketing Management* (May/June): 48–50.

Goldman, E. 2003. "Opinion: Hate Spam? Just Hit Delete." http://www.TwinCities.com (August 11): 1–2.

Gordon, J. R. 2002. "Legal Services and the Digital Divide." *Albany Law Journal of Science and Technology* 12: 809–19.

Grabner-Kraeuter, S. 2002. "The Role of Consumers' Trust in Online-Shopping." *Journal of Business Ethics* 39(1/2): 43–50.

Hagerty, J. R., and D. K. Berman. 2003. "New Battleground Over Web Privacy: Ads That Snoop." *The Wall Street Journal* (August 27): A1, A8.

Hajewski, D. 2003. "High-Tech ID System Would Revolutionize Retail Industry." *Milwaukee Journal Sentinel* (February 9): 1D, 3D.

Hays, C. L. 2004. "What They Know About You." *The New York Times* (November 14): section 3.

Hemphill, T. A. 2002. "Electronic Commerce and Consumer Privacy: Establishing Online Trust in the U.S. Digital Economy." *Business and Society Review* 107(2): 221–9.

Jamal, K., M. Maier, and S. Sunder. 2003. "Privacy in E-Commerce: Development of Reporting Standards, Disclosure and Assurance Services in an Unregulated Market." *Journal of Accounting Research* 41(2): 285–310.

Kelly, E. P., and H. C. Rowland. 2000. "Ethical and Online Privacy Issues in Electronic Commerce." *Business Horizons* (May–June): 3–12.

Kesmodel, D. 2005. "When the Cookies Crumble." *The Wall Street Journal* (September 12): R6.

Koehn, D. 2003. "The Nature of and Conditions for Online Trust." *Journal of Business Ethics* 43(1/2): 3–19.

Kracher, B., and C. L. Corritore. 2004. "Is There a Special E-Commerce Ethics?" *Business Ethics Quarterly* 14(1): 71–94.

Lager, M. 2005. "CRM in an Age of Legislation," *Customer Relationship Management* (August): 30–35.

Lans-Retsky, M. 2004. "COPPA Sets Tone for Privacy Policies." *Marketing News* (March 15): 8.

Linn, A. 2004. "Bugged By Spies: Imports Clog Computers." *USA Today* (November 1): 4D.

Loveman, G. 2003. "Diamonds in the Data Mine." *Harvard Business Review* (May): 109–13.

Loyle, D. 2003. "Privacy Under Scrutiny." *Catalog Success* (June 1); www.catalogsuccess.com, 1–7.

Mangalindan, M. 2003. "Putting a Lid on Spam." *The Wall Street Journal* (June 6): B1, B4.

Marshall, K. P. 1999. "Has Technology Introduced New Ethical Problems?" *Journal of Business Ethics* 19(1): 81–90.

McWilliams, G. 2004. "Analyzing Customers, Best Buy Decides Not All Are Welcome." *The Wall Street Journal* (November 8): A1, A8.

Milne, G., and A. J. Rohm. 2000. "Consumer Privacy and Name Removal across Direct Marketing Channels: Exploring Opt-In and Opt-Out Alternatives." *Journal of Public Policy & Marketing* 19(2): 238–49.

Murphy, P. E., G. R. Laczniak, N. E. Bowie, and T. A. Klein. 2005. *Ethical Marketing* (Upper Saddle River, N.J.: Pearson Prentice Hall), 205.

Ody, Penelope. 2004. "RFID Not Ready yet for Baked Beans." *Financial Times* (June 23): 3.

Peace, G., J. Weber, K. S. Hartzel, and J. Nightingale. 2002. "Ethical Issues in eBusiness: A Proposal for Creating the eBusiness Principles." *Business Society Review* 107(1): 41–60.

Peslak, A. R. 2005. "An Ethical Exploration of Privacy and Radio Frequency Identification." *Journal of Business Ethics* 59: 327–45.

Richtel, M. 2004. "In Texas, 28,000 Students Test an Electronic Eye." *The New York Times* (November 17): 1–3, www.nytimes.com.

Scheibal, W. J., and J. A. Gladstone. 2000. "Privacy on the Net: Europe Changes the Rules." *Business Horizons* (May–June): 13–18.

Spinello, R. 2006. "Online Brands and Trademark Conflicts: A Hegelian Perspective." *Business Ethics Quarterly* 16:3 (July): 343–67.

Swartz, J. 2004. "Is the Future of E-Mail Under Cyberattack?" *USA Today* (June 15): 4B.

Tedeschi, B. 2000. "E-Commerce Report: Giving Consumers Access to the Data Collected About Them Online." *The New York Times* (July 3): C6.

Gene R. Laczniak and Patrick E. Murphy, Marketing, Consumers and Technology: Perspectives for Enhancing Ethical Transactions, *Business Ethics Quarterly,* Vol. 16, no. 3, July 2006, pp. 313–321. Copyright © 2006 by Business Ethics Quarterly. Reprinted by permission.

Serving Unfair Customers

LEONARD L. BERRY AND KATHLEEN SEIDERS

1. Changing Focus: From Unfair Companies to Unfair Customers

Ten years ago, we published an article titled "Service Fairness: What It Is and Why It Matters" (Seiders & Berry, 1998). Therein, we argued that poor service is not always linked to unfair company practices, but that unfair company practices are always linked to customer perceptions of poor service. We also argued that companies can pay a heavy price when customers believe they have been treated unfairly because customers' responses to perceived injustice often are pronounced, emotional, and retaliatory. We concluded by providing guidelines for managers on preventing unfairness perceptions and effectively managing those that do arise.

Fairness remains a critically important topic today, for it is essential to a mutually satisfactory exchange between two parties. Perceived unfairness undermines trust and diminished trust undermines the strength of relationships. Perceived unfairness is always a negative development. The focus of our original article was company unfairness to customers. Fairness, however, is a two-way street; thus, our present focus is customer unfairness to companies. This time, we examine how customers can be unfair, why it is important, and what companies can do about it.

We are ardent champions of the customer, but we do *not* believe in the maxim that "the customer is always right." Sometimes, the customer is wrong and unfairness often results. That the customer is sometimes wrong is a dirty little secret of marketing, known to many but rarely discussed in public—or in print. What better occasion to broach this unmentionable topic than *Business Horizons'* 50th anniversary?

2. What Is Customer Unfairness and Why Does it Matter?

Customer unfairness occurs when a customer behaves in a manner that is devoid of common decency, reasonableness, and respect for the rights of others, creating inequity and causing harm for a company and, in some cases, its employees and other customers. Customer unfairness should be viewed independent of illegality because unfair customer behavior frequently is legal; repugnant, perhaps, but not necessarily illegal. Our focus in this article is legal customer behavior that is unfair, falling in the so-called "gray area" of company response.

When does a customer's bad judgment (or, when do bad manners) cross the line to "unfairness?" Three concepts are particularly useful in considering this question. The first is the severity of the harm the customer causes. The second is the frequency of the customer's problematic behavior. Figure 1 shows increasing levels of these two factors: "minor," "moderate," and "extreme" for severity of harm and "uncommon," "intermittent," and "recurrent" for frequency of occurrence. Customer behavior that reaches either the "moderate" or "intermittent" level would usually earn the unfairness label. At these levels, the customer crosses a threshold.

The third concept is intentionality. The customer who seeks to take advantage and inflict harm, who willfully disrespects the rights of other parties, will almost always deserve the unfairness label. In some cases, customers may seek to harm a company that they believe has harmed them. The customers' behavior in this case is an act of retaliation. When customers blame a company for unfair treatment, there are fair and unfair ways of responding. Intentionally unfair behavior is usually indefensible.

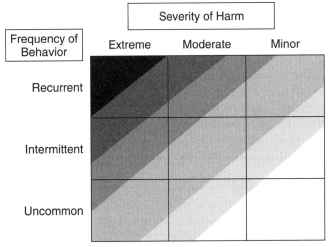

Figure 1 The threshold of customer unfairness. Adapted from Seiders and Berry (1998).

How do companies deal with unfair customers? We contacted executives from a variety of service organizations to solicit their opinions on the topic and to document examples drawn from their experiences. (We restricted our inquiries to consumer services executives based on the assumption that business-to-business services merit a separate exploration.) Our preliminary research reveals that some executives struggle with how to respond to customer unfairness. They don't want to respond in a way that confounds the company's commitment to quality service, which they and others worked hard to instill. Nor do they want to risk offending a still-profitable, albeit problematic, customer. The following comments from four executives illustrate:

- "I think there is a subservient or servant mentality to all service, and to stray from that causes confusion in taking clear and concise action that should be positive for the customer."

- "The lifetime cost of losing a guest exceeds $500, so we go to great lengths to avoid losing them, even when they're wrong. Rather than risk offending guests, we tend to let 'little things' go."

- "My philosophy is that the customer is always right to some degree. It is that matter of degree that determines the action of the company. I believe that if we ever think that the customer is 100% wrong, then we have a high risk of becoming arrogant and not being customer-focused. I know that this may sound crazy, but if we crack open the door to this idea, then I think we can very quickly go down the slippery slope."

- "We are just not used to thinking of guests 'crossing the line.' I don't know that I have ever set up boundaries. I always feel that guests have the right to say what they want and to do what they want, short of inconveniencing another guest or physically harming another guest or employee."

Our position is that companies cannot afford to ignore customer unfairness and should devise a plan to deal with it. Unfair customer behavior can exact a significant toll on employees' job satisfaction and weaken a company's overall service quality. We are not just speculating about this. Recent research by Rupp and Spencer (2006) found that customer injustice increased the degree of effort required for employees to manage their emotions in inter-personal transactions. This increased effort in what is termed *emotional labor* produces added stress, and contributes to employee turnover and overall unwillingness to perform (Grandey, Dickter, & Sin, 2004). Moreover, the injustice of one customer can negatively affect employee behavior toward other customers.

The effects of customer unfairness are often magnified because employees find it difficult to deal with customers who have treated their coworkers disrespectfully, even if the same customers treated them fairly (Rupp, Holub, & Grandey, 2007). Unfair acts are more memorable than typical encounters (Lind & Tyler, 1988), and employees may respond to customer unfairness by discussing incidents with other sympathetic employees, fostering negative word of mouth about customers.

When some customers systematically abuse company policies, such as retail return policies, companies are inclined to either clamp down with tougher rules or increase prices to cover losses. In effect, fair customers are penalized by the actions of unfair customers. Employees are put on the defensive and can become more sensitive to customer manipulation, and more inclined to question the sincerity of customers' communications and the motives that lie behind their actions (Tyler & Bies, 1990). The dynamic can turn adversarial. In short, both employees and customers pay for other customers' misdeeds.

3. Types of Unfair Customers

Over the last 30 years, justice research has focused on three types of justice. *Distributive justice* relates to the outcomes of decisions or allocations; *procedural justice* relates to the procedures used to arrive at those outcomes; and *interactional justice* relates to interpersonal treatment and communication. Interactional justice is demonstrated by interpersonal fairness (i.e., when individuals are treated with dignity and respect) and informational fairness (i.e., when communications are truthful and important decisions are explained) (Rupp & Spencer, 2006). Many studies have found that interactional injustice produces particularly strong responses.

Our exploration of customer unfairness led us to identify distinct types of problem customers. The categories we discuss are neither mutually exclusive nor comprehensive, but describe the most common and problematic types of unfair customers. Each category highlights a different facet of customer unfairness, although some behaviors may logically fit into more than one category. We exclude customers who use stolen credit cards, manipulate price tags, steal merchandise, and stage 'accidents' in service facilities (see, for example, Fullerton & Punj, 2004). The scenarios we consider involve more ambiguity than clear-cut illegality.

3.1. Verbal Abusers

Verbal abusers lash out at employees in a blatantly offensive and disrespectful manner whether in face-to-face transactions, over the telephone, or via the Internet. The verbal abuser capitalizes on the power imbalance commonly present in service encounters: the customer who is 'always right' has the upper hand by default and an opportunity to push the boundaries of fair behavior. One healthcare executive profiled this customer type as "patients and family members who belittle, demean, intimidate, and abuse staff members, and threaten litigation at the slightest lapse in service." Verbal abusers bully front-line employees who typically lack the freedom to defend themselves and, in fact, are expected not to react visibly to unfair treatment by customers. Given the importance of interactional injustice, it is no surprise that the verbal abuser's behavior can have such negative effects on employees.

Customers' verbal abuse of employees is probably more pervasive than most service industry executives would want to admit. There is no accepted protocol for managing a verbal abuse episode, and we suspect that most often this type of incident is not managed. Our favorite story involves the owner of a bicycle store well known for its dedication to customer service. A father was picking up a repaired bicycle for his daughter, who, without telling him, had approved the recommended replacement of both tires (a $40 service). Although the employee patiently and repeatedly explained that the purchase was approved and offered to further verify it, the customer made accusatory remarks and yelled at her angrily, saying at one point, "Either you think I'm stupid or you're stupid. You're trying to rip me off." At that point, Chris Zane, the store's owner, walked up to the customer and said, "I'm Chris Zane; get out of my store and tell all your friends!" After the customer wordlessly slapped $40 on the counter and stormed out, the besieged employee looked at Zane and asked "'. . . and tell all your friends'?"

Zane explained to her, and other employees who had gravitated to the front of the store, that he wanted it to be clear that he valued his employee infinitely more than a rude, belligerent customer. "I also explained that this was the first time I had ever thrown a customer out of the store and that I would not tolerate my employees being mistreated by anyone. . . . I believe that my employees need to know that I respect them and expect them to respect our customers. Simply, if I am willing to fire an employee for mistreating a customer (and I have), then I must also be willing to fire a customer for mistreating an employee."

Verbal abusers can also have a profound effect on other customers. This is illustrated by a customer who, during a lunch rush at a very busy restaurant location, insisted that his steak be prepared rare. Although a manager apologized and explained that each steak is prepared uniformly in order to maintain the best quality (and said there would be no charge for the lunch), the customer continued to voice his disapproval to the staff, creating a disturbance that distracted them and degraded the overall experience of the surrounding customers.

In another incident, two customers in a bar loudly criticized the bartender for assisting other patrons before them and then rebuked the restaurant manager who intervened to try to calm them down. The manager then went to the kitchen to check on the progress of their food; when he returned, the two customers were leaving and shouting obscenities as they walked out. A common device of the verbal abuser is the threat to report employees and/or their facility 'to corporate,' a way to prolong employee unease after the offensive incident is over.

3.2. Blamers

Whereas verbal abusers bring misery primarily to customer contact employees, blamers will indict a company's products, policies, and people at all levels for any perceived shortfall. With blamers, 'the company is always wrong.'

Because customers play a co-producer role in many services, they affect the service quality and final outcome. Blamers, however, never see themselves in any way responsible for the outcome, regardless of the scenario. Causal inferences or attributions individuals use to assess the failure of a product or service performance are based on the locus of blame and whether or not the incident could have been controlled

(Sheppard, Lewicki, & Minton, 1992). From the blamer's perspective, not only is the company always at fault, but the perceived problem is always controllable.

Blamers are not discriminate about where they voice discord, and every service provider is familiar with this type of customer. A tennis coach had been working with an adult student for about six months when the student learned that an opponent in an upcoming match had worked briefly with the same coach in the past. The student asked for and received specific advice from the coach on how to win the match by attacking the opponent's greatest weaknesses. However, the opponent had corrected these weaknesses and much to the student's chagrin, she could find no way to beat her. In the clubhouse immediately after the match, she raged at her coach for not preparing her well, giving her poor information and lousy lessons, and causing her to lose the match.

In another example, a customer called the headquarters of a national casual dining chain to complain about the price of its cocktails. It seems the gentleman had spent $86 in the bar of this restaurant having drinks and appetizers after work the previous evening. He wanted to talk to someone about what he considered the excessive price of the drinks and how unfair he thought the cost. The switchboard operator noted the caller's angry tone and put him through to the president of the company.

The man re-explained to the president and said he could not believe the restaurant had charged him $7.50 for each of the beverages that he ordered. When asked how many he had consumed, the man said that was beside the point. The president asked the number in the man's party, and the man said only two. The president asked the man when he learned that the drinks were $7.50, which he said was after he paid the bill. The president then asked what the company might do to make it right. The customer replied that he wanted all of his money back; the president responded that this was unfair, as the customer and his guest had consumed enough appetizers and drinks to total $86. A full refund would not be equitable.

The customer became extremely angry, threatening to go online and destroy the company, report it to the Better Business Bureau, and picket in front of its restaurants for the next month. He raised his voice and asserted, "You will feel the effects of my negative PR efforts for a long time to come." Frustrated at the angry customer's threats, the president asked the customer how he could resolve this negative situation without giving the customer his money back for the food and drinks he consumed. The customer calmed down, thought about it, and told the president that if the company donated double the amount of the bill to the customer's favorite charity, he would consider the situation resolved. The president agreed to do so in order to move past the situation and end the disagreement.

The blamer is a particularly difficult type of customer for the healthcare industry. Patients who fail to take responsibility for their own health status often are blamers. Many such patients believe that a treatment cure exists for every condition and thus see no need to take measures to improve their own health. In one case, a patient was referred to a hospital's patient relations department after lodging serious complaints with the president's office. The patient claimed that his wound from surgery failed to heal because the staff ignored his complaints. In reality, the patient was non-compliant with recommended diet and wound care, refused to follow his doctor's recommendations for exercise and physical therapy, and failed to return for a follow-up appointment. At each point of contact, the patient threatened to hire a malpractice attorney.

This example may sound extreme, but in fact we heard a number of such stories. One healthcare professional noted, "I have been in patient relations for more than ten years now, and I can attest to the fact that these patients are a huge burden on the healthcare system. They tie up resources that could be used to improve services for all of our patients." An executive from a different healthcare institution expressed a similar view: "I hear from the same patients over and over again, and once a resolution is offered, many times it's a prolonged argument because it's their way or no way. Unfortunately, these cases are no longer rare."

3.3. Rule Breakers

Rule breakers readily ignore policies and procedures when they find them to be inconvenient or at odds with their own goals. Rule breakers generally ignore the honor code by which other customers abide. In chronic cases, a rule breaker may be a mild version of a con artist. Rule breakers are not concerned with equity, which is the first principle of distributive justice. Equity exists in an exchange when participants' rewards equal their contributions; rule breakers seek to optimize their rewards at the expense of the company. This not only harms the company, but also puts company employees in a tenuous and uncomfortable situation as they attempt to protect their employer from customer wrongdoing.

The damage done by rule breakers varies, of course, based on the nature of the rules and polices that are being broken. A restaurant that offers "all you can eat" shrimp entrees encounters some patrons who share with their tablemates, even though the menu clearly states that the price is per person. Managers are not quick to put servers in the awkward position of having to remind guests they are breaking the rule, but will do so if the 'sharing' gets out of hand.

A retailer with a catalog operation is subject to 'customers who bend the facts' (in the words of one executive) when post-delivery complainers assert that a telephone sales associate told them that shipping was free. When this happens, a company representative will listen to a tape of the original call and will usually hear the shipping charges discussed. For smaller transactions with first-time customers, the retailer apologizes, deducts the shipping charge, and restates the shipping fee policy for future transactions. For larger transactions, the customer is told that the call was reviewed and the company is not sure why there was confusion. Once customers realize that a company representative has reviewed the call and knows what actually was said, they rarely demand a shipping refund. "It's a nice way of saying we know what happened without becoming confrontational," explains a company manager.

One type of rule breaker can be termed a *rule maker*. Rule makers expect to be exempted from the rules and demand special treatment because of perceived superior status. Both rule breakers and rule makers demonstrate unfairness to other customers who are behaving according to norms and convention. When certain customers are allowed to break the rules because of their social or financial status, the equality principle of distributive justice is defied (Grover, 1991). A hospital executive describes the rule maker in this way:

"We have had patients who believe that there is some special level of care that we are constantly holding back, and if we knew how special they were that they would get this special executive level care. This is common in the family of trustees and board members. These are families that expect to be cared for only by departmental chairmen. We have coined the concept *chairman syndrome.*"

Often, it is the family-member-turned-advocate who demands to make the rules. For example, a patient's daughter insisted, "I want all of the labs printed out each day and handed to me when I walk in in the morning." A patient's son threatened, "I am an attorney and I demand to know what is going on with my mother!" A corporate chairman transferred his child by private jet to a hospital in another city when his company's physicians (non-pediatric, without privileges to practice in the hospital) were not allowed to direct the team of hospital physicians who were treating the child. These scenarios seem almost amusing until one considers the extent to which medical staff members and other hospital patients may be adversely affected by this disregard for the rules.

3.4. Opportunists

Opportunists have their antennae up for easy paths to personal financial gain. This customer's modus operandi can be demanding compensation by fabricating or exaggerating problems or flaws in a product or service. While this type of opportunist stiffs the company, there is a second type that stiffs 'the little guy.' These penny-ante opportunists, for example, don't tip (or don't adequately tip) service employees because they don't have to; that is, they can get away with it. This behavior is distasteful because, like many cases of verbal abuse, it hurts front-line employees whose tips often represent a significant percentage of their pay.

Opportunists frequently use gamesmanship to optimize their gain. A customer observed a plumbing problem in a restaurant restroom and complained to the manager, who called a plumbing service for the repair, and sent an employee to clean up. The customer contacted the company's customer relations office, complained about the state of the restroom, and requested a refund for his party's $80 meal. In response, the company sent $30 in gift certificates, in addition to an $80 check and an apology. The customer called the company again, stating that $30 was not enough to cause him to return to the restaurant because it would not cover the cost of his dining companions' meals. He was persistent, calling several times to express his displeasure in the amount of the gift certificates. In turn, the company sent an additional $50 in gift certificates, bringing the total compensation to $160, a nice return for encountering a plumbing problem.

The opportunist may not be a chronic gold digger, but rather just someone who recognizes an opportunity to take financial advantage of a company's service failure and recovery efforts. For example, when an ambulatory surgery patient complained to her hospital that her lingerie had been lost, she was offered reimbursement. She claimed that the cost was $400 and, because this was an unusually high amount, the hospital inquired about the value of the items. The patient said she had not kept the receipts. To maintain good will, the hospital paid the $400 and apologized.

The opportunist doesn't require a service failure to take action. Some users of professional services, for example, maneuver to gain pro bono consultation from a prior provider. A communications coach periodically receives 'pick your brain' phone calls from former clients. Because these customers don't intend to pay for this 'informal' advice, the consultant is forced into an awkward position by clients attempting to exploit the relationship.

3.5. Returnaholics

This customer is a hybrid, with traits common to rule breakers and opportunists but engaged in a specific type of activity: returning products to stores. Returnaholics are rule breakers in that they don't adhere to the spirit of the company's return policies, whereby returns are accepted for defective products, a post-purchase change of mind, and gift exchange. In many cases, the returnaholic never intends to keep the product to begin with. Returnaholics are opportunists because they exploit retailer return policies for their own benefit. There are two types of returnaholics: situational and chronic.

Situational returnaholics become active under certain conditions. For example, one retailer's sales of equipment such as snow blowers, generators, and chainsaws would spike just before a major weather event but then fall precipitously shortly thereafter when many customers returned new *and* used equipment, and even products such as ice melt and flashlights, demanding refunds. It was not unusual for a store to see more than half the generators sold the week before a storm returned within two weeks after the storm. This phenomenon was a painful and expensive exercise for the retailer and its vendors. Reluctantly, the company adopted a stricter return policy covering specific items to better manage after-the-storm return rates.

Some situational returners use an item until it is damaged or worn out and then return it for a full refund or new item, claiming it is defective because it 'should have held up better.' They expect the refund to be 100% of purchase price because they believe that retailers carry a manufacturer's warranty for all items indefinitely.

Chronic, or serial, returnaholics are referred to by some store operators as "rental" customers. One customer of a men's shoe and accessories chain started shopping at two of the company's stores in 2001. The customer would often buy a product in store A and return it (after wearing it) to store B, using a different name for the return transaction. He also would complain to upper management about quality or the service he received in hopes of getting discounts on future purchases. The company realized this pattern of behavior spanned six years, once it figured out that all of this activity involved one customer rather

than two. In that period, the customer had purchased 23 pairs of shoes and returned 17 for net sales of $381 (which obviously did not come close to covering the cost of 17 pairs of worn and returned shoes). When the customer was contacted about his serial returning behavior, he became angry; he was told it was obvious the company could not please him and that it could no longer afford to do business with him.

Chronic returnaholics can be very crafty. Some purchase expensive items with credit cards to earn rewards or airline points and then return the merchandise during certain periods of the billing cycle when the points will not be removed from their account. Some purchase large quantities of items, try to sell them on the Internet or in private shops, and then return them for a refund if they don't sell. Some interior designers will purchase items for a specific event, such as an open house or a staged model home, and then return the items for a refund. These are but a few examples of how chronic returnaholics operate.

4. What Managers Can Do

Unfair customers need to be dealt with effectively. They can be a big problem for poorly managed companies with customer unfriendly policies and practices that provoke retaliatory customer behavior. Unfair customers also can bedevil well-managed companies that devote considerable energy and investment to serving customers superbly. After all, these companies build their culture on delivering an excellent experience and value to customers. As a long-time operations executive of one of America's most admired supermarket chains told us:

"I think companies that are truly committed to customer service have a difficult time dealing with unfair customers. We always [tell] our store managers that we will give the unfair customer the benefit of the doubt one or two times. The third time, we [will] fire them as a customer."

So, what should managers do about unfair customers?

4.1. Manage Customers to a Standard of Behavior

Companies cannot build a reputation for service excellence unless, in addition to serving customers competently, they treat them with respect and commitment. Treating customers with respect and commitment requires an organizational culture in which employees, themselves, are treated with respect and commitment. Managers that allow customers to behave badly (e.g., to verbally abuse employees, to create a disturbance, to rip off the company) in the name of "customer service" undermine the organizational culture upon which excellent service depends. Appeasing a customer who doesn't deserve appeasement does not go unnoticed within the organization. The bicycle shop owner who ordered an abusive customer out of the store strengthened his culture that day, rather than weakened it.

Just as managers need to manage employees, they should also "manage" customers when the situation warrants. A good manager certainly would intervene if made aware of an employee who treated customers rudely or broke important company policies. Likewise, a manager should be ready to intervene when made aware of customer misbehavior. Effective "customer management," as illustrated by the manager's intervention in the bar ruckus, demonstrated to employees and nearby customers that the disruptive party's behavior was unacceptable and would not be allowed to continue. If the customers did quiet down, the bartender could more easily interact with them because the manager, and not he, addressed their misbehavior.

4.2. Don't Penalize Fair Customers

Companies should design their business operations for the vast majority of their customers who are fair and responsible, rather than for the unfair minority. Firms should not allow unfair customer behavior to instigate needlessly restrictive policies that disrespect the good intentions of most customers. The better approach, for the business culture and reputation, is to deal fairly but firmly with unfair customers specifically.

The retailer experiencing heavy returns of outdoor power equipment following a major storm illustrates this guideline. The retailer could have done nothing, in effect enabling unreasonable customer behavior. Alternatively, the company could have installed a more restrictive return policy for all merchandise, which would have affected all customers, not just returnaholics, and likely hurt the company's reputation for customer service. The company's implementation of a more restrictive return policy for specific products with high afterstorm return rates made returns more difficult for situational returnaholics. The new policy was designed specifically to deal with opportunistic customers.

The goodwill created by *not* treating all customers as untrustworthy is an investment worth making. A supermarket operations executive illustrates this lesson with the following story:

"When I was at [Company X], we had a policy that if customers forgot their checkbook, we would let them leave with their groceries after filling out a simple IOU. The great majority of customers would immediately return to pay the amount. This policy created a great deal of positive goodwill. However, every year we had to write off a significant amount of loss because some customers would not come back to pay off the IOU. I remember one year it was in excess of $30,000. We would make attempts to recover the money, but I don't recall trying to prosecute anyone for it. Our CFO wanted to stop giving the IOUs, but I would not let him. I treated it as a marketing expense because it created so much goodwill. Interestingly, when we started accepting credit, I thought that the loss number would plunge, assuming customers would carry their credit card and use that instead of a check. However, the loss number remained the same. I believe there will always be customers who will take advantage of you. They are very intentional about their unfairness. The loss incurred by them has to be built into your financial model because you should not penalize the great customers for the deeds of a few bad customers."

4.3. Prepare for Customer Unfairness

Companies should strive to both reduce the frequency of unfair customer episodes and effectively manage specific incidents. This requires advance planning. Managers need to determine the kinds of situations that are most likely to produce unfair customer behavior, given the nature of the company's business. Managers can determine at-risk situations for unfairness by: (1) using past experiences to identify conditions in which customer and company goals might conflict; (2) soliciting employee input on causes of customer unfairness; and (3) surveying customers previously involved in unfairness incidents to gain their perspective on what happened and why. Once at-risk exchanges are identified, managers can evaluate the firm's existing practices to consider needed changes. Employee and customer input can again be helpful at this stage (Seiders & Berry, 1998).

Preparing for customer unfairness also involves investing in education and training of front-line employees and managers on how to prevent and manage the most likely types of incidents. Particular emphasis should be placed on the rationale for company policies that respond to customer misbehavior, or that may encourage it. Employees who intervene need to be able to explain the company's position effectively, which makes communications training for dealing with problem customers a priority. Contact personnel (and their managers) would benefit from focused training on the best ways to interact with verbal abusers, rule breakers, returnaholics, and other problem customers. Organizational justice researchers recommend the use of explanation as an impression management strategy (Sitkin & Bies, 1993). Explanations have been found to diffuse negative reactions and convey respect, among other positive outcomes (Seiders & Berry, 1998), although they will not always be effective with unfair customers.

Collecting pertinent information is another way to prepare for customer unfairness. Information can clarify the appropriate company response to a customer incident. The catalog retailer which captures information on every shipping transaction is better prepared to assess post-transaction claims. Has the customer complained about this issue before? If so, did the company explain its policy? What is the customer's purchase history? "Research is a great way to keep things on the up and up," explains a company executive. "It's on a case-by-case basis."

4.4. Don't Reward Misbehavior

As mentioned, companies that take pride in the quality of their service often struggle to satisfactorily resolve acts of customer opportunism. Such companies are so culturally focused on serving customers well and giving them the benefit of the doubt when problems arise that they may offer more than they should to reach resolution. Doing more than should be done for an unfair customer rewards misbehavior and encourages future incidents.

Companies need to respond to customer unfairness with fairness—and firmness. They should respond to unreasonableness with reason. It isn't easy. The case of the restaurant bathroom plumbing problem is instructive. The customer had a legitimate complaint about the state of the restroom, but then used the incident opportunistically to extract as much as possible from the restaurant. The company's first response of a full refund for the party's meal, a small gift certificate, and an apology was fair. The additional gift certificates went beyond fair. The second helping of gift certificates was excessive, reinforcing customer opportunism. Companies need to be willing to cut the cord with unfair customers.

Sometimes unfair customers recant when dealt with appropriately, as shown by a postscript to the bicycle story. The abusive customer phoned the owner to apologize three hours after being told to leave the store, explaining that he had argued with his wife prior to visiting the store. Once he returned home and verified the accuracy of the store employee's explanation, he realized he had been unreasonable. He asked that the store not blame the daughter for his actions and that he be allowed to shop in the store again. He also commented that he respected the owner for supporting his employee, even if it might mean losing a customer. The owner thanked him for the call, welcomed him back to the store, and indicated that the apology would be conveyed to the employee.

5. Rethinking Old Wisdom

Following the old wisdom—the customer is always right—has operated as the basic rule in business for so long that it has become entrenched as an "absolute truth." The practical reality, however, is that sometimes the customer is wrong by behaving unfairly.

Customer unfairness can exact a heavy cost. Company goodwill, employee relations, financial position, and service to responsible customers can deteriorate when customers engage in unfair tactics such as verbal abuse, blaming, rule breaking, opportunism, and "returnaholism."

Companies must acknowledge the unfair behavior of certain customers and manage them effectively. Some customers may need to be fired. Denying the existence and impact of unfair customers erodes the ethics of fairness upon which great service companies thrive.

References

Fullerton, R. A., & Punj, G. (2004). Repercussions of promoting an ideology of consumption: Consumer misbehavior. *Journal of Business Research, 57*(11), 1239–1249.

Grandey, A. A., Dickter, D. N., & Sin, H. P. (2004). The customer is not always right: Customer aggression and emotion regulation of service employees. *Journal of Organizational Behavior, 25*(3), 397–418.

Grover, S. L. (1991). Predicting the perceived fairness of parental leave policies. *Journal of Applied Psychology, 76*(2), 247–255.

Lind, E. A., & Tyler, T. R. (1988). *The social psychology of procedural justice.* New York: Plenum Press.

Rupp, D. E., & Spencer, S. (2006). When customers lash out: The effects of customers' interactional injustice on emotional labor and the mediating role of discrete emotions. *Journal of Applied Psychology, 91*(4), 971–978.

Rupp, D. E., Holub, A. S., & Grandey, A. A. (2007). A cognitive-emotional theory of customer injustice and emotional labor. In D. De Cremer (Ed.), *Advances in the psychology of justice and affect* (pp. 199–226). Charlotte, NC: Information Age Publishing.

Seiders, K., & Berry, L. L. (1998). Service fairness: What it is and why it matters. *Academy of Management Executive, 12*(2), 8–21.

Sheppard, B. H., Lewicki, R. J., & Minton, J. W. (1992). *Organizational justice: The search for fairness in the workplace.* New York: Lexington Books.

Sitkin, S. B., & Bies, R. J. (1993). Social accounts in conflict situations: Using explanations to manage conflict. *Human Relations, 46(3),* 349–370.

Tyler, T. R., & Bies, R. J. (1990). Beyond formal procedures: The interpersonal context of procedural justice. In J. Carroll (Ed.), *Advances in applied social psychology: Business settings* (pp. 77–98). Hillsdale, NJ: Lawrence Erlbaum Associates.

Dirty Deeds

The mortgage crisis has blighted the landscape with boarded-up houses. Now a few cities are holding giant lenders accountable for what foreclosure leaves behind.

MICHAEL OREY

On Dec. 17 in a windowless Buffalo courtroom, Cindy T. Cooper, a prosecutor for the city, buzzes among a dozen men in suits, cutting deals. "You've got to unboard [the house], go in, and clean it out," she tells one. "If all the repairs are done quickly, I wouldn't ask for any fines." To another, she says, "the gutters weren't done right," and asks to see receipts for the work. It's "Bank Day" in Judge Henry J. Nowak's housing courtroom, more typically a venue where landlords and tenants duke it out over evictions and back rent. Instead, Cooper is asking lawyers for CitiFinancial, JPMorgan Chase, and Countrywide Financial to fix problems like peeling paint, broken masonry, and overgrown or trash-filled yards at houses the city says the banks are responsible for maintaining. It may be surprising to find these financial-services giants hauled before this obscure local tribunal. In fact, Cooper and Nowak are at the forefront of a pioneering effort to deal with a vexing problem: the surging number of vacant and abandoned homes resulting from the mortgage market meltdown. The vacancies occur when lenders bring foreclosure suits against delinquent borrowers. Mere notice that such an action might be filed often sends residents packing. In Buffalo and other Rust Belt cities, the problem has been particularly acute, because in many cases banks are abandoning the houses, too, after determining that their value is so low that it's not worth laying claim to them. When city officials try to hold someone responsible for dilapidated properties, they often find the homeowner and bank pointing fingers at each other. Indeed, the houses fall into a kind of legal limbo that Cleveland housing attorney Kermit J. Lind calls "toxic title" (box, page 168). While formal ownership remains with a borrower who has fled, the bank retains its lien on the property. That opens up a dispute over who is responsible for taxes and maintenance. Even when lenders do complete the foreclosure, they may walk away from the property, leaving it to be taken by a city for unpaid taxes, a process that can take years. Orphaned properties quickly fall into disrepair, the deterioration sometimes hastened by vandals who trash the interiors, lighting fires and ripping out wiring and pipes to sell for scrap. Squatters or drug dealers may move in.

The impact goes far beyond the defaulting homeowner, as neighbors and entire communities confront a spreading blight. Vacant residences deprive cities of tax revenue and can cost them thousands to maintain. A 2001 Temple University study in Philadelphia found that simply being within 150 feet of an abandoned property knocked $7,600 off a home's value.

> **"The days are gone when you can do a foreclosure and walk away without taking care of the property."**
>
> —Cooper

In Buffalo, prosecutor Cooper is bringing lenders before Judge Nowak to hold them accountable. Wielding the threat of liens, which can hold up the lenders' other real estate transactions, she aims to make banks keep foreclosed homes in good condition until a buyer can be found. As an alternative, Cooper or Nowak may try to get lenders to donate properties to community groups or to pay for demolition when houses are beyond repair. "At least in Buffalo," says Cooper, "the days are gone when you can do a foreclosure and walk away without taking care of the property."

Those charged with violations by Cooper include participants all along the complex mortgage-industry food chain, from loan originators to servicers to the Wall Street trusts that buy up the vast majority of home loans and then securitize them. A similar initiative is under way in Cleveland, where Judge Raymond L. Pianka puts lenders on trial in absentia when they fail to respond to charges.

Even places with high property values, like Chula Vista, Calif., a San Diego suburb, are taking steps to avoid the neglect that can occur during lengthy foreclosures. "It seems like a number of the lenders aren't even doing things that are in their own best interest to preserve the asset," says Pianka—a problem he attributes to the fragmented nature of the business. "It's not an address.

It's not a property. It's just a loan number," he says. "So they'll push a button in San Francisco, and it will set things in motion to do things with [a] property that don't even make sense."

Spreading the Pain

The proceedings in Pianka's and Nowak's courtrooms offer a sobering reminder that underlying the attenuated ownership and esoteric products spun out of mortgages are actual buildings, some with leaky roofs or broken porch railings. The industry denies responsibility for properties to which it has not taken title. "The notion that a mortgage company has an obligation to make repairs on a property that it doesn't even own is very hard to comprehend," says Marco Cercone, a Buffalo attorney who represents a range of lenders before Nowak in the courtroom. Cooper says that banks and other financial firms once extolled houses as the best possible collateral for a loan. Now they're stuck with that collateral, and they don't like it.

If there ever is a national response to the messy legacy left by foreclosures, it might include something like the Buffalo system, which seeks to take action before the presence of abandoned houses hurts entire neighborhoods and which spreads the pain among many players. "We're kind of a crystal ball into what might happen" elsewhere, Cooper says.

Lenders may rue the day the State University of New York at Buffalo admitted Cooper to pursue a PhD in sociology and a law degree. The subject of her doctoral thesis, submitted in December, 2006: the role of banks in residential abandonment and why they should be accountable for property-code violations. The fourth-generation Californian says she quickly became attached to Buffalo for its history and architecture. Now 33, Cooper and her husband are rehabilitating a house that she bought after getting an IRS tax lien removed from the property. "My passion for this work is because I love this town," she says.

While researching her thesis, Cooper interned for Judge Nowak. Tall, soft-spoken, and unfailingly courteous, the judge, 39, began holding Bank Day earlier this year and schedules it once a month. The civility of the proceedings and the large number of bank lawyers in attendance belie a noteworthy fact: They are there under coercion. A few years ago, Nowak says, "the city became increasingly frustrated with the banks' role" in contributing to Buffalo's abandoned-property problem. (Estimates put the number of abandoned homes in the city at between 5,000 and 10,000.) In 2004, New York State amended the definition of "owner" in its property maintenance code to include not just titleholders but others who had "control" over a premises.

While the statute makes no reference to lenders, Nowak contends that the letters banks send to defaulting homeowners threatening to boot them from their houses show that they have begun to "assert some measure of control." On this premise, Nowak says, Buffalo began contacting banks "en masse" about foreclosed properties, but "a lot of times we'd just be rebuffed and ignored."

Cooper, as an intern, suggested a tactic that the judge adopted. When banks ignored summonses for code violations, Nowak began entering default judgments against them and imposing

---

The Story of an Orphaned Home

How properties descend into legal limbo—and how communities are trying to deal with the problem.

1. Abandonment

The borrower leaves the house. Sometimes this happens as soon as the lender sends a letter announcing that a mortgage has gone into default; sometimes it happens after the lender begins to foreclose.

2. Neglect

The foreclosure process, which gives the bank the legal right to seize the house as collateral, can take 12 months or more. If the property is left unprotected, it can become a magnet for vandalism and decay.

3. Ownership Limbo

The lender decides that the value of the loan, plus legal costs of foreclosure, back taxes, and repairs, exceeds the potential sale price. So the lender stops foreclosure efforts. The title remains in the name of the borrower.

4. Public Nuisance

Housing inspectors finally crack down. Consulting property records, they cite the borrower for violations, which can lead to fines and even jail. But the borrower appears in court and says he thought the bank took the house.

5. Resolution

Officials are expanding the definition of who owns a house. In Buffalo, prosecutors are hauling banks that abandon foreclosure proceedings into court and seeking stiff fines. If the house is unsalable, lenders may have to pay for demolition.

---

the maximum fine, which can reach $10,000 to $15,000. For a big bank, that's not much. The real pain comes because the fines give the city a lien that impedes the banks' ability to buy or sell other properties in the area. In addition, when lenders come to his court to get residents evicted from a particular property, Nowak refuses to grant the request until the bank addresses violations outstanding on other properties. Judge Pianka employs similar tactics in Cleveland. On Dec. 10, for example, he assessed a $50,000 fine against an absentee defendant, Mortgage Lenders Network USA, for 21 code violations at a home.

Even far from the Rust Belt, in places where empty houses retain significant value, the lending industry seems to have trouble preserving its collateral when homes are abandoned during foreclosure. In Chula Vista, a number of houses have been trashed by college students who have held parties in the vacant properties. In other cases, pillagers pull up in rental trucks to cart away cabinets, wood flooring, and fixtures stripped from the homes. But in October, an ordinance went into effect requiring lenders to register and maintain houses that have been abandoned during foreclosure.

Compliance, says Chula Vista code enforcement manager Doug Leeper, has been spotty. "What I need them to do is keep the water on and keep the lawn green," he says, noting that the first sign of abandonment is often a yard that has turned brown and a pool that has gone murky green.

That slide into decrepitude is exactly what Cooper is trying to head off in Buffalo. In February, she joined the city's law department, where one of her duties is prosecuting banks. She and Nowak each say their main objective is not collecting fines but bringing banks to the table to try to find constructive solutions for dealing with abandoned property. That doesn't mean borrowers are off the hook. Cooper typically charges both borrowers and lenders, and Nowak may fine homeowners or sentence them to community service. "Can both be responsible?" asks Cooper. "Absolutely."

The approach in Buffalo is paying dividends. In a case on Dec. 17, attorney Cercone addressed the status of a house that had gone into foreclosure in 2006. Cercone was representing JPMorgan Chase and Ocwen Loan Servicing (which in turn were representatives of a securitized trust that had purchased the mortgage). Cercone submitted an affidavit showing that Ocwen, which had been cited for violations in December, 2006, had spent $30,000 to repair the property, including scraping lead paint from the entire house. In September, the affidavit notes, JP Morgan Chase sold the property at a loss of $19,500, not including the cost of repairs. "The bank in this case dealt with the property as well as could be done under the circumstances," Nowak said from the bench, and he agreed not to impose any fines.

Tortuous Trails

Still, even with novel and aggressive tactics, the path to resolution for many properties in Buffalo can be tortuous and protracted. A house at 1941 Niagara St.—one of dozens of properties that Cooper examined as a graduate student—has yet to see its final chapter, though it may be close.

In 1998, Elizabeth M. Manuel obtained a $34,500 mortgage on the property from IMC Mortgage (since acquired by Citibank). By 2002, the loan had been sold into a securitization trust administered by Chase Manhattan (now JPMorgan Chase) as trustee. It also went into default, and Chase began foreclosure proceedings. In a court filing, Manuel (who could not be located for comment) said she left the home while the foreclosure action was pending. More than five years later, though, the title remains in her name. The house, although still standing, has become a fire-gutted wreck.

In May 2007, Nowak issued a default judgment against Chase for $9,000. But these cases can be notoriously difficult to untangle. Thomas A. Kelly, a spokesman for the bank, notes that Chase sold its trustee business to the Bank of New York Mellon in October, 2006, and couldn't locate anyone at Chase able to comment. But he reiterates the industry view that Chase can't be held responsible for maintaining a property it never owned. He acknowledges that if a home didn't seem worth taking as collateral, the bank may have made a decision to "just walk away."

The value of 1941 Niagara, estimate city assessors, is $4,500, of which $4,300 represents the value of the land. The home, Cooper says, is slated for "imminent" demolition.

Searching for the Top

HR professionals need to know how to tell if an executive search firm is walking the straight and narrow or crossing the line.

STEPHENIE OVERMAN

Executive search consultants, often called headhunters, wrestle with various ethical issues, but the question of whether it's OK to raid a company for candidates isn't one of them.

Executive search "by definition moves people from one firm to another. We should not feel ashamed about it," says Christopher J. Clarke, president and chief executive officer of Boyden World Corp., a global executive search firm headquartered in Hawthorne, N.Y. "We are helping market forces to operate efficiently. By providing the best leaders for clients, we are helping these firms to create growth, wealth and employment."

Industry spokesman Peter M. Felix makes a similar economic case. "You want a mobile labor market," he says, because mobility "is part of the reason you have a dynamic economy."

Felix is president of the New York-based Association of Executive Search Consultants (AESC), representing retained executive search consulting firms. It would be "ludicrous," he says, to think that "an individual can't consider an offer from an alternative employer." Besides, he continues, "you don't 'raid' a company for senior executives. You carefully and sensibly recruit them. . . . You approach a candidate in a sensitive way to find out if [the position] is appropriate for them."

The aboveboard purposes notwithstanding, executive search practitioners regularly encounter ethical issues as they gain access to clients' internal staffing matters and potential candidates' personal and professional information. In fact, for an executive search firm, an ethical concern can center on what it does with what it knows about companies or executives.

So when HR decides to enlist an executive search firm's help in filling a top slot, it becomes important to determine how a given firm does business in sensitive circumstances and how it handles inside information. In effect, HR professionals need to know whether an executive search firm's practices and assurances are ethical and not dubious.

The Ground Rules

Keep in mind that the profession is not regulated, says David Lord, founder of Executive Search Information Services, a consulting firm in Harrisville, N.H. The firm helps boards of directors, line executives and executive staffing directors evaluate, select and contract with well-qualified search consultants. It also measures search firms' performances.

"There's nothing [a firm] can get certified in," Lord says. "It is very much 'buyer beware' for companies."

Nonetheless, the AESC has developed a code of ethics for the profession, and there are executive search principles to which a firm should adhere if it is committed to behaving ethically and acting first and foremost in its clients' interests. Two major principles: confidentiality and loyalty.

The AESC's ethics code says executive search consultants should display professionalism, integrity and competence; they also should be objective and accurate, maintain confidentiality and "serve their clients loyally."

Confidentiality, in particular, "is the hallmark of our profession," says Peri Z. Hansen, a client partner in the Los Angeles office of Korn/Ferry International, a major executive search company.

The AESC's professional guidelines call on members to "use confidential information received from clients only for purposes of conducting the assignment. Disclose such confidential information only to those individuals within the firm or to those appropriately qualified or interested candidates who have a need to know the information. [Do] not use such confidential information for personal gain, nor provide inside information to any other parties for their personal gain."

To most executive search consultants, loyalty to the client means there should be no "parallel processing"—no offering of a candidate to more than one client at a time. "We see that as putting two clients in conflict over the same person," Clarke says. The practice amounts to "representing the candidate rather than the client," he says.

What's Off-Limits

Loyalty can also mean keeping the newly placed candidate and the client off-limits for future recruiting. Lord explains the rationale: "If I'm a search firm doing work for your company, I had better not be taking people out of your company."

Recruiters on Recruiting

Richard E. Barnes

The president and co-owner of Barnes Development Group in Mequon, Wis., a boutique firm specializing in manufacturing, has seen much change during two decades. "I used to jump on a plane and interview all over the country. Today, we get far more regional searches because companies don't want to relocate candidates." Candidates in manufacturing are less receptive to being contacted and considered for jobs, he says, because they receive commissions and bonuses and they're worried about "last in, first out." In other words, "people are fearful of changing from a good job where they have security to the unknown."

Peri Z. Hansen

The client partner in the Los Angeles office of Korn/Ferry International, and a member of its Legal Specialist Group, previously practiced law in Southern California. She also was associated with a national legal search firm, where she specialized in the placement of attorneys. Having been a practicing attorney "certainly helps in terms of due diligence, in understanding the work of the client and in vetting candidates" she says. "It's a matter of trust and credibility."

Linda Bialecki

The founder of Bialecki Inc., a New York boutique firm that recruits senior Wall Street talent for investment banks, hedge funds and private equity firms, says having an MBA helps establish her credibility. "You really have to understand what's going on" in the industry, she says, and her graduate degree makes clear "that my interest is finance. . . . You have to be involved in an industry that you have personal interest in."

Wendy Murphy

A leader in the Chief Human Resources Officer functional practice at Heidrick & Struggles, and managing partner in the firm's Stamford, Conn., office, has extensive HR experience, including 10 years with Organizational Dynamics Inc., a global consulting and training company, where she worked in the Asia Pacific region. Other executive positions include partner in TMP Worldwide Executive Search and managing director of the Human Resources Center of Excellence at Korn/Ferry International. "It's easier to work with HR people [as candidates] because they do understand" the process. "Their ability to answer some of the tough questions . . . tells you how effective they are."

Dr. Gilbert J. Carrara Jr.

The partner in charge of New York-based Battalia Winston International's Life Science practice conducts senior-level searches for pharmaceutical, biotechnology, health-care and health-information companies, managed-care organizations and academic medical centers. Venture capital firms have retained him to find leaders for small and medium-sized biotechnology and biopharmaceutical companies. Previously, he worked at Nicholson International and Korn/Ferry International, founded the Total Pediatric Extended Care Center and was associate medical director for a small pharmaceutical company. Being a physician helps him stay current with the technology of the life sciences, he says. Plus, "people feel more comfortable with like-thinking folks."

Tim Ward

A principal with the McCormick Group's Government Contracting Services practice in Washington, D.C., specializes in placing senior executives with providers of government information technology services. With "an even tighter IT market today," he says, he relies on the latest technology and a strong network "to keep in touch with the best and brightest." His background includes five years in mortgage sales, including two years as owner of a mortgage brokerage firm.

"Any client that we've done work for is off-limits for at least five years' as a recruiting target."

—Richard E. Barnes, president and co-owner, Barnes Development Group

---

For smaller search firms, such as Barnes Development Group in Mequon, Wis., and Bialecki Inc. in New York, establishing what is off-limits can be straightforward. "Any client that we've done work for is off-limits for at least five years" as a recruiting target itself, says Richard E. Barnes, president and co-owner of the Barnes firm. "We're small enough that we don't have a lot of problems," he says, and "we will never recruit the person we put in the company as long as he or she is with the company. That's a lifetime hands-off policy. We have search engagement details that specifically spell that out."

Linda Bialecki, founder of the Bialecki firm, agrees that "it's very simple for a small firm" to keep its clients off-limits because it deals with only a few companies. Yet other types of questions still arise: "What if the client cancels the search? Is it still off-limits? What if they paid you a retainer?" Does the search firm then keep the retainer?

A large executive search company or one that does a great deal of work in one industry finds it harder to impose areas that are off-limits because doing so would severely restrict its business opportunities, Lord says. The trend is to narrow the scope, for example, to exclude the just-placed person and immediate co-workers instead of the entire company. "But some companies really care about this. They do not want to work with a search firm that would be taking people out."

Indeed, many clients "lay a great deal of emphasis that you're not going to take their people away," Clarke says. "It's unethical to place somebody in a firm and, knowing all we do, then go back and take their people away."

Approaching a Possible Candidate

A good executive search consultant is trained to find out exactly why a candidate really wants to leave his or her current employer, says Leslie Sorg Ramsay, a principal with the McCormick Group in the executive search firm's Washington, D.C., office. "We ask, 'Can you get what you need by staying where you are?'"

If a candidate is considering changing jobs primarily for more money, the client may lose out to a counter offer from the current employer, Ramsay says, meaning that the candidate was a risky prospect from the beginning. "Part of ethics" in the executive search profession, she says, "is making sure we are not wasting people's time."

Executives who are happy where they are probably are not good recruitment candidates, says Dale Winston, chair and chief executive officer of Battalia Winston International in New York. "We recruit people who are blocked from moving to the next step, who have a problem with a new boss. There's nothing unethical about helping a frustrated person move. There's no more cradle to grave, no hidden contract on either side," to keep an employee at one company.

Winston finds that when executives make a move, there are three reasons for the decision:

First, the new post is a better opportunity, a promotion.

Second, the executive likes the people making the offer. "They don't move unless they're comfortable," Winston says.

Third is the money—but "it's third," she emphasizes, "and if the first two aren't there, you can throw in all the money in the world and the person won't take the job."

—Stephenie Overman

Large search companies are taking a closer look at who's off-limits because it's increasingly challenging to recruit great talent.

Large search companies are taking a closer look at who's off-limits because it's increasingly challenging to recruit great talent. "We want to provide diverse options," Hansen says. "We want balance, to do what's reasonable for both sides. Gone are the days of clear-cut rules [on who is off-limits]. It's more finely tailored to take into consideration the length and volume of the relationship."

No Fudging, No Shortcuts

Ethical headhunters take care not to misrepresent themselves, their clients or the candidates during the search process. They treat candidates fairly and "avoid being used as a tool to discriminate against qualified candidates" by agreeing to restrict the pool of candidates in some unfair way, Lord says. They are honest about the purpose of initial calls to potential candidates.

Barnes notes that it may be difficult to get into organizations to find names of good candidates, but "lying to get access to them" is not acceptable practice.

When a headhunter discovers that a candidate has lied—about a degree or a job title, for example—or has tried to conceal a material fact, the headhunter's responsibility is to "have the candidate help you understand how that error or omission occurred," says John Rothschild, managing director of the Chicago office of Edward W Kelley & Partners.

Sometimes, cutting corners results in what seems to be misrepresentation of a candidate. "When searches get long in the tooth, some recruiters try to get them filled. They don't care, so long as they get filled," even by a candidate who really isn't quite right, Rothschild says. "They try to force a square peg into a round hole. We can subtly direct a candidate's thinking. When we know the candidate is not best served, it's a mistake. It will end in failure at some point."

Clarke says he has heard of "lazy searchers" who "push the usual suspects. Often, these are their favorite candidates, their golf partners and, in some countries, even family or friends. They do not search the market and find the best candidates. There are, of course, cases where the client has underestimated the market rate for the position. An honest search firm will make them aware of this, rather than shoo in a weak candidate to close the case."

Many searchers try to maximize the number of searches under way, Clarke continues. "The client sees the impressive business developer, but [then] the action is handed off to a second-rate team. The biggest client complaint is of nondelivery, or the assignment taking too long because such searchers work on too many cases and give them a low priority."

Clarke adds that unethical headhunters may go so far as to attempt to advance the highest-priced candidates or push a client to increase the salary for a position to increase their own shares because headhunters' fees are a percentage of a placed candidate's annual salary.

Reasonable Expectations

HR professionals have the right to expect a search consultant to take the time and effort necessary to conduct a good search for top-level candidates, and that includes gathering a lot of information about the client.

"Studies show the more prospective candidates learn about the clients, the greater their success," says Dale Winston, chair and CEO of Battalia Winston International in New York. Before taking an assignment, her representatives meet with "the client [and] the hiring manager so we can flesh things out," she continues. "That way, when we meet with the candidate, we can give a lot of data" to help candidates and clients determine if they share the same values.

"A bad hire is worse than no hire," Winston adds, but that rarely occurs when there is plenty of upfront due diligence.

Overall, HR professionals and their companies "have a right to expect a rigorous and effective process of research, candidate appraisal and support during negotiations, by a trained and experienced search team including professional researchers and searchers," Clarke says. "This team should put the client's interests before their own and offer unbiased advice as to remuneration, candidate fit and any other important matters."

Setting Standards

Although there is no organization certifying executive search firms on the basis of performance standards (the AESC does offer certification for researchers and associates), some companies in the field have established their own standards. The Boyden firm, for example, has an internal certification program, and CEO Clarke says all firms "should go toward more certification and training. Anybody can start a search firm. You can say you're an executive search consultant" without any type of standards or quality assurance. "We need to be more professional, to have no tolerance for slack performance."

If a client suspects that a headhunter has acted unethically, Lord notes, there may be little recourse. Few search firms have ethics officers. The AESC does have an ethics and professional practices committee to investigate complaints, he adds, but "it's limited. [The AESC] does care about professionalism. [It has] worked hard to publish the code of ethics. Other than that, there is no real way to bring people to justice, if you will."

While there may be few formal mechanisms for righting perceived wrongs in the executive search industry, there's still the power of the marketplace. "What drives search firms to follow rules is the fact that their reputations are extremely important," Lord says. If a search firm does something such as violate an off-limits agreement, he says, "it's a serious problem. People get fired. It can end relationships."

STEPHENIE OVERMAN is editor of *Staffing Management Magazine*.

A Word for Older Job-Seekers: Retail

Most people still working at 65-plus are employed in stores, a new study finds.

Maria L. LaGanga

Five days a week, Max Gumbert drives up to the 95,000-square-foot Home Depot store in this leafy suburb at the northern edge of Silicon Valley, straps on an orange apron sagging with customer service badges and gets to work.

For eight hours every day, in a shift that often ends at 10:30 P.M., the flooring specialist answers questions: Hardwood or laminate? Ceramic tile or sandstone? Nylon or wool? Pergo or bamboo? Does cork absorb sound better than carpet?

But it is Gumbert's presence here on the sales floor, with his cardigan and courtly manner, that answers a crucial question perplexing demographers and policy experts: If you are 65 years old or more and you're still working in America today, what are you most likely to be doing?

Gumbert is 67, terrified of retirement and happy to go to work every day in the industry that employs more older Americans than any other: retail. Nearly 350,000 men and women 65 or older earn paychecks in the nation's stores, according to a report scheduled for release in June.

In recent years, the question of exactly where older workers were employed has baffled those who have seen conflicting trends ripple through the nation's job sites: More older Americans say they want or need to work past traditional retirement age, but employers are still reluctant to retain or hire them.

One result is that there has been little solid information about where people beyond the average retirement age of 63 work in greatest numbers, a critical issue especially now as benefits shrink and recession looms.

But statistics from the Urban Institute, a nonpartisan research group based in Washington, show for the first time that those 65 or older and still working in America are statistically most likely to do retail, farming or janitorial work, in that order.

In fact, the nation's stores employ more people 65 and over than the next two occupations combined, which worries some advocates who are trying to encourage the federal government, the country's biggest corporations and other employers to keep older workers on the payroll.

"These are not exactly the pictures of reinvention that you get in your monthly issue of Fortune, Money or AARP magazine," said Marc Freedman, author of "Encore: Finding Work that Matters in the Second Half of Life." This is "an object lesson in

the dangers of what could happen if we don't develop a compelling human resource strategy for an aging society."

But though Freedman worries that "the golden years are being transformed into the Wal-Mart decade," he does acknowledge that the retail industry provides benefits, flexibility and jobs, particularly for less-educated workers.

And there are few places better than this big-box store halfway between San Francisco and San Jose to see the effect of older employees in the workplace and few guides better than Gumbert and his colleagues.

Home Depot will not divulge complete statistics on how many older workers stride the concrete floors of its huge home-improvement stores, but the number is on the rise. The company hooked up with AARP four years ago to woo a sales force that might otherwise be golfing and says it now has 5,000 employees over 70.

They are loyal and dependable, said Tim Crow, chief human resources officer for the Atlanta-based firm. "We look at the demographics, and everyone is getting older. This is the future workforce."

In San Carlos, nearly a score of the 200-plus employees are 60 and over, from Irene Goble, 61, whose quarter-century as a bartender left retirement an unaffordable luxury—"I'm gonna be here till I'm 70 in my walker"—to Coy Deal, 72, a former Silicon Valley electrical engineer who was laid off in his late 60s.

Their reasons for regularly punching the time clock in the locker-lined employee break room include "have to," "want to" and everything in between.

Gumbert would place himself in the middle of that spectrum, a German-accented mix of need and desire. Gumbert spent most of his work life in the hotel industry, rising from waiter to director of food, beverages and catering at venues such as the San Francisco Hilton.

But by the time he hit his early 50s, the wear and tear were beginning to show. The days stretched to 18 hours. The phone would ring in the middle of the night. Contemporaries began having heart attacks and worse.

Gumbert switched to restaurant work, then left the hospitality field "cold turkey" in search of a job at which he could "punch in and punch out. I don't want to be called at 2 in the morning."

Not Retired Yet

Americans are living and working longer than ever. Here's what people 65 and older are most likely to be doing if they're still employed.

Jobs with the most workers 65 and older.

Rank	Occupation	Total 65+ Employment	Share of Workers 65+
1	Retail salespersons, supervisors	346,066	6.7%
2	Farmers and ranchers	177,383	3.4
3	Janitors and building cleaners	146,364	2.8
4	Truck drivers and driver salesmen	139,902	2.7
5	Secretaries, administrative assistants	139,829	2.7
6	Cashiers	110,508	2.1
7	Bookkeeping, accounting, auditing clerks	108,798	2.1
8	Real estate brokers, agents	92,465	1.8
9	Chief executives	89,720	1.7
10	Receptionists, clerks	81,050	1.6

Jobs with highest percentage of workers 65 and older.

Rank	Occupation	Share of Workers 65+
1	Crossing guards	27.7%
2	Models, demonstrators, product promoters	23.1
3	Farmers, ranchers, agricultural operators	22.8
4	Funeral service workers, directors	19.6
5	Tax preparers	14.3
6	Barbers	13.0
7	Tool grinders, filers, sharpeners	11.6
8	Property, real estate, community association managers	11.4
9	Animal trainers	11.4
10	Clergy, religious workers	11.3

Source: Urban Institute Graphics reporting by Maria L. LaGanga.

A newspaper ad led him to the company formerly known as Color Tile. When it went belly up, he landed at Home Depot. Nearly 11 years later he is still here in the San Carlos store, cutting carpet swatches, calling customers to cement deals, guiding do-it-your-selfers through the complexities of home renovation.

"I draw Social Security checks, but it goes right into the bank," he says, as does a small pension from his decade at Hilton Hotels Corp. "I'm not dependent on it right now, but who knows what the future brings? It's my nest egg. When I was younger, I wasn't the saving type."

Gumbert's current soapbox is the future of Social Security and the legislators he blames for poking holes in that safety net. He thinks everyone should see Michael Moore's "Sicko," an eye-opener about the state of the American healthcare system. He is an ardent fan of Illinois Sen. Barack Obama.

"I'm scared to retire," he says after weighing bamboo's eco-friendly attributes against the ease with which it can be scratched for a well-tanned man in a Hawaiian shirt. "I like to travel; I couldn't afford to.

"Eventually I think I'll have to retire," Gumbert acknowledges. "When I'm 90 I don't think I'll be selling flooring. But why not? You never know. At least I don't feel my age."

Gumbert and Deal—the 72-year-old former electrical engineer—are walking, hawking proof of another sobering statistic.

In a separate study scheduled for release later this year, the Urban Institute found that 43% of people working full time in their early 50s will change jobs before their late 60s. More than a quarter of those fifty-something full-time workers will enter a new occupation. Nearly one in four will be laid off.

"Older people really need to prepare for a work life of change," said Richard Johnson, a principal researcher on both studies. "There's a real strong possibility that you'll lose your job, and you're going to have to go out and find another one."

That's exactly what happened to Deal, a slender man with bright blue eyes who worries that he will last longer than his savings. The former engineer worked for various software companies in the Silicon Valley. One went bankrupt and was bought out by another, then that one got into serious trouble.

"I was actually let go with the reduction in force," Deal said. "I was in my 60s. I went out on unemployment. I put out 100 or more resumes. Most people want to hire some young kid out of school so they can pay them next to nothing. I gave up after I ran out of unemployment."

He went to work with his son, an electrician, and hired on at Home Depot nearly a year ago. Deal works 16 to 32 hours a week. He wishes the pay were better—he earns a little over the minimum wage—but he'll keep at it "until I really can't push myself."

And then there's James Lunsford, who turns 65 on Memorial Day, a Dennis Farina doppelganger with a pilot's license and a taste for fancy cars. Tall and athletic, he still looks like the fire-fighter he used to be, a couple of careers ago.

These days, the licensed contractor works about 50 hours a week and splits his time 50-50 between Home Depot and Echo Electric, the San Mateo electrical and construction company he owns with his wife, Sherri.

Lunsford is part of Home Depot's recently launched "master trade specialist," program, an effort to recruit skilled craftsmen with expertise in areas such as electrical work and plumbing. The pay is higher, and the specialists tend to be older than the basic sales force.

One recent Friday morning, Lunsford clambered up the packed shelves looking for the right gauge wire for Bill Hoy, an Atherton pool contractor installing an automatic gate opener.

He led a customer to the cat-door aisle, helped an elderly man read the wattage on a lightbulb that needed to be replaced and brainstormed with a builder whose solar light blinked on and off unbidden.

He and his wife could retire tomorrow, but the idea of not working bores him senseless. Most of his Home Depot check goes into the company 401(k) plan; the rest "pays for some of my toys." He is not here, he says, for the money.

"People here thank me. I don't think I've gotten one thank-you card for the over 6,000 homes I've wired," he said. "And when I come through that door, it's show time."

Psssssst! Have You Tasted This?

Mothers sound off in word-of-mouth advertising campaigns.

BARBARA CORREA

J ust hours after Emily Grant plunked down a box of Hershey's Take 5 candy bars at a PTA meeting, a teacher who sampled the chocolate treat raced out to buy a king-size bar.

On the surface, the candy bar purchase was a simple act of impulse buying.

But in reality, it was the successful application of a clever marketing tool that uses everyday people to entice friends and family to buy products.

Word-of-mouth advertising has mushroomed in recent years as companies try to reach an increasingly inaccessible consumer base—one hiding in a multimedia fog of iPods, video games and infinite Web sites and cable channels. Advertisers simply can't reach consumers with traditional television, magazine and newspaper ads in such a stratified marketing environment.

So they're turning to women such as Grant—a well-connected mom whose opinion is valued within her peer group.

Social Networking

Bzzagent Membership
www.bzzagent.com/

Procter & Gamble's Program for teens
www.tremor.com/

Procter & Gamble's Program for Moms
www.vocalpoint.com/

Word of Mouth Marketing Association
www.womma.org/

Secret-Agent Moms

Within the word-of-mouth advertising community, people such as Grant are known as "agents."

But these agents don't carry eavesdropping devices and disguises—they push household products in exchange for coupons and the very products they're promoting.

Throughout her agent career, Grant has soaked herself in a Ralph Lauren fragrance called Hot, taken Nutella samples to her sons' play dates and painted her hallway with a light-blue shade of Benjamin Moore paint.

The supplier of the products sent to her, Boston-based marketing company BzzAgent, instructs all its agents to tell people that they are getting freebies to promote them.

Grant says she doesn't see any conflict in marketing products to friends simply by sharing samples with them.

"I'm not a big sales person with my friends," she said. "There's no need to push because it's just regular stuff."

Some Worry about Ethics

Some agencies and companies do not require their agents to announce that they are in fact pushing products, preferring to leave that decision up to the individual agent. While that has some worried about the ethical implications of the practice, advocates say tell-a-friend campaigns are more honest than traditional advertising.

"Word-of-mouth is actually the most honest form of marketing because you can't con someone about the experience of a product," said George Silverman, president of Market Navigation Inc., a company that, among other things, organizes conference calls for physicians to share opinions about pharmaceuticals. "You don't expect a salesperson to be objective, but I've always found that people don't lie to their friends, and they generally won't tell a friend about something unless they genuinely like it."

Silverman says traditional advertising has been losing consumers in recent years because people feel bombarded by information and are tuning out marketing messages. "People are overloaded. I've done focus groups with everyone from Hispanic gardeners to Fortune-500 executives. They're all overloaded. Word-of-mouth is the only thing that cuts through the overload. If you want to buy something, you can spend two months researching it or you can ask a friend. Which is more fun?"

For that reason, he said, more manufacturers are turning to word-of-mouth to sell everything from coffee makers to mobile phones.

Recruiting Teens, Doctors

Most programs target big-spending groups such as moms and teenagers, and efforts vary in how aggressive they get.

Mothers, especially working mothers, are especially prized by word-of-mouth marketers because they have a large sphere of contacts: through school, their kids' activities and co-workers.

"[Women] are the ones who are controlling all the consumer spending in this country," said Kevin Burke, president of Lucid Marketing, a word-of-mouth company in Burbank specifically focused on selling to moms. "Their roles have evolved in the last 20 years. The stereotype of the male controlling certain purchases is eroding."

The certainty of that buying power prompted consumer products giant Procter & Gamble to launch a program about a year ago called Vocalpoint. To date, the program has recruited well more than half a million moms, while another unit, Tremor, has enlisted several hundred thousand teenagers to talk to their friends about new music and video games.

'Straddles a Thin Line'

However, P&G is one of the word-of-mouth marketers that doesn't require its program members to disclose their involvement. The potential for infiltration of product placement in everyday life—such as name-dropping a particular dishwashing liquid to another mom watching football practice—has sparked a storm of controversy.

"It straddles a thin line," said George Silverman, the marketing strategist. "The bad side of it is using people as shills."

P&G does not require Vocalpoint and Tremor members to disclose that they are taking products because it does not

want to tell members what to say, P&G spokeswoman Robin Schroeder said.

"They want it to be very natural," she said.

But the Word of Mouth Marketing Association, a fast-growing group founded in 2004, defines that approach as deceptive. "We were formed to take on that particular issue," CEO Andy Sernovitz said.

"Our code of ethics is, marketers have to disclose. . . . Tremor and Vocalpoint have not signed on to our code of ethics. They are conspicuously missing from the list."

Other marketing experts say companies that explicitly hide their marketing tactics are eventually found out, and the ethics surrounding word-of-mouth marketing are self-correcting.

"P&G is just hoping folks will talk about them," said Kevin Dugan, director of marketing communications at a design firm and author of a blog about public relations strategy. His wife became a Vocalpoint member when she found out about the program from him.

"There's no specific direction to go out and talk to people or to disclose. There are no talking points. The risk they have is, say my wife had Oil of Olay beauty mask. If she doesn't like it, she's going to tell someone about it. She doesn't feel compelled to talk about it because they sent it to her. With the Oil of Olay, she'll bring it up if it comes up, but it's not, 'I know we're talking about your kid's soccer game and I hate to interrupt, but I need to talk about this facial mask.'"

"It needs to be organic to be effective."

Like the recent outing of lonelygirl 15, the homeschooled girl whose fictitious YouTube identity was revealed a few weeks ago by curious fans, some companies have posed as Regular Joes online and been punished by consumers who have unearthed their true identity. Carmaker Mazda turned off some loyalists when it launched a blog hosted by someone posing as a Mazda enthusiast.

All the Talk Can Backfire

Word-of-mouth also has plenty of examples of campaigns that backfired because products were not very good. Irina Slutsky, a video blogger and host of Geek Entertainment TV, received a mobile phone from Sprint six months ago apparently in the hope that she would write about it in her blog.

"The display screen broke two months after I got it, so if I had written about it, it would be all bad stuff," Slutsky said. "I thought, 'That's a silly marketing plan.'"

Folgers hired BzzAgent to create hype about its home brewing machines. The problem was the machines didn't work well, reportedly leaking water and emitting smoke.

Such backfire worries have kept some big companies from engaging in word-of-mouth marketing.

"Companies are very scared of it," Silverman said. "Nuclear power is very efficient and clean if it's handled right, but you'd better know what you're doing, or you're going to blow up the place. Marketers are control freaks, and you can't control a lot of aspects of word-of-mouth marketing."

Barbara Correa—barbara.correa@dailynews.com (818)713-3662

Swagland

Where the writers are gluttons, the editors practice ethical relativism and the flacks just want to get their clients some ink.

DAVID WEDDLE

Swagland. It's not a mythical over-the-rainbow realm, an Eastern European country, a theme park. You might call it a state of mind, a wondrous alternate universe concocted by publicists, funded by corporations eager for media coverage of their wares and frequented by journalists who have cast off concerns about conflicts of interest and embraced a new creed of conspicuous consumption.

In Swagland, the streets are paved with freebies, from promotional T-shirts, CDs and DVDs, to designer clothing, jewelry and perfume, to spa treatments, Broadway show tickets and suites in five-star hotels, to cellphones, laptops and luxury sports cars on loan. Travel writers accept tree trips to exotic foreign lands. Automotive reviewers take junkets to Switzerland or the sun-dappled hills of Italy to drive the latest high-end roadsters. Entertainment hacks hobnob with stars and directors at the Four Seasons in Los Angeles. High-tech audio and video reviewers max out their home-entertainment centers with LCD HDTV screens, surround-sound systems and five-digit turntables, which they keep for months at a time—for research purposes. Surfing journalists travel to remote South Pacific atolls and stay with supermodels on "floating Four Seasons" luxury cruisers where the champagne never stops flowing.

Fashionistas have long been infamous for raking in the loot—the currency of Swagland. Designers lavish magazine editors with the latest styles because they're "celebrities in their own right," explains an editor at a major fashion daily. "They're gifted quite a bit because they are friends with these designers and they have a lot of access. They may get photographed with those items, and that influences what people buy. All the top editors take free clothes."

In recent years, Los Angeles has become the R&D capital of swag culture. The now-ubiquitous promotional gift bag grew out of Hollywood's plethora of award ceremonies and premiere parties. A gift bag may contain a T-shirt or coffee mug, or it might be crammed with thousands of dollars worth of goods. Whatever it may hold, the gift bag has an uncanny power to bring out the greedy 2-year-old in some members of the media. Many have come to view it not as a perk but a birthright. "When

I'm holding an event," says Susie Dobson of the Los Angeles firm Susie Dobson Global PR, "the magazine editors call and ask if there's going to be a gift bag. 'Will there be gift bags?' Yes. 'Will they be good?' Yes. 'Oh, great! I'll be there.'

At some events, journalists are allowed to pack their own gift bags. If the "merch" runs low, things can get ugly. "At the 2003 Environmental Media Awards," says freelance journalist Kyle Roderick, "there was a frenzy at the booth for Under the Canopy, which is this organic fiber fashion line. There was a jostling fight. . . . People were yelling, 'I want my T-shirt!' There were some shoulder blows. The sign was up that said 'Please take one.' People were grabbing three or four or five."

The abundance of swag fuels a thriving underground economy. Writers fence their T-shirts, designer duds and movie and automotive promotional memorabilia to a loose network of used-clothing stores (such as Decades in L.A.), entrepreneurs and Internet vendors. "I have editors calling me all the time and bringing me bags of stuff—designer shoes, jewelry, dresses, everything from Chanel to Gucci," says Keni Valenti, owner of Keni Valenti Retro-Couture, a vintage designer clothing store in New York's Garment Center.

Some journalists steal swag outright from photo shoot sets or magazine fashion closets. "I've had editors call me up and say, 'I have two fur coats here in a bag. I'm at 38th and 7th Avenue, right on the corner. If you can bring me X amount of dollars in cash, they're yours,'" Valenti says. "I said to one editor, 'What exactly are you going to say to the company?' She said, 'I'll just send back the bag empty and blame it on the messenger.'"

Others shake down merchants. Mary Norton, designer of Moo Roo handbags, was flabbergasted when an anchor for a prominent Los Angeles newscast walked into her showroom during the 2003 Oscar season and pointed to three of her creations. He told her that Moo Roo would never be mentioned on his show—ever—if she didn't give them to him.

Anne Rainey Rokahr, director of Red PR in New York, had a similar experience. A magazine writer offered to promote her clients' products on a TV morning show if Rokahr would pay her. "I was shocked and insulted," Rokahr says.

She's not alone. The guardians of journalistic ethics are horrified and dismayed by this subversion of all the values they hold dear. "There are no ifs, ands or buts about it, you put yourself in a compromising position if you accept any gift or free trip or anything from somebody you're writing about," says Edwin Guthman, a Pulitzer Prize-winning journalist and former editor of the Philadelphia Inquirer and national editor of the Los Angeles Times, who is now a senior lecturer at USC's Annenberg School. "It's something that a self-respecting journalist shouldn't do. There isn't any question about it, it's wrong. I'm sorry to hear that it's fairly prevalent."

Ethicists argue that the proliferation of swag has undercut the integrity of the press, blurred the lines between advertising and editorial and encouraged some publications to mislead their readership. "Very few readers have any idea how editorial staffs decide what gets reported on," says Jeffrey Seglin, an associate professor at Emerson College in Boston who writes a weekly column on ethics for the New York Times. "They don't know what the policies are at the magazines about accepting freebies. Readers need to be aware of this issue, especially when they're reading travel pieces and product reviews. There should be a clear distinction between what's advertising and what's editorial. Because when you purchase a magazine, you presume you are buying objective editorial. But that's not always the reality."

The perception that journalists can be bought contributes to an overall distrust of the media. A recent Gallup poll found that only 21% of those surveyed rated newspaper reporters' ethical standards as high or very high. Journalists ranked lower than bankers, auto mechanics, elected officials and nursing home operators. Kelly McBride, the ethics group leader at the Poynter Institute, a training school for professional journalists in St. Petersburg, Fla., laments that the press is "losing ground" in the battle for the public's respect, and believes that swag is a factor. "For people who are concerned about media bias, it is one more straw on the camel's back."

For publicists who practice giveaway marketing, however, such hand-wringing is futile, even a little comical. As far as they're concerned, the battle's already been won. The glittering utopia of Swagland is governed by one supreme precept, and Kelly Cutrone, founder of the firm People's Revolution, sums it up: "Here's the deal: Everything's a commercial."

The Age of Ethical Relativism

The rise of swag culture is no accident, according to McBride. "Corporations are spending a higher percentage of their annual budgets on marketing, and larger portions of those budgets are directed specifically at journalists, because marketing executives realize that ink on any given product is better than advertising," she says. "We've always known that, but they realize now, particularly in this age of an inundation of advertising, that advertising is limited in its ability to reach an audience. It's much more effective to create the elusive buzz about a product that everyone's after."

And the schizophrenic ethics policies of American publications make them an easy target. Many magazines and tabloids either turn a blind eye or encourage their writers to score freebies as a method of cutting expenses. The Robb Report, Motor Trend and Powder routinely send their contributors on junkets. Many others have strict rules against it. Travel + Leisure posts its policy in each issue, stating that its writers do not accept free trips. Most major newspapers and news magazines forbid employees and freelancers to accept merchandise or services from potential subjects, and some high-end glossies—Playboy, Harper's Magazine, Forbes, Fortune—have similar policies.

But even publications that enforce strict ethics policies do not have entirely clean hands. Most, including the Los Angeles Times, commission stories from freelance writers who operate as independent contractors. Freelancers are the migrant farmworkers of journalism—cheap labor that fills the gaps left by editorial downsizing and dwindling advertising revenue. As they scramble from publication to publication to make a living, some practice ethical relativism. If they're writing a story for a newspaper where accepting giveaways is forbidden, they adhere to that policy. But when they're on assignment for a lifestyle magazine that encourages them to accept free hotel rooms and airfare to cut expenses, they shift into high freebie mode. Thus, even the most scrupulous publications end up employing freelancers who may have accepted copious swag on other assignments.

> When fashion writers come to town, they don't stop at taking a free hotel room. 'You ask them to come to an event,' says Kelly Cutrone, founder of the firm People's Revolution, 'and they say, "Can you send me a car?" or, "I don't have anything to wear. I'd really like to wear your designer to the show." You can smell a fashion editor who's looking for a free ride. They'll come to your showroom and they light up, saying, "Ohhhh, loooovvvveee!!! Oh my God, I've got to get one of these. I just love it, love it! Do you think there's any way I can get a deal on one of these?" That's classic.'

"There is an entire set of problems that comes with freelancers that does not come with staff writers, because there's a limited amount of control you can have over them," observes Stephen Randall, deputy editor of Playboy and an adjunct faculty member at USC's Annenberg School. "You don't know what freelancers are doing on other assignments. You don't know what hidden agendas they might have."

Some editors worry about ethics creep. Rick Holter, arts editor for the Dallas Morning News, points out that if an automaker decides to debut a new model in Germany, "there's no way my paper is going to pay for me to go to Germany." But what happens if five freelancers take the junket and come back with terrific stories, which they then submit to the paper? "If you're the car reviewer at Dallas Morning News, you look bad. Here's a freelancer coming in with a great story that you didn't get. Editors get tempted not to ask the tough questions of the freelancers they're buying something from."

Even more problematic are the pseudo-ethics policies of some publications. "One of the worst things that happens is when there is a policy and the publications don't enforce it," says Seglin. "On paper it may say, 'We will not do this.' But the staff and the freelancers see that everybody takes freebies and no one enforces the ethics code. It sends a message that the code is worthless."

Last month the editorial staffs of Jane, Details, Women's Wear Daily and W were banned from receiving gifts "of value" from advertisers. The New York Daily News reported that rebellious employees of Fairchild Publications planned to circumvent the ban by having publicists mail swag to their home addresses. Fairchild spokeswoman Andrea Kaplan averred that this would be against company policy and was quoted as saying, "We are not aware that this is happening."

Truth in Labeling

Many lifestyle scribes shrug off traditional ethics with the rationalization that they aren't really journalists. Julie Logan, a former editor for Glamour who has written for Self and InStyle, refers to fashion and beauty magazines as "service books." "I don't consider service books to be journalism," Logan says. "I consider it copy writing with a narrative. The function of a service book is to deliver readers to the advertisers. If the advertisers could find a way to put the magazine out without writers, they would. We're there because of their largess, not the other way around."

Yet the mastheads of service books list editors and correspondents and look identical to those of hard news publications. "They have all the trappings of regular journalism," McBride says. "They're doing what passes for consumer journalism—writing about products, places and things that people spend money on." And when consumers purchase a magazine, Seglin argues, "they expect objectivity. They don't expect the magazine to show favoritism. As readers, we want consumer journalists to do the legwork and review all of the available products, not just the ones they got for free."

Logan thinks service book readers could care less about the intricacies of objectivity. "These are people who look at advertorial the same way as they would editorial. These are not rocket scientists."

McBride counters that readers would care if they knew that not all magazines adhere to the same ethical standards. "If you're about to spend a lot of money on a vacation in a foreign country and are trying to decide what hotels to stay at, you would certainly want to know if a reviewer is raving about a place because he got a free room, or because he really did his homework on all the hotels in that area."

Seglin believes the solution is truth in labeling. Magazines should disclose their policies on freebies on the table of contents or masthead. "If editors argue that it's not a big deal to accept gifts and it doesn't affect the integrity of their reporters,

then why not tell the reader exactly what your policy is? Then the readers can make an informed decision about how to interpret the magazine's content."

But publications that allow acceptance of gifts have little or no incentive to do any such thing. McBride thinks there will always be a spectrum of publications and writers who take swag, and she sees this as an inevitable byproduct of a free market society. "Part of the beauty of American journalism is it's not licensed. Standards are voluntarily applied. There is no regulation," she says. "So I think the only thing we can do is put as much peer pressure as we can on our brethren and, in the spirit of a free market, give the readers the information they need to make intelligent choices."

The History of Swag

One of the most brilliant tactical breakthroughs in swag culture was developed in Los Angeles. In the late 1990s, publicists realized that the Academy Awards—a fashion vortex that draws the world's finest designers and jewelers and the international press together for one dizzying media-saturated weekend—presented an unprecedented opportunity to raise awareness for their clients' products. Thus the "swag suite" was born. Consortiums of designers rented out entire floors of such chic hotels as the Chateau Marmont, Raffles L' Ermitage and Le Meridien, and filled the suites with samples of their wares. They enticed celebrities and their stylists—and the media—with free champagne, facials, massages, makeup and hair styling, yoga classes and, of course, gift bags. The concept proved fantastically successful.

"Have you ever gone to a 99-Cents store on a welfare payday?" asks Kelly Cutrone. "It's basically like that. [Writers] will try to get four extra gift bags—one for their nanny, one for their sister in Oklahoma and one just in case they need to give it away for a Christmas present."

Cutrone's company, People's Revolution, has organized swag suites during the Oscars and the Golden Globes, and she's seen media greed escalate with each passing year. "It's gotten to the point where the vendors have to nail the stuff down. We've had to create a color-coded gift band system. The different editors and writers won't really know they're a part of it until they arrive. There will be different color codes: a silver bracelet, a gold bracelet and a white bracelet. The gold bracelet would be the highest rank. That means: This person is very, very credible and has a lot of power and you should gift accordingly. The silver one might mean: Give them a T-shirt. The white one is: Don't give them anything. They just need to be in here to feel important and we need their body to fill the space."

The swag suites proved so successful that they soon popped up at the Grammys and New York and LA's fashion weeks. At the Sundance Film Festival the swag suites have exploded into swag lodges, lounges and houses sponsored by Michelob, Skyy Vodka, Mystic Tan, Gap, Chrysler, Diesel, Tommy Hilfiger, Reebok, Ray-Ban and Black & Decker. Last year Volkswagen offered morning yoga classes, treated celebs and select members of the press to, free rides around town in its luxury Phaeton sedan and handed out $1,000 gift bags. The once sleepy main street of Park City, Utah, which used to host a quiet counterculture film festival, has become a gaudy carnival midway where New York fashionistas such as publicist Lara Shrift man hawk their clients' wares and writers for Women's Wear Daily, Us Weekly and the New York Post's Page Six hammer out exultant prose about the swagathon.

Juicy Couture is a textbook example of how swag suite marketing can propel a fledgling company into the limelight almost overnight. Founded in L.A. in 1994 by Gela Nash-Taylor—wife of John Taylor, bass player for Duran Duran—and Pam Skaist-Levy, it started as a T-shirt line and soon became known for low-cut, hip-hugging sweatpants with the words "Juicy" emblazoned across the butt. The product was hip, if no hipper than dozens of other start-up clothing lines that debuted and quickly vanished at around the same time. But Juicy had the marketing savvy of Nash-Taylor and Skaist-Levy.

"They really know how to work it in terms of getting free product into the hands of people," says Rose Apodaca, West Coast bureau chief for Women's Wear Daily. "Early on [in 2001], Juicy did a suite at the Chateau Marmont. It lasted all day. It was crazy chaos. Celebrities, media editors and all kinds of It Girls were there. Most people were given one free outfit. Others got more than that, I'm sure. Their track suits retail for about $175. The cashmere ones go for $500. Advertising Age wrote about the event as a case study. It put their name out there in a big way. They also sent a lot of swag to editors and celebrities and got the Juicy name out there on the people who mattered."

It cost Juicy anywhere from $20,000 to $100,000 to stage swag fests from L.A. to New York, but they proved to be extremely cost-effective. "In the fashion world it is much more impactful to see editorial than to see an advertisement," Nash-Taylor explains. "If you see an advertisement in Vogue, our customer will riffle past that. If the editor says 'Editor's Pick,' you're going to pay attention to that." Juicy's giveaway events generated articles in People, Women's Wear Daily, Us Weekly, the New York Post's Page Six, New York Daily News, Angeleno, OK!, Brntwd, New York magazine, Allure, Elle, Glamour, Harper's Bazaar, InStyle, Marie Claire, Vogue, W, the Los Angeles Times, Los Angeles magazine and the Boston Globe. In 2002 the advertising value equivalency of these articles was estimated to be $41,966,494.

In 2003 Nash-Taylor and Skaist-Levy sold the company to Liz Claiborne for an initial cash payment of $39 million, which may climb to $98 million after a required earn-out payment. And late last year they launched their first Juicy boutique, at the Caesars Palace Forum Shops in Las Vegas—chartering three planes to fly celebs and press to the opening night party.

"I don't know if they gave outfits to people," says Los Angeles Times fashion critic Booth Moore, who covered the opening. "Obviously, I didn't take the plane." (Los Angeles Times staffers and freelancers are not allowed to accept gifts of any kind, including travel, so she drove.) "But a lot of people at the opening were dressed in Juicy, and I don't imagine that they paid for it."

The Prehistory of Swag

Before the swag suite and the gift bag, there was the travel junket. Like D.W. Griffith's perfection of the close-up, the junket was a revolutionary breakthrough in its field. Developed by resorts and travel bureaus after World War II, it has become a surefire way of generating reams of ink.

The junket gives travel bureaus, resorts and hotels the biggest bang for their buck, far more than they could get by taking out ads in major magazines or newspapers. Full-page ads in national magazines run into the hundreds of thousands of dollars. In contrast, it might cost a grand to fly a writer to a hotel or resort for a week-end junket, and the results are far more effective. Kim Marshall, a fanner freelance writer who now runs a PR firm, the Marshall Plan, that organizes "press trips" for luxury resorts such as the Bora Bora Nui and Triple Creek Ranch in Montana, explains that "objective" copy in the form of an article is "seven times more believable. Because an ad is what you say about yourself. A third-party endorsement is far more credible in the mind of the reader."

Publicists refuse to admit that junkets compromise the integrity of participating journalists. "I'm a professional and I work with professionals, and they can't be bought," Marshall says. She claims the correspondents on her junkets adhere to back-breaking schedules to take in all of the sights and activities of the locales she promotes. Nevertheless, she expects at least half of them to get stories into print—"a minimum 50% return rate." Those who don't won't be invited on her next trip.

The spectacular success of travel junkets has led to the "Junketization" of a wide spectrum of industries. Movie studios were the first to realize the potential, and they began flying journalists to exotic locations to schmooze with movie stars. In 1969, more than 500 members of the press congregated on Grand Bahama Island for Warner Bros.' International Film Festival, which was in reality a giant junket to promote the studio's most prestigious summer films, among them "The Wild Bunch" and "The Rain People." The same approach was later applied to the music business.

Today, when auto companies debut their latest models, they invariably fly journalists in for the event. When Acura showed off its 2004 Acura TL in Seattle, dozens attended the junket at the W Hotel, where they were put up for two nights, treated to two dinners and cocktails, attended technical briefings on the car and test drove it. According to Mike Spencer, Acura's public relations manager, only a handful paid their own way. "Hopefully, we'll get at least 100 stories out of it," he says.

Jaguar held a junket in Scottsdale, Ariz., where the freebies included rounds of golf. Rolls-Royce offered reporters a drive up the coast from Santa Barbara to a private winery, where the vino flowed freely. Land Rover has held junkets on a ranch in Colorado and other rural settings where writers could practice skeet shooting, fly-fishing and falconry. According to a PR rep for the automaker—who asked not to be identified for fear that this article would reflect negatively on the industry—this isn't bribery but merely a way of contextualizing the product: "It's not just about what the vehicle physically does, it's also about the culture of the vehicle. The optional activities . . . are everything that you picture someone who ultimately would purchase a Land Rover would do."

Many auto magazines allow or even encourage their writers to take free junkets because, they claim, they can't afford to pay the costs themselves. "An airline ticket or hotel room is not, in this parlance, in our space, in any way a gift," says Matt Stone, executive editor of Motor Trend magazine. "Business travel is a tool necessary for us to do our job."

A veteran freelancer now employed by a major daily newspaper agrees. "To take the high road and accept no freebies is very, very expensive," he says. But, he adds, "the argument that this doesn't affect journalists' judgment is crap. Of course it does. And I'm an old hand at this. I've been to Europe maybe 50 times on product launches. They'll fly us into Frankfurt or Rome, the south of France. It'll be spectacular, right? Then they'll say, 'OK, drive this car. What do you think?' 'Gee, I don't know. Here I am bathed in the warm light of the Riviera. The car looks pretty good to me.' It really takes some doing to resist that tendency to be favorable."

How to Talk Swag

The gift bag, swag suite and junket paradigms have been adopted by almost every conceivable industry. Cosmetic companies fly beauty editors to Paris to present their new product lines. At the 2004 Republican National Convention, journalists received booklets full of discount tickets for New York retailers and were treated to martinis by Time Warner. Chris Mauro, editor of Surfer magazine, and Tom Bie, editor of Powder, say that their contributors accept free travel and product from manufacturers and promoters in the surf and ski industries, but without any guarantee of giving them ink.

"Outdoor writers are the biggest whores in the business," says the veteran free lancer. "I've seen outdoor writers who've had boats delivered to their house from manufacturers. Theoretically they're testing them, but the boat sits in the guy's yard—they just keep it, a 25- to 30-foot boat. There are $50,000 bass boats."

The freebie culture has engendered a sense of entitlement. Publicists love to do imitations of journalists who have tried to scam them. "Our company represents the Tribeca and SoHo Grand hotels," Cutrone says. "I get 10 e-mails a day from journalists who are coming to New York from all over the world. I'm talking about everyone from the Daily Telegraph to the Shanghai Times. They call and say, 'Hi, we're going to do this big, huge blowout story. We can only pick one hotel in New York City. Can you offer a press rate?' As a publicist, this is how I would translate that: 'We're sending this e-mail to every cool hotel in New York. This is a huge [tourist] market for you. We're not going to come out and say that we want a free hotel room.' So what I'm going to say to my client is: 'Can we offer these people a comped room? I think it could turn out to be a great story for us.' "

When fashion writers come to town, they don't stop at the free hotel room. "You ask them to come to an event," Cutrone explains, "and they say, 'Can you send me a car?' Or, 'I don't have anything to wear. I'd really love to wear your designer to the show.' You can smell a fashion editor who's looking for a free ride. They'll come to your showroom and they light up, saying, 'Ohhhh, loooovvvveee!!! Oh my God, I've got to get one of these. I just love it, love it! You knoooow, we're actually working on this amazing issue, which I think that this would be perfect for. But you know what, I'm going away with my boyfriend for the weekend. We're going to St. Bart's. Do you think there's any way I can get a deal on one of these?' That's classic."

Of course, publicists have no one to blame for this but themselves. They're the ones who addicted journalists to freebies in the first place. Many fashion publicists offer a "media discount" on their clients' products, which can range from 20% to 70%, depending on the client and the writer's clout. (A writer for a national glossy might get a larger discount than a reporter for a regional publication.) And then there's the "gifting" of designer clothing, shoes, purses, jewelry, sunglasses, watches and so on. Again, the status of the byline and the circulation of the publication calibrate the value of the gift. A junior editor at a regional publication might receive a $500 starter purse, while an editorial superstar could receive a $5,000 status bag.

Product is sometimes dispersed as part of a wider campaign to raise public awareness. Cutrone explains: "We'll go to the designer and say, 'Listen, we think that the green leather bag is a very cute must-have item for this season. What I'd like to do is order an extra 35 bags and do a gifting program to the editors.' Then the costs are rolled into production. Then the editors show up at fashion shows wearing it." And a trend is born.

No wonder Juicy Couture's Nash-Taylor proselytizes the virtues of swag. When I interviewed her for this story, I asked if she rewards journalists who write favorable articles with follow-up gifts. "You'd better believe it, David!" she exclaimed. "At the end of the conversation, we always say, 'Do you have Juicy? Do you want something for your wife?' We'll put you on with Kate and say, 'Kate, send David a great box.' Some journalists are not allowed to accept anything." And I was one of them, I informed her. "Oh, you are?" Nash-Taylor groaned. I admitted that my wife and daughter would be angry that I turned her down. She emitted a throaty laugh. "They're bumming. As a journalist, if you were allowed to do that, you'd understand our product better. So why not? That's how I look at it. Why not? I'm sorry I can't send you something for your wife and your daughter. They're going to be saying, 'You should have done it, Dad!' You too, David. We've got great men's stuff."

DAVID WEDDLE last wrote for the magazine about his daughter's college course work in film theory.

UNIT 5

Developing the Future Ethos and Social Responsibility of Business

Unit Selections

Key Points to Consider

- In what areas should organizations become more ethically sensitive and socially responsible in the next five years? Be specific, and explain your choices.

- Obtain codes of ethics or conduct from several different professional associations (eg, doctors, lawyers, CPAs). What are the similarities and differences between them?

- How useful do you feel codes of ethics are to organizations? Defend your answer.

Student Web Site
www.mhcls.com

Internet References

International Business Ethics Institute (IBEI)
http://www.business-ethics.org/index.asp
UNU/IAS Project on Global Ethos
http://www.ias.unu.edu/research/globalethos.cfm

© Eyewire/Getty Images

Business ethics should not be viewed as a short-term, "knee-jerk reaction" to recently revealed scandals and corruption. Instead, it should be viewed as a thread woven through the fabric of the entire business culture—one that ought to be integral to its design. Businesses are built on the foundation of trust in our free-enterprise system. When there is a violation of this trust between competitors, between employer and employees, or between businesses and consumers, the system ceases to run smoothly.

From a pragmatic viewpoint, the alternative to self-regulated and voluntary ethical behavior and social responsibility on the part of business may be governmental and legislative intervention. From a moral viewpoint, ethical behavior should not exist because of economic pragmatism, governmental edict, or contemporary fashionability—it should exist because it is morally appropriate and right.

This last unit is composed of articles that provide some ideas, guidelines, and principles for developing the future ethos and social responsibility of business. The first article, "Creating an Ethical Culture," discloses how value-based programs can help employees judge right from wrong. "Hiring Character" presents a look at business leader Warren Buffett's practice of hiring people based on their integrity. The next article, "The True "Measure of a CEO," elucidates how Aristotle provides us with a set of ethical questions to ponder. The last article, "Green Is Good," covers how environmentalists have actually embraced market-based solutions.

Creating an Ethical Culture

Values-based ethics programs can help employees judge right from wrong.

DAVID GEBLER, J. D.

While the fate of former Enron leaders Kenneth Lay and Jeffrey Skilling is being determined in what has been labeled the "Trial of the Century," former WorldCom managers are in jail for pulling off one of the largest frauds in history.

Yes, criminal activity definitely took place in these companies and in dozens more that have been in the news in recent years, but what's really important is to take stock of the nature of many of the perpetrators.

Some quotes from former WorldCom executives paint a different picture of corporate criminals than we came to know in other eras:

> "I'm sorry for the hurt that has been caused by my cowardly behavior." —*Scott Sullivan, CFO*

> "Faced with a decision that required strong moral courage, I took the easy way out. . . . There are no words to describe my shame."
>
> —*Buford Yates, director of general accounting*

> "At the time I consider the single most critical character-defining moment of my life, I failed. It's something I'll take with me the rest of my life."
>
> —*David Myers, controller*

These are the statements of good people gone bad. But probably most disturbing was the conviction of Betty Vinson, the senior manager in the accounting department who booked billions of dollars in false expenses. At her sentencing, U.S. District Judge Barbara Jones noted that Vinson was among the lowest-ranking members of the conspiracy that led to the $11 billion fraud that sank the telecommunications company in 2002. Still, she said, "Had Ms. Vinson refused to do what she was asked, it's possible this conspiracy might have been nipped in the bud."

Judge Jones added that although Ms. Vinson "was among the least culpable members of the conspiracy" and acted under extreme pressure, "that does not excuse what she did."

Vinson said she improperly covered up expenses by drawing down reserve accounts—some completely unrelated to the expenses—and by moving expenses off income statements and listing them as assets on the balance sheet.

Also the company's former director of corporate reporting, Vinson testified at Bernie Ebbers's trial that, in choosing which accounts to alter, "I just really pulled some out of the air. I used some spreadsheets." She said she repeatedly brought her concerns to colleagues and supervisors, once describing the entries to a coworker as "just crazy." In spring 2002, she noted, she told one boss she would no longer make the entries. "I said that I thought the entries were just being made to make the income statement look like Scott wanted it to look."

Standing before the judge at her sentencing, Vinson said: "I never expected to be here, and I certainly won't do anything like this again." She was sentenced to five months in prison and five months of house arrest.

Pressure Reigns

While the judge correctly said that her lack of culpability didn't excuse her actions, we must carefully note that Betty Vinson, as well as many of her codefendants, didn't start out as criminals seeking to defraud the organization. Under typical antifraud screening tools, she and others like her wouldn't have raised any red flags as being potential committers of corporate fraud.

Scott Sullivan was a powerful leader with a well-known reputation for integrity. If any of us were in Betty Vinson's shoes, could we say with 100% confidence that we would say "no" to the CFO if he asked us to do something and promised that he would take full responsibility for any fallout from the actions we were going to take?

Today's white-collar criminals are more likely to be those among us who are unable to withstand the blistering pressures placed on managers to meet higher and tougher goals. In this environment, companies looking to protect themselves from corporate fraud must take a hard look at their own culture. Does it promote ethical behavior, or does it emphasize something else?

In most companies, "ethics" programs are really no more than compliance programs with a veneer of "do the right thing" messaging to create an apparent link to the company's values.

184

To be effective, they have to go deeper than outlining steps to take to report misconduct. Organizations must understand what causes misconduct in the first place.

We can't forget that Enron had a Code of Ethics. And it wasn't as if WorldCom lacked extensive internal controls. But both had cultures where engaging in unethical conduct was tacitly condoned, if not encouraged.

Building the Right Culture

Now the focus has shifted toward looking at what is going on inside organizations that's either keeping people from doing the right thing or, just as importantly, keeping people from doing something about misconduct they observe. If an organization wants to reduce the risk of unethical conduct, it must focus more effort on building the right culture than on building a compliance infrastructure.

The Ethics Resource Center's 2005 National Business Ethics Survey (NBES) clearly confirms this trend toward recognizing the role of corporate culture. Based on interviews with more than 3,000 employees and managers in the U.S., the survey disclosed that, despite the increase in the number of ethics and compliance program elements being implemented, desired outcomes, such as reduced levels of observed misconduct, haven't changed since 1994. Even more striking is the revelation that, although formal ethics and compliance programs have some impact, organizational culture has the greatest influence in determining program outcomes.

> **Leadership must know how the myriad human behaviors and interactions fit together like puzzle pieces to create a whole picture. An organization moves toward an ethical culture only if it understands the full range of values and behaviors needed to meet its ethical goals.**

The Securities & Exchange Commission (SEC) and the Department of Justice have also been watching these trends. Stephen Cutler, the recently retired SEC director of the Division of Enforcement, was matter of fact about the importance of looking at culture when it came to decisions of whether or not to bring an action. "We're trying to induce companies to address matters of tone and culture. . . . What we're asking of that CEO, CFO, or General Counsel goes beyond what a perp walk or an enforcement action against another company executive might impel her to do. We're hoping that if she sees that a failure of corporate culture can result in a fine that significantly exceeds the proverbial 'cost of doing business,' and reflects a failure on her watch—and a failure on terms that everyone can understand: the company's bottom line—she may have a little more incentive to pay attention to the environment in which her company's employees do their jobs."

Measuring Success

Only lagging companies still measure the success of their ethics and compliance programs just by tallying the percentage of employees who have certified that they read the Code of Conduct and attended ethics and compliance training. The true indicator of success is whether the company has made significant progress in achieving key program outcomes. The National Business Ethics Survey listed four key outcomes that help determine the success of a program:

- Reduced misconduct observed by employees,
- Reduced pressure to engage in unethical conduct,
- Increased willingness of employees to report misconduct, and
- Greater satisfaction with organizational response to reports of misconduct.

What's going to move these outcomes in the right direction? Establishing the right culture.

Most compliance programs are generated from "corporate" and disseminated down through the organization. As such, measurement of the success of the program is often based on criteria important to the corporate office: how many employees certified the Code of Conduct, how many employees went through the training, or how many calls the hotline received.

Culture is different—and is measured differently. An organization's culture isn't something that's created by senior leadership and then rolled out. A culture is an objective picture of the organization, for better or worse. It's the sum total of all the collective values and behaviors of all employees, managers, and leaders. By definition, it can only be measured by criteria that reflect the individual values of all employees, so understanding cultural vulnerabilities that can lead to ethics issues requires knowledge of what motivates employees in the organization. Leadership must know how the myriad human behaviors and interactions fit together like puzzle pieces to create a whole picture. An organization moves toward an ethical culture only if it understands the full range of values and behaviors needed to meet its ethical goals. The "full-spectrum" organization is one that creates a positive sense of engagement and purpose that drives ethical behavior.

Why is understanding the culture so important in determining the success of a compliance program? Here's an example: Most organizations have a policy that prohibits retaliation against those who bring forward concerns or claims. But creating a culture where employees feel safe enough to admit mistakes and to raise uncomfortable issues requires more than a policy and "Code training." To truly develop an ethical culture, the organization must be aware of how its managers deal with these issues up and down the line and how the values they demonstrate impact desired behaviors. The organization must understand the pressures its people are under and how they react to those pressures. And it must know how its managers communicate and whether employees have a sense of accountability and purpose.

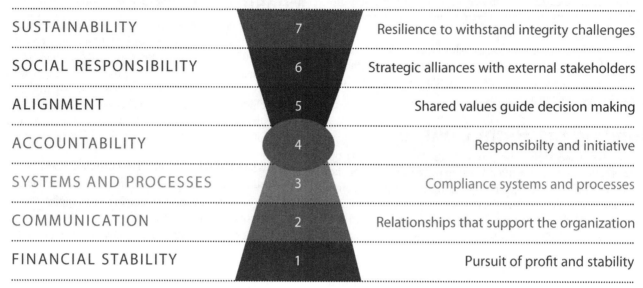

SUSTAINABILITY	7	Resilience to withstand integrity challenges
SOCIAL RESPONSIBILITY	6	Strategic alliances with external stakeholders
ALIGNMENT	5	Shared values guide decision making
ACCOUNTABILITY	4	Responsibilty and initiative
SYSTEMS AND PROCESSES	3	Compliance systems and processes
COMMUNICATION	2	Relationships that support the organization
FINANCIAL STABILITY	1	Pursuit of profit and stability

© Working Values, Ltd. Based on Cultural Transformation Tools © Richard Barrett & Associates

Figure 1 Seven levels of an ethical organization.

Categorizing Values

Determining whether an organization has the capabilities to put such a culture in place requires careful examination. Do employees and managers demonstrate values such as respect? Do employees feel accountable for their actions and feel that they have a stake in the success of the organization?

How does an organization make such a determination? One approach is to categorize different types of values in a way that lends itself to determining specific strengths and weaknesses that can be assessed and then corrected or enhanced.

The Culture Risk Assessment model presented in Figure 1 has been adapted from the Cultural Transformation Tools® developed by Richard Barrett & Associates. Such tools provide a comprehensive framework for measuring cultures by mapping values. More than 1,000 organizations in 24 countries have used this technique in the past six years. In fact, the international management consulting firm McKinsey & Co. has adopted it as its method of choice for mapping corporate cultures and measuring progress toward achieving culture change.

The model is based on the principle, substantiated through practice, that all values can be assigned to one of seven categories:

Levels 1, 2, and 3—The Organization's Basic Needs

Does the organization support values that enable it to run smoothly and effectively? From an ethics perspective, is the environment one in which employees feel physically and emotionally safe to report unethical behavior and to do the right thing?

Level 1—Financial Stability. Every organization needs to make financial stability a primary concern. Companies that are consumed with just surviving struggle to focus enough attention on how they conduct themselves. This may, in fact, create a negative cycle that makes survival much more difficult. Managers may exercise excessive control, so employees may be working in an environment of fear.

In these circumstances, unethical or even illegal conduct can be rationalized. When asked to conform to regulations, organizations do the minimum with an attitude of begrudging compliance.

Organizations with challenges at this level need to be confident that managers know and stand within clear ethical boundaries.

Level 2—Communication. Without good relationships with employees, customers, and suppliers, integrity is compromised. The critical issue at this level is to create a sense of loyalty and belonging among employees and a sense of caring and connection between the organization and its customers.

The most critical link in the chain is between employees and their direct supervisors. If direct supervisors can't effectively reinforce messages coming from senior leadership, those messages might be diluted and confused by the time they reach line employees. When faced with conflicting messages, employees will usually choose to follow the lead of their direct supervisor over the words of the CEO that have been conveyed through an impersonal communication channel. Disconnects in how local managers "manage" these messages often mean that employees can face tremendous pressure in following the lead established by leadership.

Fears about belonging and lack of respect lead to fragmentation, dissension, and disloyalty. When leaders meet behind closed doors or fail to communicate openly, employees suspect the worst. Cliques form, and gossip becomes rife. When leaders are more focused on their own success, rather than the success of the organization, they begin to compete with each other.

Level 3—Systems and Processes. At this level, the organization is focused on becoming the best it can be through the adoption of best practices and a focus on quality, productivity, and efficiency.

Level 3 organizations have succeeded in implementing strong internal controls and have enacted clear standards of conduct. Those that succeed at this level are the ones that see internal controls as an opportunity to create better, more efficient processes. But even those that have successfully deployed business processes and practices need to be alert to potentially limiting aspects of being too focused on processes. All organizations need to be alert to resorting to a "check-the-box" attitude that assumes compliance comes naturally from just implementing standards and procedures. Being efficient all too often leads to bureaucracy and inconsistent application of the rules. When this goes badly, employees lose respect for the system and resort to self-help to get things done. This can lead to shortcuts and, in the worst case, engaging in unethical conduct under the guise of doing what it takes to succeed.

Level 4—Accountability

The focus of the fourth level is on creating an environment in which employees and managers begin to take responsibility for their own actions. They want to be held accountable, not micromanaged and supervised every moment of every day. For an ethics and compliance program to be successful, all employees must feel that they have a personal responsibility for the integrity of the organization. Everyone must feel that his or her voice is being heard. This requires managers and leaders to admit that they don't have all the answers and invite employee participation.

Levels 5, 6, and 7—Common Good

Does the organization support values that create a collective sense of belonging where employees feel that they have a stake in the success of the ethics program?

Level 5—Alignment. The critical issue at this level is developing a shared vision of the future and a shared set of values. The shared vision clarifies the intentions of the organization and gives employees a unifying purpose and direction. The shared values provide guidance for making decisions.

The organization develops the ability to align decision making around a set of shared values. The values and behaviors must be reflected in all of the organization's processes and systems, with appropriate consequences for those who aren't willing to walk the talk. A precondition for success at this level is building a climate of trust.

Level 6—Social Responsibility. At this level, the organization is able to use its relationships with stakeholders to sustain itself through crises and change. Employees and customers see that the organization is making a difference in the world through its products and services, its involvement in the local community, or its willingness to fight for causes that improve humanity. They must feel that the company cares about them and their future. Companies operating at this level go the extra mile to make sure they are being responsible citizens. They support and encourage employees' activities in the community by providing time off for volunteer work and/or making a financial contribution to the charities that employees are involved in.

Level 7—Sustainability. To be successful at Level 7, organizations must embrace the highest ethical standards in all their interactions with employees, suppliers, customers, shareholders, and the community. They must always consider the long-term impact of their decisions and actions.

Employee values are distributed across all seven levels. Through surveys, organizations learn which values employees bring to the workplace and which values are missing. Organizations don't operate from any one level of values: They tend to be clustered around three or four levels. Most are focused on the first three: profit and growth (Level 1), customer satisfaction (Level 2), and productivity, efficiency, and quality (Level 3). The most successful organizations operate across the full spectrum with particular focus in the upper levels of consciousness—the common good—accountability, leading to learning and innovation (Level 4), alignment (Level 5), sustainability (Level 6), and social responsibility (Level 7).

Some organizations have fully developed values around Levels 1, 2, and 3 but are lacking in Levels 5, 6, and 7. They may have a complete infrastructure of controls and procedures but may lack the accountability and commitment of employees and leaders to go further than what is required.

Similarly, some organizations have fully developed values around Levels 5, 6, and 7 but are deficient in Levels 1, 2, and 3. These organizations may have visionary leaders and externally focused social responsibility programs, but they may be lacking in core systems that will ensure that the higher-level commitments are embedded into day-to-day processes.

Once an organization understands its values' strengths and weaknesses, it can take specific steps to correct deficient behavior.

Starting the Process

Could a deeper understanding of values have saved WorldCom? We will never know, but if the culture had encouraged open communication and fostered trust, people like Betty Vinson might have been more willing to confront orders that they knew were wrong. Moreover, if the culture had embodied values that encouraged transparency, mid-level managers wouldn't have been asked to engage in such activity in the first place.

The significance of culture issues such as these is also being reflected in major employee surveys that highlight what causes unethical behavior. According to the NBES, "Where top management displays certain ethics-related actions, employees are 50 percentage points less likely to observe misconduct." No other factor in any ethics survey can demonstrate such a drastic influence.

So how do compliance leaders move their organizations to these new directions?

1. **The criteria for success of an ethics program must be outcomes based.** Merely checking off program elements isn't enough to change behavior.

2. **Each organization must identify the key indicators of its culture.** Only by assessing its own ethical culture can a company know what behaviors are the most influential in effecting change.

3. **The organization must gauge how all levels of employees perceive adherence to values by others within the company.** One of the surprising findings of the NBES was that managers, especially senior managers, were out of touch with how nonmanagement employees perceived their adherence to ethical behaviors. Nonmanagers are 27 percentage points less likely than senior managers to indicate that executives engage in all of the ethics-related actions outlined in the survey.

4. **Formal programs are guides to shape the culture, not vice versa.** People who are inclined to follow the rules appreciate the rules as a guide to behavior. Formal program elements need to reflect the culture in which they are deployed if they are going to be most effective in driving the company to the desired outcomes.

Culture may be new on the radar screen, but it isn't outside the scope or skills of forward-thinking finance managers and compliance professionals. Culture can be measured, and finance managers can play a leadership role in developing systematic approaches to move companies in the right direction.

DAVID GEBLER, J. D., is president of Working Values, Ltd., a business ethics training and consulting firm specializing in developing behavior-based change to support compliance objectives. You can reach him at dgebler@workingvalues.com.

From *Strategic Finance*, May 2006, pp. 29–34. Copyright © 2006 by Institute of Management Accountants (IMA). Reprinted by permission via Copyright Clearance Center.

Hiring Character

In their new book, ***Integrity Works,*** authors Dana Telford and Adrian Gostick outline the strategies necessary for becoming a respected and admired leader. In the edited excerpt that follows, the authors present a look at business leader Warren Buffett's practice of hiring people based on their integrity. For sales and marketing executives, it's a practice worth considering, especially when your company's reputation with customers—built through your salespeople—is so critical.

DANA TELFORD AND ADRIAN GOSTICK

This chapter was the hardest for us to write. The problem was, we couldn't agree on whom to write about. We had a number of great options we were mulling over. Herb Brooks of the Miracle on Ice 1980 U.S. hockey team certainly put together a collection of players whose character outshined their talent. And the results were extraordinary. We decided to leave him out because we had enough sports figures in the book already. No, we wanted a business leader. So we asked, "Who hires integrity over ability?"

The person suggested to us over and over as we bandied this idea among our colleagues was Warren Buffett, chairman of Berkshire Hathaway Inc.

Sure enough, as we began our research we found we had not even begun to tell Buffett's story. But we were reluctant to repeat his story. Buffett had played an important part in our first book. And yet, his name kept coming up. So often, in fact, that we finally decided to not ignore the obvious.

Perhaps more than anyone in business today, Warren Buffett hires people based on their integrity. Buffett commented, "Berkshire's collection of managers is unusual in several ways. As one example, a very high percentage of these men and women are independently wealthy, having made fortunes in the businesses that they run. They work neither because they need the money nor because they are contractually obligated to—we have no contracts at Berkshire. Rather, they work long and hard because they love their businesses."

The unusual thing about Warren Buffett is that he and his longtime partner, Charlie Munger, hire people they trust—and then treat them as they would wish to be treated if their positions were reversed. Buffett says the one reason he has kept working so long is that he loves the opportunity to interact with people he likes and, most importantly, trusts.

> **Buffett loves the opportunity to interact daily with people he likes and, most importantly, trusts.**

Consider the following remarkable story from a few years ago at Berkshire Hathaway. It's about R.C. Willey, the dominant home furnishings business in Utah. Berkshire purchased the company from Bill Child and his family in 1995. Child and most of his managers are members of the Church of Jesus Christ of Latter-day Saints, also called Mormons, and for this reason R.C. Willey's stores have never been open on Sunday.

Now, anyone who has worked in retail realizes the seeming folly of this notion: Sunday is the favorite shopping day for many customers—even in Utah. Over the years, though, Child had stuck to his principle—and wasn't ready to rejigger the formula just because Warren Buffett came along. And the formula was working. R.C.'s sales were $250,000 in 1954 when Child took over. By 1999, they had grown to $342 million. Child's determination to stick to his convictions was what attracted Buffett to him and his management team. This was a group with values and a successful brand.

Arnie Ferrin, longtime friend of Child, said, "I believe that [Child] is a man of extreme integrity, and I believe that Warren Buffett was looking to buy his business because he likes to do business with people like that, that don't have any shadows in their lives, and they're straightforward and deal above-board."

This isn't to say Child and Buffett have always agreed on the direction of the furniture store.

"I was highly skeptical about taking a no-Sunday policy into a new territory, where we would be up against entrenched rivals open seven days a week," Buffett said. "Nevertheless, this was Bill's business to run. So, despite my reservations, I told him to follow both his business judgment and his religious convictions."

Proving once again that he believed in his convictions, Child insisted on a truly extraordinary proposition: He would personally buy the land and build the store in Boise, Idaho—for about $11 million as it turned out—and would sell it to Berkshire at his cost if—and only if—the store proved to be successful. On the other hand, if sales fell short of his expectations, Berkshire could exit the business without paying Child a cent. This, of course, would leave him with a huge investment in an empty building.

You're probably guessing there's a happy ending to the story. And there is. The store opened in August of 1998 and immediately became a huge success, making Berkshire a considerable margin. Today, the store is the largest home furnishings store in Idaho.

Child, good to his word, turned the property over to Berkshire—including some extra land that had appreciated significantly. And he wanted nothing more than the original cost of his investment. In response, Buffett said, "And get this: Bill refused to take a dime of interest on the capital he had tied up over the two years."

And there's more. Shortly after the Boise opening, Child went back to Buffett, suggesting they try Las Vegas next. This time, Buffett was even more skeptical. How could they do business in a metropolis of that size and remain closed on Sundays, a day that all of their competitors would be exploiting?

But Buffett trusts his managers because he knows their character. So he gave it a shot. The store was built in Henderson, a mushrooming city adjacent to Las Vegas. The result? This store outsells all others in the R.C. Willey chain, doing a volume of business that far exceeds any competitor in the area. The revenue is twice what Buffett had anticipated.

As this book went to print, R.C. Willey was preparing to open its third store in the Las Vegas area, as well as stores in Reno, Nevada, and Sacramento, California. Sales have grown to more than $600 million, and the target is $1 billion in coming years. "You can understand why the opportunity to partner with people like Bill Child causes me to tap dance to work every morning," Buffett said.

Here's another example of Buffett's adeptness at hiring character. He agreed to purchase Ben Bridge Jeweler over the phone, prior to any face-to-face meeting with the management.

Ed Bridge manages this 65-store West Coast retailer with his cousin, Jon. Both are fourth-generation owner-managers of a business started 89 years ago in Seattle. And over the years, the business and the family have enjoyed extraordinary character reputations.

Buffett knows that he must give complete autonomy to his managers. "I told Ed and Jon that they would be in charge, and they knew I could be believed: After all, it's obvious that [I] would be a disaster at actually running a store or selling jewelry, though there are members of [my] family who have earned black brits as purchasers."

Talk about hiring integrity! Without any provocation from Buffett, the Bridges allocated a substantial portion of the proceeds from their sale to the hundreds of coworkers who had helped the company achieve its success.

Overall, Berkshire has made many such acquisitions—hiring for character first, and talent second—and then asking these CEOs to manage for maximum long-term value, rather than for next quarter's earnings. While they certainly don't ignore the current profitability of their business, Buffett never wants profits to be achieved at the expense of developing ever-greater competitive strengths, including integrity.

It's an approach he learned early in his career.

Warren Edward Buffett was born on August 30, 1930. His father, Howard, was a stockbroker-turned-congressman. The only boy, Warren was the second of three children. He displayed an amazing aptitude for both money and business at a very early age. Acquaintances recount his uncanny ability to calculate columns of numbers off the top of his head—a feat Buffett still amazes business colleagues with today.

At only six years old, Buffett purchased six-packs of Coca-Cola from his grandfather's grocery store for twenty-five cents and resold each of the bottles for a nickel—making a nice five-cent profit. While other children his age were playing hopscotch and jacks, Buffett was already generating cash flow.

Buffett stayed just two years in the undergraduate program at Wharton Business School at the University of Pennsylvania. He left disappointed, complaining that he knew more than his professors. Eventually, he transferred to the University of Nebraska–Lincoln. He managed to graduate in only three years despite working full time.

Then he finally applied to Harvard Business School. In what was undoubtedly one of the worst admission decisions in history, the school rejected him as "too young." Slighted, Buffett applied to Columbia where famed investment professor Ben Graham taught.

Professor Graham shaped young Buffett's opinions on investing. And the student influenced his mentor as well. Graham bestowed on Buffett the only A+ he ever awarded in decades of teaching.

While Buffett tried working for Graham for a while, he finally struck out on his own with a revolutionary philosophy: He would research the internal workings of extraordinary companies. He could discover what really made them tick and why they held a competitive edge in their markets. And then he would invest in great companies that were trading at substantially less than their market values.

Ten years after its founding, the Buffett Partnership assets were up more than 1,156 percent [compared to the Dow's 122.9 percent], and Buffett was firmly on his way to becoming an investing legend.

In 2004, Warren Buffett was listed by Forbes as the world's second-richest person (right behind Bill Gates), with $42.9 billion in personal wealth. Despite starting with just $300,000 in holdings, Berkshire's holdings now exceed $116 billion. And Buffett and his employees can confidently say they have made thousands of people wealthy.

We often ask business leaders one simple question: Which is more dangerous to your firm—the incompetent new hire or the dishonest new hire? It's the part of our presentation where attendees sit up straight and start thinking.

We always follow the question with an exercise on identifying and hiring integrity. Though it becomes obvious that many of the executives and managers haven't given employee integrity much thought, most of the CEOs in the audiences are increasingly concerned about hiring employees with character.

So, how do you hire workers with integrity? It's possible, but not easy. It is important to spend more time choosing a new employee than you do picking out a new coffee machine. Here are a few simple areas to focus on:

First, ensure educational credentials match the resume. Education is the most misrepresented area on a resume. Notre Dame football coach George O'Leary was fired because the master's degree he said he had earned did not exist, the CEO of software giant Lotus exaggerated his education and military service, and the CEO of Bausch & Lomb forfeited a bonus of more than $1 million because he claimed a fictional MBA.

It is important to spend more time choosing a new employee than you do picking out a new coffee machine.

Job candidates also often claim credit for responsibilities that they never had. Here's a typical scenario:

Job candidate: "I led that project. Saved the company $10 million." Through diligent fact checking, you find an employee at a previous employer who can give you information about the candidate:

Coworker: "Hmm. Actually, Steve was a member of the team, but not the lead. And while it was a great project, we still haven't taken a tally of the cost savings. But $10 million seems really high."

How do you find those things out? Confer with companies where the applicant has worked—especially those firms the person isn't listing as a reference. Talk to people inside the organization, going at least two levels deep (which means you ask each reference for a couple more references). Talk to the nonprofit organizations where the person volunteers. Tap into alumni networks and professional associations. Get on the phone with others in the industry to learn about the person's reputation. Check public records for bankruptcy, civil, and criminal litigation (with the candidate's knowledge). In other words, check candidates' backgrounds carefully (but legally, of course).

We find that most hiring managers spend 90 percent of their time on capability-related questions, and next to no time on character-based questions. In your rush to get someone in the chair, don't forget to check backgrounds and be rigorous in your interviewing for character. Hiring the wrong person can destroy two careers: your employee's—and your own.

Ask ethics-based questions to get to the character issue. We asked a group of executives at a storage company to brainstorm a list of questions they might ask candidates to learn more about their character. Their list included the following questions:

- Who has had the greatest influence on you and why?
- Who is the best CEO you've worked for and why?
- Tell me about your worst boss.
- Who are your role models and why?
- How do you feel about your last manager?
- Tell me about a time you had to explain bad news to your manager.
- What would you do if your best friend did something illegal?
- What would your past manager say about you?
- What does integrity mean to you?
- If you were the CEO of your previous company, what would you change?
- What values did your parents teach you?
- Tell me a few of your faults.
- Why should I trust you?
- How have you dealt with adversity in the past?
- What are your three core values?
- Tell me about a time when you let someone down.
- What is your greatest accomplishment, personal or professional?
- What are your goals and why?
- Tell me about a mistake you made in business and what you learned from it.
- Tell me about a time when you were asked to compromise your integrity.

It's relatively easy to teach a candidate your business. The harder task is trying to instill integrity in someone who doesn't already have it.

Of course, we don't want to imply that it's impossible. Sometimes people will adapt to a positive environment and shine. Men's Wearhouse has certainly had tremendous success hiring former prison inmates, demonstrating everyone should have a second chance.

But integrity is a journey that is very personal, very individual. An outside force, such as an employer, typically can't prescribe it. It's certainly not something that happens overnight. That's one reason many of the CEOs we have talked with prefer promoting people from inside their organizations when possible.

Don Graham, chairman and CEO of the Washington Post Company, said, "There's a very good reason for concentrating your hires and promotions on people who already work in your organization. The best way to predict what someone's going to do in the future is to know what they've done in the past—watch how people address difficult business issues, how they deal with the people who work for them, how they deal with the people for whom they work. You may be able to put on a certain face for a day or even a week, but you're not going to be able to hide the person you are for five or ten years."

Graham tells a story about Frank Batten, who for years ran Landmark Communications and founded The Weather Channel. "Frank is a person of total integrity," Graham says. "Frank once said, 'When you go outside for hire you always get a surprise. Sometimes it's a good surprise. But you never hire quite the person you thought you were hiring.' "

What do you look for in a job applicant? Years of experience? College degree? Specific skill sets? Or do you look for character? If so, you're in good company.

Years ago, Warren Buffett was asked to help choose the next CEO for Salomon Brothers. "What do you think [Warren] was looking for?" Graham asks. "Character and integrity—more than even a particular background. When the reputation of the firm is on the line every day, character counts."

Don't like surprises? Then hire people who have integrity. Want to ensure a good fit with the people you hire? Then hire people who have integrity. Want to ensure your reputation with customers? Then hire people who have integrity.

Are we saying that nothing else matters? No. But we are saying that nothing matters more.

From *Integrity Works: Strategies for Becoming a Trusted, Respected and Admired Leader* by **DANA TELFORD** and **ADRIAN GOSTICK**.

The True Measure of a CEO

Aristotle has something to say about that.

JAMES O'TOOLE

In 400 B.C., Aristotle argued that a leader's task is to create conditions under which all followers can realize their full human potential. In this view, leadership is not about the leader's needs for wealth, power, and prestige—rather, it is about the leader's responsibility to create an environment in which followers can develop the capabilities with which they were born.

Today, given the nature of 24/7 work conditions, and the commitment to long hours that American corporations demand of employees, the only place where most people have the opportunity to develop their capacities is at work. Hence, if corporations and their CEOs do not provide the opportunity for their employees to grow, they effactully deny them their basic humanity. That is why creating a culture in which the true and basic needs of employees are addressed is the core ethical issue in corporate leadership today.

Aristotle provides us with a set of ethical questions to determine the extent to which an organization provides an environment conducive to human growth and fulfillment. And, he would say, not only does an ethical leader create that environment—he does so consciously, and not coincidentally. Motivation is important in ethics. Miami hoteliers cannot claim credit for sunny days, and leaders in Silicon Valley get no ethical credit for providing jobs that are accidentally developmental. Just because working with computers may be inherently a developmental task, one is not necessarily a marvelous employer for providing people with that opportunity.

Aristotle also asks the extent to which we as leaders observe decent limits on our own power in order to allow others to lead and develop. He says that too many leaders turn their people into passive recipients of their moral feats. In practice, celebrity CEOs such as Citigroup's Sandy Weill and Sun's Scott McNealy have behaved as if there were only one leader in each of their respective organizations—themselves—and not only have garnered credit for all good decisions made in their companies but have amassed for themselves the best opportunities to learn through leading. Worse, they have dismissed and discouraged executives who have challenged their authority, particularly upcoming stars who shined too brightly and thus threatened the CEO's status as the sole source of organizational enlightenment.

In essence, here are the questions that Aristotle asks CEOs and other leaders to ask themselves:

- To what extent do I consciously make an effort to provide learning opportunities to everyone who works for me?
- To what extent do I encourage full participation by all my people in the decisions affecting their own work?
- To what extent do I allow them to lead in order to grow?
- To what extent do I measure my own performance as a manager or leader both in terms of realizing economic goals and, equally, creating conditions in which my people can fulfill their own potential in the workplace?

I do not pretend that it is easy for leaders to create ethical cultures. Tough sacrifices and trade-offs are demanded. For starters, leaders must behave courageously and consistently to meet their ethical responsibilities to employees. For example, during the extended 2001–04 recession, when hundreds of thousands of American workers were losing their jobs, most corporate leaders assumed they had no other choice but to lay off workers. But out in Silicon Valley, the CEO of Xilinx Inc., Wim Roelandts, believed that there had to be other alternatives, even when his company's profits plummeted by 50 percent in 2001. His own board and some of his top executives argued that the only way he could stem the flow of red ink was to lay off workers. But driven by his stated communitarian values of respect for employees and commitment to their development, he charged a task force of managers with finding alternatives to layoffs. They came up with a dozen programs that were put into place, including funding educational sabbaticals for workers and paying them modest stipends for volunteering in nonprofit organizations.

I do not pretend that it is easy for leaders to create ethical cultures.

A year later, Xilinx came roaring back, with its workforce intact and committed to making their company a financial success. Significantly, Roelandts is a self-described "geek"

Aristotle on CEO Pay

No matter how one cuts the figures, even moderately well-paid CEOs of large corporations make about as much in a day as their workers make in a year. Even if the point of reference is the more modest salaries of CEOs of midsized American companies, the average for them is some 34 times that of industrial workers (the comparable ratios are 13-to-1 in Germany and 11-to-1 in Japan). Keep in mind, too, that the $35,864 earned by the average American worker is exactly that, *an average*, one that includes the astronomical salaries of CEOs, sports figures, and Hollywood celebs on the high end and the minimum-wage earners on the low end, who, if employed full time, make about $9,888 per year before taxes.

Averages also conceal extreme behavior, such as Kmart CEO Charles Conway drawing down some $23 million during his two-year reign, during which time he terminated some 22,000 employees with zero severance. In 2001, while Wal-Mart CEO H. Lee Scott was receiving something like $17 million in total compensation, many of his lowest-paid hourly employees were suing the company because they claimed they were forced to punch out at the end of their eight-hour day, then made to continue working overtime without additional compensation.

Few American executives appear to apply the same standards of justice they demand and expect for themselves to compensation issues relating to their subordinates. In 2002, employees of Hershey Foods went on strike after the company raised their share of health-insurance premiums at a time when the company's sales and profits were up. The workers thought this hefty increase was particularly unfair because it occurred the year after the company's new CEO earned $4.6 million in salary, bonuses, and stock options—in just nine months on the job. Assuming Hershey's CEO was entitled to what he earned, the Aristotelian question is, *Was he virtuous in reducing the benefits of those who earned far less?*

Admittedly, it is hard to reckon what is just and fair. But it is not impossible. For example, Disney's board compensated its CEO, Michael Eisner, with $285 million between 1996 and 2004. We can't pretend to have all the data required to decide how much Eisner deserves, but, thanks to Aristotle, we have a question that a virtuous member of the Disney board's compensation committee might ask in making that decision: Is the CEO's proportionate contribution to the organization really ten—or a hundred, or a thousand—times greater than that of a cartoon animator at the company's Burbank studios or the operator of Disneyland's Space Mountain ride? Alas, I sincerely doubt the Disney board has ever examined the ethics of its pay policies in this way.

Although asking such a question is practically unheard of in the boardrooms of giant companies, a few small- and medium-sized companies have done so and established ratios as low as 20-to-1 between the compensation of their highest-paid executive and average worker. That may sound unrealistic, but when you run the numbers it makes some sense. If the average worker makes $20 an hour, the CEO of even a "low-paying" company can make a million dollars a year. This ratio is "unrealistic" only because the current ratio in Fortune 500 companies approaches 500-to-1.

Creating an ethical corporate culture turns out to be a far more difficult task than the authors of Sarbanes-Oxley anticipated. As smart as Aristotle was, even he couldn't provide a clear moral principle for the just distribution of enterprise-created wealth. He admits that it's harder to distribute wealth fairly than it is to make it. Nonetheless, here are some Aristotelian questions that virtuous leaders might ask themselves, particularly before awarding themselves large bonuses at the same time they are outsourcing jobs to contractors who don't pay health benefits:

- Am I taking more in my share of rewards than my contributions warrant?
- Does the distribution of goods in the organization have a negative effect on morale?
- Would everyone in the organization enter into the employment contract under the current terms if they truly had other choices?
- Would we come to a different principle of allocation if all of the parties concerned were represented at the table?

We will all answer such questions differently, and that is to be expected, but if we want businesses that are perceived as fair in their dealings with employees, then CEOs must start asking them.

—James O'Toole

engineer who, in discovering the importance of ethical analysis, learned that leadership requires moral imagination, which begins with spotting ethical issues, asking oneself tough questions about the consequences of one's actions, and finding better alternatives when all those available have unacceptable consequences.

Of course, this runs against prevalent assumptions not only about corporate finance but also about leadership. In the dominant philosophy, there is only one dimension: A leader is simply measured in terms of her effectiveness at achieving a goal, whether that goal be profits or personal power. Jack Welch proudly proclaimed that he should be judged solely by the criterion of how much wealth he created for shareholders. The leadership philosophy of Roelandts and others like him stands in stark contrast. While they are as concerned as Welch with their effectiveness at producing financial results, they believe they must also be judged by the extent to which they create a corporate culture in which the ethical principle of respect for people is never violated.

Very few CEOs today set such high standards for themselves. Indeed, many successful and admired corporate leaders consciously reject such ethical measures of performance as inappropriate, impractical, and irrelevant to the task their boards have hired them to do, which is to create wealth. They say their responsibility is to their shareholders, not their employees, and if the social responsibility of employee development interferes with profit-making, then workers' needs must be sacrificed. Aristotle would answer that virtuous leaders have responsibilities to both their owners and their workers and, if there's a conflict between the two, it is the leader's duty to create conditions in which those interests can be made the same.

This two-dimensional standard of leadership is doubly hard to meet because it entails practicing what one preaches—that is, consistency between word and act. That consistency is known as integrity, and it leads to the most important element in creating an ethical corporate culture: trust. Unfortunately, it is in the realm of integrity that too many corporate executives are failing today. For example, at one of the nation's fastest-growing financial-services companies, the CEO speaks enthusiastically and proudly about his "values-based leadership," the value of his people being at the top of his list of things he says the company holds dear. The company is a success. It has basically doubled its sales and its profits over the last couple of years. While doing so, it has halved its workforce through domestic outsourcing and by selling off divisions and then contracting for the services of its former employees—naturally, at lower rates.

In essence, the policy of the company is to find ways to pay people less for doing the same work and, now, with fewer benefits. Significantly, it has not been driven to do so by foreign competitors paying lower wages. What is interesting is that no one in top management, as far as I can discern, sees this as an ethical issue. It is simply considered what a company must do in order to succeed in business. But what is the effect on employee trust, morale, and the senses of community and commitment?

I don't know, and a precise answer is impossible, but I do know that the consequences may be indirect and unexpected. For example, in January, near Los Angeles, a suicidal motorist drove his Jeep Cherokee onto railroad tracks. At the last moment, he thought the better of it and abandoned the SUV, and seconds later, a full commuter train crashed into the vehicle, killing eleven people and injuring 120. The accident occurred directly behind a Costco store. Almost immediately, the blue-collar Costco employees organized themselves into an emergency brigade and, armed with forklift trucks and fire extinguishers, set out to rescue trapped passengers and to deliver first aid to the wounded.

It is not coincidental, I believe, that Costco's culture stresses the importance of each worker, rewards individual initiative, and trusts frontline employees to solve problems in the absence of supervision and detailed rules. Costco is among the retail industry's leaders in terms of investing heavily in the training and development of its workforce. Hence, if the train accident had to occur, I believe the passengers were at least fortunate that they ended up near a group of people whose skills and instincts had been well primed to spring to their aid. Of course, we cannot know what might have happened had the accident occurred outside a store owned by one of those retail chains that has adopted the currently more-prevalent HR strategy: viewing employees as simply factors of production, the cost of which needs to be minimized—if their jobs cannot be eliminated altogether.

Here I will go out on a limb: I cannot help but suspect that people who are treated as fungible, told simply to obey their supervisors, and whose development is not seen as a corporate responsibility would be far less prepared than the Costco people to respond to an emergency as quickly, effectively, and appropriately.

In the 1990s, many corporations abandoned the Costco approach of paying living wages, providing decent health care, and treating employees with dignity and respect by rewarding them for participating in self-management. Numerous companies—to cite the most obvious example, Wal-Mart—went in the opposite direction, believing that investing in workers is too costly and leaves the company vulnerable to low-price competitors. Sometimes that is true, but in many cases, executives have had room for choice. For example, while FedEx has moved to a low-cost model for its drivers (even contracting out), its competitor UPS has stayed with its commitment to long-term employment, high pay, and individual development. And UPS believes that its drivers are key to corporate success, and that having informed and committed workers is the best way to serve customers. It is also true that the leaders of UPS are former drivers themselves and so have moral empathy with their workers. They understand that the lowliest worker in the organization is as human as they are, with much the same basic needs.

This kind of understanding lies at the root of Aristotelian leadership. But many large corporations today have become depersonalized; not only do the executives not know their workers personally—they come from different educational backgrounds and live in different neighborhoods. That makes moral empathy increasingly rare. For example, a few months ago I witnessed a two-hour discussion among corporate board members in which they debated what portion of their expected record-high profits should go to top management, and what portion should go to shareholders, profits that could lead to a windfall of as much as a million dollars to each of the company's top people. At the end of the discussion, they reviewed the prime risks facing the company, one of which was a possible increase in the minimum wage in China to $71 per month. Since all the company's manufacturing was in China, that event would greatly increase labor costs. The CFO proposed a solution: The company could reduce this increase's bottom-line impact by charging employees more for their room and board. That settled, the board and the executives present went on to other matters.

It happened so quickly that it was easy to miss what had occurred. In effect, the board decided to reduce the net take-home pay of their poorest workers so that the top people's bonuses would not be reduced by a few percentage points. If that isn't an ethical issue, I don't know what is. But the CEO and members of the board not only failed to address it—they didn't even recognize it.

Unfortunately, this is probably not that extreme an example. In my frequent interactions with executives from large U.S. corporations, it is clear from what they say—and do—that the prevalent assumption is that the only part of the workforce that is indispensable, and therefore the part in which an investment in development is justified, is the few highly trained and skilled people at the top of the hierarchy. Moreover, in too few of those large corporations do managers believe they have a moral responsibility to address the needs of workers; instead, the assumption is that if workers do not like the conditions being offered, they are free to quit and look for employment elsewhere.

Certainly, Aristotle would have something to say about that.

JAMES O'TOOLE is research professor at the Center for Effective Organizations at the University of Southern California's Marshall School of Business, Mortimer J. Adler Senior Fellow at the Aspen Institute, and author of, most recently, *Creating the Good Life: Aristotle's Guide to Getting It Right,* from which this article is adapted.

Green Is Good

No, it's not just greenwash. Business in the U.S. really has become cleaner and greener. Environmentalists actually have embraced market-based solutions. And the politics are about to get very interesting. As a result, the changes that have swept through business are huge. So is the economic opportunity. Here is a look at what could be the business story of the 21st century.

MARC GUNTHER ET AL.

Big business and environmentalists used to be sworn enemies—and for good reason. General Electric dumped toxins into the Hudson River. Wal-Mart bulldozed its way across America. DuPont was named the nation's worst polluter. The response from the environmental movement: mandate, regulate, and litigate. Those days are mostly over.

Today big companies and activists are at least as apt to hammer out a partnership over a cup of sustainably grown coffee as to confront one another in court. No, they do not always see eye to eye, but the areas of common ground are getting broader. Why? For one thing, because there is money to be made. "The opportunity to provide environmental solutions is going to be one of the big four or five themes of our generation of business leadership," Jeffrey Immelt, the chief executive of GE, told the 25th anniversary dinner of the World Resources Institute.

Like Immelt, FORTUNE sees big changes ahead. For the past 30 years, most of what passed for environmentalism in corporate America was driven by two things: compliance and efficiency. Industry stopped polluting the air and water after it became illegal or unprofitable to do so. Going a step further, some companies also recognized that by reducing their consumption of energy and materials, they could save money, help the planet, and maybe clean up their image. Now we're at the threshold of a different era, one in which smart companies are trying to figure out how to profit by solving the world's big environmental problems. This era won't be about efficiency—although there are still lots of gains to be made there—but about increasing revenues and inventing entirely new businesses. That, at least, is what DuPont has set out to do, albeit with mixed results. That's also why GE is selling wind turbines as fast as it can produce them.

Global warming is the game changer. A number of influential FORTUNE 500 CEOs, including GE's Immelt, Wal-Mart's Lee Scott, the heads of America's four biggest carmakers, and utility industry leaders like Jim Rogers of Duke Power and Peter Darbee of PG&E, have agreed that climate change is real and that national action is required to slow, stop, and then reverse the growth of greenhouse-gas emissions. That is a very tall order.

Transitioning to a low-carbon economy will require new ways to generate power, run our cars, grow our food, and design, build, heat, and cool our homes and offices. Only business is capable of innovation on that scale.

> **Increased 500% wind-power installation in the U.S. since 1999, to 11,600 megawatts. That's enough electricity for about 2.5 million homes.**

And many businesses are taking up the challenge with verve. On the following pages we identify ten companies that are ahead of the learning curve on the strategic value of environmentalism in their industries. Selecting them was difficult—another sign of how the world is changing. We began by soliciting nominations from environmentalists and consultants who have worked in the trenches of corporate America (see a partial list of sources on page 50). They nominated nearly 100 companies. We decided to concentrate on bigger firms because their environmental footprint is more important. (We could not, however, overlook the remarkable story of Patagonia, on page 62.) We also left out two very big companies, GE and Wal-Mart, whose environmental initiatives have been widely covered.

> **Increased 10% U.S. coal production since 1990; coal accounts for about half the U.S. power supply.**

Like Arnold Schwarzenegger (page 72), FORTUNE is basically optimistic. As the statistics show—and we highlight a few of them—the U.S. has made enormous progress in some areas, while backsliding in others. Change for the better is certainly possible; building a sustainable economy is a plausible goal.

10 Green Giants

These companies have gone beyond what the law requires to operate in an environmentally responsible way.

Company	Location	Year Founded	Revenue	Employees	Note
Honda	Japan	1945	$84.2 Billion	145,000	The most fuel-efficient auto company in the U.S.
Continental Airlines	Houston	1934	$13.1 Billion	44,000	Worked with Boeing to engineer more fuel-efficient aircraft
Suncor	Canada	1917	$13.6 Billion	5,500	Measures the environmental impact of each project
Tesco	Britain	1919	$71 Billion	380,000	Cut energy use and is trying to get customers to think green
Alcan	Canada	1902	$23.6 Billion	68,000	Investing in clean, efficient manufacturing
PG&E	San Francisco	1852	$12.5 Billion	20,000	Strategic investments in efficiency and renewables
S.C. Johnson	Racine, Wis.	1886	$7 Billion	12,000	Three generations of committed environmental stewardship
Goldman Sachs	New York	1869	$69.4 Billion	24,000	Bold climate-change policy shapes major investments
Swiss Re	Switzerland	1863	$24 Billion	10,500	Developing financial tools to deal with the risks of climate change
Hewlett-Packard	Palo Alto	1939	$91.7 Billion	156,000	Silicon Valley's longtime industry leader in eco-sensitivity

And what is sustainability? The ability to meet our present needs without compromising the ability of future generations to meet theirs. Getting there won't be easy—and business will have to help take us on the journey.

—Marc Gunther

While other automakers gripe, Honda attacks the issues of fuel economy and emissions with relish. Working independently, it is focusing on three alternative fuel technologies: gas-electric hybrid, clean diesel, and fuel cell. Honda has also taken a crack at solving a problem other automakers have left to the oil companies: creating an infrastructure for hydrogen. Honda's solution is for individual refueling stations that provide heat and electricity for the home as well as hydrogen for a fuel-cell-powered car. Long term, Honda wants to be the world's cleanest, most efficient manufacturer. It has promised to reduce CO_2 emissions from its factories as well as its vehicles by 5 percent between 2005 and 2010—on top of the 5 percent it achieved between 2000 and 2005.

—Alex Taylor III

Amid rising concern about aviation pollution, British Airways introduced a "CO_2 emission calculator" on its website, letting passengers pay to offset the carbon dioxide generated by their flights. Lufthansa recently equipped an Airbus A340 with a 1.5-ton mobile laboratory to track gases and compounds. But it is American airline Continental that's gone furthest to green operations. Besides spending more than $16 billion over the past ten years to replace its fleet with more efficient aircraft, it installed fuel-saving winglets that reduce emissions by up to 5 percent on most of its Boeing 737s and 757s, and reduced the nitrogen oxide output from ground equipment at its Houston hub by over 75 percent since 2000. Its 13 full-time staff environmentalists work with engine manufacturers, design green terminals, and track carbon emissions and chemical recycling daily. Even all the trash from company headquarters is later sorted for recyclables.

—Barney Gimbel

Finding black gold is a dirty job—particularly when it's buried in tar sands. But Suncor still stands out for how it does the job. Its environmental and social efforts have earned it membership in the Dow Jones sustainability index and the British equivalent, the FTSE4Good. In a survey of 23 global oil companies last year, Jantzi Research, a Canadian consultancy, named Suncor a top performer, noting its environmental and greenhouse-gas management programs. Specifically, it has improved emissions intensity (the amount of oil it extracts per ton of greenhouse gases emitted) 25 percent since 1990. Ditto for energy, sulfur dioxide and nitrogen oxide. Suncor is part of an initiative to develop carbon-capture techniques. And while Suncor hopes to double its production by 2012, its water management is so advanced that it expects to draw no additional water from Alberta's Athabasca River.

—Cait Murphy

Wind-powered stores, high-tech recycling, biodiesel delivery trucks—Tesco does all that. Last year the company pledged to cut the average energy use in its British buildings in half by 2010; now it says it will get there two years early. State-of-the-art trains that have lower-than-normal noise and pollution reduce the use of trucks, slashing thousands of tons of carbon dioxide emissions; in a major store initiative, Tesco will estimate the "carbon costs" of each item. To ensure that its leadership walks the talk, Tesco now determines senior-management bonuses partly on meeting energy- and waste-reduction targets. Tesco is also encouraging customers to be greener by awarding points, redeemable for merchandise, to those who bring their own reusable shopping bags.

—Matthew Boyle

When Alcan took over French rival Pechiney in late 2003, the Montreal-based aluminum maker also landed world-class smelting technology. Because of Pechiney's proprietary methods (and an aggressive push by Alcan to track emissions), the company has been able to reduce its greenhouse-gas output by 25 percent since 1990, while production increased 40 percent. Alcan's latest goal is to install a high-capacity process that increases energy efficiency by as much as 20 percent and lowers emissions. A pilot plant in Quebec is already testing the technology. "It's inherent to the engineering culture to respond to problems like these," says Alcan's Corey Copeland. "It's what makes engineers tick."

—Jia Lynn Yang

PG&E played a big role in getting mandatory controls on greenhouse gases enacted last year in California, and CEO Peter Darbee is now pushing for federal legislation.

The utility generates 56 percent of its retail electricity sales from non-greenhouse-gas-emitting sources, and it aggressively helps customers become more efficient. For instance, it subsidizes homeowners who buy energy-efficient appliances with $75 grants. PG&E is also experimenting with a variety of clean power alternatives. It is seeking permission to develop generation projects that could convert wave energy off the Pacific Coast into electricity. It is bullish on solar thermal technology, and it has a pilot project in the San Joaquin Valley in which cow manure is turned into electricity. "That's a dung good idea," cracks Darbee.

Jokes aside, Darbee is seriously excited about the prospect of plug-in hybrids that would draw power from the electricity grid at night and then feed power back into the grid during the day when demand peaks. These clean cars would burn less gasoline, pollute less and take advantage of the utility industry's capital-intensive infrastructure. "The energy industry," Darbee concludes, "is on the brink of a revolution."

—Marc Gunther

In 1935, long before sustainability became a corporate buzzword, H.F. Johnson Jr. led a 15,000-mile expedition to Brazil in search of a sustainable source of wax, the carnauba palm tree, for his company's first product, Johnson's Wax.

His grandson and the current CEO, Fisk Johnson, has continued that legacy at S.C. Johnson, a family-owned company that makes Windex, Pledge, Ziploc bags and Raid. Its most notable innovation is its Greenlist process, a classification system that evaluates the impact of thousands of raw materials on human and environmental health. By using Greenlist, S.C. Johnson eliminated 1.8 million pounds of volatile organic compounds (VOCs) from Windex and four million pounds of polyvinylidene chloride (PVDC) from Saran Wrap, which is now PVDC-free. (VOCs and PVDC are both pollutants.) The company licenses Greenlist royalty-free to other firms that want to use it. It is also cutting back its reliance on coal-fired power, recently building its own power plant that runs on natural gas and methane piped in from a nearby landfill. Glenn Pricket of Conservation International says that when it comes to the environment, "Fisk Johnson is probably the most personally committed CEO I've met."

—Marc Gunther

When Goldman Sachs announced a groundbreaking environmental policy in 2005, critics said chief executive Hank Paulson was imposing his green ethos. Wrong. The bank has become even more planet-friendly since Paulson left. Why? Because it is doing lots of green business.

Goldman's investment of $1.5 billion in cellulosic ethanol, wind and solar have paid off. Texas Pacific and Kohlberg Kravis Roberts turned to Goldman, which had built bridges to environmental groups, as they prepared a bid for Texas energy company TXU. Research clients are pleased that Goldman's equity analysts in Europe now factor environmental, social and governance issues into their reports. "The world's changing," says one Goldman official. The company is too—some cars that take bankers home are hybrids.

—Marc Gunther

Swiss Re's main product is insurance for insurers, so its products never come near a smokestack. And Swiss reinsurance companies are not exactly known for boldness. Even so, Swiss Re has been way ahead of the pack on climate change, warning as early as 1994 about the bottom-line threat in the form of higher claims from storms and other weather-related disasters.

In addition, Swiss Re has pioneered products like weather-based derivatives to hedge these risks. Buyers can bet on future heat waves or cold snaps with puts and calls on specific periods of time and temperatures, much as conventional options have a preset strike price for a stock. So a farmer in India might be able to buy insurance from a local insurer in case the usual monsoon rains fail to arrive or, conversely, his fields are flooded. Swiss Re was also among the early supporters of the Chicago Climate Exchange, an emerging hub for traders in derivatives linked to carbon emissions.

—Nelson D. Schwartz

High tech is falling all over itself to go green. It may be that Prius-driving engineering types are more eco-sensitive than the rest of us, or maybe they're simply battling for competitive advantage. The fact is, as more of modern life goes digital, the environmental impact of those computers and gadgets has gone from negligible to considerable. Hewlett-Packard has done the most to mitigate that. HP owns massive e-waste recycling plants, where enormous shredders and granulators reduce four million pounds of computer detritus each month to bite-sized chunks—the first step in reclaiming not just steel and plastic but also toxic chemicals like mercury and even some precious metals. HP will take back any brand of equipment; its own machines are 100 percent recyclable. It has promised to cut energy consumption by 20 percent by 2010. HP also audits its top suppliers for eco-friendliness, and its omnibus Global Citizenship Report sets the standard for detailed environmental accountability.

—Oliver Ryan

Test-Your-Knowledge Form

We encourage you to photocopy and use this page as a tool to assess how the articles in *Annual Editions* expand on the information in your textbook. By reflecting on the articles you will gain enhanced text information. You can also access this useful form on a product's book support Web site at *http://www.mhcls.com*.

NAME: DATE:

TITLE AND NUMBER OF ARTICLE:

BRIEFLY STATE THE MAIN IDEA OF THIS ARTICLE:

LIST THREE IMPORTANT FACTS THAT THE AUTHOR USES TO SUPPORT THE MAIN IDEA:

WHAT INFORMATION OR IDEAS DISCUSSED IN THIS ARTICLE ARE ALSO DISCUSSED IN YOUR TEXTBOOK OR OTHER READINGS THAT YOU HAVE DONE? LIST THE TEXTBOOK CHAPTERS AND PAGE NUMBERS:

LIST ANY EXAMPLES OF BIAS OR FAULTY REASONING THAT YOU FOUND IN THE ARTICLE:

LIST ANY NEW TERMS/CONCEPTS THAT WERE DISCUSSED IN THE ARTICLE, AND WRITE A SHORT DEFINITION:

We Want Your Advice

ANNUAL EDITIONS revisions depend on two major opinion sources: one is our Advisory Board, listed in the front of this volume, which works with us in scanning the thousands of articles published in the public press each year; the other is you—the person actually using the book. Please help us and the users of the next edition by completing the prepaid article rating form on this page and returning it to us. Thank you for your help!

ANNUAL EDITIONS: Business Ethics 09/10

ARTICLE RATING FORM

Here is an opportunity for you to have direct input into the next revision of this volume.
We would like you to rate each of the articles listed below, using the following scale:

1. **Excellent: should definitely be retained**
2. **Above average: should probably be retained**
3. **Below average: should probably be deleted**
4. **Poor: should definitely be deleted**

Your ratings will play a vital part in the next revision.
Please mail this prepaid form to us as soon as possible.
Thanks for your help!

RATING	ARTICLE	RATING	ARTICLE
	1. Thinking Ethically: A Framework for Moral Decision Making		26. Trust in the Marketplace
	2. Create a Culture of Trust		27. Survey: Unethical Behavior Unreported
	3. Business Ethics: Back to Basics		28. Congress Stops Playing Games with Toy Safety
	4. Building an Ethical Framework		29. Does It Pay to Be Good?
	5. Ethical Leadership: Maintain an Ethical Culture		30. Women and the Labyrinth *of* Leadership
	6. Truth or Consequences: The Organizational Importance of Honesty		31. Avoiding Green Marketing Myopia: Ways to Improve Consumer Appeal for Environmentally Preferable Products
	7. How to Make Unethical Decisions		32. The New E-spionage Threat
	8. Best Resources for Corporate Social Responsibility		33. Global Diversity: The Next Frontier
	9. Your Privacy for Sale		34. Trouble In Toyland
	10. Are You Too Family Friendly?		35. Cracks in a Particularly Thick Glass Ceiling
	11. Con Artists' Old Tricks		36. How Barbie Is Making Business a Little Better
	12. Help! Somebody Save Our Files!: How to Handle and Prevent the Most Common Data Disasters		37. Is Marketing Ethics an Oxymoron?
	13. ID Thieves Find a Niche in Online Social Networks		38. Truth in Advertising: Rx Drug Ads Come of Age
	14. Gender Issues		39. Marketing, Consumers and Technology: Perspectives for Enhancing Ethical Transactions
	15. Hiring Older Workers		40. Serving Unfair Customers
	16. The War Over Unconscious Bias		41. Dirty Deeds
	17. Reflecting on Downsizing: What Have Managers Learned?		42. Searching for the Top
	18. Fear of Firing		43. A Word for Older Job-Seekers: Retail
	19. Protecting the Whistleblower		44. Pssssst! Have You Tasted This?
	20. Learning to Love Whistleblowers		45. Swagland
	21. On Witnessing a Fraud		46. Creating an Ethical Culture
	22. His Most Trusted Employee Was a Thief		47. Hiring Character
	23. Erasing 'Un' from 'Unemployable'		48. The True Measure of a CEO
	24. The Parable of the Sadhu		49. Green Is Good
	25. The Ethics of Edits: When a Crook Changes the Contract		

ANNUAL EDITIONS: BUSINESS ETHICS 09/10

NO POSTAGE
NECESSARY
IF MAILED
IN THE
UNITED STATES

BUSINESS REPLY MAIL
FIRST CLASS MAIL PERMIT NO. 551 DUBUQUE IA

POSTAGE WILL BE PAID BY ADDRESSEE

McGraw-Hill Contemporary Learning Series
501 BELL STREET
DUBUQUE, IA 52001

ABOUT YOU

Name

Date

Are you a teacher? ☐ A student? ☐
Your school's name

Department

Address   City   State   Zip

School telephone #

YOUR COMMENTS ARE IMPORTANT TO US!

Please fill in the following information:
For which course did you use this book?

Did you use a text with this ANNUAL EDITION? ☐ yes ☐ no
What was the title of the text?

What are your general reactions to the Annual Editions concept?

Have you read any pertinent articles recently that you think should be included in the next edition? Explain.

Are there any articles that you feel should be replaced in the next edition? Why?

Are there any World Wide Web sites that you feel should be included in the next edition? Please annotate.

May we contact you for editorial input? ☐ yes ☐ no
May we quote your comments? ☐ yes ☐ no